...w Service ... Aeria... Service 150 Limited. 134

CORAL SEA

PAPUA.

THURSDAY I.

—QUEENSLAND—

Administration

Defence

Development

Commercial Aviation

YORK.

COOKTOWN.

CAIRNS

P A C I F I C

O C E A N

Townsville.

12

16

20

24

28

Burketown

Cloncurry

RAILWAY

AIR MILES

Diamantina

Birdsville

Betoota

WINDORAH

Cooper Creek

LIA

Winton

LONGREACH

RAILWAY

BLACKALL

Charleville

Thargomindah

Cunnamulla

St George

DIRRANBANDI

RAILWAY

Clermont

Rockhampton

TROPIC OF CAPRICORN.

Springsure

ROMA RAILWAY

Toowoomba

Brisbane

WARWICK

Tenterfield

N S W   S O U T H   W A L E S.

142   146   150   154

THE DEFEAT OF DISTANCE

THE DEFEAT OF DISTANCE

QANTAS 1919-1939

JOHN GUNN

University of Queensland Press

ST LUCIA • LONDON • NEW YORK

First published 1985 by University of Queensland Press
Box 42, St Lucia, Queensland, Australia

Typeset by University of Queensland Press
Designed by Horsley Dawson
Printed in Australia by Globe Press Pty Ltd., Melbourne

Distributed in the USA and Canada by the University of Queensland Press,
5 South Union Street, Lawrence, Mass. 01843 USA

Cataloguing in Publication Data

National Library of Australia

Gunn, John, 1925–   .
  The Defeat of Distance: QANTAS 1919 to 1939.

  Bibliography.
  Includes index.

  1. Qantas Airways — History.
  2. Aeronautics, Commercial — Australia —
History. I. Title.

387.7'065'94

Library of Congress

Gunn, John, 1925–   .
  The Defeat of Distance: Qantas 1919 to 1939.

  Bibliography: p.
  Includes index.
  1. Qantas Airways — History. I. Title.

HE9889.Q33G86   1985   387.7'065'94   84-11978

ISBN 0 7022 1707 7

To Paul McGinness, Hudson Fysh and Fergus McMaster, founders of Qantas

... we shall in one bound be loosened from the fetters imposed by our remoteness and brought in close touch with the western world.

William Hughes, *Hansard*, 22 November 1921

Contents

Illustrations

Preface

Qantas is, in terms of Australian history, an unusual institution. It had its roots in our pioneering outback tradition, in western Queensland, in the unusual and sustained contribution of Australia to the early years of aviation and in the national experience and aftermath of World War I. As it grew, it combined the enterprise, tenacity and idealism of individuals with, from the start, intimate involvement with Federal politics and the bureaucracy of government. Qantas was at times both a catalyst and a mirror to the development of our relationship with the Empire, the Commonwealth, and with other nations as it increasingly provided an instrument with which to shrink the immense distances that for so long had isolated Australia from the world.

I was not a contemporary of the early Qantas, by any means, but I knew some of the people who were; I have known many more who worked for or did business with the postwar Qantas. Although I have had many and long discussions with people who were at the very centre of the events with which this history deals, it has been their perspectives on those events and their recollections of their fellows, and not their memories of what happened, in all its detail and complexity, that most helped me. For that, I have gone to the written word of the day and, almost always, to the wealth of primary sources; to the personal and business letters of those involved, to the official and unofficial correspondence of ministers and their advisors, to the analyses and reports of the time by senior civil servants and airline people, to secret Cabinet submissions and public government pronouncements.

xiii

A great deal of this material comes from the private papers of Fergus McMaster, first chairman of Qantas, Hudson Fysh, its first managing director, and Edgar Johnston, who joined the Civil Aviation Branch in Australia in 1919, went on to head it in the thirties and was, after World War II, an advisor to Qantas. The McMaster papers are in the possession of Qantas, the Fysh papers are in the Mitchell Library, Sydney, and the Johnston papers are still in Edgar Johnston's possession in Melbourne. The Fysh papers are by no means fully indexed, the McMaster and Johnston papers are not indexed at all. Consequently, though I have attempted to read them all (I was my own research assistant), I may have missed some relevant or enlightening detail in the tens of thousands of letters and documents available. In addition to these private collections, the archival material of the company itself exists (in raw form) in such volume that the periodical additions made to it are transported in trucks. Within the present operating departments of Qantas extensive and useful records are also retained. Board papers and minutes over decades in themselves provide a rich source of material. In the archives of the Royal Air Force Museum at Hendon, in England, I found much relevant and fascinating correspondence. To complement these written sources I have recorded and transcribed interviews with many people in England and Australia. (United States material is almost all relevant to Qantas history subsequent to the period covered by this volume.)

It is from all this material that I have tried, in the main, to find out what happened and to set aside the myths and prejudices that survive. As I immersed myself in the material, it seemed that both the facts from the past and what could be recaptured of the atmosphere of the time and the outlook, values, and personalities of the human beings involved, could best be set down (where this was possible at all) in the words of the participants themselves. Although this approach cannot entirely rule out inclusion of my own comments, judgments and prejudices — either directly or in the process of selection — it does present much of the hard evidence of actuality. Where it has been necessary, I have tried to supply the broader context and, with the advantage of hindsight, relate events to the particular slice of Australian history that the emerging Qantas provided.

I have many people to thank, some of them involved in the very beginning of Qantas, others who were great or central

figures in Australian or international aviation. I found Frank
Cory, who supplied the early Qantas office free and acted as
company secretary in 1920, in a nursing home in Toowoomba, Queensland, and I am particularly grateful to him for the
time and effort that he gave before his recent death. In
Sydney, still active and vigorous, I found Jack Hazlett, who
flew as mechanic on the first-ever scheduled return flight by
Qantas from Cloncurry to Longreach in 1922. Norman
(G.P.N.) Watt, a former secretary of the Treasury, vice-
chairman of Qantas, chairman of TAA and chairman
of British Commonwealth Pacific Airlines, was ninety-
two when we talked in Melbourne and though he was to die
only months later (and knew it) his mental grasp of complex
past events and his lucidity were astonishing. In England, I
spoke with A.J. Quin-Harkin, who was chief accountant of
Imperial Airways in 1934 (when a young C.O. Turner was
selected to train with them and join Qantas); Sir George
Edwards O.M., former chairman of British Aircraft Corporation; and Sir Ross Stainton, former chairman of BOAC, who
had joined Imperial Airways some fifty years previously. Also
very helpful were Sir Keith Granville, another former BOAC
chairman and Imperial Airways employee from the early
1930s; Ralph Robins (director, Civil Engine Group, Rolls-
Royce, London); and Derek John (marketing director,
Military Engine Group, Rolls-Royce, London). At Rolls-
Royce in Derby I spoke with Alec Harvey Bailey, who
established the Rolls-Royce engine overhaul plant at Mascot
in the 1950s, and with Malcolm Muir, who had a long and
close involvement with Qantas. Jim Cownie, at Derby, went
to great trouble to facilitate these and other meetings. In
Australia, Ken Wright, vice-chairman of Rolls-Royce of
Australia Pty. Ltd., provided much valuable background on
the Rolls-Royce–Qantas relationship. I was also much helped
in England by Robert Gardner of British Aerospace, who
arranged meetings for me with those who, in the predecessor
companies that came together to form British Aerospace, were
involved in the sometimes torrid battles to sell British aircraft
to Australia.

I am, of course, very grateful to many past and present
members of Qantas, among them Capt. R.J. (Bert) Ritchie, a
former chief executive; G.U. (Scotty) Allan, a most
remarkable pioneer airman and airline executive; Capt. Bill
Crowther and Capt. Russell Tapp (whose early Qantas careers

form part of this first volume). Many other people who served Qantas gave me generous help. As this first volume was being prepared for publication, research for the subsequent period has continued and many more people (this time mainly in Australia and the United States) have been interviewed. I thank them, too, and will acknowledge their assistance more appropriately in the following volume. Brian Reed gave much practical and erudite assistance in the selection and captioning of photographs and close reading of the manuscript. Ian Gunn not only typed the manuscript but also assembled the bibliography and the references.

Of all those who have helped I am especially indebted to Edgar Johnston, who made available to me the comprehensive collection of his own papers and correspondence and the records of the early years of the Civil Aviation Branch (and much else of value); he is a central character in the latter part of this first volume. I am also deeply grateful to John Fysh, son of Sir Hudson Fysh, for permission to consult the papers of his father in the Mitchell Library, Sydney. Without the trust and assistance of Edgar Johnston and John Fysh this history would have lacked much richness of detail.

Although the publication of the history has been strongly supported by Qantas, and I have been given full access to the records of the company, there have been no constraints of any kind on what I have chosen to include. It was agreed from the outset that final editorial responsibility would lie with myself.

Qantas is the second oldest airline in the world. It has endured throughout the whole of that turbulent period in which the world was changed by man's conquest of the air. This present volume covers the history of Qantas from 1919 until the outbreak of World War II in 1939.

Prologue
An Unlikely Meeting 1919

The fat bullocks that ran on the black soil plains of western Queensland in 1919 were worth big money. Devoncourt Station, near Cloncurry, carried a herd of 10,000 head of cattle that year, but it was a small herd compared with those run on neighbouring stations. On the paddock hoof each beast was worth up to fifteen pounds.[1]

It was a good year, too, for sheep, with some seventeen million in the state, each one of them yielding wool to the value of nine and sixpence.[2] With a bale of wool bringing between twenty-five and thirty-five pounds, towns like Longreach were prosperous.[3]

The fickle patterns of the seasons, that in some years turned battlers into men of substance and in others drove proud families from their land, were soon to show their harsher aspect. Drought was to combine with a world economy no less inconstant than the weather to trim severely the earnings of station owners and again make more familiar the swagman on the road.

But wool was not yet unsaleable and a cattle slump hardly imaginable to those sharp stockmen engaged in the practice of poddy-dodging. There were, across the country, enough of them almost to make an industry of it for in substantial numbers they were collecting the unbranded calves of the cattle owners and selling them to "receivers" for up to three pounds a head. A shearer had to shear a hundred and fifty sheep to earn as much.[4]

So widespread was the practice, and so vast the area of coun-

1

try involved, that neither government nor police could control it. A Cloncurry dairyman who objected to the poddy-dodgers harvesting his land found his waterholes poisoned and almost all his cattle dead. In one of the valleys of the Selwyn range they collected all the new calves and, in an act of sheer bloody-mindedness, shot the sixty Devoncourt cows that had borne them.[5]

That remote area had long since forced on those who peopled it a tradition of self-help. All the big stations came together to wipe out this threat to their livelihood and prosecute the men behind it; a co-operative organization was formed to hunt them down. At times as many as eighty horses were in the association's mustering camp, with twenty riders and black trackers to help them. The chairman of the new Anti Cattle Duffing Association, at the time managing Devoncourt Station for his brother who was in hospital with typhoid, was Fergus McMaster. Given his discharge from the AIF in London early in 1919 he was, in his own words, "one of the few who were given the privilege of paying their own fare and choosing their own time and route for return to Australia". He spent some months touring and on the day of his arrival in Sydney, still on the boat, received an urgent telegram about his brother's illness and a request that he go immediately to Cloncurry.[6] Though he did not know it then, he was soon to become chairman of an unlikely commercial enterprise for those parts. With three employees, no premises, and uncertain prospects it would grow with the decades into a great international airline and its founder chairman would be knighted for his services to his country.

Fergus McMaster returned to an Australia much changed by the impact of the Great War on its population, then approaching 5.5 million. Most of them were of English, Scottish, or Irish stock, though they were led by a fiery and diminutive Welshman, Billy Hughes. It was an Australia that had sent 330,000 troops overseas to fight for England, all of them volunteers. Because they quickly established for themselves a reputation as shock troops and were used as such, their casualty rate far exceeded that of England; 59,258 were killed in action or died of wounds and a further 173,815 were wounded; only three men out of every ten were to return unharmed.[7]

In the eight months of attack and counterattack that followed the landing at Gallipoli on 25 April 1915, more than ten thousand Australian and New Zealand troops were killed. In

1916, after regrouping and reinforcement in Egypt when Gallipoli was evacuated, the four infantry divisions moved between March and June to France while the Australian and New Zealand Light Horse, with the Camel Corps and one squadron of the Flying Corps, remained, under General Harry Chauvel, in the Middle East.[8]

Three of the Anzac divisions, used in the first Battle of the Somme in July, suffered 23,000 casualties in five weeks, wounded or dead. The figures mounted with Ypres, Passchendaele, and a dozen other French battlefields. Under Australia's greatest soldier, John Monash, the seasoned Australian divisions made a contribution out of all proportion to their numbers in the final moves against the Hindenburg line. In the eight months before the Armistice of 11 November 1918 they defeated thirty-nine enemy divisions, captured almost a quarter of the prisoners taken, and were responsible for more than one-fifth of the ground recovered. At the time, they constituted less than one-tenth of the numerical strength of the British Army.[9]

In the Middle East, Chauvel went on the attack against the Turks early in 1916. Slowly, over the ensuing two years, they were driven from Sinai, Palestine, and Syria until, with much-needed reinforcements and under the command of General Sir Edmund Allenby, a final offensive forced the defeated Turkish army to sign an armistice. The Anzac cavalry of Chauvel was by then part of the Desert Mounted Corps, in an army of five divisions with units from Britain, France, and India. Never before had there been assembled for modern warfare so extensive a body of cavalry.[10]

While men on horseback fought across the desert wastes, men in aircraft engaged in strange new battles above them. The new technology of war, fought in the cloudy corridors of the skies, was romanticized in the public mind. Like the spectacle of cavalry at the gallop, both were far removed from the known realities of the mud, the maiming, and the mass slaughter of infantrymen in the trenches. Flight itself, fathered in ancient myth, was still only yesterday's achievement; Orville and Wilbur Wright had made the world's first controlled and sustained flight by a power-driven, heavier-than-air machine on 17 December 1903; though it lasted a mere twelve seconds, it was to change the world.

The Englishman, Sir George Cayley, who died in 1857 after years of experimentation, became accepted as the man mainly responsible for discovering the basic principles of heavier-than-air flight but, for a long time after his death, the balloon or airship seemed the logical way to the heavens. Though half a world away, Australia had its share in the history of these endeavours. As early as 1851 a member of the New South Wales Legislative Council, Dr William Bland, designed a hydrogen-filled, steam-driven semirigid airship ninety feet long and with a loaded weight of five tons. A model and drawings were shown at the Crystal Palace, London, in 1852 and at the Paris Universal Exhibition in 1855.[11] The first balloon ascent in Australia, by Englishman William Dean, was made from Cremorne Gardens in Melbourne on 1 February 1858. Sixty feet high and with an inflated diameter of forty feet, it travelled seven miles before descending.[12]

Two papers "On the flight of birds and aerial navigation", by Henry Sutton of Ballarat, Victoria, were printed in the 1878 annual report of the Aeronautical Society of Great Britain (now the Royal Aeronautical Society). Sutton gave details of his experimental, clockwork ornithopter which, he wrote, could fly in a circle of about twelve feet.[13] Interest in flying was high and in earnest; Melbourne bookshop proprietor, E.W. Cole, offered a prize of £1,000 on 31 October 1882 for the invention within two years of a flying machine propelled electrically, chemically, or mechanically, which could fly one hundred miles.[14]

But it was Lawrence Hargrave, born in England in 1850, who made Australia's major contribution to practicable, heavier-than-air flight. Hargrave came to Australia when he was sixteen, a year after his father was appointed a Supreme Court judge. He made the study of human flight his life's work. Apart from remarkably successful experiments with flapping wing models, variously powered by clockwork, rubber bands, or compressed air, he also experimented with air screws and their motive power. He designed the rotary engine in model form and used it with success. Hargrave became a member of the Royal Society of New South Wales in 1877 and in nineteen lectures read before its members between 1884 and 1909 he covered in much detail all his wide-ranging work. On his successful experiments with box kites were founded the basic designs of the early European aeroplanes.[15]

There was much activity in aviation matters in Australia in 1909. On 28 April, the Aerial League of Australia held its inaugural meeting in the Hotel Australia, Sydney. Hargrave was one of its five vice-presidents.[16] George A. Taylor, its honorary secretary, opened what he claimed to be the first aeroplane factory in the southern hemisphere at Surry Hills, Sydney, six months later. On December 5, Taylor made the first flight in Australia in a heavier-than-air machine, though not a powered one. His flight, and twenty-eight others that day, were made at Narrabeen Heads, NSW using a glider built by Taylor. Described by him as a Voisin, it had a Hargrave box kite tail and a wing span of eighteen feet. Others who flew the Voisin were Edward (later Sir Edward) Hallstrom, Charles Schulz, Florence Taylor (George Taylor's wife), and Mrs Schulz. Mrs Taylor was the first woman to fly in Australia. The best distance covered was 110 yards, by George Taylor.[17]

Four days later, at Victoria Racecourse, Sydney, Colin Defries covered a distance of 115 yards, at a height of from two to fifteen feet, in a Wright Biplane, though he did not manage to turn or control the aeroplane in flight. His aircraft, the first imported powered aeroplane to arrive in Australia, was acquired by L.A. Adamson, headmaster of Wesley College, Melbourne. It arrived in Sydney on 15 November, but had a short life. Defries, who had been sent to England and France by Adamson and who purchased a Bleriot as well as the Wright Biplane for him, made a second attempt at flight on 18 December. Again, his height varied only between two and fifteen feet, and his flight path was a straight line. But this time, grabbing for his hat which had been caught by the wind, he lost control and crashed into a ditch, extensively damaging the aeroplane.[18]

The first controlled, powered flight in Australia was made by F.C. Custance when he flew for five minutes twenty-five seconds in a Bleriot at Bolivar, near Adelaide, South Australia, on 17 March 1910. On the same morning, in a second attempt in which he reached an estimated height of fifty feet, he crashed.[19] One day later, at Diggers Rest near Melbourne, Victoria, the magician Harry Houdini (Ehrich Weiss) made three successful flights in a Voisin aeroplane of from one to three and a half minutes. On 20 March, Houdini made two more flights, one a short one of twenty-six seconds, the other of three minutes forty-five seconds, when he covered between three and four miles and reached a height of one hundred feet. The following day, in a seven minute thirty-seven seconds flight, he covered some six miles. Houdini made his last attempt in his Voisin at Rosehill Racecourse near Parramatta, NSW on 18 April but ended a flight of some four to five minutes with a crash landing. He was not injured.[20]

Louis Bleriot, of course, had flown across the English Channel on 25 July 1909 and Henry Farman, on 3 November, made his flight of 144 miles in a little over four hours. Though these were exciting spectacles, the aeroplane was widely regarded as a sporting machine, with perhaps some military potential; only a dedicated few glimpsed its promise for civil application.

In England, in September 1910, a postal service was conducted by air between London and Windsor for three weeks to commemorate the coronation of King George V and some 115,000 letters and postcards were carried. In Germany, Count Zeppelin had, in October 1909, formed a company to operate six airships for the regular carriage of passengers. Though three were wrecked, the company (DELAG) made 881 flights, covered 65,000 miles, and carried 19,100 passengers between March 1912 and November 1913. In Florida, in the United States, the St Petersburg-Tampa Airboat Line began a twice daily flying boat service in 1914 across Tampa Bay which continued for four months, now credited as the first attempt to operate a regular passenger service with aeroplanes.[21]

Australian interest in flying remained intense, with many individual efforts at aircraft design and construction. L.J.R. Jones, of Sydney, tested a monoplane of his own construction at Emu Plains in May 1911, but it was wrecked.[22] C.W. Mackay of Dulong, Queensland, patented an "aviation machine" in January 1911 designed to "keep upright in the air in any weather" and "able to hover or poise". Its horizontal propeller, which could "serve the purpose of a parachute", was inspired in principle by a study of the flight of the seeds of the hickory tree.[23] In Cloncurry, Queensland, in the same month Auriol Barker applied for a patent on his "helio-copter" which he claimed would be capable of vertical take-off, having its main driving propeller in a cylindrical cage, from which was suspended the passenger "car".[24]

The British Colonial Aircraft Co. (later Bristol Aircraft) sent Joseph J. Hammond to Australia in 1911 to try to interest the Australian government in buying aeroplanes for defence purposes. In a remarkably sustained series of displays in his two Bristol Boxkites, Hammond made some seventy-two flights covering 765 miles between January and May 1911.[25] A Parramatta dentist, W.E. Hart, bought a Bristol Biplane from Hammond and was given flying lessons by Leslie McDonald, who had accompanied Hammond to Australia as a representative of the Bristol Aeroplane Co. On November 16, Hart completed the series of tests prescribed by the Royal Aero Club for the issue of an Aviator's Certificate and became the first pilot to qualify in Australia.[26]

A young H.J.L. (Bert) Hinkler exhibited his second glider at the Bundaberg Show in Queensland in April 1912.[27] In England an Australian called Harry Hawker was beginning a career that would identify his name with one of Britain's greatest makers of aircraft. On 24 October, flying a Sopwith-Wright biplane, he established a British endurance record of eight hours twenty-three minutes, which stood for many years. Hawker visited Australia in 1914 with a Sopwith Tabloid biplane which he had designed as chief designer for the Sopwith Co. and Hinkler, now in England, took a job with the Sopwith Aeroplane Works in March when he could not raise seventy-five pounds to join the London Flying School.[28] He became no. 318 on the list of accepted volunteers for the Royal Naval Air Service on 7 September.[29]

This ferment of aviation activity, stretching from Russia, through Europe and Great Britain to America, and across the world to Australia was concentrated by the demands of war. Though the application of the aeroplane was narrowed, its technical development was greatly accelerated and aircraft were produced in great numbers. The young men who were trained to fly them provided the postwar pilots on which the world's airline industry was founded.

One of them was Paul McGinness, who served with No. 1 Squadron of the Australian Flying Corps in the Middle East; he was to be the driving force behind the beginnings of Qantas. His observer, Hudson Fysh, was later to become its manager and for over four decades to remain at its head. Their flight sergeant, Arthur Baird, was to found and nurture the airline's long tradition of engineering excellence.

No. 1 Squadron of the Australian Flying Corps, under the command of Maj. Richard Williams, was among the Allied squadrons that played so devastating a part in the final Turkish defeat of the long desert campaign. Williams later became chief of the Air Staff at the age of thirty-one, Australia's first air marshal and, finally, director-general of civil aviation. His two lieutenants, McGinness and Fysh, had served with distinction in the Australian Light Horse before joining the Flying Corps. Both had landed at Gallipoli, only two weeks after the Anzacs had stormed ashore. They landed

7

without their horses, for horses were not needed on that terrible terrain. McGinness won the Distinguished Conduct Medal at Gallipoli, in an action at Pope's Hill. Fysh, following their return to Egypt after the Gallipoli evacuation and subsequent action with the Light Horse against the Turks, was commissioned in the field. He replaced his own section officer, Lt. Ross Smith, who had transferred to the Flying Corps. Ross Smith was to end the war as Australia's most decorated flyer and then complete the first flight from England to Australia. Both McGinness as pilot and Fysh as observer were to win the Distinguished Flying Cross.[30]

The impetus to aviation brought about by the volume and diversity of military aircraft design and production continued directly and dramatically into the early years of peace; 1919 was a year crowded with experiment, ferment, high hopes, and uneconomic, unco-ordinated muddle.

The first day of civil flying in the British Isles after World War I was 1 May 1919, when a DH9 aircraft of Aircraft Transport and Travel took off from Hounslow before dawn carrying newspapers for Bournemouth. The flight ended with a forced landing on Portsdown Hill in fog, but it was the first flight ever from an officially appointed civil aerodrome in the United Kingdom and the first from London.[31] Between 16 and 27 May, a United States Navy flying boat made the first successful crossing of the North Atlantic by air, via Halifax, Newfoundland, the Azores, Lisbon, and Spain to Plymouth. On 14–15 June, Alcock and Brown made the first direct flight across the North Atlantic by air, taking fifteen hours fifty-seven minutes for the crossing between Harbour Grace, Newfoundland to Clifden, Ireland. Both men were knighted for their flight.

On 21 June, the British secretary of state for air appointed a Standing Advisory Committee on Civil Aviation under the chairmanship of Lord Weir to advise and report on the best method of organizing Imperial Air Routes. On 2 July, the British rigid airship R34 set off on the first east-to-west crossing by air of the North Atlantic, returning successfully on 13 July to complete the first two-way crossing by air. On 25 August there was a meeting of the International Air Traffic Association (IATA) at The Hague, resulting in an agreement, signed on 28 August, forming the first free association of international airlines.

Meanwhile, in Australia, a ground survey party organized by a company called Aerial Services Ltd. left Sydney on 31 January 1919 using motor cycles and side-cars to survey an air route across Australia to Calcutta, Port Said, or Baghdad. The party travelled north through Singleton, Tenterfield, Roma, Charleville, Longreach, Winton, Camooweal, Brunette Downs, Newcastle Waters, and Katherine, arriving in Darwin on 10 June. It was an ambitious effort, led by Reginald Lloyd as managing director and with J.C. Marduel as his aeronautical expert, to determine a route suitable for inclusion in a London–Sydney air service.

Marduel, as long ago as October 1914, had flown from Richmond to Centennial Park, Sydney, and back again. He had taken control of an aviation school at Richmond started by fellow Frenchman, Guillaux, but he left it in December to volunteer for active service.

On 10 March 1919 the acting prime minister of Australia announced in the House of Representatives, which was then in Melbourne, that the Commonwealth government had decided to offer a prize of £10,000 "for the first successful flight to Australia from Great Britain of a machine manned by Australians". Competitors were required to supply their own aircraft and the flight was to be completed within 720 consecutive hours by midnight on 31 December 1920. The aircraft and all components had to be constructed within the British Empire and the rules and regulations for the contest were drawn up, at the request of Prime Minister W.M. Hughes, by the Royal Aero Club of the United Kingdom.

Marduel heard about the government competition in a telegram from his wife on 21 March, addressed to him at Mahoney's Imperial Hotel, Longreach, in western Queensland. It excited him and, in a letter he wrote to her that night, he said:

> I am very pleased you sent me that wire . . . it may alter our plans after we get to Burketown . . . In my opinion our survey is a farce and I want R.L. [Reginald Lloyd] to go to England as soon as possible with me and get a Bus (sic) to fly back, before anyone else does it. He is dead anxious to get to Burketown and make a big fuss in the papers, saying we have crossed Australia . . . I keep drumming into him that what we are doing is not worth a tinkers curse . . .[32]

Lloyd's ambitious plans were never to be realized and Marduel was not to be one of the five competitors that attempted the England–Australia challenge. Even Lloyd's choice of a landing site, on the racecourse at Darwin, was to be rejected as unsuitable, in October 1919, by the former Flying Corps lieutenant, twenty-three-year-old Hudson Fysh.

Five days before the announcement of the £10,000 government prize in March, Lts. Paul McGinness and Hudson Fysh had sailed from Egypt by ship, their military flying days over, for the journey back to Australia and the unknowns of civilian life. They knew nothing of the race until their arrival in Hobart in April and, though the idea of participating excited them, their prospects were negligible. Fysh, who had partly trained as a wool-classer before his war service, returned to his Launceston home wondering, like tens of thousands of other ex-servicemen, how he was to earn his living. McGinness, not a man for worrying or wondering, went on to Melbourne determined to find a way of trying for that £10,000. He had reminded Fysh that one of the Bristol Fighters of No. 1 Squadron had been presented to it by a wealthy grazier from New South Wales, Sir Samuel McCaughey, and that they had flown it. The link was more than enough to spur McGinness and he set off for Yanco in western New South Wales to seek financial backing from Sir Samuel. His personality, his record of war service in the Light Horse and the Flying Corps, and the energy and enthusiasm that had brought him from Melbourne to western New South Wales were more than enough to sway the old philanthropist. He agreed to back a McGinness team and gave him a letter promising support.

A delighted McGinness telegraphed Fysh in Launceston and their old flight sergeant, Arthur Baird, in Melbourne. Baird abandoned the garage business he had started; Fysh sold his car and said quick goodbyes to his people; passages were booked to England. The chance of fame and fortune was now within their grasp. Then, sadly and suddenly, Sir Samuel McCaughey died.

Though it was a great blow to them, it was soon softened by an offer from the Defence Department to survey a possible air route for the race contestants between Longreach, in western Queensland, north to the Gulf of Carpentaria and then via Katherine in the Northern Territory to Darwin, where the airmen were to land. Baird was not part of this venture, and he returned to Melbourne. McGinness and Fysh, barely used to their civilian status, were brought back into the Defence Department "on special duties". Just under a year after the end of the war, on 14 August 1919, they arrived in Longreach to wait for the utility-backed Model T Ford car which was to

10

come to the railhead from Brisbane. In uniform again they were, as airmen, of much public interest. "I can best describe the experience", Fysh wrote later, "by comparing it to what would happen if two of our present-day spacemen walked along a street in full space rig-out." Pilots returned from the wars, he added, often regarded themselves as quite apart from the ordinary run of men — though he excused McGinness and himself to some extent: "Ginty and I were perhaps saved from being entirely objectionable through our service in the Expeditionary Force as one of the mob before we took to the air."[33]

They engaged a driver and handyman, George Gorham, and with McGinness as senior officer and leader, set out on 18 August on a journey of 1,354 miles for the Katherine River railhead in the Northern Territory. The task of recording their observations, of sketching and mapping was left to the methodical and painstaking Fysh. McGinness, neither then nor later, was one for pen and paper. Both of them, however, saw on their maps the wide plains between the unconnected railheads of Charleville, Longreach, Winton, and Cloncurry,

Survey through the Gulf Country, mid-September 1919 (taken by Hudson Fysh). Paul McGinness is guiding two borrowed horses to tow the Model T Ford. George Gorham is at the wheel. Between Robinson River and Borroloola Settlement, the Ford frequently needed towing to negotiate soft sand and steep river banks.

experienced the lack of made roads and bridges, and were told that heavy rains each year made the black soil plains impassable. It was utterly unlike the settled and civilized countryside of England and Europe, where the main thrust of pioneering air travel was concentrated, but to McGinness and Fysh its empty and unconnected distances made it the perfect, logical match for the aeroplane. New ambitions stirred in the ever-optimistic McGinness.

It took them only six days to reach Burketown, on the Gulf of Carpentaria. The next stage was through country that had never been crossed before by motor car, an area "as big as Tasmania and with, perhaps, fifteen white residents".[34] Even before they left Brisbane, however, they had decided against this northern route for the air race contestants. The owner of Brunette Downs station and an authority on north Australia, A.J. Downs, had described the area to them as dense in timber, without telegraphic communications and with few open spaces that could be turned into landing grounds. They had wired these observations to the Defence Department, but had been ordered to proceed according to plan. It took them a further forty-five days of effort and adventure to complete the journey from Burketown to the Katherine railhead, where they arrived on 8 October. (Many years later, Hudson Fysh acknowledged that "McGinness with his enterprise and optimism was the one who got us through".)[35] Their earlier judgment had been confirmed. They advised the chief of the General Staff, Maj.Gen. James Legge, that the Gulf route should be condemned and that the race contestants should fly inland on a central route across the Barkly Tableland (the route surveyed earlier by Reginald Lloyd's party). McGinness was instructed to return to Cloncurry by this inland route, choosing and establishing landing grounds as he went; Fysh was ordered to remain in Darwin and prepare landing grounds there and at the Katherine River.

In a report to General Legge dated 30 October, Fysh rejected the Darwin racecourse landing ground site favoured by Lloyd. It was, he said, in a depression, could not be extended, and required extensive clearing of stumps and saplings. Fysh chose, instead, a site at Fanny Bay, two miles to the north of Darwin and only some four hundred metres from the shore on its western edge. He wrote:

> . . . the greater length of the ground runs north-west, which is the direction of the prevailing wind at the present time of year. A run of some 800 yards can be got in this direction . . . The area has

been cultivated with rice and other crops while a portion of it is natural grass. The soil carries a good quantity of gravel and is hard and even ... The present obstructions which are being cleared are 700 yards of wire fencing, two banyan trees, two large earth mounds and several small trees on the edges of the site.[36]

He was much concerned at the cost of labour for both the Darwin and Katherine landing grounds. The superintendent of public works, Mr Kellaway, advised him that the work would have to be done by casual day labour at the rate of four shillings per hour. There was some urgency for he was told that "the wet season starts in the district about the first week in December and continues till sometime in March. Very heavy rains fall ... heavy weather sets in from the north-west and storms are expected from the south-east ... A machine out in the open at the landing place would stand a good chance of being wrecked."[37]

The Fanny Bay ground was completed at a cost of £700 and on 10 December 1919, as the official representative of the Defence Department, Hudson Fysh greeted the winners of the £10,000 government prize when they touched down at five minutes past three in their Vickers Vimy. In command was his old colleague from the Light Horse and Flying Corps, Capt. Ross Smith, with his brother, Keith, and with J.M. Bennett and W.H. Shiers as mechanics. They had taken off from Hounslow on 12 November in Vickers Vimy G-EAOU, with its two Rolls-Royce 360-horsepower Eagle VIII engines, and

Darwin residents at Fanny Bay aerodrome, 10 December 1919, crowd around the Vickers Vimy, the first aeroplane to fly from Britain to Australia.

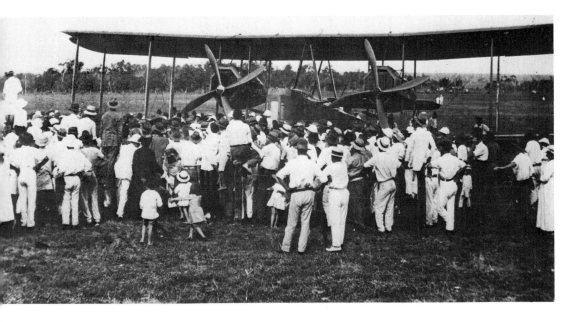

Hudson Fysh (right) at Fanny Bay aerodrome, 10 December 1919, welcomes Ross Smith to Australia. Fysh has just handed him a bundle of telegrams which can be seen in Smith's left hand.

flown some 11,500 miles in 135 hours 50 minutes, with an elapsed time of 27 days 20 hours. It was, wrote Hudson Fysh, "one of the most moving sights I can remember — the termination of one of the greatest flights, if not the greatest, in the history of aviation, and a great initial fillip for civil aviation in Australia, for no one had ever flown across the world before".[38]

There was a less publicized but hardly less remarkable flight to Darwin that arrived on 12 December, two days after the Vimy. Capt. H.N. Wrigley and Sgt. A.W. Murphy, commissioned by the Defence Department to survey an air route between Melbourne and Darwin for the race competitors, had left Point Cook, Victoria, on 16 November in a BE2E biplane and had covered the 2,500 miles in forty-six flying hours. It was the first crossing of the Australian continent by air.[39]

Paul McGinness, though he played no part in the Darwin preparations, made his contribution to the epic flight of the Smith brothers on his return journey to Cloncurry. At New-

castle Waters he organized the start of work on north Australia's first cleared aerodrome, had stones removed for a landing
area at Brunette Downs, approved a landing site at
Camooweal, and completed his outback car trip of 2,300 miles
at Cloncurry where he booked in at the Post Office Hotel to
await the flyers, on their way south to Sydney and Melbourne.

By then his new ambitions had crystallized and he set out to
arouse as much interest as he could in the establishment of a
local air service. The drama of the air race from England, and
the preparations for the passage of the competitors through
Queensland, ensured that aviation was a topic of intense
interest. McGinness, as its most glamorous embodiment in
Cloncurry, was no stranger to the sociable picnics that were
often held under the trees that shaded the banks of the
waterholes along the sandy Cloncurry River. He had time
enough to discover who were the local men of means and
influence.

And so it was that one hot, Sunday afternoon he left the Post
Office Hotel to pick up a young lady in his motor car and join
a picnic party. He did not make it to the picnic. Trudging up
the deserted street towards him in the oppressive heat was a
blue-eyed man, close on six feet tall, whom he recognized as
the chairman of the Anti Cattle Duffing Organisation, Fergus
McMaster. He was surprised, because this group had concluded its Sunday meeting in his hotel only a short time before.
McGinness, knowing the calibre of this man, decided to wait.

Their conversation, when McMaster stopped at his car, was
not rushed. Fergus McMaster, for all his Scottish ancestors
and his proudly Scottish name, spoke with the slow, easy
drawl of a western Queenslander. A drawn-out "Y-e-s",
repeated slowly, was his habitual response to any pause that
invited acknowledgment. The voice and the blue eyes had a
steady authority.[40]

The two men had met before, but did not know one another
well. McMaster, learned McGinness, had been on his way
back to Devoncourt Station when the front stub-axle of his car
had snapped as he tried to cross the Cloncurry River. Fergus
McMaster was never to forget McGinness's response to his
predicament. Twenty years later he wrote: "I did not know
McGinness very well and was surprised when he said he
would make arrangements for his friend to attend the picnic
with someone else, and that he would give me a hand to fix up
my car."[41]

They visited one garage after another but all were deserted

15

and locked. Not once did McGinness talk of flying or the desirability of a local air service. But, despite the sultry heat, over a period of some hours his energy and ingenuity were unflagging. McMaster recalled: "If there was a door that it was possible to open, or a sheet of iron that could be removed to give access to a garage well, he was in. I was so impressed with the help and alertness of McGinness — and so grateful for his assistance — that the ground was prepared for my ready help when he and Hudson Fysh later submitted their ideas to me in Brisbane."[42]

McMaster finally got back to Devoncourt that night. He did not see McGinness again until they met in Brisbane in the middle of the following year. But their Sunday meeting in Cloncurry was to have consequences every bit as important to Australian aviation history as the arrival in Darwin of the Vickers Vimy.

Flying in Formation
1920 to 1921

There were no consolation prizes for the four other con- **1**
testants who sought their place in aviation history by setting
out from London to cross the world by air. R. Douglas and
J.S.L. Rose, flying an Alliance PZ Seabird, left on 13
November and crashed at Surbiton only minutes later; both
were killed. H.G. Wilkins, V. Rendle, D.R. Williams, and
G.H. Potts, flying a Blackburn Kangaroo, made their departure from Hounslow on 21 November but after a forced landing in Crete on 8 December, abandoned the flight. C.E.
Howell and C.H. Fraser, in a Martinsyde Type A Mark 1, left
on 4 December but crashed at St George's Bay, Corfu, on 9
December. They were both drowned. Only the Sopwith
Wallaby, piloted by G.C. Matthews and T.D. Kay, came near
to completing the flight. After leaving Hounslow well before
the others, on 21 October, they persevered with great courage
for some six months before reaching Bali; but here, on 17
April, their flight came to an end when they crashed on a
banana plantation.

Hudson Fysh, in Darwin, watched the grass on the Fanny
Bay landing ground grow monstrously while he waited for the
arrival of Matthews and Kay. In less than two months after
Ross Smith had touched down on a smooth, cleared surface, it
had grown to a height of eight feet. Fysh commandeered all
the scythes and sickles in Darwin and, with labour from the
occupants of the Fanny Bay gaol, cut a long landing strip
through it. It was not to be needed. The news of Matthew's
crash in Bali ended his early endeavours at airport

maintenance as well as the requirement for his presence in Darwin.

Transport facilities for departing residents of Darwin hardly matched those of Europe in 1920. There was a monthly boat for Brisbane which had to round Cape York and pass down through the Great Barrier Reef waters, or there was an overland route south to Adelaide, part of which was made by horse or camel. Fysh chose neither but, instead, joined a car party leaving for Cloncurry and traversing much of the hard country crossed by McGinness through Newcastle Waters, Borroloola, Anthony Lagoon and Camooweal. He left in an old Ford on 27 May on a journey that was as rugged and remarkable as McGinness's had been. At one time the car was towed by a team of horses; punctures became so constant that they ran first with sacking in the front tyres and then with long grass, stuffed in tightly and lashed with greenhide. Their last stop before Cloncurry, after heavy going in rain and mud, was at the homestead of a great pioneer, Alexander Kennedy, who in 1869 had come to the region by bullock train; his partner had been speared by a group of Kalkadoons. Now in his vigorous eighties, Kennedy was full of interest and support for the notion of a local air service. Paul McGinness had fired his enthusiasm.

This grand old man was to become one of the original shareholders of Qantas, after participating in the legal guarantee that enabled the founders to raise finance pending the first share issue. He was also, at the age of eighty-four, the airline's first paying passenger.

"Mr. and Mrs. Kennedy took us in", wrote Fysh, "and we slept in dry beds that night, with our wet clothes steaming before a big wood fire in the kitchen."[1]

The following day, after a final few hours in the old Ford, they reached Cloncurry and McGinness and Fysh were reunited. He found an impatient McGinness, full of optimism and with a plan of action. Convinced, after his sustained contacts with the local people, of widespread interest, McGinness wanted to start an air taxi service, supplemented by joy-rides. The key person for the successful business implementation of his plan was the influential and respected Fergus McMaster, then visiting Brisbane. Swept along once again by his old pilot's drive and decisiveness, Fysh responded. They set off for Brisbane together.

Country men who, like McMaster, depended on a sound rural economy for their prosperity, were becoming a cohesive

18

and increasingly influential force in the young federal Parliament. Anti-Labor in their general outlook as the Great War ended, they nevertheless became more and more disenchanted with the leader of the National Party, Prime Minister William Hughes who, for his part, did not attempt to hide his contempt for them. Their intrinsic and enduring political strength emerged when, campaigning for the first time as a separate political party in the 1919 general elections, they won eleven seats in the House of Representatives.[2] With Hughes re-elected as prime minister, these two parties were seen in the public mind as staunch supporters of Britain and the Empire, for the war had brought a passionate and widespread belief that national survival was impossible without imperial unity and the protection of Britain. Indeed, these two conservative parties "tended to place loyalty to Britain above local patriotism".[3]

There had been a radical change across the nation in self-perception. "The old digger replaced the bush-worker as the symbolic embodiment of the national identity."[4] The nationalist of the nineties and the prewar years had been transformed by a great world war from an independent and assertive youth to a cautious adult, conservative and imperialist in outlook. The resulting federal political mix, with its rural influence, was to prove useful to the handful of graziers who supported the idea of a new air service in outback Queensland.

McMaster was staying at the Gresham Hotel in Brisbane when McGinness and Fysh called on him. "It was", he wrote, "about June 1920. They gave me an outline of a proposition for joy-flight and taxi air work in Western Queensland and the Northern Territory. This close personal appreciation of myself for McGinness had been established . . . I was quite prepared to assist, not only personally, but to raise sufficient capital to finance the venture."[5]

Though that meeting between the two airmen and the station owner saw the birth of Qantas it was, in terms of contemporary world airline activity, of little significance. Overseas, there had been a proliferation of new aviation companies. In England, Aircraft Transport and Travel, formed as far back as 5 October 1916, had begun "operations suggestive of airline practice" in February 1919.[6] A route to Amsterdam was opened on 17 May, followed on 25 August 1919 by the opening of the world's first daily commercial service on international routes between Hounslow and Le Bourget. Another

English company, Handley Page Transport, was incorporated on 14 June 1919 and began regular services to Paris on 2 September. A third air transport company, British Aerial Transport Company (BAT) began operating on 30 September and a fourth, S. Instone & Company, converted its private air service to a public one on 15 May 1920, flying London–Paris. Three other British companies operated scheduled services in this first year of sustained activity.

The Qantas beginnings were, however, remarkable in retrospect. Except for KLM Royal Dutch Airlines, registered in October 1919, Qantas is the only airline in the world from those pioneering days that is still in existence.

KLM began life with solid financial backing from the Dutch business and banking fraternity, a grant from Her Majesty Queen Wilhelmina of the "Royal" prefix, and the support and authority of the Dutch government.[7] The initial funds for Qantas were put together less institutionally.

When McGinness and Fysh left McMaster in the lounge room of the Gresham Hotel, he saw that a grazier friend was in the room. "I looked across", wrote McMaster, "and noticed A.N. Templeton, a woolgrower from the Longreach district. I explained the proposition, the good work that Fysh and McGinness had put up in Palestine, that there was no doubt in my mind that, although the venture of an air service in the outback was not a gilt-edged investment, aviation should be encouraged."[8]

McMaster made his first convert. Templeton was won over and undertook to match any contribution that McMaster himself made. Greatly encouraged, McMaster decided to follow up his success.

> Not having any business engagements for the afternoon [he wrote] I strolled over to John Thompson's Bookshop at 311 Queen Street. He and I had been in the A.I.F. together, and I gave John the whole story. He parted with a cool £100.
>
> From Thompson, I went across Eagle Street and told the story to Mr. Alan Campbell, managing director of the Queensland Primary Producers Association Ltd. He also parted up and, as well, undertook to act as secretary pro-tem until the venture got on its feet.
>
> Fortunately, after leaving Campbell, I met Mr. T.J. O'Rourke in Queen Street. He was the largest shopkeeper in Winton and also a man with considerable personal interests. Generous to the needy, he had the reputation of being very careful regarding investments. I placed the proposition before him with little hope of support. To my surprise, he suggested I walk back with him to

his hotel — where he drew a cheque for £250, and said that there was another one there for the same amount if required later on.[9]

Though seemingly casual, those encounters marked the beginning of a sustained commitment by McMaster. He was well aware that McGinness had marked him out and just as aware that there were sound reasons for his doing so. He had warmed to the carefree style of the aviator but had seen behind it an energy and sincerity that he respected. Now, in the proposition put to McMaster, McGinness had demonstrated his sincerity in generous measure by putting up £1,000 in cash for the venture; Fysh, too, had committed £500. These were substantial amounts at a time when the basic wage for an adult man was only a little over £4 a week.

McMaster arranged another meeting at the Gresham with Ainslie Templeton, Alan Campbell, McGinness, and Fysh where they agreed on the basis of a prospectus for a company, which he undertook to draw up. McGinness and Fysh were authorized to proceed to Sydney and investigate the purchase of suitable aircraft.

There was no complex legal documentation of their initial agreement; not even a separate business bank account. McMaster's personal account was used. "Qantas", wrote McMaster, "was founded on trust and co-operation, and that

Ainslie Templeton, one of the first Qantas directors, Acacia Downs, Longreach (left).

Fergus McMaster, first Qantas chairman, Moscow station, Winton.

GRESHAM HOTEL

BRISBANE
AUSTRALIA

T. M. AHERN,
Proprietor

Advantages offered to an aerial
Co in N.W. Queensland

(A) Climatic Conditions.

In the climate of N.W.
Queensland, almost every day of the year should
be a flying day. No fogs and stormy weather
conditions such as are met with on the
coast and in the South are experienced in the
N.W. Local thunderstorms are of little
hindrance to flying. Owing to the above
facts it should be far more easy to establish
a regular service in N.W. Q'land than in the
Southern States.

During wet weather the Company's
machines will be able to operate between
the wildernoots when all car traffic is held
up owing to the boggy unsettled roads.
On occasions the car traffic is held up for
weeks and the roads are bad.

(B). Country flown over.

Before any regular aerial

Draft notes on stationery from Brisbane's Gresham Hotel in Hudson Fysh's handwriting, written following the discussions between McMaster, Templeton, Campbell, McGinness, and Fysh in mid-1920 which led to the registration of Qantas on November 16 that year.

is what stuck to it through the first severe years of its pioneering life."[10]

In Sydney, McGinness and Fysh soon fully committed all the initial capital. Joined there by Arthur Baird, who once again had abandoned his garage business to become their engineer, they met with Nigel Love, who headed the Australian Aircraft and Engineering Company, agents in Australia for the British firm of A.V. Roe. Love had himself been a pilot with the Australian Flying Corps. With his colleagues, he had chosen Mascot as the site for the company operations and as Sydney's first aerodrome, building the first hangar there on the tidal flats.

The Australian Aircraft and Engineering Company was building, and modifying, the much-used Avro 504K biplane, replacing its unreliable rotary engine with the water-cooled Sunbeam Dyak, a vertical six-cylinder engine of 100 horsepower. It had a fabric-covered, wooden structure, was twenty-eight feet eleven inches long, and had a wingspan of thirty-six feet. It could carry, besides the pilot, two passengers at a cruising speed of sixty-five miles per hour. McGinness and Fysh ordered two of them, at £1,500 each.

That order, dated 19 August 1920, was placed in the name of "The Western Queensland Auto Aero Service Ltd". The basis of the Qantas acronym was still three months away. It was not until 16 November 1920 that the certificate of incorporation was given under seal at Brisbane for "Queensland and Northern Territory Aerial Services Ltd.". Its initials, including the full-stops,* provided the name Q.A.N.T.A.S. "coined", wrote McMaster, "with Anzac as its inspiring factor".[11]

After the exhilaration of buying their first aircraft, there was an almost immediate let-down. The Sunbeam Dyak engines, which had to come from England, were delayed. Without any income, and with hotel and travel expenses which they met themselves, the two airmen grew anxious. Alternative aircraft were considered. Their pro-tem secretary, Alan Campbell, received a rough quote for "the Westland Limousine Machine":

... the Limousine, with the 200 Hispano Suiza Engine is about £2,700 in England, and with the Rolls-Royce Falcon Engine

---

*In early documents and correspondence, the company's initials, Q.A.N.T.A.S., were capitalized and separated by full stops. Gradually this gave way to the now familiar "Qantas", though both forms were used.

about £3,500. The firm are also bringing out a large machine with a 450 Napier Lion Engine and this comes out at about £5,000 in England. This machine carries a pilot and five passengers, or the equivalent weight in goods. The touring speed is about 100 to 105 miles per hour, and the petrol capacity is 96 gallons, or about five hours flying.[12]

Another possibility was the new Avro Triplane. In England, Avro had won a £10,000 prize for its design in a competition sponsored by the *Daily Mail* for "the best commercial aircraft". The Triplane had a payload of four passengers, or 1,206 pounds, and a price tag of £2,798. "The cabin", wrote *The Morning Bulletin*, Rockhampton, "is as roomy as a railway carriage of the box type, furnished with four comfortable chairs."[13] For a proposed Longreach–Winton service it could manage a schedule of one hour forty minutes for the 108 miles.

Despite misgivings from the prudent McMaster but after "making the fullest enquiries in Melbourne and London", a decision was made to order a Triplane. "Personally," McMaster wrote to Alan Campbell on 30 September, "I would sooner have let this machine stand over until the Company had got further ahead . . ."[14]

Although the Triplane purchase went ahead, some financial caution prevailed. One of the two Avro Dyaks was cancelled. Now, they were in the hands of the suppliers and they could only wait.

McMaster threw himself wholeheartedly into the business arrangements, single-handedly preparing the draft prospectus and urging Campbell to try to sell more shares (then a perfectly legal activity). Solicitors were engaged to draw up the Articles of Association of the company, in preparation for its registration. In the same letter of 30 September expressing caution about the Triplane, he had written:

> Under separate cover I am posting you a copy of the prospectus, which I have handed to the printers. Knowing you to have a contrary kink in your constitution I feel that you will go out of your way to pull this document to pieces . . . I have dealt with the proposition much more fully than in the draft we drew up in Brisbane. I would like to get the Articles of Association printed and everything, as far as you can, pushed along. The sooner we get the Company registered and in order the better. Also, try and get as many good Australians as you can to take shares. I hope you will appreciate the typing. There are a few mistakes but I have been going at a hell of a pace — fully ten words a minute.[15]

He followed up with an urgent telegram: "Hope you

pushing on articles. Can you get the necessary signatures for registration in Brisbane?'' Campbell wired back. The Articles were on their way from the solicitors. He had no new subscribers though he required seven names for registration, each taking up a minimum of fifty shares. "I know of no-one," he said in a follow-up letter, "excepting Messrs Thompson and Kennedy in Brisbane and, of course, myself . . . I could allot Mrs Campbell fifty of my shares, but there would still be three names short. Perhaps we will be able to do something when a supply of prospectuses comes along."[16]

There was some slapstick between them. Having roused Campbell's expectations for the text of the prospectus and, with the authority of friend and chairman, exhorted him to greater effort, McMaster reappraised his typing and found it insufficiently elegant for the printer. So he did not send Campbell the promised prospectus. Campbell sent an urgent telegram, all anxiety, to which McMaster, on 6 October, responded: "Yours of the 4th I received today; also your telegram — which I promptly did not answer."[17]

"Consider yourself sacked", responded his friend. "I have been raising Cain here and shaking the Postal Department to its foundations . . . One can never get anything out of you, even when one knows where you are."[18]

When the elusive prospectus was finally printed it bore the date 14 October 1920 and revealed that the modest plans of McGinness and Fysh for joy-riding and aerial taxi work had, under McMaster's hand, become vastly more ambitious. First, there was to be the establishment of "aerial service centres at Longreach, Winton and Cloncurry", said the document. Warming to his task, McMaster then sketched in what would have been the longest direct air service in the world, "an aerial mail service from Longreach to Port Darwin, connecting at Winton, Cloncurry, Avon Downs, Anthony Lagoon, Newcastle Waters and The Katherine". Federal ministers, he affirmed, were considering the proposition and "it is expected they will assist in establishing the route . . . one that would be required in connection with the aerial defence of Australia".

His enthusiasm was boundless. Such an air route would be valuable to the federal government in the administration of Port Darwin, he wrote; it would help the development of the large pastoral and mineral areas by making them accessible to the providers of capital; it would allow mails for Europe and elsewhere to connect at Darwin. "A regular mail service along this route would do more to develop commercial aviation . . . than any other in Australia."[19]

In fact, the first official approach by the new company to the federal government for support was not made until 23 February 1921. By then, the immediate postwar boom, fuelled by the soaring prices for export commodities and providing a favourable trade balance of £50 million for the year ending mid-1920, was over. Wholesale prices peaked in August then began a sharp slide. Deflation in Britain and the United States curtailed spending and there were savage price reductions for Australian exports, compounded by a bad season that cut the actual volume of agricultural products. The turnabout in the trade balance in that 1920–21 year brought recession and, as credit was restricted, interest rates rose. Wages were reduced, wool became almost unsaleable, and cattle followed. It was a tough period in which to bid for government financial support. Responding to the Qantas request for support the government "had no hesitation in saying 'No' ".[20] (In England, Mr Winston Churchill, secretary of state for air, was telling the operators of Britain's pioneer air services not to expect financial subsidies from the state; European governments, more enlightened, were more generous.)

The fledgling company, with its immodest prospectus and modest capital, though formally registered in Queensland on 16 November 1920 with its head office at Winton, still lacked aircraft. The Sunbeam Dyak engines arrived on the wharf in Sydney one week after registration and sat there for a further week. Nigel Love estimated that he could deliver the Avro early in December; McGinness and Fysh hoped for mid-December; Alan Campbell, who met them all passing through Sydney, more cannily judged that Christmas would pass before it would be ready. He was right.

It was not until 25 January that McGinness was able to wire McMaster that the final tests of the aircraft were satisfactory and he had taken it over. On 31 January, three months after the arrival of the engines, McGinness left Mascot in the Avro Dyak for Winton. The first aircraft ever to be owned by Qantas was on its way.

For Hudson Fysh there had been additional anxieties. Cancellation of the order for the second Avro had, at least temporarily, threatened him with redundancy. McGinness was by far the more experienced pilot, with some five hundred flying hours to his credit compared with Fysh's meagre thirty-five. Indeed, Fysh, who had proved himself a fine observer,

had only just managed to win the coveted pilot's wings before
the war had ended. Maj. Richard Williams had given a promise that all observers, after a tour of duty, would be given the
opportunity to train as pilots. Fysh managed to complete his
training on 28 February 1919 in Egypt, only one week before
his ship left for Australia. He had done most of his flying in an
Avro 504K, but had managed thirty minutes and one landing
in a BE2E biplane. Now he was to try the BE2E again;
Longreach stock and station agent, Charles Knight, had
bought one of two BEs imported by the Perdriau Rubber
Company for publicity purposes. (The aircraft, with
Perdriau's chief pilot, Jack Butler, had made the first-ever
flight between Australian capital cities in one day when on 9
July he flew it from Sydney to Brisbane.) Knight wanted
Qantas to deliver the machine to Longreach and the job went
to Fysh. Arthur Baird went with him, as passenger. "When I
took the aeroplane over," wrote Fysh, "the problem of my
own temporary redundancy was solved."[21]

McMaster had been preparing for their arrival. Three and a
half tons of petrol and three cases of engine oil were stored at
the private home of Longreach stock and station agent, Frank
Cory, awaiting transfer to "the shed at the rear of the Mar-
supial Board's offices".[22] The press were primed, and low
fares were promised between Winton and Longreach when
the Triplane arrived. That, said McMaster, would be about a
week after the first aircraft.[23] He had investigated all proper
insurance policies, though not without some problems. The
State Government Insurance Office told him that it could not
give cover under the Workers' Compensation Acts to his
pilots because "their remuneration exceeds £400 a year".
Within the meaning of the act the pilots, he was informed,
"are not workers".[24]

Storm clouds were massing along the coast to the north of
Sydney as McGinness and Fysh (with Baird as passenger)
opened their throttles to take off for Winton. Their immediate
destination, before nightfall, was the New South Wales country town of Moree, along a route that took them north over the
relative safety of coastal waters to Newcastle, and then inland.
In noisy cockpits, they were buffeted by wind and subject to
constant turbulence as the sky darkened. There were few flying aids. Each aircraft had a magnetic compass that swung all
too easily with the erratic motion, an inclinometer, a counter
for engine revolutions, and an air speed indicator. Stalling

speed was a mere twenty-five miles per hour below top speed. The propeller, as it spun, drove air backward in a spiral pattern so that it exerted pressure on one side of the aircraft fin and forced the pilot to push constantly on the left rudder to avoid turning. Sustained blind flying in turbulent cloud was impossible.

McGinness managed to fly through gaps in the thickening cloud but Fysh had less luck. Hoping to break through into clear air, he plunged into the blackness ahead of him and, tossed about by turbulence, was almost immediately disoriented. The aircraft stalled, with the nose swinging, and began to enter a spin. As it did so, he broke cloud base over a valley, but "with the clouds on the ground all round".[25] Recovery from the incipient spin, now that his confused senses had some visual reference, was rapid and straightforward but there was no way out through the encircling clouds. Fysh glimpsed a bushy hillside near a pithead, turned in towards it and, somehow, managed to land on the uphill slope. He came to rest next to a miner's cottage. Neither he nor Baird was hurt and the BE2E, miraculously, was undamaged. It was a very near thing. No records exist of the reaction of the miner's wife but they learned, while she gave them tea and they waited for the weather to lift, that they were at Red Head coal-mine. They turned the aircraft around, cleared some of the bushes from the ground ahead of it and, when the clouds began to break, took off — downhill.

It was the only unpremeditated landing of the flight. Fysh joined up with McGinness, who had arrived safely at Singleton, and they flew on uneventfully over the following days northward to Queensland through St George, Charleville, and Blackall to Barcaldine, the last stop before Longreach. McMaster, who had caught the train from Rockhampton on Queensland's north coast, was waiting there for them.

It was hot, and he was apprehensive, for the plan was that he should fly the last legs with them to Longreach and Winton and grace what, it was hoped, would be an impressive and historic arrival. While he waited, he inspected the landing ground and found it was a small clay-pan in a scrub of gidyea stumps. Away to the west, towards Longreach, he could see willy-willies that spiralled whirling columns of dust across the mile-wide, parched stock route. He sent a telegram to his Rockhampton friends: "Everybody happy but father."

The Avro 504K and the BE2E came into sight on schedule

and landed safely, though "with only inches to spare", on the clay-pan. Pilots, passengers, and spectators adjourned with McMaster to the bar of the Shakespeare Hotel. There, "the immediate future was mapped out".[26]

McMaster had flown only once before, on a short joy-ride at Hendon in England. Now, only the conviction that his personal prestige in the district was at stake sustained his determination to undertake the sixty-five mile flight ahead. As he settled himself in the hot cockpit, he noted that McGinness seemed, as usual, utterly without care. The engine roared, they bumped forward across the hard clay and climbed slowly through the thin and no less bumpy air. He nerved himself to enjoy "the splendid view of the surrounding country". Settled on course, he soon found himself flying over Kelso, one of his properties between Longreach and Ilfracombe, and was able to count the five dams. "I could see every one of them at once and could tell the quantity of water in each", he wrote to his friend, Campbell. But great sheets of lightning began to fill the sky to the south-west and approaching storm clouds were massing ominously as they landed, in late afternoon, before cheering crowds at Longreach.

Despite the welcome, and the knowledge that they had beaten the mail train from Barcaldine by twenty minutes after giving it two hours start, he faced the final flight to Winton with misgivings. They were not unjustified.

The BE2E aircraft of Longreach stock and station agent, Charles Knight. Hudson Fysh flew the BE2E from Sydney to Longreach in company with McGinness, who flew the Qantas Avro 504K. Knight travelled from Longreach to Winton with Fysh on 7 February, 1921 and returned the following day, when this photograph was taken. Knight is sitting in the front cockpit.

On Monday morning, 7 February 1921, McGinness led the two aircraft off the ground on the final leg for Winton. McMaster's grazier friend, Ainslie Templeton, shareholder and director of the company, was now his fellow passenger in the Avro. Fysh, following immediately in the BE2E, had the aircraft's owner, Charles Knight, as passenger. A flight of one and a half hours, that should have posed no difficulties, lay ahead of them. It was to take considerably longer. "Templeton and myself", wrote McMaster, "were supposed to know every road and track between Longreach and Winton. We didn't. In high, and other, spirits and with a tail wind, the Avro and BE were easily doing 100 miles an hour. But up in the air it was impossible to tell a road from a ploughed fire track, and the country was a maze of tracks. We went wrong."[27]

Half an hour out from Longreach, when there should have been open downs country around them, he saw only the hills and rough country of the Opalton Range. It was far too windy and noisy to shout to McGinness, so McMaster contrived to write him a pencilled note. It had no effect. "He was cool; too cool for Templeton and myself", wrote McMaster. "He kept pointing to his compass, which showed west."

McMaster tried again with another note. "One hour from Longreach. Too many mountains on our right." His pilot remained cheerful but unmoved.

"Should be open downs country on the right", said a third note. The helmeted McGinness continued calmly on his course. With some desperation, McMaster scribbled again. "Winton", he said, trying a new line of persuasion, "is north north-west of Longreach."

This time McGinness, who had been steering west for two hours instead of north of north-west, reacted. He came round a little to the right, then more, then more again until, retracing his track, he was steering east. Far ahead — "as far as the eye could see" — McMaster sighted a faint discolouration on the ground. Slowly, very slowly, it became recognizable as open downs country. At its centre he began to make out a "slate-coloured patch, the size of a dinner plate". In turn it grew, became some kind of settlement, and then a town. Ainslie Templeton passed a note to McMaster: "Thank blazes we are somewhere!" They had now been airborne for three hours on a flight that should have taken half that time; but the town ahead was Winton.

On the hill to the north of Winton's artesian bore, a large

crowd had assembled. They knew that the aircraft were due by eleven o'clock because a telegram had been sent after the departure from Longreach "requesting smoke on the landing ground" by that time, to indicate wind direction. Intently and anxiously, the crowd scanned the sky in the direction of Longreach as the minutes dragged by. Then a speck was seen, far to the south of the expected direction. Two aircraft became distinguishable, drew closer, and then began circling the town as they lost height. McGinness came in with the Avro first, touching down only feet from the sheet that had been pegged out on railway hill to indicate the landing area. Fysh followed, with another perfect landing. They had fuel in their tanks for only fifteen minutes more flying. "Much relieved," wrote McMaster, "we had a drink."

The town's welcome was a hearty one and "the aerial party was . . . entertained at a smoke concert at the North Gregory Hotel".[28] The king was toasted. Speeches recalled the days when "Cobb & Co's coaches were the most up-to-date method of rapid transport", when "it was the usual thing to see station owners and managers arrive in Winton by buggy, with a mob of spare horses driven behind by a couple of black boys". McMaster, in his resounding voice, reminded them of the links between aviation and defence. "Australia", he warned, "lies open to all from the air. The only reason that Australia is held by us today, gentlemen, is because we are fortunately a part of the greatest Empire in the world." As he reached his peroration, carried away by the company and the drama of the day, the single Avro 504K became for him the symbol and heart of the security of their vast and empty continent.

"This commercial aviation company", he urged across the smoke-filled room, "should get your support as Australians, not investors; not for the dividends it is likely to bring in, but for the great influence it must have in the administration, development and defence of Australia."[29] Possibly, out on railway hill in the darkness, the lone Avro blushed.

The Imprint of Honesty
1921 to 1922

2   Despite the euphoria of the arrival at Winton, the two aircraft left next day to return to Longreach. There has been, ever since, a desultory but amicable debate between the two places to claim the honour of providing the birthplace of Australia's international airline. The records, however, are specific.

Though Alan Campbell was "pro-tem" official secretary of the company, he lived in Brisbane. The routine chores of secretary were first carried out in Winton. Harriet Rylie did them, free of charge, from the office of her father, who was a stock and station agent.[1] Miss K. Tighe of Winton did the book-keeping, also free of charge.[2] The address of the company when it was formally registered on 16 November 1920 was Winton. The first meeting of directors (a "special meeting") was held at the Winton Club on 10 February 1921, though it proved to be the only meeting of directors ever held at Winton.[3] In the words of Fergus McMaster, as father of the airline, Winton was "the official birthplace of Qantas".[4]

The baby, however, needed intensive care from the start; it was moved immediately to the more promising operational environment of Longreach. From Longreach commercial operations began, first in Eagle Street and then from an office in the little Cory building of wood and galvanized iron in Duck Street. It was provided free of charge.

On the day of the return flight to Longreach, the Qantas fleet doubled. The owner of the BE2E, Charles Knight, though he had survived without enthusiasm the diversions and delays of the prolonged flight from Longreach to Winton, decided after the return flight that he had had enough. Hudson Fysh, after leaving Winton, lost his way and, in conditions that were very rough, missed Longreach by twenty miles and had to track back to it along the Thompson River. Knight was very sick. He vowed (probably while still in the air, according to an amused McMaster) never to fly again.[5] When he offered the BE2E to Qantas, they bought it for £450 (though McMaster insisted that part of the purchase price take the form of shares in the company).

With two operational aircraft now in Longreach and the expensive Triplane nearing its delivery date in Sydney, there were three urgent priorities. All fell neatly under one heading — financial. The company needed immediate cash to pay bills, and this could only come from flying operations; it needed longer term financial security which could only come from government subsidy of some kind; and it needed more capital, from the sale of shares, to expand.

"Please do your best to absolutely nail any prospective passengers, as well as shareholders", wrote Frank Cory to Alan Campbell. Get any interested shareholder, he urged, to sign the form of application "then and there, so you have some hold on him".[6]

Passengers, though, were very few. The only continuing source of revenue from February 1921 was joy-rides at

The ill-fated Avro Triplane at Mascot aerodrome, Sydney in late February 1921. It had been ordered in September the previous year and was to prove a costly disappointment for Qantas. The area where it is standing in this photograph is now part of the Qantas Jet Base at Sydney Airport.

£1.1s.0d for ten minutes.[7] Very aware that this was a limited and temporary source of cash, McMaster turned his sights on the government. Less than a fortnight after the Winton arrival he was wiring McGinness, in Sydney checking the Triplane, to go to Melbourne "to see Rodgers, Colonel Williams, Guthrie and any others possible". (Guthrie was a Queensland senator and Arthur Rodgers a minister in the government.) "Let them know we have actually started operations. Keep the position fully before Federal Ministers", urged McMaster.[8]

The "operations" referred to by McMaster meant joy-flights by Hudson Fysh in the BE2E. As the aircraft could carry only one passenger, and as Fysh took along with him on flights between towns, "the proprietor of the Western Motor Works, Herbert Avery" as mechanic, only local joy-rides were possible. Nevertheless, the industrious Fysh was able to report to his chairman that in the last week of February, in a trip that included Blackall, Muttaburra, Isisford, and Wellshot, he had carried seventy-eight paying passengers and "cleared £100 off the BE". On one flight he had taken up an Aboriginal (without charge) and on another carried a Mr Murray who "shot two turkeys from the machine". His report was as conscientiously concerned with the grey necessities of business as with the adventure and eventfulness of flying. "I think we should have a bank account here [Longreach] as soon

Joy-riding at Winton in early March 1921. Some of the staff and a young patient from the Winton hospital with Arthur Baird (left) and Paul McGinness (second from right) in front of the Qantas Avro 504K. The engine cowling of the Avro shows evidence of modifications by Baird to improve cooling in the high temperature conditions of western Queensland.

as possible. I am sure Longreach is the best headquarters."
His worries included his own finances. "I hope you got my
wire", he concluded. "As you understand, I have all my
money in the company and I should like to pay my hotel bill
here."[9]

As Fysh was concluding his successful first tour, McGinness was active in Melbourne. He wired on 28 February that
McMaster should join him at once. On the advice of Rodgers,
he thought prospects were bright. McMaster responded at
once and joined him but it was a false alarm and there were no
immediate results. McMaster, however, considered it "the
first shot fired at the then Federal Government".[10]

More pressing and potentially disastrous matters were soon
occupying them. Writing with some pride to Campbell on the
company's new letterhead ("Head Office: Winton; District
Office: Longreach"), McMaster advised that McGinness and
Baird had left for Sydney to bring the five-seater Triplane up.
When it arrives, he said, "we will get the regular service
started between Winton and Longreach in conjunction with a
motor service which will take all excess baggage".[11] The
Triplane never came; McGinness had crashed it in Sydney. A
telegram advised McMaster (with considerable underem-
phasis) that on a practice landing with full load the undercarriage had sheared off and the aircraft was "damaged slightly".
A follow-up letter next day was equally sanguine in tone and
stated that the flight ended in "damaging the undercarriage,
propeller, radiator and one wingtip". In fact, the aircraft, in
which was invested almost half the capital of the company,
was massively damaged.

It was a substantial blow. In Longreach, Frank Cory had
been expecting valuable revenue from it. There was lots of
passenger work offering, he told Campbell, because of the wet
weather. Longreach had had over six inches of rain and all the
creeks and rivers were flooded. The Triplane, besides, had
commercial and passenger attractions. Fares for the Avro
504K, which only carried two passengers, had been calculated
at £10 a head for the Longreach–Winton trip. Fares for the
Triplane, with four passengers, would be only £6.6s.0d each.
And, said Cory, "in a car you take six or seven hours on the
best of roads and are charged up to £4.4s.0d and you have the
expense of extra meals".[12]

Campbell had a letter from McMaster that same week. It
was quite clear that neither economic recession, government
procrastination, broken aircraft, or weather patterns could

deter him. "I am pleased in a way", he wrote, "that we are up against it for a start, because it will make the business stand on its own feet." If it could carry on under present difficulties then, he said, "when a more generally prosperous time comes it should be a very good commercial as well as national investment — and the latter is, as far as we are concerned, the principal [one]. It [Qantas] will have to be something stronger than a hot-house plant."[13] In the same letter he advised Campbell that Senator Guthrie had taken shares and concluded: "Britain got her great sea power during the last war from her mercantile marine. So will every country get its aerial strength from the machines, pilots, mechanics and ground organisation used in commercial aviation." He was to back his words with almost total involvement in the small and precarious company. He was, said Cory, "the moving spirit of the thing. Absolutely."[14]

Meantime, and somewhat nearer the coal face, McGinness and Fysh were attending to the "future aerial strength of the country" by joy-riding. Fysh set off to the south in the BE2E to work the Lower Diamantina and Cooper's Creek area but business was not good.[15] "I am cutting out every possible risk", wrote Fysh, "and am not taking up any children." McGinness, going north, made Urandangi his centre for a tour of the middle and upper Georgina country. A special target was the gathering at Urandangi for the Picnic Race. He took up a lot of passengers and won some helpful notoriety by riding the winner in one of the main races.[16]

In that same month, pioneer aviator Bert Hinkler demonstrated how air travel could shrink the vast Australian continent. Hinkler flew his Avro Baby aircraft nonstop over the 800 miles from Sydney to Bundaberg, in Queensland, taking only nine hours. The flight was widely and deservedly acclaimed. At the same time Fergus McMaster, on the ground, once more proved the fallibility of the motor car. He wrote to Campbell on 12 April:

> I had a pretty rough trip back. The roads were extra rough and I had a job to get to Kyuna the first day. I spent the second, until three o'clock, on repairs. I went pretty rotten setting sail for McKinlay, then damn rotten when I struck a creek seven miles out. Had to foot it into McKinlay and get the assistance of three good horses to pull the car out. Then I set sail for El 'Rita [one of his properties] and had a rotten time out to the ten-mile creek — known as Snake Creek. Damn me if I didn't get stuck again, and had to walk the ten miles back. Quite a nice Sunday afternoon's walk.[17]

36

In the same letter he told his friend that the aviation business was paying its way — "something to be thankful for these days".

In fact, it had, in bad economic conditions, done surprisingly well. In his chairman's address at the first general meeting of the company on 21 May in Longreach, McMaster was able to report that the "Aerial Service" had been established on a permanent footing. Everywhere the aircraft went there was enthusiasm that, he said, "must eventually warrant . . . opening centres in Charleville and Cloncurry". That, when it occurred, would be a big step towards opening up "what must eventually be one of the greatest aerial routes in Australia".

The report of the provisional directors showed that, to 15 May 1921, there had been applications for 6,850 shares for which there were cash receipts of £6,075. The company's plant was shown as one Avro Dyak Biplane three-seater, one BE2E Biplane two-seater, and one Avro Triplane five-seater. The cost of the plant was set down as £5,671.18s.11d, including spares. Apart from £100 on the BE, it was declared clear of debt — with the exception of repairs to the Triplane "owing to an accident in Sydney during the trial flights". There were also some "incidental charges" of about £200.

This somewhat casual reference to the Triplane crash and its implications would not nowadays win an annual report award for frankness, compounded as it was by the obscurity of the chairman's statement that "your directors decided to allow her to remain in Sydney until August next" and then return to

Longreach in 1921, taken by Paul McGinness from a balcony looking along Eagle Street. A complete block of shops and houses, including Qantas's first office, was destroyed by fire forcing the airline to move into temporary premises in Frank Cory's small building in Duck Street from about April 1921 until May 1922.

Qantas's second office in Longreach in mid-1921 and probably the best-known office of all in the company's history. It was owned by Frank Cory and located in Duck Street. The building to the left in the photograph is the Longreach Club and across the street to the left of the club was the site of the Graziers Building. Qantas moved its head office to the Graziers Building in May 1922 and this remained the headquarters until the move to Brisbane in 1929.

operate in the wet months. As, however, the biggest shareholder in the company, McGinness, had crashed the aircraft himself and as his fellow directors, Templeton, Fysh, and McMaster, followed him in their financial commitment as shareholders, perhaps their reluctance to emphasize the setback can be overlooked. (Of the 6,850 shares issued, McGinness then held 1,450, Templeton 1,000, Fysh 600, and McMaster 500. There were no free "promoters' shares" and no directors' fees or expenses of any kind were paid.)

McMaster reported that the pilots had "absolutely put safety first". McGinness, in the Avro Dyak, had flown 7,400 miles and been in the air 111 hours, taking up 285 passengers and making 130 landings. Exclusive of pilots' salary, it had cost forty-eight shillings per hour to keep the aircraft in the air, or eight and a half pence a mile (four and a quarter pence per passenger-mile with two passengers). Fysh, in the BE2E had "done exceptionally good work". The machine had already made "a gross return of double the purchase price". It had flown 6,370 miles, been in the air 98 hours, and carried 296 passengers. The flying cost had been forty-one shillings per hour, or seven and a half pence per mile. The Avro had averaged sixty-seven miles per hour, the BE2E, sixty-five miles per hour.

"Considering the serious financial times that the country

has gone through", McMaster concluded, ". . . the position of the company must be considered satisfactory."

He wrote to Campbell on 29 May promising a copy of the report and of the address of "the most noble chairman, which will tell you very little in a big lot of oratory". The head office, he advised, "has been shifted from Winton to Longreach, with Mr Cory as secretary". (The bank account was officially transferred to the Bank of NSW, Longreach.) Net profit was "about 600 pounds", and the new directors were "A. Templeton, P. McGinness, H. Fysh, F.W. Bode, T.B. McIntosh, G. Morgan Reade, Norman White, Dr Hope Michod, and myself". McMaster concluded: ". . . now that we are up against what we think are hard times, we are as fretful as a lot of spoilt children. No, dear friend, don't think for one moment that yours of the Mobile Artillery is down and out . . ."

For a small company it was, in McMaster's words "a pretty hefty" board, "but as no fees, travelling, hotel or other expenses were being paid it didn't matter".[18]

Of great moment to the company's ultimate survival, in the report of the provisional directors, was this sentence: "Your directors placed a proposition for an Aerial and Motor Service to operate between the railheads of Longreach and Winton, before Capt. Edgar Johnston, one of the officials of the Air Board, who lately visited the district." He was "very interested" and "advised that an application should be lodged before June 30".[19] Intense efforts to persuade the federal government to support the company were now to dominate their thoughts. McMaster told Fysh that he had suggested to McGinness that a move in regard to getting a subsidy should be made without further delay. "I would like to see you", he said, "push this particular matter and try either to get a straight out subsidy or a mail contract."[20] There were hopeful signs on government thinking; the Department of Defence had invited tenders, to close on 30 July, for an air route in Western Australia from Geraldton to Derby (via Carnarvon, Onslow, Roebourne, Port Hedland, and Broome).

Financial assistance from the government of the Commonwealth was "the big picture". Less grand, but indicative of the true scale of the financial parameters, was Frank Cory's request to McMaster on 15 June for £4.10s.0d to secure "a proper cabinet for the files, instead of filing correspondence in a folder in my own cabinet". Cory also urged that they get a cheque book "properly printed with the company's name . . .

39

as is done by other companies". His plea was heard and in the balance sheet for the year ended 30 June 1921, office furniture was listed among the company's assets at £6.5s.3d.

While Qantas was, for the first time, dipping its toe in the restless sea of federal politics, aviation decisions were being taken in England that greatly interested the Australian prime minister. Introducing the estimates of the Air Ministry on 1 May, the air minister, Mr Winston Churchill, announced "a melancholy decision". As the need for economy was so great, he said, Britain could not further develop both airships and aeroplanes; it had best give up on airships and concentrate on aeroplanes. He offered, to any private company willing to take over the government's airships and run them for commercial purposes, "all the airships free of charge". That airships could be commercially attractive was not doubted by some authoritative commentators. The magazine *Aeronautics* observed that the P&O Company had raised their rates for the voyage to India, charging a second-class fare to Bombay of over £70.[21] "Were the R36 [airship] now ready to carry passengers to and from Karachi at £100 a head, there would", commented the magazine, "probably be a daily queue outside the booking office in India."

Churchill was offering "as a free gift" seven airships in the possession of the ministry, including two Zeppelins surrendered by Germany. The other five "represented expenditure of several million pounds". They were huge structures. The R33 was 640 feet long, with a cubic capacity of 2 million feet of gas and a disposable lift of twenty-nine tons. To Prime Minister Hughes the opportunity seemed too good to miss. He was to urge the Parliament later that year to take them, because "Australia would be at one bound brought to the shores of Europe".[22]

The general news from England on civil aviation was not encouraging. Though the War Ministry reported that British aircraft had flown more than a million and a half miles between "the opening of civil aviation in May 1919" and the close of December 1920 (with a fatality rate of one passenger per ten thousand miles), the industry was in trouble. Churchill gave one reason for its failure: "Travelling by air does not mean travelling from one city to another but from one aerodrome to another", and aerodromes were "on the outside of the cities".[23] Trains, on the other hand, said Mr Churchill, ran into the heart of cities. The authoritative commentator,

Lieutenant Colonel Holt, wrote: "Private aviation having come to nought, there is only one other way to keep a large civil aviation organisation in being, and that is to establish an air mail service in England."[24]

The Qantas financial problem, in the outback of a vast continent on the other side of the world, was therefore not unique. A "somewhat dampening" letter from Rodgers at Parliament House advised them on 14 July that there was no immediate likelihood of a Charleville–Cloncurry aerial service, though there were prospects of a limited subsidy for a trial service.[25] The situation held some hope, however, and the Civil Aviation Branch was, under Edgar Johnston's direction, active in providing aerodromes and emergency landing grounds between Adelaide and Sydney and Melbourne and Sydney, as well as northward through New South Wales to Charleville and Cloncurry. And the Department for Home and Territories was negotiating for the purchase of aerodromes in Melbourne, Sydney, and other cities.

The philosophy behind this activity on behalf of commercial aviation included the possible necessity for the sudden expansion of the RAAF. Parliament had voted £100,000 for civil aviation but, as the staff of the Civil Aviation Branch of the Department of Defence had been organized for only four months of the financial year, only a little over half of the vote had been transferred into approved recommendations for expenditure and, of this, "it had only been practicable to expend usefully £6,700".[26]

With government assistance still little more than a gleam in McMaster's eye, the Avro and BE again concentrated on

The Qantas Avro 504 in Townsville, 7 July 1921, after registration lettering was applied for the first time. The painting of the lettering was done by Richardson's Signs of Longreach.

Ingham, 1 August 1921. McGinness is standing second from the right. During a flight from Ingham the next day, McGinness experienced engine failure and had to force land the Avro in a sugar cane field. It was extensively damaged and had to be sent to Sydney for repair.

custom from joy-rides and trips to race meetings. Fysh considered a four-day taking of £49.10s.0d "a very good trip and a profitable one" but in the hard times, "no passengers were obtainable at our usual rates". "If my charge was four pounds an hour instead of eight pounds I am sure", he wrote, "that trips would come along at a great rate."[27]

McGinness had had one particularly interesting job just before the meeting of directors. On 16 May, with Arthur Baird, he had flown the Avro to Elderslie Station to pick up the owner, C.J. Brabazon, who wanted to examine potential grazing country in the Northern Territory. They flew to Austral Downs and a hundred miles beyond and, though the country proved unpromising, Brabazon congratulated McMaster "on having secured so capable a man as McGinness". Baird, too was praised, as "thoroughly careful, wonderfully so".[28] Bad luck, though, lay ahead for McGinness. While Fysh worked the southern districts, McGinness went north again and during a July trip took up a total of 138 passengers, plus eight on a joy-ride from Ingham. His engine failed, he reported, and he was forced down in a field of tall sugar

cane.[29] Though no one was injured, the damage to the Avro
was extensive. The aircraft was dismantled and shipped to
Sydney for repairs. It was their first major operational crash
and their modest profits to date all went on repairs.[30] With the
wrecked Triplane still in Sydney (it never saw operations),
they were left with the old BE and a total passenger carrying
capacity of one.

With remarkable resolution, the board decided in August to
intensify their efforts to secure fresh capital and so enable the
company to buy suitable aircraft to tender for the hoped-for
Charleville–Cloncurry route, if tenders were called. Fysh, in
the BE, was to tour the south and south-west yet again, but
this time with the prime objective of selling shares; McGinness, by car and then aircraft when the Avro was repaired, was
to cover northern towns, assisted towards the end by
Clarkson, a professional "sharegetter".[31] A leaflet with the
title "Flying's the Thing" was printed, stressing the link
between the government subsidy for commercial aviation and
national defence. Fysh wrote articles for the local press. A
second prospectus, dated 18 August, was issued to raise a
further £15,000 and, following a meeting of directors at
Longreach on 30 August with Dr Hope Michod in the chair,
"a propaganda committee" was formed.

The pace was hectic, and the commitment intense.
McMaster, after addressing meetings in Rockhampton on 16
September, took a steamer to Townsville and joined McGinness there for more meetings. They drove inland to Charters
Towers where, after addressing two enthusiastic gatherings,
the mayor formed a supporting committee. McGinness then
went across by car to the north-east coast while McMaster
took the train to Hughenden where the mayor chaired a
meeting of town and country people. Then it was on to Cloncurry where "the project had a splendid reception".[32] The
Cloncurry Chamber of Commerce and Mines and the Cloncurry Shire Council passed a strong resolution calling for
immediate action to connect the town and district "to the
southern pastoral centres and with the south by means of a
regular Government-subsidised Aerial Mail Service".

This political ground swell was backed by individual financial commitment. "Over £13,000 was subscribed in a very
short time", wrote McMaster.[33] One letter from W.J. Bell, a
railway fettler said: "[I have] read your advocacy . . . and I beg
to state that I, a common worker, am willing to take up 10, 20

SECOND PROSPECTUS

— OF —

QUEENSLAND AND NORTHERN TERRITORY AERIAL SERVICES LIMITED.

(INCORPORATED IN QUEENSLAND UNDER "THE COMPANIES ACTS, 1863-1913.")

CAPITAL:

£100,000 divided into 100,000 Shares of £1 each.

DIRECTORS:

FERGUS McMASTER, ESQ., (Chairman), Moscow, Winton.
A. N. TEMPLETON, ESQ., Acacia Downs, Longreach.
DR. F. A. HOPE MICHOD, Longreach.
NORMAN F. WHITE, ESQ., Warrandaroo, Longreach.
G. MORGAN READE, ESQ., Winton.
FRED. BODE, ESQ., Winton.
T. B McINTOSH, ESQ., Wologorang, Burketown.
LIEUT. P. J. McGINNIS, Longreach.
LIEUT. HUDSON FYSH, Longreach.

HEAD OFFICE: LONGREACH, QUEENSLAND.

BANKERS:

BANK OF NEW SOUTH WALES, LONGREACH.

SOLICITORS:

CANNAN AND PETERSON, LONGREACH AND BRISBANE.

SECRETARY:

F. R. CORY, LONGREACH

PILOTS:

LIEUT. P. J. McGINNIS, D.F.C., D C.M   LIEUT. HUDSON FYSH, D.F.C.

ENGINEER:

SERGEANT BEARD, M.M. ex-A.F.C.

Proposed Issue of 15,000 Ordinary Shares of £1 each.

The minimum number of Shares of the present issue that will be issued by the Company to any one Shareholder will be £10. Shares are to be applied for as per accompanying form of application and to be paid for with application or within one month of acceptance of application.

PROSPECTUS.

The Company has been duly incorporated and has carried on business with the abovenamed pilots and engineer since the seventh day of February, 1921, with a plant consisting of an Avro Biplane and a B. E. 2 E. Biplane. The number of miles flown have been 21,450. The number of passengers carried have been 950. The number of special trips to stations have been 62 covering a distance of 5,800 miles. In all 789 landings have been safely effected as against two landings which were unsuccessful. On these latter occasions only minor damages occurred and no personal injuries were sustained. The balance sheet for the period ended 30th June, 1921, may be inspected by any intending shareholder at the office of the Company or with any director.

The second prospectus of Qantas Ltd. issued on 18 August 1921.

COMMONWEALTH GOVERNMENT SUBSIDY.

The Commonwealth Government have set apart an amount not to exceed £25,000 for the purpose of subsidising an Aerial Mail Service which will operate along a route touching Charleville, Blackall, Longreach, Winton and Cloncurry and probably other towns on the way. It is obvious that this service, if established, will be of incalculable benefit to Western and Northern Queensland. To secure it any company or firm submitting a tender must show that they have the necessary plant and equipment to maintain same.

The service is part of a scheme of Aerial Defence of the Commonwealth and from a patriotic standpoint and in the best interests of the Commonwealth it should be encouraged and supported by every good Australian.

From a district standpoint it will at once be seen that such a service will bring the towns mentioned and the districts surrounding them very much closer to the southern centres of population, business and finance for passengers as well as for mails. Fares will compare more than favourably with those charged on other modes of transport, in addition to securing enormous saving of time. For instance Cloncurry will be brought within ten hours of Charleville including stops. This will tend to popularise and advertise Central and Northern Queensland and will add to the value of both town and country properties. This aspect the Directors would stress as a reason for asking the support of the residents of the district served. It is impossible to place a limit on the benefits which are likely to be conferred on these districts.

As the Government will provide and pay for all landing grounds along the route, risk of accidents will be practically eliminated.

After this service had been proved, an effort could be made to connect with Mungindi—a railhead on the borders of New South Wales. This would bring Sydney within thirty-six hours of Cloncurry.

The Company proposes, if sufficient capital can be raised, to tender for such service and if same is accepted (which is confidently expected) to procure the necessary plant and start running over the route mentioned.

It will be a condition of the contract that a service at least once a week each way between Cloncurry and Charleville shall be carried out. In addition to this, the Company would run a bi-weekly service between Longreach and Winton connecting with mail trains.

To carry out the conditions of such tender and service, the Company will require to raise an additional £15,000. This sum is required to obtain the necessary extra plant to carry out such service and such plant and its cost is estimated as follows :—

3 Aeroplanes	£9,000
Spares and Accessories	2,200
Hangars, Workshops, and other Plant ...	3,400
Other items including oil and petrol ...	400
	£15,000

The Company already own the following plant :—

Avro Triplane costing	£2,750
B. E. 2 E. Biplane costing	450
Avro Biplane costing	1,500
Spare tools, etc.	743
Buildings, etc.	276
	£5,719

The Company proposes to tender for the above service at a figure which will cover complete running cost of the machines engaged. It is believed that the Government in considering tenders will place the greatest weight upon the ability of the tenderer to carry on and the efficiency of his plant and staff.

The following is an estimate of receipts and disbursements for twelve months on this and other work to be obtained.

LOW ESTIMATE OF RECEIPTS.

Income from all sources	£18,500

HIGH ESTIMATE OF DISBURSEMENTS.

Salaries	£3,330	
Secretary, Office, and General Expenses ...	1,800	
Petrol and Oil	2,200	
Depreciation—50% on machines and spares	8,200	
10% on plant	380	
		£15,910
Balance profit on a very conservative basis		£2,590

45

The Directors therefore ask for the Subscription of a further £15,000 of Capital.

To raise this amount they propose to issue shares in sums of not less than £10 to any one shareholder. This minimum amount is within the reach of practically everyone but it is hoped that large individual issues will be asked for.

If the proposed contract is not obtained from the Commonwealth Government, any moneys paid by applicants under this present prospectus will be refunded.

While the Directors are of opinion that the business is a good commercial proposition and capable of development, owing to the favourable nature of the country operated over and the special facilities it offers for travelling, they would make a special appeal to the patriotism of the people in the districts served and urge the great benefit it will be to such districts and to the Commonwealth as a whole. The service will ensure the quickest possible means of transport of mail and passengers. The personel of the Company will become members of the Australian Air Force Reserve. The pilots have now had six months experience in pioneer flying over the said route and the districts served. This is important on the question of efficiency.

Applications should be made on the form enclosed and forwarded with remittance, if any, to the Secretary, Bankers, or Solicitors of the Company, or to any Director. From any of these, prospectuses and forms of application can be obtained.

Longreach, 18th August, 1921.

APPLICATION FOR SHARES.

THE QUEENSLAND AND NORTHERN TERRITORY AERIAL SERVICES LIMITED
(Incorporated in Queensland under the Companies' Act, 1863-1913).

CAPITAL: 100,000 Shares at £1 each.

ISSUE of 15,000 SHARES—payable on application or within one month of acceptance of application.

TO THE DIRECTORS—

I request you to allot me... of the abovementioned SHARES upon the terms of the COMPANY'S SECOND PROSPECTUS (dated 18th August, 1921.) I agree to accept such SHARES and I authorise you to register me as the holder of the said SHARES and to pay for same as set out above.

Dated the..... ....day of....................................192

NAME IN FULL.......

ADDRESS...........

DESCRIPTION...........

SIGNATURE ....

Theo F. Barker, Printer, Longreach

The second prospectus of Qantas Ltd. issued on 18 August 1921 (cont.).

46

or 30 pounds' worth . . . so you can fire away." Touched, but aware that risk was involved, the board wrote to him accordingly: "Your letter", Bell responded, "bears the imprint of honesty."[34] He cut his application by half.

Some subscribers were won over more dramatically. Fysh flew his BE2E into Tambo just after the owner of a local property, Minnie Downs, had left town. "I jumped into a car and raced after him", wrote Fysh.[35] It took an hour to catch him but, in the dust by the side of the road, he signed up for 200 shares. When a Sydney man, who owned a station at Longreach, left his satchel in the Longreach Club when he caught the train south, McGinness took off with it in the Avro, caught the train, and circled it until the driver stopped. The satchel was dropped from the air and its owner, Mr C. Foy, later took up a total of 750 shares.[36]

The new Qantas prospectus and the all-out efforts to raise capital attracted mild reproof from the controller of civil aviation, H.C. Brinsmead. He advised them gently but firmly that though he thought a Queensland service linking the western rail terminals would be of great value, it should be clearly understood that any subsidy would depend on the size of the grant in aid of civil aviation approved by Parliament. "I have to suggest that perhaps the time is a little premature to call for subscriptions to ensure financial backing to place a tender." He noted, however, that Qantas had promised to refund all moneys in the event of the contract not materializing.[37]

The political pressure stimulated by McMaster was growing. In October, over a dozen shire and municipal councils plus the Charleville, Charters Towers, Townsville, and Rockhampton chambers of commerce and the New Settlers league at Cloncurry sent telegrams to the prime minister. McMaster urged on his parliamentary friends, A.J. Hunter and Donald Cameron, and McGinness was sent to Melbourne. By the end of October there were hopeful signs and McGinness wired from Geelong Railway Station on October 29: "Absolutely vital our subsidy McMaster come Melbourne immediately."[38]

McMaster went at once and, after preliminary meetings with Brinsmead and others arguing his case, an impressive deputation of all Queensland members of the House of Representatives and Senate accompanied McMaster for an interview with the prime minister on 10 November.

It took place in Mr Hughes's private office in the basement of Melbourne Parliament House and the atmosphere was tense. Herbert Brookes, president of the Nationalist Party Organisation, was present, emphasizing the uneasy and unfriendly relations between Hughes and the Country Party. Hughes, wrote McMaster, had a very narrow majority in the House but the Country Party had been voting almost solidly with Labor as each item was challenged in the estimates and division after division called for.[39] Dr Earle Page, minister for defence and responsible for civil aviation, had indicated he would move a vote of no confidence. It was in this atmosphere that McMaster's friend, A.J. Hunter (Country Party member for Maranoa in Queensland) introduced the deputation.

"Mr Hughes," wrote McMaster, "bristling like an old war horse, raked the Country Party from stem to stern."[40] For the whole week, roared Hughes, they had been voting solidly with Labor for reductions in all items of the estimates. Now, a prominent member of the Country Party had the audacity to lead a deputation asking for increased expenditure.

The broadside lasted some twenty minutes then Hughes, reaching for the large device on his desk that he used to assist his hearing, indicated that McMaster should speak.

"I am reputed", wrote McMaster, "to have a very loud, resounding voice. Possibly on that occasion it was not absolutely under control. Our wartime Prime Minister was sitting there at his table holding a great, clumsy black box affair to his ear. After I had been speaking for a few minutes, Mr. Hughes put his black box on the table. My reaction was that he had decided not to listen further."[41]

It was a wrong interpretation. After a short time Hughes interrupted: "Excuse me, Mr McMaster, I know I am deaf, but I am not as deaf as you evidently think."

There were some short, supporting speeches when McMaster concluded, then a dead silence. Then, wrote McMaster, "Mr. Hughes shot a question to me out of the blue".

Prime Minister: "When are you going back to Queensland?"

McMaster: "As soon as we secure your reply."

Prime Minister: "You have it now. The Government has no money. My reply is no!"

McMaster, confident that his backers would continue the fight, replied that he would not accept that answer. But the interview was over. "We filed out," he wrote, "leaving Mr. Hughes alone, like a conquering bull, still with the black box on the table."[42]

48

Though the prime minister could find no money on 10 November for the Queensland Air Service and its Country Party advocates, tenders for government-subsidized carriage of mails by air between Sydney and Brisbane and Sydney and Adelaide closed the following day. And only a week before, Mr Hughes was praised in London by the British Member of Parliament, Mr A.B. Raper, for his "enthusiasm for an England–Australia [Airship] service".[43] There was, in fact, no doubt about the prime minister's underlying interest in aviation. He urged the House, less than a fortnight after the McMaster deputation, to take advantage of Mr Churchill's offer of the airships. "That they can make the passage from England to Australia", he said, "I am as certain as that I can walk down the steps of this building."[44] For a two-year experimental service to Australia, the cost would be £1,647,000 of which Great Britain would pay half and the Dominions the other half. The government, he said, must pioneer the way and then "the development of this means of communication must rest on a business basis".

In the same week, in London, the agent-general for Tasmania, Mr A.H. Ashbolt, was also advocating a service by airships, in a lecture to The Royal Society of Arts: "Our first step must be Egypt, which is destined to become the Clapham Junction of the Imperial Service."[45]

Meanwhile, as Fysh and the Longreach Committee "were hard at it trying for all the cash possible" McGinness gathered the Qantas supporters in Melbourne together and, with them, put an alternative proposal to the prime minister.[46] The government, he suggested, should give Qantas some of the war surplus DH9 aircraft that were available from Britain. But this second proposal, also, was turned down.

These two setbacks did not deter McGinness. "He was still out for a fight", wrote McMaster, and when he learned that "a certain member of the Government would be travelling on the Melbourne-Sydney train" he suggested he should be on it too.[47] Exact details of this McGinness initiative, like so many of his activities, were never recorded but there were results.

"During the early hours of a Saturday morning," wrote McMaster, "I had a telephone call from McGinness from a railway station somewhere between Melbourne and Sydney. If it were possible to get the Country Party to ease up its opposition to the Estimates, sufficient money would probably be made available for a service between Charleville and Cloncurry."[48]

The response was quick. Mr Hunter told the House on 22 November that if certain unexpended funds could be used for subsidizing commercial air services throughout Australia "it would probably induce Honourable Members to pass these Estimates as they stand". Already, he said, there had been an arrangement entered into with a West Australian company involving a sum of £25,000 and tenders had been called for Sydney–Brisbane and Sydney–Adelaide services. In addition, he said, a deputation had asked "for a similar service through Central Queensland . . . Since February last, a Company [Qantas] has been operating in the interior of Queensland with headquarters at Longreach . . . It has been found impossible to carry on if dependent on passengers only."[49]

The Labor Party was indignant, sensed betrayal in the air, and accused the Country Party of gross inconsistency. But the Country Party "to support civil aviation" voted with the government.[50] The battle seemed won.

Within a week of the Country Party about-face in Parliament, McMaster was advised that tenders for a Charleville–Cloncurry service would be called at "an early date".[51] The company now had to follow through the consequences of political success. To tender convincingly it had to raise the remainder of the required capital and, aware that the Civil Aviation Branch would press for bigger and more experimental aircraft for the route, it faced big and urgent commitments. The board decided, at a meeting on 7 December "that a Manager should be secured".

Though no official word had come through to Qantas about tenders, McMaster knew that McDonald had received a letter on the 19th from the Air Council advising that tenders would be called and there would be a maximum subsidy of £12,000 a year. He felt sufficiently certain of his sources to call on the bank on 8 December, told the manager that the federal government had sanctioned a £12,000 subsidy for the new service and requested an extension of the company overdraft limit to £1,000 until the middle of January. A circular was prepared and sent out on 14 December on the company letterhead over Frank Cory's signature seeking more shareholder funds.

As a result of the good work done in Melbourne by our Messrs McMaster and McGinness [it said], the Federal Government are prepared to subsidise the Aerial Route from Charleville to Cloncurry to the extent of £12,000. To be in a satisfactory position to tender for this contract, it is necessary to sell 10,000 more shares

. . . There are 240 shareholders at present and if each persuades
an acquaintance to take up even ten shares we would have another
2,400 sold. We enclose an Application Form. A person buying
shares is merely asked to pay ten per cent of the value of the
application, balance by arrangement.[52]

Formal advice from the government that approval had been
granted for "the establishment of a weekly [return] aeroplane
service between Charleville and Cloncurry, Queensland" was
received in a letter dated 15 December from the secretary of
the Prime Minister's Department. Qantas, it said, "now has
the opportunity of tendering under conditions similar to those
approved for the contracts already granted, viz Geraldton–
Derby, Sydney–Adelaide and Sydney–Brisbane".[53]

Hudson Fysh was able to tell Campbell on 19 December
that "the capital is coming in well". He sent him thirty
booklets "which deal with propaganda work for the raising of
the rest of our required capital" and advised that he would be
canvassing in Brisbane and Sydney in the New Year. On the
same day he wrote to McMaster urging that, if they won the
tender, they should run the service "with small machines
from the start. I find it hard to believe", he said, "that the
Civil Aviation people will want us to put big machines on a
service such as this. It would be a bad business risk."[54]

The scale of operations envisaged was set down in a brief
financial forecast, outlining proposals to acquire three Bristol
Tourers (or similar) at a cost of £9,000. Spares, workshops,
and hangars were costed at £5,600 and plant in hand valued at
£5,719 to "bring total capital to £20,319".[55]

Running costs were estimated at £15,849 for one year. A
total of four aircraft, flying a combined 884 hours of 70,720
miles, would consume petrol and oil worth £2,043. The old
BE2E and Avro would be limited to 100 hours per year.
Pilots' salaries were put at £1,500, engineers' and mechanics'
at £1,830, with remuneration for the secretary of £300.

"Possible revenue" was headed by the item Government
subsidy: for 70,720 miles it would, at the anticipated 4s.0d per
mile, amount to £14,144. By contrast, passenger revenue
forecasts were modest: for Winton–Longreach, 260 at £4
(£1,040); for Cloncurry–Winton, 104 at £10 (£1,040); for
Charleville–Longreach, 104 at £12 (£1,248). Other work at
3s.6d a mile was forecast at £1,000, bringing total revenue to
£18,472.

January 1922 was dominated by the requirements of tendering. Though Qantas had put their capital and effort into pioneering an aviation company for western Queensland, had mustered widespread financial and local government support for a service, and had been largely responsible for convincing the government of its necessity, they now found that this was insufficient to win them the contract and subsidy for the Charleville–Cloncurry mail service. The tender was an open one, and there was strong competition, particularly from The Larkin Aircraft Supply Company and its associate Australian Aerial Services Ltd.

The Larkin interests had won contracts for both the Adelaide–Sydney and Sydney–Brisbane services but Larkin, like Norman Brearley who had won the contract for the Geraldton–Derby route for Western Australian Airways Ltd., on 2 August 1921, was not popular with the Civil Aviation Branch. Both were aggressive, quick to complain, and never satisfied with departmental decisions. Fysh, by contrast, was regarded as helpful and co-operative.[56] Larkin's company held the Australian agency for the big Handasyde aircraft, a new but untried light-passenger machine. Though he put strong pressure on Qantas to buy it, even offering to withdraw his competition for the Charleville–Cloncurry tender if it was ordered, the company considered it too big, too experimental, and too expensive.[57] The Qantas first choice was the much smaller DH9C.

The form of tender with its conditions, was sent to them on 6 January, but they had already, two days earlier, cabled London for aircraft quotations. As Qantas had no representation there, the cable was sent through Dalgety and Company, whose Queensland general manager, A.D. Walsh, was a personal friend of McMaster. Westland Aircraft of Yeovil was asked to give prices on three aeroplanes suitable for the 600-mile route and able "to carry three passengers and luggage, one hundredweight of mails and pilot". The McMaster touch was evident for the cable (the first ever sent to London by the company) expressed expectation that the service would be extended northward from Cloncurry to the Katherine, and southward, from Charleville, to Mungindi in New South Wales, "a total distance of 1,600 miles and the longest direct air service in the world".[58]

The directors met on 7 January and decided to request that the bank increase the overdraft limit to £3,000 (with the same nine guarantors). It was agreed that Fysh should go to Melbourne to "make enquiries as to suitable machines and report by telegraph, complete the tender in all respects and lodge same on behalf of the company with the Defence Department."[59]

Despite what seemed a bewildering number of aircraft types to be considered, the choice soon narrowed. McMaster, in mid-January, had passed on to Fysh information received from the controller of civil aviation, Lieutenant Colonel Brinsmead, on Vickers, de Havilland, Handley Page, Beardmore, and Handasyde aircraft. It was known that Brinsmead strongly favoured the Vickers machine, the Vulcan. By Qantas standards and needs it was enormous. A biplane with a wingspan of forty-six feet, it could carry eight passengers and pilot and cruise at ninety miles per hour. It was expensive, costing £3,700. Fysh asked the controller for permission to tender with two aircraft, instead of the three specified. It was refused, and it seemed that Qantas would have to tender with three eight-seater aircraft for a service on which their December analysis had estimated total passenger traffic for the year at under five hundred.

Fysh sent a last minute telegram to McMaster on 29 January 1922 saying that he had been advised, confidentially, of strong opposition.[60] One tenderer had proposed four of the big Vulcans. Larkin had undertaken to extend the proposed service to Cunnamulla, in southwest Queensland, without subsidy. Fysh, wrote McMaster, "thought these Vulcans the only thing" for the Qantas tender.[61]

It was too much for McMaster. In what was meant to be the final decision they "decided to risk it with two Vulcans". Then Fysh, he said, at the very last moment, added a smaller DH4 "and put the tender in hoping for the best".[62] (The Triplane, though included on the tender document, was not considered appropriate.)

The tender price was four shillings per mile flown. For a one-year contract it was, for the company, a substantial commitment.

They did not have to hold their breath for too long. The Qantas tender was accepted on 2 February "against heavy opposition".[63] A condition was the appointment of a third pilot, from England, with experience "in handling big machines".[64]

Brinsmead congratulated them. "I have little doubt", he wrote, "that if you had not pushed so hard for such a service that it would have meant waiting at the earliest until the next financial year."[65] Their choice of the aircraft he had favoured

This aerial view of Longreach was one of a series taken from the Qantas BE2E early in 1922. The street in the foreground is Duck Street where the Qantas office was then situated in Frank Cory's premises, just out of this photograph to the right. The Graziers Building is shown in the corner on the lower right, facing the camera.

had obviously played a part. Brinsmead wrote: "I feel sure you will have no reason to regret having decided in favour of the Vickers type . . . it should prove to be a much better financial proposition than any other machine designed for war purposes." Qantas was soon to find out that he was wrong.

The Bravest of the Brave
1922

McGinness, who remained in North Queensland with Clarkson canvassing for shares, took no part in these heady affairs. Clarkson's success, though, meant that his services were no longer needed. (The board decided on 7 January to give him notice of termination; he left on 22 April.) Fysh followed through in Melbourne, on the day of the tender acceptance, with an inspection of a DH4 aircraft owned by Ray Parer. "I believe that it is fitted up well with a cabin, and is in perfect order. We should purchase this at once. The Rolls-Royce engine alone is worth £1,200 and I think we can purchase the machine complete for £1,500."[1] He inspected the DH4 in the afternoon, and then set out for Sydney to discuss contracts for the Vickers Vulcans with William Adams, the Australian agents.

It was a busy month for Hudson Fysh. The board agreed on 12 February 1922 to cable £2,000 to Vickers in London as a deposit on the Vulcans and sent Arthur Baird to join him in Sydney to expedite the return of the Triplane when repairs were complete. They were instructed to ship the DH4 to Longreach as soon as possible if the purchase went ahead.

Fysh also occupied himself with requirements for the Longreach, Charleville, and Cloncurry landing grounds and the selection of a manager for the company, while arranging with the Air Council for their representative in London to see that the appropriate tests on the Vulcans were carried out. He also fitted in for himself flying instructions on heavier aircraft at Point Cook.

3

With board approval, Fysh bought the DH4 from Parer on 7 March for £500 cash and £1,000 in three months ("the best terms I could get").[2] A week later, on 15 March, the company contracted with Stewart and Lloyds in Brisbane for the supply and erection of a hangar at Longreach for £1,637 and asked the Department of Defence for permission to spend £100 on behalf of the government in clearing and improving the Longreach aerodrome. On that same day, Frank Cory finished up as temporary secretary.

Cory, from his stock and station agent office, had worked hard and conscientiously for the company, without fee. "They needed someone, though, with book-keeping skills", he said, "and I never had any of that."[3] He was not altogether unhappy to part company. Hudson Fysh, he thought, was hard to get on with. "He had a fair idea of his own importance", said Cory. For McMaster he had only respect. "He was the moving spirit. Absolutely. He was a strict, upright Scotsman and a big man in the cattle industry. But he spent the whole of his time on Qantas." McMaster did not approve of drinking, particularly for pilots. "Old Fergus was a bit hard that way", said Cory. On that count, Fysh "got on with Fergus". Fysh was no drinker.

McMaster's views on drinking complicated the search for an English pilot to fly the Vulcan. A board memo that required Qantas pilots to sign "the pledge" together with some strict conditions for dismissal, did not appeal to English aviators.

In the week following Cory's departure, Marcus Griffin was appointed manager of the company. A former army captain and winner of the Military Cross, Griffin had returned from the war to find that the manufacturing business which his brother had looked after in his absence had failed completely and was deeply in debt. Griffin, with no legal obligation to do so, personally met all liabilities. He was a good accountant and capable organizer and came to Qantas highly recommended for his integrity and abilities.[4] When he arrived in Longreach he found, to his concern, that the company was living entirely on its capital.

Fysh, in Sydney, communicated his anxiety to McMaster about the possible lack of engine power for the heavy Vulcan aircraft to which they were committed.[5] The extreme heat of western Queensland had already proved the limitations of engines fitted with radiators appropriate to English conditions. Engine power was reduced, as the hot air was less dense and less effective for combustion. Fysh urged that Vickers should be warned, as their contract guaranteed that the Vulcan should be capable of climbing to 10,000 feet with full load in thirteen and a half minutes, a rate of climb that the company considered the minimum acceptable.

This problem of engine power had been evident in the Triplane which now, a year after McGinness had crashed it, was finally repaired and ready for testing. Hudson Fysh did the honours with some apprehension, on 17 May. "It was indeed a strange looking machine", he wrote, "with its high cockpit and towering tiers of wings, its stove-pipe exhaust topping all." The tests were successful so Fysh, anxious as always for revenue, advertised joy-rides over Sydney — "No wind, noise or oil. Every comfort. Don't miss it." It was in fact the only cabin aeroplane then in Australia but Fysh thought it overweight and an aerial monstrosity.[6] He flew the Triplane in the Aerial Derby of New South Wales and came second, after Nigel Love, with a speed of sixty-nine miles per hour.

Though in flying condition, Fysh thought it only safe on perfect aerodrome surfaces with good landings in good weather and condemned it for commercial use. The Civil Aviation Branch agreed and withdrew its certificate of airworthiness. Including repairs, it had cost the company almost three thousand pounds and its final demise meant the loss of almost half the company's paid-up capital. Its Beardmore engine went to Longreach as a spare and its fuselage and cabin ended as a suburban hen-house.[7]

Brinsmead paid the company a visit at Longreach on 10 May 1922 in his capacity as controller of civil aviation, inspected the landing ground and promised that immediate steps would be taken to prepare it for the start of services. On 24 May, Qantas moved into its new offices in the Graziers' Building. Despite the loss of the Triplane, the company seemed set to progress from the uncertainties of joy-riding to regular, subsidized, scheduled operations and the prospect of stemming the mounting losses. Then came a crisis which was to threaten the existence of the company.

As early as 19 April there had been cause for concern about the Vulcans. Industrial disputes in England had delayed the delivery of the Vulcan engines, though Rolls-Royce was able to offer replacement engines that had run a few hours (but were guaranteed for 900 hours).[8] The directors were undecided about these engines but Fysh, urging that "your delay

Lt. Col. H.C. Brinsmead,
Controller of Civil Aviation,
1922.

means loss of £50 every day" won their approval to accept the offer.[9]

Then on 26 June, Griffin wired McMaster, who was in Sydney, that the delivery of the Vulcans would be delayed a further three months. Immediate efforts were made to buy or borrow two DH9s from the Department of Defence and, on Brinsmead's advice, a telegram was sent to the prime minister asking for his assistance.[10]

It was not possible to get the DH9s but approval was given for the purchase of two Armstrong Whitworth aircraft. Brinsmead wired the company on 6 July that "to enable you to commence service early September Minister approves purchase Armstrong Whitworth Machines and spares owned [by] Miller [and] Simpson, price not exceeding £700 each inclusive spares ... Repayment to Department to be effected by deducting proportion subsidy over six months second year your contract. If you concur, agreement will be drawn by

Crown Solicitor to ensure only Vulcan and DH4 machines utilised [on] main service after arrival and test . . ."[11]

Baird was sent to Melbourne to inspect the Armstrong Whitworth machines. Like the Avro 504K, they had a wooden structure and were fabric covered, but they were bigger. Though the wingspan, at 43 feet 6 inches, was only 7 feet 6 inches more than the Avro's, the 2811-pound maximum weight was a full 1,000 pounds more. Both had single, water-cooled six-cylinder engines but the AW FK-8's Beardmore engine delivered 60 more horsepower than the Avro's 100 horsepower Sunbeam Dyak. The AW carried three passengers, the Avro two.

The financial position of the company was precarious. It had a subscribed capital of £31,917 at 8 July, of which £22,749 was fully paid, but operations for 1922 showed a loss of £4,400. The company was living entirely on capital, and faced further expenses as the big Longreach hangar was completed, early in August. (The old hangar, at the showground, was dismantled and re-erected at the new aerodrome, as an office and store.) Their troubles compounded. Vickers cabled that no English pilot would agree to the proposed employment contract clauses that set out the Qantas grounds for dismissal

The Longreach aerodrome about mid-August 1922.

and the company's requirement that pilots should "sign the pledge" to abstain from alcohol.[12]

The DH4 aircraft that Fysh had bought arrived at Longreach on 12 August by train and was completely dismantled and overhauled by Baird. (The aircraft log book, completed in Baird's neat handwriting, indicates the painstaking detail and range of skills that he brought to the company. The cabin was removed and ring bracings placed in the fuselage; new compression struts were attached and a new top section constructed and fitted. Completely new ply and fabric covering was fitted to the fuselage top and the undercarriage was completely dismantled. A new tail skid was fitted and shock absorbers renewed throughout the machine. The engine bearers and fuselage were tuned up and a Rolls-Royce engine No. 158 was installed.)

Overhauling a Beardmore engine from an FK-8 in the Longreach hangar, late 1922. From left: Frank McNally, Arthur Baird, and Jack Hazlett. The object in Hazlett's hands is the camshaft from the engine.

Bigger than both the Avro and AW aircraft, with a 42-foot wingspan and maximum weight of 3472 pounds, its Rolls-Royce Eagle VIII V-12 engine was, at 360 horsepower, more than twice as powerful as the AW's. It had a clumsy, four-bladed propeller and a steel ladder fixed to the outside of the passenger cabin. Though ungainly and able only to carry two passengers it was to have a long and useful life.

While they were waiting for the Armstrong Whitworth aircraft, emergency landing grounds were selected. McGinness, in Cloncurry, let a contract to prepare two of them, one four miles and one eleven miles east of Cloncurry. A third, fifteen miles east, was being readied by the government and south from it towards Winton, more emergency grounds were being selected. South of Longreach, the company had men preparing four grounds, with plans for an additional two on the stock route between Longreach and Winton.[13]

Brinsmead had endorsed a timetable for the service requiring completion of the Charleville–Cloncurry journey in one day but Fysh and Griffin, strongly against flying in the hot, thin afternoon air of the summer months, opposed it, proposing an overnight stop at Winton.

There were many other details to attend to. A Talbot truck was bought for £275 for carrying spares and stores between aerodromes and emergency grounds. Construction of hangars at Charleville and Cloncurry was started. Petrol and oil depots were established to provide about a ton of fuel at Charleville, Blackall, Winton, and McKinlay.

On 9 September, when the directors met to approve an increase in capital to £40,000, a cable was received from Vickers Limited advising that they had at last engaged a pilot for Qantas.[14] He had considerable flying experience and his name was Capt. Geoffrey Wigglesworth. Vickers were also now advising that one Vulcan would be shipped from England on 19 September and the second one at the end of the month.

Hudson Fysh, meantime, had tested the first Armstrong Whitworth aircraft (which had been fitted with the Beardmore engine from the Triplane) on 6 September and then, nine days later, the second. Both tests were successful, though the engine radiators were considered too small and larger ones were ordered.

McMaster, with some optimism and much faith, had informed Brinsmead on 11 September that the DH4 and two AW FK-8 aircraft would be ready to commence the Charleville–Cloncurry service on 26 September.[15] They were to be used for six weeks until the big Vulcans, so consistently urged by Brinsmead, arrived.

It was a rash forecast, as the overhaul work on the DH4 was extensive. McMaster wired Brinsmead on 26 September that start of the service would be delayed until 5 October "to allow for unforeseen contingencies".[16] He asked if Qantas could substitute the Avro for the DH4. The reply from the controller of civil aviation was angry and withering. The Avro substitution was unacceptable.

"The delay in the commencement of the service", wrote Brinsmead, "is deplored." It was his view and that of his technical assistants, he said, "that two Armstrong Whitworths and an Avro of considerable age are not sufficient to ensure a reasonable guarantee of reliability of service, even for six weeks".[17]

Those first six weeks, he said, were "the most critical period of your undertaking". With unconcealed sarcasm he quoted McMaster's phrase, "the doing up of the DH4" and suggested that this "should not have been an unforeseen contingency to your technical staff . . . the responsibility for the delay must be taken by them". Brinsmead asked that work not essential to the airworthiness of the DH4 should be postponed "to obviate the disastrous delay of six weeks that is otherwise inevitable".

It was not possible, however, to ready the DH4 quickly, and a new starting date of 2 November was set. To add crisis to confusion, the company was advised by the Department of Defence liaison officer in London that the Vickers Vulcans, on test, had fallen well short of specifications. They were much heavier than had been calculated.

At the close of the second annual meeting of the company on 2 October 1922, the directors met and agreed that the liaison officer be instructed through Brinsmead not to take delivery of the Vulcans until they came within 5 per cent of the specifications supplied. A cable was sent to "stress the absolute importance of full climbing capabilities".[18] It was also, ominously, agreed that all further correspondence about the Vickers aircraft should "be passed through the hands of the company's legal advisers".[19]

Brinsmead tried to head off this confrontation with Vickers. "Do you realise", he wired, "that owing to the loose draft of your contract with Vickers the machines need not be fully loaded when tested for performance?"[20] But McMaster remained firm. The matter, he insisted, was now in the hands of the company's solicitors.[21]

On 21 October, Brinsmead passed to the company a telegram from the liaison officer in London. Vickers had been informed that "Qantas [was] apprehensive stability Vulcans for proposed work owing increased weight and inferior performance, particularly climb. Qantas refuse acceptance unless machines answer within 5 per cent of contracted estimated performance with 2375 lb load."[22]

There was now no chance of any early availability of the big

Vickers aircraft. However, Griffin advised his chairman on 21 October that both of the AW FK-8s had been finally tested and proved satisfactory in all respects. Four days later, on 25 October, the DH4 was tested and approved. Brinsmead was advised that the company was ready to start services on 2 November.

On that same day, Paul McGinness shocked them all. He sent a telegram to the company tendering his resignation.[23] It was only a week before the realization of their vision of a government-supported, scheduled air service.

Fysh had been aware that McGinness seemed "to be getting on the outer". Certainly, in all the detailed work of tendering and the selection of aircraft Fysh, his old observer and junior officer in the Flying Corps, had carried the flag. Though McGinness had shone in persuasiveness and the perception of political opportunity on that critical train journey between Melbourne and Sydney, he had not been able to "add any showing of administrative ability".[24] McMaster had always warmed to his personal qualities. McGinness, wrote McMaster, "was adventurous, quick and daring", with a restless, energetic nature that needed "something out of the ordinary as an occupation".[25] He could not tolerate constraint, and he had chafed under the nondrinking decree. He had

Repairs to the DH4, purchased as a reserve aircraft for the forthcoming Charleville-Cloncurry service, were completed on 25 October 1922. Qantas staff and several Longreach residents who assisted in the preparations pose for Hudson Fysh's camera. From left: Unknown, Cormack Hurst, George Dousha, Jack Hazlett, Marcus Griffin (manager), George Beohm, Arthur Baird.

63

sought to have it rescinded but when he made his proposal to the board that pilots be allowed to drink alcoholic beverages not stronger than lager beer, no one supported him.[26] While his days with Clarkson, the professional share canvasser, had been stimulating and opened up new possibilities and horizons, he was no longer on such close terms with Fysh.[27] The leader-follower relationship that had its beginnings in the junior observer's admiration of his daring and battle-proved pilot, and that had been carried over in peace into their rugged survey work in the north, was past. The methodical, tenacious, painstaking Fysh, who carried through the dull but necessary work of taking notes, making maps, writing letters, reports, and press stories, and worrying about the pennies and small problems was now, more and more, the pivot of events. Fysh could begin to see where his future and commitment lay, while McGinness was finding barriers in the very circumstances that gave the enterprise — based as it was on painstaking regularity — any meaning. To the carefree and venturesome elements of his temperament, the slog and detail of daily administration and bureaucratic sword-crossing were impossibly pedestrian. The dawning truth that his romantic vision of airline operations had at its centre the combined reality of a railway timetable and a cash book, that adventure and risk must subside into routine, repetitive perseverance, was disillusioning. He decided to follow Clarkson, in a new share-getting venture, in Western Australia.[38]

Though the trio of Roman Catholic McGinness, Presbyterian McMaster, and Anglican-educated Fysh was to split, McGinness agreed to stay on long enough to fly the opening service. "We desire to place on record", McMaster wrote to him on behalf of the board, "our appreciation of your services to the company, both in regard to the initial inauguration and the subsequent work in obtaining the subsidised contract and the raising of capital, and the directors view with regret the step you have taken . . ."[29]

McGinness was then twenty-six. He was, wrote Fysh, "the bravest of the brave [while] I was a much quieter, fearful type, who counted the odds. He was an extrovert. I was still deep in my retiring complex, an introvert. We never quarrelled."[30]

McGinness flew the Armstrong Whitworth aircraft G-AUDE, with Baird, to Charleville, in readiness for his last contribution to Qantas; he would pilot its first service as a scheduled airline operator.

Qantas Inaugural
1922 to 1923

The mayor and leading citizens of Charleville rose at dawn on 2 November 1922. In the still, sweet air they assembled at the aerodrome where Baird had fuelled and readied the Armstrong Whitworth FK-8, filling the fifty-gallon tank. It held the Australian Certificate of Airworthiness No.36 and was boldly identified with the registration letters G-AUDE. It had flown for almost exactly a year on joy-riding flights in Western Australia before Fysh, with Baird as his passenger, had taken it up on 9 September at Longreach on its first Qantas test. Charleville had already seen it, as Fysh and McGinness had each flown it there in September and October. Now the atmosphere was different. McGinness, in his flying clothes, addressed the attentive gathering. Australia, he said, was keeping pace with Europe and America. This service, whose start they were to witness, was destined to link Australia to Asia, Africa, Europe, and Great Britain. A cheer went up when, with McGinness in the cockpit, Baird swung the propeller and the engine roared into life. It was 5:30 A.M. and, with 108 letters on board, they rolled forward to begin the first Charleville–Cloncurry Aerial Mail Service.

McMaster was at Longreach with the chairman of the Longreach Shire Council and a crowd of townspeople to welcome them when, ahead of schedule, and after a stop at Blackall, they touched down at ten fifteen. Their passenger for the onward flight next day to Cloncurry, eight-four-year-old Alexander Kennedy, was waiting with McMaster. His first journey to Cloncurry, fifty-three years previously, had taken

4

65

The directors of Qantas and the first passenger in Longreach, 2 November 1922, with the Armstrong Whitworth FK-8 which had just completed the first section of the inaugural airmail service. From left to right are: Arthur Baird, N.F. White (director), Dr. F.A. Hope Michod (director), Marcus Griffin (manager), Alexander Kennedy, Paul McGinness, Fergus McMaster (chairman of directors), Hudson Fysh, and T.F. Barker (director).

him eight months. He had taken shares in Qantas after a promise by McMaster that he should be the first farepaying passenger. Now, after travelling by train from Brisbane for the occasion, he was ready for a different dimension of pioneering.

Fysh flew the Longreach–Cloncurry sector next day. Again, to take advantage of the cooler air, they started at first light. Baird, as engineer, joined their first revenue passenger in the second Armstrong Whitworth FK-8 but its Beardmore engine refused to provide maximum revs and, after three attempts to take off, they transferred to G-AUDE. As they readied for take off, half an hour later, Kennedy in cap and goggles with the wind tossing his beard shouted, "Be damned to the doubters".[1]

They landed at Winton, 107 miles on, with mail and drank tea while the aircraft fuelled, then took off against head winds for their intermediate stop 132 miles away at the bush town of McKinlay. There was a brief stop and then they set out on the final 71-mile leg for Cloncurry, landing at 11:30. The first Qantas service, Charleville to Cloncurry, had taken seven and three-quarter hours in flying time for the 580 miles.[2] There were three cheers for the success of the service from the waiting crowd, and three more for its exhilarated first passenger.

The triumph of that inaugural flight was not the beginning of great things, nor even a first step towards stability and steady improvement. With aircraft that were entirely unsuit-

66

able, the year ahead was to bring a succession of unfinished trips and forced landings, crashes, and major damage.[3] The Vulcan, for all its gorgeous blue velvet trim and hat racks, was to be a flop. Orders for replacement DH9 aircraft took precious months for their fulfilment. And there were staff tensions and changes.

The departure of McGinness from Qantas in mid-November 1922 (after two more trips between Longreach and Charleville with a newly appointed mechanic, Jack Hazlett) left Hudson Fysh as the sole employee from the company's dreamtime days. It was a distinction that would always lend an added aura to his public reputation.

A new pilot, Fred Huxley, was engaged on 4 November as a temporary replacement for McGinness. The board gave McGinness a formal letter of thanks and a cigarette lighter to mark his departure. "There was no big deal about it", said Jack Hazlett. "He just left."[4]

A third pilot, T.Q. Back, joined them on 4 December. Other problems soon eclipsed their regrets at the loss of McGinness for Marcus Griffin, the manager, soon followed him. Though he had worked conscientiously and efficiently, Griffin's very forcefulness and impatience to get matters decided and done had made him less than tactful with his directors. The board did not like it and, through their chairman, told him so. On 5 January 1923 he wrote to McMaster: "From the conversation we had yesterday afternoon I am led to believe that my

Charleville, 2 November 1922, just before the departure of the first aerial mail in Queensland. From left: Mr Head, Charleville's postmaster and his son; Paul McGinness, Mr H.J. Carson, George Herriman, Qantas's agent in Charleville, two unidentified women, Arthur Baird, Mr C. Fitzwalter, Mrs Head (last two persons unknown).

The first airmail flight landing at Longreach 2 November 1922. A group of Qantas staff are running from the left toward the aircraft. Dr Michod, in white shirt and trousers with a white tropical helmet, is near the propeller and Hudson Fysh stands between the wing and tail fin.

resignation from the position of manager of Q.A.N.T.A.S. Ltd is expected by yourself and fellow directors . . . I now beg to tender such resignation."[5]

His resignation, to be effective on 7 February, was to prove of major significance for Hudson Fysh. Crombie, a director, wrote to McMaster: "I would like to see Mr. Fysh get a trial in the management position."[6] McMaster and the board concurred and, on 5 February, appointed him manager. In a phrase that summarized the personality and enduring attitude of the new manager throughout his subsequent career, Fysh assured the chairman of "my earnest endeavour to do the best possible for the company and to make a success of my new position".[7]

January had seen the cancellation of the joint and several guarantees made to the bank, following the financial commitment of the Commonwealth government; the installation of "late letter" boxes at agents' offices and acceptance of "a scheme of advertising by means of slides to be shown at Picture Shows at the various towns on the mail route".[8] Also from January, Hudson Fysh was granted a £50 salary increase that took him to £550 a year. An excess of passenger enquiries over available space kept confidence high but, over all, hung the shadow of the capacious and suspect Vulcans.

Fysh wrote to Brinsmead on 31 January "with the thermometer at 110 degrees in the shade" arguing that as it would be "positively unsafe to fly either the Avro Dyak or the A.W. between 11 a.m. and 5 p.m. . . . could there be any hope for

68

the Vulcans on a hot day?". Even loaded to only half its specified capacity it had, he said, no better performance than an Armstrong Whitworth. "Unless the Vulcans will climb fully loaded to 6,000 feet in 13½ minutes it is impossible for me to advise their acceptance", he told Brinsmead. "The first aim of this company is absolute reliability of machines and safety to passengers. It is only on those conditions that commercial aviation can be built."[9]

Brinsmead, whose advocacy alone had thrust the Vulcans on Qantas, now at last wavered. On 13 February he replied to Fysh, agreeing on the necessity for reserve power and good climb.[10] Still hopeful that the Vulcan, now at Point Cook in Victoria in process of erection, would prove suitable he put the proposition that it might work year round as a four-seater and possibly, in the colder months, as a six-seater. If, however, Fysh decided on cancellation there would be no objection.

The company, despite its newly won mail contract, was in a grave position. Prevented by the Civil Aviation Branch from tendering with the aircraft of its choice, the DH9, it was operating with what engineer Jack Hazlett described as "beaten up old Armstrong Whitworths and their most unsuitable engines, with tiny little radiators built for cold

Hudson Fysh, second from left, signs for the mails at Longreach prior to departure in the Qantas DH4 behind the group. Arthur Baird stands in the background between Fysh and the Postmaster.

climates".[11] The engines, mockingly, were called "the boiling Beardmores" (until the ingenious Baird made successful modifications). Meant only as stop-gap equipment pending the arrival of the Vulcans, Fysh now was facing the prospect of the Vulcan's unacceptability. On 25 February a bad situation worsened. Fysh responded to an emergency call to fly a worried father from Barcaldine to Rockhampton, where his small son had become critically ill. Taking off after a stop en route at the town of Jericho on 26 February the old AW (G-AUCF) could not clear the trees ahead. Fysh banked to the left, hauled the nose up, stalled, and crashed. He was not injured but the damage to the aircraft meant they were even more critically dependent on the outcome of the imminent Vulcan tests.

Fysh wrote to McMaster on 12 March 1923, the day the assembled Vulcan finally left Point Cook for its demonstration flight at Longreach: "We are fast approaching the end of our tether in respect of our present plant. There could be a temporary suspension of service if the Vulcan is refused." He hoped, he told McMaster, that some kind of settlement with Vickers could be effected and that they could put the Vulcan "on the run". Brinsmead, he added, was officially silent about their dilemma and seemed "to be leaving us to fight Vickers rather on our own".[12]

The aircraft on which so much depended, though christened because of its external appearance "The Flying Pig" was, internally, a flying palace for its day; it was a splendour of dove-grey upholstery, hat racks, and satin braid. Its name was appropriate enough because of the massive body volume and short undercarriage but the fuselage, in fact, more nearly resembled the shape of a great pear, swollen monstrously at its fore-end (where sat a dainty propeller and tiny enclosed engine). It tapered dramatically at the other extremity and the twin aerofoil surfaces of the tail planes crossed, top and bottom, the two spaced fins and rudders.

The pilot of this aerial monstrosity matched it in eccentricity. Test pilot Geoffrey Wigglesworth, wrote aviation pioneer Horrie Miller (from whom Qantas had bought one of its two Armstrong Whitworth FK-8s) "was afraid of nothing and nobody. He neither boasted nor bluffed. He was simply indifferent to the feelings of his fellow men."[13] In white collar and dark tie and dust coat, his symmetrical features were slackening around jaw and chin with well-established signs of his liquid appetites while his hair, shamming discipline with short back and sides, dropped carelessly down a broad forehead over his right eye. Reporters were allowed to board the Vulcan for its flight to Longreach but Wigglesworth made them clean and brush their boots before entering and "brusquely reprimanded them for fingering the upholstery".[14] On the first stage of the flight from Victoria some, in the bumpy conditions, were violently sick. Horrified at the defilement of lush carpet and upholstery, Wigglesworth turfed out the offenders at the first stop. "The machine", wrote Miller, "got little further publicity."

The flight to Longreach, with the departmental Bristol Tourer as escort, was completed without further incident. The aircraft attracted crowds, its pilot notoriety. On the evening of his arrival, after some hours at work on the Vulcan's Rolls-Royce engine, a grease-covered and dirty Wigglesworth entered the hotel's crowded little bar and "surveyed the assembly with open contempt". His audience, as tough and as hard-living as any mere test pilot, waited. "What", roared Wigglesworth, "are all you convict bastards drinking?" Neither the man nor the question was considered in the least offensive. "All named their drinks quietly."[15]

On 27 March, after further work on the engine by Wigglesworth, the chairman and directors of Qantas assembled for the test flight, as unimpressed by the old carpet slippers that Wigglesworth wore as by their knowledge of his very heavy "night-before".[16] With trepidation they allowed themselves to be shut inside the stuffy cabin. "We were for it," wrote McMaster, ". . . in an aeroplane we all knew to be unairworthy for Western Queensland conditions."[17]

Wigglesworth kept them waiting while he eyed the sky. Finally he climbed into the high cockpit, the engine was started, and without any preliminary checks or taxiing, roared into its take-off run. "It took an awful long run", said Jack Hazlett, who was on board watching, through small windows between cabin and cockpit, the engine revolution counters.[18] Barely clearing the fence, and with engine revs hard on 1,950 (1,850 was the designed maximum, with 1,950 allowable only for five minutes in emergencies) the Vulcan clawed its way to 500 feet and stuck there.[19] "The heat and noise in the cabin were", wrote McMaster, "almost overpowering; and whenever we looked down our eyes were attracted either to the hospital or the cemetery."[20] Wigglesworth sighted some circling kites and joined them in their current of rising air. After forty-five minutes, with only half payload on board, the

71

The ungainly Vickers Vulcan during its return flight from Longreach to Melbourne in late March 1923 after an unsuccessful demonstration flight for the Qantas board of directors.

Vulcan had not exceeded 5,750 feet. By now it was apparent that the aircraft could do no better. Wigglesworth landed. "The Board members did not wait for any formality", wrote McMaster, "and with one impulse set off, the Longreach Club as the objective."[21]

Two days later there was a meeting of directors at which Wigglesworth was present. A resolution was carried that "as the local test of the Vickers Vulcan had proven unsatisfactory, and that as both local and English tests had demonstrated that the machine was not in compliance with the contract, acceptance of the Vulcan be refused".[22] So ended Qantas's first involvement with an aircraft built primarily for commercial purposes, and the first commercial machine to arrive in Australia. Vickers accepted the verdict and there was no unpleasantness.[23] Qantas received £1,000 in damages.

Apart from the old BE2E and Avro 504K, both unsuitable for route service except in dire emergency, they were now reduced to one uncertain AW FK-8, G-AUDE, and the reliable DH4. A new secretary, R.D. Miller, was taken on but there was pilot trouble; Huxley and Back were at odds over their seniority. Huxley triumphed and Back, formerly a major in an English squadron, began to demonstrate his resentment by treating with open contempt any advice given him by Fysh.[24]

Fysh had flown to Sydney to sort out details of the Vulcan cancellation with Vickers' agents, William Adams Ltd., and then to Melbourne to discuss the company's predicament with a now-anxious controller of civil aviation. Brinsmead approved an emergency plan by Fysh to buy a Bristol Fighter from Horrie Miller.

"Huddy," said Miller, when the proposal was made to him, "you're stuck with an air service and no aircraft and I'm stuck with an aircraft and no service. Maybe we can help one another out."[25]

The price agreed was the Vickers' cheque — £1,000. The condition was that Miller deliver the Bristol to Longreach at his own risk — and fast.[26] On 19 April 1923 Fysh wired that the new aircraft would be on its way to Longreach at the weekend. They had bought a fighter aircraft for their airline, a Bristol F2B. A single-engined biplane, manufactured by the Bristol & Colonial Aeroplane Co. Ltd. of Filton, Bristol, it had a fabric-covered wooden structure, an empty weight of 2,070 pounds, and a maximum weight of 3,000 pounds. Cruising speed, from the 300-horsepower, water-cooled V-8 Hispano-Suiza engine, was ninety miles per hour. Apart from

The Bristol Fighter—purchased by Qantas as a stop-gap aircraft following the failure of the Vickers Vulcan to meet Qantas's performance specifications — at Longreach soon after it was delivered by Horrie Miller on 28 April 1923.

Qantas pilot Fred Huxley and Arthur Baird stepped unhurt from this spectacular accident at Guilford Park Station, south-west of Longreach, on 6 June 1923. The propeller cut a low telephone wire as they were landing to assist Hudson Fysh, who had been grounded in the Avro 504. Despite the apparent destruction of the aircraft, it was rebuilt, flying again in May 1924.

the pilot it could carry one passenger who, because the engine was lubricated with pure castor oil that enveloped him in penetrating fumes, was invariably sick. Its performance, however, even in the hottest conditions, was superb.

The Bristol was meant as a stopgap and the board, on 19 May, approved the purchase of two de Havilland DH9C aircraft, the type originally favoured by Qantas when forced to tender with Vulcans. Though a converted war-time type, the DH9C could carry three passengers plus pilot. Heavier than the Bristol (the empty weight was 2,600 pounds and the maximum weight 3,300 pounds), it was of similar construction and its single Siddeley Puma engine of 240 horsepower (a water-cooled in-line six cylinder) was less powerful but adequate. The cruising speed was eighty miles per hour.

It seemed now — with the Vulcan issue settled and the crashed AW FK-8 replaced by the Bristol — only a question of waiting for the DH9Cs. But Huxley (who had tendered his resignation on 19 May) crashed the main aircraft of "the fleet", the workhorse DH4 through a bush telephone line, on 6 June, landing at a station called Guildford Park. Neither he nor his passenger, Arthur Baird, was hurt but the aircraft was seriously damaged.

To add to the problems of the overworked Fysh, Back was getting "quite out of hand", showing continual hostility both to Fysh and the rest of the staff.[27] Fysh wrote to McMaster: "He has been flying the Bristol — the best machine on the service — but when Hazlett declared her unfit on Monday and

74

he was asked to take the Avro, he made quite a scene . . . and a lot of silly accusations about our staff, particularly Baird.''[28] Fysh asked for his resignation, with one month's notice, but Back decided to leave almost immediately. Fortunately their new pilot Fred Haig (engaged to take Huxley's place) had arrived the day before. A former No. 1 Squadron pilot and an expert on Bristols, he had been captured by the Turks after landing behind enemy lines in an attempt to fly out comrades who had been shot down.

Fysh who, on his promotion to manager had written in mid-February to McMaster that "Last Sunday was my last trip so far as regular flying goes", now had to report that Back's departure left "Haig and myself to carry things on. I will have to do my share of the flying. I am fairly stuck for a new pilot . . ."[29]

Their two DH9C aircraft, formally ordered through Brinsmead on 11 June, were not due on the route for three months. With almost crushing problems, Fysh assured McMaster: "No effort will be spared to keep things going."[30]

Survival became precarious and liquidation of the company a real possibility. Good pilots were as hard to get as suitable aircraft, and did not stay long in the harsh conditions. Fysh was relieved when G.C. Matthews, who had demonstrated remarkable skill and stamina in 1919 in the epic England–Australia race attempt that had ended in Bali, joined them in July. But even the best pilots, combined with the dedication of Baird and his staff, could not make old machines faultless. On 13 September 1923, Matthews was flying the AW G-AUDE, near Blackall when the engine failed and, in the forced landing that followed, the undercarriage, wing, and propeller were damaged. The aircraft had to be railed to Longreach. Of their fleet of four route aircraft, only one — the Bristol Fighter — was now serviceable. (Both AWs and the DH4 were in the workshops for repair.) The old BE2E and Avro 504K were available for taxi work. With misgivings, Fysh was forced to do one run from Longreach to Cloncurry with the Avro when the shade temperature was 114 degrees. Though he had only himself and two four-gallon tins of petrol on board, he never got above 1,000 feet on the whole trip and, for most of the time, was at half that height.[31]

By 29 September 1923 the vice-chairman, Dr Hope Michod, formally referred to the possible demise of Qantas. Referring to the decision of the directors to heavily depreciate the second-hand machines purchased and therefore show

TRAVEL AND COMMUNICATION UNPRECEDENTED.

The Queensland and Northern Territory Aerial Services, Limited.

Time Table and Fares for Aerial Services.

CHARLEVILLE TO CLONCURRY.

SUMMER SERVICE.

Northern Trip Read Down.	Inter Town Mileage			Southern Trip Read Up.	
Depart 5.30 a.m.		Charleville	Miles	Arrive 10.25 a.m.	
Arrive 7.10 a.m.	105	Tambo	105	Depart 8.45 ,,	
Depart 7.40 a.m.				Arrive 8.15 ,,	
Arrive 8.35 ,,	60	Blackall	165	Depart 7.20 ,,	
Depart 8.55 ,,				Arrive 7.0 ,,	
Arrive 10.25 ,,	100	Longreach	265	Depart 5.30 ,,	
Depart 5.30 ,,				Arrive 11.10 ,,	
Arrive 7.10 ,,	110	Winton	375	Depart 9.30 ,,	
Depart 7.40 ,,				Arrive 9.0 ,,	
Arrive 9.45 ,,	135	Mackinlay	510	Depart 6.55 ,,	
Depart 10.5 ,,				Arrive 6 ,,	
Arrive 11.10 ,,	70	Cloncurry	580	Depart 5.30 ,,	
	580		580		

(Thursdays / Fridays — Northern Trip) (Mondays / Sundays — Southern Trip)

FARES.

Charleville to Cloncurry, 9d. per mile			£21
Charleville to Longreach, 10d. per mile			11
Longreach to Cloncurry, 9d. per mile			41
Charleville-Tambo			£4 15 0
,, Blackall			7 10 0
,, Winton			15 10 0
,, Mackinlay			21 0 0
Tambo-Blackall			2 15 0
,, Longreach			7 0 0
,, Winton			11 0 0
,, Mackinlay			16 10 0
,, Cloncurry			19 10 0
Blackall-Longreach			4 10 0
,, Winton			9 10 0
,, Mackinlay			13 10 0
,, Cloncurry			17 10 0
Longreach-Winton			4 0 0
,, Mackinlay			11 0 0
Winton-Mackinlay			6 0 0
,, Cloncurry			9 0 0
Mackinlay-Cloncurry			3 0 0

Children under 12 years, half-price.
One child under 3 years, free.

N.B.—For Winter Service times will be approximately 2 hours' later.

LUGGAGE:—35 lbs. free when in compact package, but the Company reserves right to refuse, or charge extra, for bulky luggage.

BRISBANE-CHARLEVILLE Mail arrives Charleville 1 p.m. Wednesdays. **Aerial Mail** leaves 5.30 a.m. Thursdays. **ROCKHAMPTON-LONGREACH** Mail arrives Longreach 3.50 p.m. Wednesdays. **Aerial Mail** leaves at 5.30 a.m. on Fridays.

THE UP SERVICE connects with the Blackall-Rockhampton Mail, leaving Blackall at 12.50 p.m., and the Longreach-Rockhampton Mail, leaving 11.40 a.m. on Thursdays, and the Winton-Townsville Mail leaving at 10 a.m. on Fridays.

THE DOWN SERVICE connects with the Longreach-Rockhampton Mail, leaving at 11.40 a.m., and the Charleville-Brisbane Mail, leaving at 1.45 p.m. on Mondays.

THE AIR MAILS.

Wherever you may reside, write by Air Mail and save days. Mark letters " By Air Mail " and post in usual way. Total Postage required 5d. per ½ oz.

AERIAL TAXIE SERVICE.

Machine always available at Longreach or whilst on tour. Urgent trips carried out at a moment's notice. Tariff 2s. 3d. per air mile for hire of machine over approved routes.

GOODS AND PARCELS.

Parcels from the South should be addressed to our Charleville Agent who will forward them for delivery to any town on the Aerial Route. You pay on delivery. Ordinary parcels should be handed to local agent together with payment.

Rates—(In parts of 1 lb. only)—
Up to 100 lbs. 8d. per lb. up to 110 miles.
1s. per lb. from 110 miles to 350 miles.
1s. 6d. per lb. from 350 miles to 580 miles.
Over 100 lbs. by arrangement.

AGENTS:

Charleville—G. HERRIMAN	Blackall—SMITH'S GARAGE.	Mackinlay—J. L. HARDGRAVE.
Tambo—J. LOW.	Winton—H. RILEY & CO.,	Cloncurry—D. S. McGILLIVRAY.

For any further information apply to any of the above Agents or to Q.A.N.T.A.S., Ltd., Longreach.

HUDSON FYSH, Manager.

Saved Time Means More Time for Work or Leisure. —— It Pays.

Qantas timetable issued in 1923; note Hudson Fysh's name appears as the manager.

them in the books at a low figure, he told the third annual
general meeting which he chaired, that their true value "if we
are compelled to go into liquidation" was "not at all low. The
heavy depreciation shown, the heavy wage bills for
mechanical staff required to keep old machines flying, low
revenue from a public yet to be educated to the advantages of
quick transport for themselves, mails and parcels" and the fact
that "only for two thirds of the year have we been earning any
revenue at all"[32] had resulted in a loss for the year. In each of
the three years since the formation of the company in 1920,
there had been losses.

There was worse news. Dr Michod had told the directors on
the same day: "There is a rumour that Mr. Fergus McMaster
contemplates resignation from the Board." There was
unanimous dismay at the prospect that they might lose the
man who had played the central part in the formation of the
company and hopes were expressed "that the rumours are
without foundation". McMaster, the meeting recorded, was a
tower of strength and they all hoped that he "would continue
to guide the destiny of the company".

Though the first eight months of operation under government subsidy had in fact been marginally profitable, Fysh
described the position as "very bad" in his October manager's
report.[33] "It is doubtful", he wrote, "that the service can be
maintained until the arrival of the new machines." The only
serviceable aircraft were the Avro, the BE2E, and one AW. It
had even "been necessary to use the BE on the mail route".
To McMaster, on the following day, he wrote: "We have been
generally running ourselves into a hole because of second-
hand plant and lack of spares."[34] He had held up repair work
on the AW that Matthews had force-landed on 13 September
and concentrated on "getting the DH4 and Bristol in the air".
He believed "it will pay us to scrap G-AUDE [the AW]. The
first DH9C is expected to be flying by 25 October and the
second by 10 November." The repaired DH4 was expected
back in service by the end of November.

Fysh wrote again to McMaster on 25 October 1923 of "our
present struggle for existence".[35] Brinsmead had visited them
and had expressed dissatisfaction with the mechanical staff.
Though Fysh acknowledged that Baird was more inclined to
do a job himself than see someone else do it properly, he
defended the staff and put "the recent crop of forced
landings" down to faultiness of the engine in the last AW.
Pilot strength remained an uncertainty. Haig's wife disliked

the West and Haig intended leaving in January. Matthews, said Fysh, "is ageing and will not stand up to another year of flying". The two pilots had not complained but the "disorganisation of the past and flying inferior machines" had had their effect. Fysh had certainly done his best to minimize their burdens. "Neither has been asked to fly the Avro", he reported, though he himself had done over forty hours in it in the previous two months. The only good news in his report was Brinsmead's disclosure that their Charleville–Cloncurry contract would be renewed for a further year at the same subsidy of four shillings a mile.

The McMaster rumours were to prove only partly true. McMaster had poured his energies into every aspect of the company since its formation but he had also found the demands of "added pastoral interests and unfavourable seasonal conditions" increasing.[36] He also had other business interests. With his friend Alan Campbell he discussed an idea for promoting dried onions, the concept of a Primary Producers Bank, his belief in the need for secondary industries in Queensland, his decision to "throw in my lot with the Woollen Mills project", and his intention to go into "that other great project, the Co-operative Meat Works". He maintained his political contacts and was always sympathetic to innovative ideas. One such involvement, in the proposal for a vertical-lift aeroplane, drew a wry response from Campbell. "I appreciate the humour of you asking me anything about Mr. Val Rendle [Rendle had proposed the idea]", he wrote, "considering that in consequence of you having wished him on me I had to hand him out fifteen lovely quid to prevent his heart from breaking."[37]

The idea of dehydrated onions was only part of a venture involving the erection of a factory in a Sydney suburb to package dehydrated "cabbage, carrots, pumpkins, eschalots and every vegetable you like to mention", wrote McMaster who, with Dr Michod, had provided a bank guarantee for the enterprise. "The Doctor, in his Longreach home, gave dinner after dinner to his friends . . . sampling dehydrated vegetables of every nature. I did the same in Winton. Naturally the household arrangements at both Longreach and Winton were somewhat strained."[38] The company eventually went into liquidation and its two stalwart supporters had to meet its liabilities.

Fysh observed that McMaster "has momentarily lost impetus" and so it seemed, at least as far as Qantas was con-

Dr F.A. Hope Michod,
Longreach. Dr Michod took
over from Fergus McMaster as
chairman of directors 1924–26.

cerned.[39] He relinquished his position as chairman and at a meeting of directors on 17 November Dr Hope Michod was elected to succeed him. To the relief of his colleagues he remained on the board and, as McMaster did nothing by halves, continued to make a significant contribution. Only two weeks later he let it be known that he would like to see a DH50 aircraft ordered as early as possible. Though it cost £1,000 more than a DH9C for the carriage of only one extra passenger it was, he argued, worth it. The DH9Cs were old and faulty while the DH50 would be "of all new material. The landing speed of 38 m.p.h.", he observed, "is very desirable as against the 60 m.p.h. of the DH9C."[40]

His comments, as usual, were sound. The two DH9C aircraft ordered had arrived early in November and though both had proved satisfactory when tested by Fysh, the three-ply used in their construction was of inferior quality and, reported Fysh, "would require renewing at an early date".[41]

Hudson Fysh had other important matters, quite unconnected with the uncertainties of Qantas, on his mind that month. At the 17 November meeting of directors he had requested leave from 29 November 1923 to 5 January 1924. He planned to marry, in Sydney, on 5 December. The board approved his leave, granted him a bonus of £100, and increased his salary to £600 per year.

In the first year of subsidized, regular operation Qantas had, in the face of the most harrowing difficulties, completed 204 of 205 scheduled flights. On these they had carried 156 passengers, almost 13,000 letters, and just over 1,000 pounds of freight. In 71,108 miles of flying there had been, despite accidents, no injuries to passengers or crew. It had though been for the company and its employees, a near thing in 1923. Now, with the arrival of the two DH9C aircraft and the renewal for a further year of their government contract, prospects were more hopeful.

Always Worth the Money
1924 to 1926

The journey back from Sydney to Longreach took Hudson Fysh and his new wife three days by train. The secretary, Doug Miller drove the company's Model T Ford to the station to meet them. It was a sweltering day, well over a hundred degrees. Little whirlwinds of dust were the only signs of activity along the deserted streets and even the hardy Longreach goats had taken shelter. Miller was attired Mother Country fashion in the way that most Australian businessmen dressed in summer's heat, ". . . sitting upright in the driver's seat, his high collar and white, starched shirt cuffs were fairly glowing in the powerful rays of the December sun", wrote Fysh.[1]

The capital of the Central West of Queensland and the centre of the Mitchell grass sheep area, Longreach, had some three thousand inhabitants, schools, a good club, and little else. A desolate place of dust and gibbers, its few trees were often gnawed and ring-barked by the indestructible goats. A small dairy provided milk but vegetables came, mostly by rail, from the coast. The water from the local bore was unfit both for human consumption and lawns and gardens. Tank water, or muddy river water, met domestic needs. "There was ample hot water, but no cold", wrote Fysh.[2] An ice man called each day at the rented Fysh house in Kingfisher Street, with its galvanized iron roof, its unpapered wooden interior walls, and its lean-to kitchen at the back that caught the full blast of the afternoon sun. Compared with that of the average Longreach inhabitant, however, the Fysh income was handsome enough.

5

Their social standing, with his Geelong Grammar and service background and his position as pilot and manager, was enough to give access to all that was pleasant in the town community and among the surrounding station owners but Fysh, deeply introverted, shunned business and social groups whenever he could.[3]

Though Fysh was soon immersed in Qantas problems there was good news at last. The DH9C aircraft had operated well and carried a total of forty-five passengers in December and January though the Bristol, in an accident on 18 December with a new pilot, Captain Vigers, at the controls was now out of action for some months ahead. The directors were sufficiently confident to resolve, at their 2 February meeting, "that one DH50 aeroplane be ordered".[4]

The Bristol Fighter after its crash at Longreach on 18 December 1923.

It was an aircraft type that was to play an important role not only in the operations of Qantas, but in civil aviation in Australia. Both the other airlines operating under subsidy —

Western Australian Airways (WAA) and Larkin Aircraft Supply Company (Lasco) — ordered it. WAA, whose 1211-mile route between Geraldton and Derby in Western Australia commenced operations on 5 December 1921, was the first airline in Australia to undertake regular scheduled services. As Qantas set out in 1924 to emerge from the critical uncertainties of its beginnings, WAA was extending its route southward from Geraldton to Perth. But Lasco had not done so well. Though tendering successfully on 1 November 1921 for the Adelaide–Sydney route, it was not to start actual operations until 2 June 1924.

The DH50 airliner that Qantas now wanted had its official trials in England in November 1923. With a 230-horsepower Siddeley Puma engine it had, besides the pilot, a usable load of 982 pounds and a total weight when loaded of 3,900 pounds. In operational terms this meant a passenger capacity of four, a climb rate from the ground in good conditions of 600 feet per minute, and a speed of 102 miles an hour at full throttle. Of importance to Qantas, the distance to take-off was 180 yards, and the range some 375 miles when fully loaded. It was the first aeroplane type specifically built for civil work to be used by Australian airlines, and had a genuine passenger cabin.

For Fysh, however, flying in February and March 1924 still meant long hours in the old BE2E. The prolonged dry spell had, in mid-February, at last broken. Rain deluged the black soil plains, turning them into a grey expanse of water. Road travel was impossible. While Matthews and Vigers flew the regular service, Fysh flew Dr Michod on medical trips to isolated stations, took station owners on stock inspections, flew in urgent supplies to hard-pressed homesteads, and plucked intending train passengers from marooned properties to make their rail connections. He replenished by air the West Longreach pub, after shearers flown in for a local job had drunk it dry, and flew in one passenger "perched on a small keg of rum".[5] The board formally expressed its appreciation "of the strenuous work put in by Mr. Fysh during the wet weather".[6]

McMaster, meanwhile, was looking ahead. Writing to Fysh he urged pressure on the Civil Aviation Branch for a speedy extension of the route from Cloncurry through Duchess and Mount Isa to Camooweal.[7] Mount Isa Mines, he said, would in a short time become one of the largest mining centres in Australia.

While McMaster was predicting a population of sixteen

83

thousand within two years for Mount Isa, Queensland graziers were counting their losses from the drought. Sheep numbers had been reduced and were not much above the 1920 level, interest bills were rising, the amount of wool on the surviving sheep was down, and shearers were pressing for an increase in wages. For graziers, the two years ahead were needed simply to get back the money they had spent on fodder or agistment to keep their surviving sheep alive.[8]

Far away on the other side of the world in early 1924, the uneconomic proliferation of competing British airlines was, under government pressure, on the verge of rationalization. Four airlines — Handley Page, Instone, Daimler, and British Marine Air Navigation — were merged into a new company, Imperial Airways Limited, on 31 March 1924. Britain thus became "the first major power to sponsor its own unified national airline".[9] This new British airline was, ten years later, to join on equal terms with Qantas in initiating regular England–Australia services on one of the great air routes of the world.

The first proposed extension to the Qantas route, the Cloncurry–Camooweal section urged by McMaster, was submitted to the Civil Aviation Branch in April while Qantas in the same month at last acceded to Brinsmead's urging that they modify their Charleville–Cloncurry timetable to eliminate the overnight stop and fly the route in one day. Concurrently, both their route pilots resigned, Matthews leaving at the end of April and Vigers a month later. Their departure marked the end of the years of wearisome instability amongst flying staff. Matthews' replacement, P.H. Moody, was to stay with the airline for six years while L.J. Brain (a cadet from Point Cook) who succeeded Vigers, was to become a nationally known figure in Australian civil aviation, leaving Qantas only after World War II when he became the first general manager of Trans-Australia Airlines. Lester Brain was the first nonwartime pilot to join Qantas. "He seems", wrote Fysh with prescience a few days after Brain joined them, "a keen and sensible sort of fellow."[10]

In fact, the worst was over for the company. The two DH9C machines had, since their introduction in November, been a great success. Their freedom from noise and excessive wind coupled with mechanical reliability and complete absence of accidents had combined to attract passenger traffic. The situation in the month before their arrival, when revenue was under ten pounds and operation on the verge of collapse had changed marvellously for the better.[11] As May ended Fysh told McMaster he could not "see a profit smaller than £1,500, in spite of the bad months towards the end of last year's contract".[12] He was also able to report that the DH4 had been tested satisfactorily and that Baird's staff had fitted "a nice new cabin . . . after the style of the DH9Cs". It was better looking, and longer exhaust pipes had been substituted, to cut noise. The news from Brinsmead was good. He had responded to their request for an extension to Camooweal, and favoured it.

The close of the financial year on 30 June, coinciding with the first eight months of their renewed government contract, brought the best possible blend of airline figures — a marked jump in passengers carried despite a dramatic decline in miles and hours flown. In the first full contract year from 2 November 1922 they had flown 71,108 miles (955 hours) and carried 156 passengers. In only eight months of the second contract year from 2 November 1923 they had carried 203 passengers yet had done so by flying only 44,412 miles (573 hours). In the first year there had been seventeen forced landings. In the eight months to 30 June 1924 there had been only three. Fysh totalled up the operations record from the very beginning of flying in 1921 and noted that there had been no injuries to passengers in 2,285 flying hours involving 165,537 miles in the air. In an article in *The Graziers' Review* he sought more converts. "Increased speed of transport", he wrote, "is always worth the money. Riding on horseback is always cheaper than travelling by rail or hiring a car. But what would we think of the man who preferred that mode of transport for a journey of any length? In time, people will realise that aerial travel at 90 miles per hour will practically always pay them."[13]

The early promise of 1924 was sustained by the DH9C aircraft and augmented by the introduction in October of their first DH50 (G-AUER). This specialized civil air transport plane, with its enclosed cabin for four, marked the end of the era of cap and goggles for passengers. It had a better all-round performance than the DH9C and an appreciably bigger payload. Fysh, testing it on 4 October, found it easy to fly, with no vices, and "a very great advance on anything we have from almost any point of view".[14] Its introduction was timely. On 31 October the prime minister, S.M. Bruce, on a tour of western Queensland, was in Winton, planning to motor with his wife and party to Longreach. A thunderstorm and downpour of rain cut the road and Fysh found himself called on to fly his prime minister in the DH50, while Moody flew the luggage and lesser members of the party in the DH9C.

October saw Fergus McMaster receive his first financial reward from the airline. On the fourth, the secretary wrote to him enclosing a cheque for £10.14s.3d "being your proportion of the sum set aside for reimbursing the directorate".[15] Fysh did considerably better. At the end of the year his salary was raised to £750. Baird's rose to £500, plus a £50 bonus.

Baird had built up a skilled staff that had dealt quickly and efficiently with the constant influx of damaged aircraft and failed engines. As the year drew to a close and the heavy programme of repairs from the early months was near completion, it became evident that with the reliability of the new aircraft, work was getting short. There had, in fact, been no crashes of any kind for a full year. They now had a hangar floor of concrete, some modest wood-working equipment and a link, at last, with the town's light and power supply. The board did not want to lose this skilled team and in January 1925, after discussions with Brinsmead and de Havillands, an important decision was made. Qantas would build its own DH50 aircraft at Longreach, under licence, paying an initial royalty to de Havillands of one hundred pounds per aircraft, later reducing to fifty pounds.

Arthur Baird had been the backbone of Qantas throughout those precarious early years. The demands of day-to-day maintenance on old airframes and unreliable engines were heavy enough but, added to them, was the increasing programme of major engine overhauls and the unpredictable rhythm of crisis when aircraft crashed in remote places. The old Talbot truck was always at the ready, shear legs and hoisting gear on board for lifting out and changing entire engines on some distant clay-pan; iron rations and engineering kit were packed and on hand. His hangar team, now gearing up to build modern airlines, could still turn their hand to sewing up asbestos-lined, fire-resistant mailbags or turn out supplies of cardboard air-sick boxes. Baird's fox terrier, Kelly, rode with him on the bonnet of the Talbot truck and his black cat slept in the fuselage of the BE2E. A bachelor, Arthur Baird's whole life centred on the Longreach hangar.

At 6:00 A.M. on 7 February 1925 pilot Lester Brain took off from Cloncurry in the DH4 on the first official flight of their

route extension to Camooweal. There was sunlight on the peaks and hilltops around Cloncurry as he climbed, with one passenger and engineer Frank McNally, and a cargo of ice and butter, heading for the patches of open downs country among the hills some forty miles out. The McMaster property, Devoncourt, passed below them and Duchess, the mining town, bared its disused mine shafts in the clear air, a witness to its dependence on markets in distant countries and the decline in copper prices. Turning northwest, the DH4 passed over Alexander Kennedy's former property of Bushy Park, where the old pioneer and his wife had given Hudson Fysh their hospitality on the last night of his overland car trip back from Darwin. At 7,000 feet, the workings and shafts of Mount Isa itself were visible along the ridge and then, beyond it, came the yellow tones of the grassed downs and the last stage of the flight to Camooweal. The Qantas route network was now officially 248 miles longer and totalled, from the rich pastoral country of Camooweal and the Barkly Tablelands, an imposing 825 miles. Camooweal was impressed with the DH4 but ecstatic at the sight of the ice.

This extension of the original subsidized route on which the airline was founded, together with the introduction of the new DH50 and the reliable performance of the DH9Cs, marked the arrival of financial stability and maturity. The company profit for the year to 30 June 1925 was an impressive £2,847. Fysh met with Brinsmead in Melbourne in June and came

The Bristol Fighter, repaired after its crash in December 1923, is prepared for an engine run in late 1924. The original V-8 Hispano-Suiza engine was replaced by a Siddeley Puma engine which also powered the DH9s introduced in November 1923. The rear cockpit had been fitted with a cover during its rebuild at Longreach.

87

away with an agreement that abolished one recurring uncertainty. The year-by-year contract with the government was, from November, to become a three-year contract and, though the subsidy rate was to reduce from four shillings a mile in the first year to three shillings and sixpence in the third, it was a decisive change for the better. To temper this positive development, however, Brinsmead made it clear that the government did not sympathize with the airline's new ambitions to extend south from Charleville to Brisbane and north from Camooweal to Darwin. There would, said Brinsmead, be no more route extensions.[16]

There was a minor setback on the Camooweal operation on 25 July when Lester Brain, stationed in Cloncurry to operate the route, responded to an emergency call at Maxwelton. Not reaching his destination until sunset, he crashed his DH9C when approaching darkness made a forced landing unavoidable. Though there was damage to the undercarriage, propeller, and leading edge of the wing, it was not serious and normal operations were soon resumed.

Brain's duties involved many short taxi flights and some long and important charter jobs. On one of these he flew an American mining engineer, L.J. Stark, into an area some 150 miles south of Newcastle Waters, inhabited only by tribal Aboriginals, on a pioneering aerial survey that, while hazardous, proved the worth of this new role for aviation. Brain actually landed in this remote and rough terrain to allow his intrepid passenger to assess conditions on the ground. The Aboriginals helped them clear a path for take-off. Later in 1925 Brain found himself flying Fergus McMaster and his brother, Francis, on a different kind of pioneering venture. On 1 November they set out on a one-week election tour by candidate Francis in the DH9C "with pilot Brain at the rudder". After calls at Kynuna and Middleton they landed at Boulia where, wrote McMaster to Alan Campbell, "Mr. Francis again used God's open air to convey messages of warning and hope to the seething masses gathered from far and wide in the empty spaces".[17] Like a modern day presidential candidate they sped on to McKinlay and Cloncurry where "Francis did battle with the people for two hours to such effects that shouts of 'Windbag' were heard, it being the evening of the great [horse] race known as the Melbourne Cup . . .". From Cloncurry they flew north to Normanton and took the opportunity "to have a look at the blue waters of the Gulf" before heading back three hundred miles to Julia Creek. In all they covered some fifteen hundred miles. "Francis", McMaster summed up, "is a good candidate. But the odds are too great in this electorate for truth and reason to prevail." And so it proved. His brother was not elected but the tour did McMaster no harm amongst his influential Country Party friends.

McMaster used Brain and the DH9C as a weapon against the deepening drought in the following February. For week after week, from January 1926, temperatures had stood between 100 and 115 degrees in the shade. Passengers between Longreach and Cloncurry saw piles of dead horses on the outskirts of McKinlay and Kynuna, and there were dead sheep and cattle in growing numbers along the route.[18] North-west Queensland was in the grip of its worst drought for many years, with rainfall at Longreach totalling only 375 points over an eleven-month period to February. The search for agistment and relief country among hard-pressed property owners was keen and competitive. "Mr. Fergus McMaster", said a Qantas circular, "used Q.A.N.T.A.S. services to look. Knowing that the Gulf of Carpentaria country . . . had recently had up to seventeen inches of rain, he determined to see if he could secure land for his own use."[19]

McMaster left Winton at midday on 25 February for Cloncurry and Brain, in the DH9C, flew him on to Normanton where they breakfasted next day on "salt water Gulf fish, considered a great luxury to Westerners". Already, said the circular proudly, McMaster had flown 465 miles in just over five hours flying time and "was ready for business". He at once went on by truck some forty miles to the property he had in mind and completed agistment arrangements for thirty thousand sheep. Next he "energetically utilised the rest of the day by securing another block of 80,000 acres further up the Flinders River". He inspected this block by air on 27 February, leaving with Brain at 6:00 A.M. His pilot flew "to within a few feet" of the open downs so that "they could see the seed on the Mitchell grass [the great fodder grass of Western Queensland], and the position and state of the stock watering places". Satisfied, McMaster headed for Cloncurry where, after checking the condition of the stock route that he would have to use, he landed in time for breakfast. He was back at his starting point in Winton at 9:00 A.M. on 28 February, having flown 930 miles in ten hours of flying, all "in under three days". The Qantas circular recounting this feat was headed with the motto "Transportation is Civilisation".[20]

Two Qantas engineers engaged in "doping" the linen fabric which has been used to cover the wing of a DH50 under construction in the Longreach hangar (1926). Other components, including a lower right wing, can be seen against the wall in the background.

The airline's new-found operational reliability and a contract for three years ahead now brought a perspective of sound future financial results. The energies of board and management, for so long concentrated on mere survival, now turned to plans for expansion southward to Brisbane. All their considerable political support was mustered, Fysh was sent to Melbourne in March, and McMaster's friend, D.C. Cameron, brought together all the Queensland members of the federal Parliament in a deputation to the minister for defence, Sir Neville House V.C., to argue the benefits of their proposal. Longreach, said Fysh, would be brought within twelve hours of Brisbane, instead of forty-two hours by train; a considerable reduction in subsidy would be possible; Qantas would make Brisbane its base and provide a workshop for the overhaul of aeroplanes. Though Sir Neville promised to put the matter before Cabinet, they had little hope for Brinsmead, their close friend and supporter in so many ways, was against the plan. The minister was not only opposed to an extension of aerial services while railways existed; he was, publicly and privately, against all forms of aviation. Subsidies for civil aviation, he told Fysh, were a waste of money. Defence, said the minister for defence, was a waste of money.[21] He was to remain unbudged on the Brisbane extension, and a bane in all aviation matters to Brinsmead, until 2 April 1927 when his term of office ceased. Brinsmead wrote privately to Fysh in October 1926: "If it were not for Qantas and the Aero Clubs I would resign immediately. It has been a continual and nerve-racking fight to get anything done . . . I can't thank you sufficiently for your unswerving support and straight dealing, even when we do not quite see eye to eye on certain matters."[22]

Of considerable consolation to Qantas were the financial results for the year to 30 June 1926. There was a profit of £6,370, representing a 20 per cent return on capital and turning the accumulated deficits of the early years into a surplus of £3,849. They transferred £2,249 to contingency reserve, their first-ever reserve, and Dr Michod was supported by the board when he recommended that the profits should be applied, not to dividends but to expansion. It was decided "to put the money towards the support of any new form of the

Alexander Kennedy, who was the first passenger to travel on a regular Qantas service, is seen here in mid-1926 about to fly from Longreach in one of the DH9C aircraft. The pilot, Capt. Eric Stephens, who is taking a suitcase from Arthur Baird, joined Qantas in early 1926 and the aircraft, G-AUEF, was written off at Cloncurry on 22 September 1926.

Company's operations or any new aircraft venture which may seem likely to assist in the development of civil aviation in Queensland".[23] The editor of *Aircraft* magazine, E.J. Hart, commented: "Here we see the true pioneer spirit. It is the only spirit in which the millenium of an unsubsidised air transport service . . . may be anticipated."[24]

While Fysh, amongst the details of his working days, pressed the airline's pilots on matters of timetable observance, flight reports, and log book entries he spent his evenings at home "trying desperately to acquire some degree of managerial and business ability".[25] His efforts included a course in Pelmanism. Pelmanesque notices and memos began to circulate. "Are you known as a man who has practical ideas?" asked one, on business ability. "Do you often have well worked out suggestions to make?" Another, advising on how "to secure advancement in life" in the context of Qantas's requirements, listed pep and progressiveness, loyalty, and (possibly with the bruising experience of Back in mind) a willingness to carry out instructions.[26]

These commercial preoccupations were interrupted for Fysh when Alan Cobham called in at Longreach on his great double flight from England to Australia and back to England. Cobham left London on 30 June 1926 in a DH50 with floats, which were changed to wheels for the overland flight when he reached Darwin. His Longreach arrival was spectacular. He flew in so low, wrote Fysh "we almost thought his aeroplane was a motor car".[27] Cobham was the first to use the route across Australia originally surveyed by McGinness and Fysh since the flights in 1919 and 1920 by Ross Smith, and Parer and McIntosh. He was also the first pilot to fly out and back from England and the public attention accorded his achievement prompted other pilots, in ensuing years, to attempt major new pioneering ventures. (Cobham completed his return journey on 1 October, landing on the Thames.)

A less spectacular but no less important influence on the overseas air links between Australia and England in 1926 was the policy that emerged from the Imperial Conference in London of developing air communications among the members of the British Commonwealth "with as much expedition as practicable". This policy "had far reaching effects on the development of the Australian internal network of aerial routes".[28] The Australian prime minister, S.M. Bruce, announced in the House of Representatives on his return from Britain that the 1927–28 budget allocation for the develop-

Capt. Lester Brain demonstrates winter flying gear at Eagle Farm, Brisbane in March 1927. Captain Brain was the chief flying instructor of Qantas's Brisbane Flying School when it opened on 26 March 1927. The Flying School was equipped with two of the new DH60 Cirrus Moths, registered G-AUFL and G-AUFR (pictured).

ment of civil aviation in Australia would be increased from £115,000 to £200,000 and outlined long-range plans.[29]

Qantas had, of course, clearly recognized that their Queensland route was well placed (as Cobham's flight had emphasized) on the aerial highway from England to the eastern capitals of Australia. In any commercial development of that long highway there was either the opportunity for significant Qantas expansion, or the distinct possibility that their Charleville–Camooweal route would be absorbed in some grander international plan that would put Qantas out of business. This awareness was the motivating force in the company's growing preoccupation with Brisbane. An advisory board was established there in October 1926 consisting of Hope Michod, Alan Campbell and F.E. Loxton, a director of the Burns Philp company. McMaster, on 30 October 1926, resumed his old position of chairman of the company.[30]

The Qantas presence in Brisbane was strengthened in an operational way by the company's move into the provision of flying schools for private pilots. The de Havilland Moth, now in production, made private ownership and operation of a personal aircraft just as practicable, for those who could afford it, as the operation of a motor car except that there were no flying schools in Queensland to train pilots for private licences. Fysh, at a board meeting on 19 May 1926, had suggested the need for a more economical, light aircraft for the company's taxi work, and the potential with such an aircraft for private pilot training. With board approval and supported by the Queensland Aero Club he met Brinsmead in Melbourne in September and got agreement to open flying schools at both Longreach and Brisbane. Pilot strength was more than adequate to absorb these additional duties. Two new Point Cook-trained pilots, A.D. Davidson and Arthur Affleck (later of Flying Doctor fame) and an experienced aviator, C. Matheson, had joined them during 1926 and two more pilots, E.J. Stephens and C.W.A. Scott came later in the year. (Scott, a man of great gifts and personality, was to become one of a growing band of individualistic flyers who captured public attention in the glamour period of pioneers and publicity-seekers.) The Longreach school, under Matheson,

Qantas's first DH50, the British built G-AUER, suffered considerable damage when it overturned during take-off from the rain-sodden aerodrome at McKinlay, near Cloncurry, 20 February 1927. Pilot Lester Brain escaped injury and G-AUER was transported back to Longreach for repairs. It was flying again on 25 April 1927.

opened on 27 December 1926 but the hot, gusty, and bumpy summer conditions took their toll in crashes; the supply of pupils, like local incomes in the dry conditions, dried up. The Brisbane school, inaugurated on 26 March 1927 with an aerial pageant, flourished with Lester Brain in charge until, in May 1929, it was handed over to the Queensland Aero Club. Joy-rides, taxi trips, and commissions from aircraft sales to private owners brought in additional revenue from the school.[31]

Brain, after his forced landing at Maxwelton in 1925, had had two subsequent and serious accidents. On 24 September 1926 the engine of his DH9C, G-AUEF, had cut on take-off at Cloncurry causing undercarriage, propeller, and general damage. Five months later, flying the DH50A G-AUER, he had turned over when taking off from McKinlay on boggy ground. This time Fysh had put the blame solely on the pilot. He was "of the opinion that Mr. Brain made a serious error of judgement . . . in not taking sufficient care on soft ground". Mr. Brain, Fysh reported to the board, "is worthy of censure in this case".[32] But, added Fysh, Brain had for three years carried out with success flying on the most difficult sections of the route and the most hazardous taxi trips, acquiring skill and ability. There was general damage to the aircraft but it was in the air again at the end of the month.

Completely repaired after its accident at McKinlay on 20 February 1927, Qantas's first DH50, G-AUER before being taken up for a test flight at Longreach, 25 April 1927. The name *Hermes* is new though it was renamed *Victory* when it became the first Flying Doctor Service aircraft in May 1928. Note the fitting of a four-bladed propeller, probably intended to improve the take-off performance.

95

Far more serious than this accident, and overshadowing the inauguration of the Brisbane flying school, was the crash of DH9C G-AUED at Tambo on 24 March. The aircraft was a total loss and the pilot, A.D. Davidson, and his two passengers were killed. It was the company's first fatal accident. Though young and relatively inexperienced, with some five hundred flying hours to his credit, Davidson had in fact done much more flying when he joined Qantas than Brain had done.[33] "All technical staff", wrote Fysh, "emphatically agreed that the cause was stalling on approach . . . the most common cause of fatal aircraft accidents."[34]

Lester Brain and engineer T. Young were, with the opening of the Brisbane school, now permanently stationed there. "The Brisbane Branch", Fysh reported to his directors, "is a new sphere of operations for us and is now firmly established. Our hangar at Eagle Farm is nearly complete. You have set up an organisation on which can be built the larger operations of the future."[35]

In Jeopardy
1927 to 1928

Ross and Keith Smith, Parer and McIntosh and Alan Cobham had, with their flights between England and Australia, sown the first seeds for what Fysh called "large operations". Then, on 20 May 1927, Charles Lindbergh flew solo from New York to Paris, entered the American consciousness as a new type of hero, initiated mass support in his dynamic country for civil aviation, and excited the whole world. The thrust of such individual endeavour, the romanticism, enterprise, and private ambition of individual aviators in a world still largely motivated by private enterprise, compounded. Australian Bert Hinkler, the least egotistical and most lovable of those driven men, was continuing his pioneering flights that were to lead in February 1928 to the first solo flight to Australia from England. Kingsford Smith and Ulm, in the same year, were to make the first crossing by air of the Pacific Ocean. Building on their initiatives, the substance of civil aviation was growing. Imperial Airways took over from the Royal Air Force the operation of the Cairo–Baghdad route to implement British policy on the extension of international routes, while the Dutch airline, KLM, under Albert Plesman, began its test flights to Batavia in the closing years of the decade. But, nearer home in Australia, the Qantas advances excited neither national acclaim nor international notice. On 1 July 1927 the company inaugurated its service from the modest centre of Cloncurry, north to the even more modest centre of Normanton. It was with some pride though, that they did so with a subsidy rate of three shillings and sixpence a mile, down sixpence on the rate of four shillings when their operations began in 1922.

In the seventh annual report and balance sheet of 1 October 1927 the directors were able to state that "after payment of all expenses of management, the establishment of two flying schools, the establishment of the extension service Cloncurry-Normanton ... and after allowing £3,821 for depreciation, £410 in respect of [the] Tambo [accident] and £1,800 for the Taxation Account, operations for the twelve months ending 30 June gave a net profit of £4,020". This result had been achieved despite "continuation of the disastrous drought conditions over practically the whole of the pastoral districts in which the Service is operating, and also the depressed conditions in the mining areas served".[1] The new Normanton destination had attractions for the governor-general, Lord Stonehaven, who flew there with Arthur Affleck as pilot towards the end of the year to enjoy the shooting and fishing. As Maj. John Lawrence Baird and a member of the Air Board in the last years of the war he was both knowledgeable and supportive of civil aviation. He had flown first with Qantas, with Fysh as pilot, in July 1926 and again, in the following month, on an inland flight with Moody to Newcastle Waters. His wife, Lady Stonehaven, had christened the first aircraft built by Qantas at Longreach, the DH50A *Iris*, on 18 August 1926.

The aircraft building programme was in full swing in 1927. The federal government, through the collector of customs, approached Australian aircraft manufacturers early in the year to seek their views on the imposition of a 25 per cent tariff on imported aircraft. Qantas, as an airline, "viewed with alarm" the proposition, which would have made its imported aircraft considerably more expensive.[2] Qantas, as aircraft manufacturer, saw little financial benefit in such a tariff. Fysh told the collector of customs that two DH50A aircraft were under construction at Longreach but "engines, instruments, bracing wires, wheels and all metal parts and fittings were imported from England. Also linen fabric for covering wings, aero tyres and other specialised parts. The majority of the plywood is imported, and the spruce logs. All timber work is carried out in our factory and thus forms the main portion of our construction work, together with the actual assembling of the machines." A DH50A imported complete from England cost, he added £2,400; a DH50A constructed at Longreach cost £2,350.[3]

By 1 August 1927 the third DH50A *Pegasus* (G-AUGD) was ready for christening, this time by Mrs S.M. Bruce, wife of the prime minister. (Fysh then flew the Bruces in the new aircraft to Winton and Hughenden.)

Though wonderful aircraft for Qantas compared with previous machines, the Puma-engined DH50A had no performance in reserve for conditions in western Queensland. Arthur Baird recommended a change to the DH50J, which had as its power plant the 450-horsepower Bristol Jupiter Mark VI radial engine. It still carried one pilot and four passengers, with a little luggage and urgent freight, as there was no increase in payload or volumetric capacity, and it was much more expensive to build than the DH50A. But with almost double the horsepower, the rate of climb nearly doubled, cruising speed increased to 105 miles per hour, and extra petrol tanks provided greater range. The extra power also permitted an increase in gross weight from 3,900 to 4,200 pounds. Above all, the Jupiter was a much more reliable engine and big cost savings accrued from the increased period between overhauls.[4] Two DH50Js (*Atalanta*, G-AUHE and *Hermes*, G-AUHI) were built in 1928, one DH50A (unnamed, G-AUJS) and DH50J (*Hippomenes*, VH-ULG) in 1929. Then the DH61 and other types superseded the DH50s. They were too big for Qantas to build and the completion of *Hippomenes* in September 1929 saw the end of the Qantas venture into aircraft manufacture. Some idea of the reliability of the DH50J type under Qantas conditions is apparent from *Atalanta*'s first nine months of operation. The aircraft flew 26,000 miles in 348 hours with total replacement costs for the period of less than one pound. By contrast, the Siddeley Puma engine in the DH50As seldom lasted more than 75 hours without serious attention.[5] Though the government decision did not finally impose any tariff on imported aircraft, a customs proclamation in 1928 forbade the import of aircraft not accompanied by a certificate of airworthiness issued in, or validated by, a signatory state to the 1919 Paris Convention on International Air Navigation. This had the effect of preventing direct importation of aircraft manufactured in Germany or the United States.

Though a significant testimonial to the professional excellence of Baird and his hangar staff, the manufacture of aircraft was peripheral to Qantas activity as an airline. Growth in that activity depended ultimately on extensions to the route network and these rested on government decisions and government subsidy. Airline competition was in essence for new routes and a bigger slice of the available subsidy cake. It came from the two other subsidized operators, West Australian Airways and Lasco.

Operationally, Qantas had done well since its beginnings, in comparison with West Australian Airways. In passenger and freight transport, to mid-1928, it had a superior record in terms of miles flown and was the only company which had an excess of passenger-miles over machine-miles in this period.[6] It had, in other words, carried more than one passenger on each mile flown by its aircraft. "From the inauguration of the subsidised routes to 30 June 1928 its [the Qantas] ratio of passenger miles to miles flown was 1.085 as compared with 0.92 for Western Australia Airways and 0.644 for Lasco", wrote analysts Hocking and Cave.[7] They were remarkably low figures, particularly as four-passenger aircraft were the most common types employed. "Qantas, on the average with one passenger weighing, say 160 pounds, plus 70 pounds of freight and 30 pounds of letters, had an actual payload of about 260 pounds as compared with a maximum payload of nearly 1,000 pounds. The two factors of low load factor combined with low average plane utilization", concluded Hocking and Cave, "explain the high cost of air transport, in spite of high subsidisation, and its inability to operate successfully where alternative land transport was available."

In an effort to achieve growth independently of government support, Qantas launched a regular daily air service with a DH50A on 9 May 1928 on the seventy-mile route between Brisbane and Toowoomba, charging £2.15s.0d for the fifty-minute trip in competition with the first class rail fare of £1.0s.1d for the four-hour trip by train. It was a brave experiment but, after initial encouraging passenger traffic volume from the curious, Fysh had to report that the figures "appear to have taken a permanent drop below that allowing a profit".[8] The service was discontinued in December.

Of much more importance that year was the government decision to call tenders for services between Brisbane and Charleville and, in the north, between Camooweal and Daly Waters. The forcing of tenders, utterly unexpected by Qantas, now gave competitors the opportunity to intrude at both the northern and southern extremities of Qantas's Charleville-Camooweal route. "Our very existence", wrote Fysh, "was in jeopardy."[9]

Two of the big, eight-passenger DH61 aircraft were ordered from England for delivery in January and February of 1929 and it was with these aircraft, which met the government's contract conditions, that Qantas tendered. Their price was three shillings and three pence a mile for the first year, one penny above the subsidy rate on the Charleville–Camooweal route, but reducing by twopence a mile for the second year and a further threepence for the third. Lasco undercut them, offering the lower Qantas third year price from the outset.

It was a dangerous situation but the Qantas DH61 order saved them: Lasco could only tender with DH50 and ANEC III aircraft, which did not meet the requirements of the government contract. Fysh was able to telegraph McMaster on 26 September that, although there was no official news, the prime minister was reported in the press as announcing that Qantas had secured the Brisbane–Charleville service. Lasco, however, had been granted Camooweal–Daly Waters. It seemed that the enduring Qantas dream of an eventual Brisbane–Darwin route had been shattered. "This is unpleasant news", wrote Fysh to his chairman. "I feel we should make a systematic and strong protest without overstepping the mark."[10]

Lasco had won on price. Qantas, knowing the conditions in that far outback area, had tendered at four shillings and three pence a mile, reducing to four shillings by the third year. Larkin had offered three shillings four and a half pence a mile, well under the subsidy rate he received for his Victorian services which, even at the higher rate of three shillings and nine pence, were unprofitable. Now he was faced with operating an aircraft thousands of miles from his centre of operations in the south of Australia, in an area where petrol was expensive and passengers few. From Melbourne on 23 November Fysh wrote to McMaster: "I have not been able to get to the bottom of the Camooweal–Daly Waters service. The whole thing is regarded amongst aviation people down here as a great blunder, and as a huge joke with the joke on Larkin."[11]

Though the decision to put Lasco on the remote run at the northern extremity of the Qantas route was a cause of grave unease in their future hopes for Darwin, winning the southern extension of the route to the city of Brisbane was of critical significance and by far the most important event of 1928 for the company. Civil aviation in Australia in 1928 was in a weak economic position and the capital city connection granted to

101

Qantas was to enable it to match the continuous expansion of the industry as a whole throughout the coming years of the Depression.

By the end of 1928 the three subsidized companies had in their fleets a total of fifteen of the four-passenger, 100 mile per hour DH50s aircraft. (Lasco had three of them but also operated three ANEC IIIs, the only six-passenger aircraft in operation in Australia before the close of 1928.) In terms of aircraft utilization, Western Australian Airways flew six DH50s a total of 428 hours in the three months ending 30 September 1928 on their subsidized route, which was an average utilization of less than one hour a day. Qantas, also with six DH50s, only managed a total of 322 hours in the same period. The reserve aircraft capacity inferred by these figures was the price paid for regular timetable performance. It cost less to keep spare aircraft along the route than to pay additional maintenance staff to man intermediate landing points. Later, when frequencies were doubled on major routes, only negligible extra capacity was needed.[12] The aircraft fleets of the subsidized companies were all British-made, as required by the government proclamation prohibiting import of aircraft from nonsignatory nations to the 1919 Paris convention.

On international comparisons, Australian aviation did remarkably well in 1928. Great Britain's only regular operating company, Imperial Airways Ltd., flew 1,032,842 miles in the twelve months to 31 December 1928. Australia's total for the year to 30 June 1929 in civil aviation flying was almost double this, at 1,992,070 miles, of which 430,852 miles was flown by the regular subsidized services. On a per capita basis, Australia was considerably more air-minded than Great Britain.[13]

Comparisons with the United States for the period are just as flattering. There were some 70,000 miles of regular air route operations throughout the world and the Australian contribution to the total was 5,800 miles. It therefore, with some four-thousandths of the world population, operated one-twelfth of existing regular air routes. With one-twentieth the population of the United States, Australia had over one-third that country's air route mileage and one-eighth as many airports. Air miles flown in 1928 in Australia were more than one-fifth of the total for the United States.[14] This extraordinary progress in civil aviation was in every way an honourable match for the international acclaim accorded

Kingsford Smith and Ulm, and Hinkler, for their pioneering flights.

Qantas in 1928 — in addition to its flying operations, flying schools, and aircraft manufacture — began a unique, romantic, yet extraordinary practical venture with John Flynn and the Australian Inland Mission to provide an air ambulance plane and pilot for an experimental Flying Doctor service based at Cloncurry. The service, conceived by Flynn and the AIM, was an extension of their great work to bring medical care to the isolated families who peopled inland Australia. Its implementation had awaited two technical achievements: the availability of an aircraft that could carry doctor, nurse, and stretcher patient, and the ability to provide a cheap and reliable means of radio communication between remote homestead and Aerial Ambulance centre. The aircraft was available as early as 1924, when Qantas imported its first DH50, but the wireless, an ingenious foot-pedal power-generating set that linked outlying stations with Cloncurry, took another three years to develop. On 27 March 1928, an agreement was signed under which Qantas, in return for the provision of an ambulance aircraft and pilot, was guaranteed twenty-five thousand flying miles at two shillings a mile under a one-year contract. (The Civil Aviation Authority paid half this rate; Qantas agreed to a rebate of tenpence a mile for every unflown mile.) The first Flying Doctor pilot was Arthur Affleck; the first flying doctor, Dr St Vincent Welch; and the first aircraft was the DH50A, G-AUER, but named *Victory*. It was by far the most risky of all Qantas flying operations.[15] Station owners were all sent instructions on "How to Make Your Own Landing Ground and How to Receive an Aeroplane". An ever-present dilemma for Affleck (and, from 1931, pilot Eric Donaldson) was to balance flight safety and medical need; the clear realization that safety was paramount often meant refusal to fly, under pressure from doctor and patient, when the risk was judged too great. In its first year Qantas flew 17,479 miles for the service and there were no accidents.

"The work of the whole Qantas staff during the past year", Fysh reported to his directors in early September 1928, "cannot be spoken of too highly . . . [it had been] far busier than in past years, owing to the vastly increased amount of work without proportionate increase in staff." He singled out Brain as "an untiring, loyal worker who, besides his piloting ability, has shown sound business knowledge". Operations, he noted

103

Adelaide, August 1928. Royal Air Force Air Marshal, Sir John Salmond — second from right — with members of his party and the Qantas crew after a taxi trip from Darwin, using the Qantas DH50J *Hermes*. C.W.A. Scott — third from right — was the pilot and George Nutson — first on left — was the engineer. The aircraft crashed soon after take-off from Adelaide on 4 September 1928 and was destroyed by fire.

proudly, "were considerably in excess of any other commercial company in Australia".[16]

This substantial company achievement was marred by the crash, on 4 September, of C.W.A. Scott and engineer G. Nutson in the *Hermes*, six miles north-east of Parafield, South Australia. Scott had been the pilot for a long tour of North Australia by Lord Stonehaven earlier in the year. It was followed by an equally extensive tour of the north by Sir John Salmond who was visiting Australia from Britain as a guest of the Commonwealth government to advise on aerial defence. The Salmond tour ended in Adelaide and Scott, soon after an early morning take-off on the return trip to Longreach, crashed in bad weather in hilly country and the *Hermes* caught fire. Scott broke his jaw and was badly burned and shocked. Nutson, dragged clear of the aircraft by Scott despite his injuries, died on the way to hospital. The aircraft was a total loss.

It was, in addition to the tragedy of Nutson's death, a heavy financial blow and a severe disruption to the company's operations, particularly the planned Brisbane service. On 7 September, Fysh asked the directors "to decide on the question of Mr. Scott's future employment".[17] Scott, he wrote, "has given valuable service and he is a brilliant pilot, is possibly the hardest worker we have yet employed and has the physical qualities to stand up to this". (Scott, a poet and musician and man of great personal charm, had also been heavyweight boxing champion of the Royal Air Force.) However, said Fysh, despite repeated notifications and personal instructions Scott had not attained "the standard of care and safety we demand". His personal behaviour had been the subject of criticism, though he was popular and a good man to work with. "I find on present evidence that the pilot [Scott] committed a serious error of judgement in leaving Parafield Aerodrome in weather which was unsuitable . . . and when there was no need for hurry." Scott had also, Fysh reported, placed fourteen tins of petrol in the cabin of the aircraft without proper reason.

Scott had, in fact, promptly offered his resignation. But he was offended and angered by the swift judgment passed on him by Fysh without hearing his own evidence and that of the official Air Accident Investigation Committee. He withdrew his resignation, explaining in a letter to McMaster on 12 October that it had been offered "as the only decent thing to do . . . in that feeling of good fellowship that can exist between employer and employee".[18] He had, he said, expected a fair hearing, adding, "I must mention certain letters that I received from the managing director and their effect on my attitude". Scott disputed the facts concerning the take-off as set down by Fysh. "I am no novice", he wrote indignantly, "to such flying conditions."

His letter to McMaster was written, with Fysh's consent and knowledge, after a long meeting between the two men on 10 October, following Scott's return to Longreach. On 16 October Fysh reported to McMaster that in his interview with Scott he had "gained nothing that would tend to make us take a more lenient view of his general behaviour and the Adelaide crash". In fact, wrote Fysh, Scott had made matters worse by saying that the petrol was placed in the cabin to enable him to return via Broken Hill and Thargomindah "right across more or less unknown country, and without even informing us". Fysh recognized that Scott had acted "quite openly with us" and admitted, "I could certainly use Scott later on . . . If he can be got on to safe flying he will make an excellent man for us." He suggested the board consider Scott's suspension without pay for two months, a salary reduction, a strict undertaking to carry out company rules, and that Scott must sign an undertaking to go teetotal both on and off duty.[19]

McMaster weighed Fysh's report and Scott's letter. On 21 October his characteristic firm, fair-mindedness was evident in his reply. He had, he said, considered fully all Scott's points but "the fact remains that you were a pilot employed in commercial aviation and you did not put safety first. You took a risk that you should not have taken."

"I quite realise", he wrote, "that for a young man such as yourself, with unlimited energy, ambition and skill it must come hard to sit down and not act . . ."

McMaster then soundly reprimanded him for his off-duty conduct. "It was common street talk that only a few days previous to you leaving Longreach for Hughenden to pick up Sir John Salmond you had been drinking heavily. Your conduct was anything but desirable both as regards your own interests and the interests of commercial aviation." McMaster acknowledged that "street talk" was not something ordinarily to be listened to but, he said, "the talk was common at the Hotel, the Club and the Golf Links". He concluded: "I sincerely regret losing your services and am only too willing to place your letter before the Board."[20]

The board considered Scott's letter, formally interviewing him, and made the decision that he be allowed to continue flying with Qantas. (Scott made no reference to these disciplinary events in his autobiographical book published in November 1934, though he writes vividly of the crash and the spin from eighteen hundred feet in cloud into the ground. "I returned to flying duties", he wrote, "at the end of January 1929.")[21] Fysh thought him "a brilliant but over-volatile pilot . . . too brilliant to be stable".[22] From this disruptive and tragic episode came a set of "Rules for the Observance of Pilots" which Fysh put into operation in November.

The directors' report for the financial year ended 30 June 1928 showed a net profit of £3,843 and a recommendation that it be placed in the Reserves Accounts. This brought contingency reserves to a healthy total of £10,112 and the directors recommended that £1,897 be set aside for the payment of 6 per cent dividend. There was justifiable satisfaction at such sound results. The airline, during the year, had carried an impressive 3,825 passengers and, following the start of the Cloncurry–Normanton extension, freight had increased by a massive 19,203 pounds to a total of 26,139 pounds. Four complete aeroplanes, said the report, were built under licence, two

DH50A-type with the Puma engine and two DH50Js with Jupiter engines. The order for two DH61 eight-passenger machines with Jupiter engines and "the latest Handley Page Slotted Wing Safety device" was recorded and the date for the opening of the Brisbane service set for April 1929. The *Hermes* crash at Adelaide had delayed this all-important event in the company's history by six months, with the company fully staffed to undertake the new run but without enough suitable aircraft.[23] The result, wrote Fysh, was that "at the present moment operations are not at all on an economic basis".[24] Further, the Brisbane Flying School was showing a loss and Fysh had also to recommend cessation of the Brisbane–Toowoomba service from the end of December, with a view to restarting in April.[25]

Despite these problems, Qantas ended 1928 in sound financial condition, with two big new airliners about to be delivered and the crucial Brisbane link only months away. But the necessity to tender for this extension, and the inclusion of Lasco on a section of the route between Brisbane and Darwin, were grim reminders that the future existence of the company depended on government decisions. These, in turn, could be influenced by the performance, growth, and public stature of their two subsidized competitors. There was plenty of

In-the-field repairs to the fabric covering on the wings of a Qantas DH50 at Vindex station near Winton in 1928.

107

political fight left in financially hard-pressed Lasco while, on the other side of the continent, West Australian Airways was poised to link Perth with Adelaide and so push Qantas into second place in Australian aviation with a single 1,453-mile route that matched the total Qantas route mileage. Two mighty names in aviation, Kingsford Smith and Ulm, were soon to link and emerge as even more formidable competitors. They were to do so without benefit of any government subsidy, in a major new airline enterprise.

The Brisbane Connection
1929 to 1930

Fysh, however, was thoroughly optimistic as the new year
began. "Undoubtedly", he wrote in his 31 January report,
"prospects are bright for the future." Until now, he said,
"work has been almost entirely of a pioneering nature" but
"the constant tendency for aircraft to become safer, more
economic and more foolproof must indicate with certainty
that commercial aviation, not only in Queensland but the
world over, has a future at least equal to any other mode of
transport."[1]

The immediate future, so far as Qantas was concerned,
involved preparation of the two new DH61 aircraft for the
inauguration of the Brisbane–Charleville route on 17 April,
clarification of legal requirements on the removal of head
office to Brisbane, and consideration of revised plans by Baird
for the hangar, workshops, and office there. Under investigation was "a scheme for the insurance of our fleet against flight
risks", submitted by Lester Brain as a result of his London
visit in the hope that it could be put into effect before the
DH61s were commissioned.[2] Important, if less pressing, was a
letter to the minister for defence, Sir William Glasgow,
"pointing out the advantage and saving in time in continuing
the proposed England to Australia air service down the Qantas
route instead of down the West Australian coast".[3]

On 16 April, before assembled guests from the civic and
commercial life of the city of Brisbane, Lady Goodwin, wife of
Queensland's governor Sir John Goodwin, christened one of
the gleaming DH61 airliners, naming it *Apollo*. (The second

7

The passenger cabin of a Qantas DH61 at Eagle Farm aerodrome, Brisbane in April 1929. This photograph was taken from the forward end of the cabin and shows four of the seven seats. The pilot sat in an open cockpit behind the passenger area. Note the small hole in the rear wall near the ceiling. This allowed the pilot to see into the passenger compartment and to communicate with them as needed.

DH61 was called *Diana*.) On 17 April, Skipper Moody took it out from Brisbane on the inaugural service to Charleville. Among his passengers was veteran Qantas supporter, white-bearded Alexander Kennedy, now ninety-one, in a three-piece suit and felt hat. Of some historical importance, installed in the DH61 was the first in-flight lavatory. The era of "sprinting for the little tin shed" after landing was coming to a close.[4]

For McMaster, 17 April "marked the biggest step in the welfare of Qantas since the commencement of the original mail route from Charleville to Cloncurry".[5] Fysh, in his manager's report, said it was "the culmination of four years of endeavour to secure the objective of a city connection. Directors will remember that our campaign was started in the face of great difficulties, the first being the lack of all official support . . . the second, the expressed policy of the Commonwealth Government that no subsidised airlines would be operated parallel to railway lines."[6]

Insurance of the fleet against accident as from 10 April was concluded with T.C. Bowring & Co. of London, insurance brokers to Imperial Airways, for a yearly premium of £1,000, with Qantas liable for the first £2,000 of breakages during the year.[7]

Within a week of this first air route link with the capital city of Queensland, Qantas was caught up in a national aviation drama that put it on the front pages of almost every newspaper. The drama had its origins in the airline ambitions of C.E. Kingsford Smith and C.T.P. Ulm, already household names throughout Australia for their great pioneering flights in 1928. They had conquered the Pacific Ocean; crossed the Australian continent from Point Cook in Victoria to Perth in Western Australia; and made a double crossing of the Tasman Sea, to and from New Zealand, all in the three-engined Fokker monoplane, *Southern Cross*. In that same year they had together founded Australian National Airways (a quite separate company with this name was founded in the 1930s). On 30 March 1929, again in the *Southern Cross*, they left Sydney flying westward across the continent en route for England for negotiations on behalf of ANA for aircraft. They crossed the Overland Telegraph Line in Central Australia with Wyndham as their first planned stop but then, their radio out of action, seemingly disappeared. In fact, bad weather had forced them down near the Glenely River in Western Australia.[8]

The DH61 *Apollo* made the inaugural flight on the Brisbane to Charleville service on 17 April. It is shown here immediately after coming to a halt; pilot "Skipper" Moody is standing in the cockpit wiping his brow in the mid-morning heat.

The crew of the *Southern Cross* are driven in triumph through the streets of Brisbane on 9 June 1928, after completing the first crossing of the Pacific Ocean by air. From left: Charles Kingsford Smith, Harry Lyon, James Warner (standing), Charles Ulm (seated in front).

A massive air search was organized but a full week went by with no sightings. Public concern intensified and dominated all other news. Then the tragedy compounded. On 7 April their old comrade, Lt. Keith Anderson, took off from Sydney with mechanic H.S. Hitchcock in the unsuitable and ill-prepared Westland Widgeon *Kookaburra* to join in the search. Their compass was inaccurate and they carried no special rations for emergencies. They, too, were headed for Wyndham where they were expected on 11 April but, after leaving Alice Springs on 10 April, engine trouble forced them down

south-east of Wave Hill in Central Australia. The ground was
unsuitable for take-off, and they were trapped.[9] On the same
day, 12 April, that the Citizens Search Committee (formed to
back the search for Kingsford Smith and Ulm) also became
concerned for the safety of Anderson and Hitchcock, the
Southern Cross was sighted, with no casualties and undamaged.
But day followed day with no sight of the *Kookaburra*. Qantas
was asked by the Citizens Search Committee if it would
provide an aircraft to assist in the search and on Friday 19
April the DH50 *Atalanta*, hastily fitted with a special short-
wave wireless transmitter, set off from Brisbane. Lester Brain
was the pilot and F.W. Stevens, deputy director of radio
station 4QG Brisbane, went as wireless operator. There were
now seven planes engaged in the search.

On the afternoon of Sunday 21 April the director of 4QG,
J.W. Robinson, received a radiogram from Stevens. They had
sighted Anderson's machine, intact on the ground, in desert
country eighty miles west-by-north of Powell's Creek, a
station on the Overland Telegraph Line. Circling low, Brain
saw a man lying under the wing, apparently dead for some

Lester Brain in front of DH50J
Atalanta at Eagle Farm,
Brisbane in early 1929.

days. There was no sign of the second occupant of the *Kookaburra*. "We dropped a can of water attached to a small parachute", said the radio message. "The machine appeared undamaged and stands at the east end of a large red patch of ground, lately burnt off and still smoking. A pack horse party is setting out from Wave Hill without delay."[10]

Qantas DH50J *Atalanta* tied down on a clay-pan in the Jervois Range, 170 miles north-east of Alice Springs, while on a charter flight in September 1929 with a survey party of mining engineers from Brisbane. Flown by Lester Brain, the *Atalanta* has been fitted with extra wheels to facilitate landings and take-offs from sand-covered or stony areas.

Brain could not land the *Atalanta* because of the dangerous sand (this was later rectified by the addition of extra wheels) and returned to Wave Hill. At daylight he set out again. There was no change at the scene of the *Kookaburra*. In bumpy conditions Brain searched in the vicinity of the aircraft but found nothing. He set off, against strong head winds, for Powell's Creek but the wind there was across his landing path and too powerful and he continued on to Newcastle Waters. There, after refuelling, he was joined by three Air Force machines and they returned together for a further extended search. There was no sign of the second man and Brain surmised that "the first man to die was buried by the other".[11] One of the RAAF search aircraft, a DH9A, crashed later that day near Tennant Creek and was destroyed, though without loss of life. Brain brought the *Atalanta* back to Longreach on the Tuesday, ending the Qantas involvement in the tragedy. The *Southern Cross*, with Kingsford Smith and Ulm, eventually landed back at Richmond, near Sydney, on 27 April, four weeks after setting out on what *Aircraft* magazine called "the stunt which has cost Australia too much". It was, wrote the magazine, "a publicity stunt and an ill-advised one at that".[12] But *Aircraft* emphatically dissociated itself from the rumour that began to spread through the Commonwealth that the crew had lost themselves deliberately to gain publicity. "The failure of the non-stop flight from Sydney to Wyndham", it wrote, "was unpremeditated."[13]

Both Kingsford Smith and Ulm were called before an Air Inquiry Committee which sat in Sydney in May and June. An agreement between them and Sun Newspapers Ltd. was produced in evidence in which, in exchange for the exclusive Australian rights to the story of their proposed flight, they were to be paid £500 "upon the Airmen reaching England in less time than Hinkler occupied on his flight [sixteen days], but if they do not complete the flight within the period of sixteen days then they shall only be paid the sum of 250 pounds".[14] Ulm told the inquiry: "We had to go to England on the business of our company [Australian National Airways Ltd.] but the flight was not in any way financed or backed by our company. It was a separate venture ..." They went by air, he said, "not only for the reason of getting there quickly but for other reasons, amongst which was that our then proposed flight to England was an exploration and pioneering flight. We believe that in the very near future we can help considerably towards the establishment of a regular route between here and England."[15]

That was, indeed, their vision and one towards which Ulm, in particular, was to strive with gifts of intellect, organization, and the written word that his more glamorous colleague did not share. In this transition year of their careers, from pioneer aviators to major airline entrepreneurs, the pressures on both men for continuous and recognized public performance were immense. In a word they needed, for the most practical of reasons, publicity. Reputation required public awareness and, in their chosen profession, reputation was the very rock on which they had to build the support of financial backers and the esteem of government ministers. It was so too, of course, with others, including Qantas. A month after the *Kookaburra* episode, Lester Brain was involved, successfully, in another dramatic search in the *Atalanta*, this time for a Vickers Vellore aircraft that had crash-landed at Cape Don lighthouse after crossing the Timor Sea on the last leg of a flight from England by Flight Lts. J.J. Muir and H.C. Owen. Brain was awarded the Air Force Cross for his achievements. Fysh pointed out to his directors that "the helpful publicity which we have received through the success of the two search trips could probably not have been bought for money".[16]

Important as publicity was for particular interests and individuals, the great sweep of events in which they played a part was guided by more fundamental and complex issues and pressures. The strategic and political need to minimize the isolation of Australia's western capital, Perth, from the centre of government and the cities on the other side of the continent was a powerful influence in the allocation of federal government resources for competing air links. The allocation of a subsidy for the Perth–Adelaide route had been opposed by Brinsmead, for the same reason that he had fought against the Qantas Charleville–Brisbane link. "I am quite convinced", he said, "that as long as the mileage subsidy is paid, any new aerial lines should be opened up entirely for the benefit of people who require quick transport to railheads only. I am not and never have been in favour of aircraft being subsidised merely to save a few hours of discomfort to passengers who can travel by existing railways."[17]

The Imperial Conference of 1926 and its recommendation that air services should receive early consideration "with a view to ultimate creation of a complete system of Imperial Air Routes", was eventually to override Brinsmead's restrictive philosophy.[18] At that conference, the British secretary of state for air, Sir Samuel Hoare, had pointed out that the prime ministers of Australia and New Zealand had had to spend over sixty days travelling to and from the meeting. Australian Prime Minister S.M. Bruce remarked that an air route between Adelaide and Perth would alone cut the journey time to England from the eastern states by three or four days. Such a link would, if the eventual air route from England crossed the Timor Sea to Wyndham in Western Australia (the shortest way), also be necessary to link New Zealand by air with England. For Australia the opening of this Perth–Adelaide service, by West Australian Airways, on 2 June 1929, was the first direct outcome of the Imperial Conference.[19]

Norman Brearley's West Australian Airways (a new company formed, in 1926, with the assets of the old Western Australian Airways, amid a modest uproar over the manner of bonus share allocations in the new company) was awarded the

contract for the service. Not only was it the first five-year contract ever awarded, it was also the first to be based on payment
per pound of mail carried instead of mileage. There was a
guaranteed weight minimum of six hundred pounds per trip
at the rate of twelve shillings and eight pence per pound. This
minimum guaranteed weight loading was to double if, after
four consecutive months, the weight of surcharged mails
carried averaged eight hundred pounds. The effect of such an
increase for WAA in money terms was a jump in guaranteed
income per trip from £380 to £760. It was almost an open
invitation to ensure, somehow, that mails would indeed
average eight hundred pounds per trip. They did. By extraordinary coincidence, which occasioned press comment and
departmental wrath, there was from almost the outset of the
service a quite unpredicted quantity of weighty land sale
catalogues from Perth. New and hastily introduced Post Office regulations dried this artificial river of gold, but such a
manipulation of subsidy possibilities was not unnoticed by the
government and its officers.[20]

Sordid commercial matters were far from the minds of the
fifteen thousand Adelaide people and the vice-regal and other
guests on the beflagged dais at Adelaide's Parafield aerodrome
on 1 June for the christening by Lady Hore Ruthven, wife of
South Australia's governor, of WAA's three-engined Hercules
airliner, *City of Adelaide*. "Thirty uniformed members from
the private orchestra of Holden's Motor Body Builders Ltd.
gave up their half holiday to brighten the occasion and
discoursed popular melody", wrote *Aircraft*, as Her Excellen-
cy shattered a red-and-white silk-corded bottle of Australian
Romalo against the central propeller boss.[21] The governor,
Lord Hore Ruthven, reminded them that it was less than sixty
years since Lord Forest had travelled from Perth to Adelaide
in five months of severe hardship, "a journey that could now
be accomplished in thirty hours, including a rest period of
twelve hours". And he added, reflecting an attitude to
England held by most Australians and their leaders that would
ultimately influence the airline structure joining the two
countries, "every hour by which we can shorten the journey
between the Old Country and the New will further the
progress and prosperity of the Empire".[22] (The prime
minister himself, Mr Bruce, stressed the British link at much
the same time when he responded in Parliament to an attack
on the administration of the RAAF and civil aviation by
Queensland's ex-Labor Premier Theodore, who had criticized

outdated Air Force aircraft. "When the British Government has decided on the most suitable [aircraft] type and made a final selection [for the Royal Air Force] we shall probably adopt it", he said.)[23] By the end of July, *Aircraft* reported, the transcontinental service was functioning smoothly and efficiently. West Australian Airways was now the country's premier airline; Qantas had been overtaken.

Financial results for Qantas for the year were disappointing. Profit was down as a direct result of the Adelaide crash and its effects. The Aerial Medical Service had shown a modest profit but the Brisbane Flying School, which had been handed over in May to the Queensland Aero Club, had lost money. The unsubsidized Brisbane–Toowoomba service had not lived up to expectations and, after a depreciation charge of £350, had shown a loss for the period of its operation between May and December, of some £45. It had carried 445 route passengers, 23 taxi passengers, and 1,146 joy-riders. It had, however, done much to establish the Qantas presence in Brisbane.[24]

Net profit to 30 June was £3,856 and a 6 per cent dividend agreed. Poor seasonal conditions coupled with the Depression had had their effect. The directors could only describe the results as "satisfactory".[25]

Qantas was now running into serious trouble with the engines of its new DH61 airliners. Fysh told the directors, in a letter of 5 July 1929, that "the culminating point was reached when the engine fitted to *Diana* broke a piston at Charleville, and later broke a connecting rod. The action has been taken of withdrawing the machines from service pending a full enquiry."[26] The DH61s were powered by the Bristol Jupiter Mark XI engine which, unlike the earlier and excellent Mark VI version, suffered constantly from overoiling of plugs, collapse of pistons, seizures, and excessive oil temperatures.[27]

Though the DH61s were in fact to continue operating, troubles persisted and there were frequent forced landings. "The whole position has been unsatisfactory in the extreme," Fysh wrote to McMaster on 1 October, "but the makers are not legally responsible and feel they have done everything possible by sending a man all the way from England, loaning a Mark VI engine and rebuilding two engines to equal to new."[28]

In that same letter he reported what was an unusual and puzzling decision by the Defence Department, and a reminder that their immediate future, as well as their destiny, lay in the hands of the federal government. The secretary of the depart-

ment had informed them that their contracts on the main
Charleville–Camooweal route, and on the Cloncurry–Normanton extension, had been renewed from 4 December to 7
June 1930, a mere six-month period. It "leaves us entirely in
the dark concerning the Government's policy after 7 June
next", wrote Fysh.[27]

The motives of the government soon became clear. "The
Minister for Defence", Fysh reported to McMaster on 22
November, "has issued a statement [on] the desire to more
closely co-ordinate the R.A.A.F. and the Subsidised Companies to provide for closer working in war time. The
R.A.A.F. services will link up with Qantas, whatever this
means." A scheme was under consideration, Fysh added, for
an exchange and intermingling of the RAAF and the staff of
the subsidized services.[30] The new government, he said, had
leanings towards nationalization. Further, it was intended to
do away with all the routes operated by Lasco "as being of no
utility".[31]

This attitude to Lasco was not unexpected as the Commonwealth auditor-general, in his report for the 1928–29 financial
year, had recommended withdrawal of subsidies to the Larkin
Aircraft Supply Co. But that same report had recognized that
the Perth–Derby route in Western Australia and the Qantas
routes in Queensland provided "facilities for the carriage of
mails, passenger transport and urgent freight in a manner
which is of great value", because of the immense distances,
and absence of railways and frequent postal services.[32] The new
notion of RAAF involvement seemed to Qantas as ridiculous as
it was unexpected.

The possibilities were frightening. One was that Qantas
would be forced to re-tender for all of its routes, which would
then be run wholly by RAAF personnel. Another was that
RAAF staff would be seconded to the airline and Qantas staff
obliged to operate with the RAAF. Fysh tried to canvass the
alternatives logically and concluded: "If the R.A.A.F. must go
into commercial aviation then it will be my endeavour to
influence a separate trial to show which is the best scheme.
But the trouble may be that they want private capital to stand
up to the experiment. It is just the thing Larkin would rush
into, as the losses would not hit his parent company and a
market would be secured for his machines."[33]

McMaster responded on 24 November: "I consider our best
policy is to keep absolute control of all services operated by
Qantas but in the event that this is impossible, and provided

no undue financial risk is forced on Qantas, we should work in with Government policy as much as possible — and risk readjustments being made in our favour later."[34] He also urged Fysh to push Qantas interests for Darwin, Alice Springs, Sydney, and Canberra services.

That Qantas was held in high public esteem was without doubt. In an article in *Aircraft* on 30 November, the respected commentator E.R. Peacock acclaimed "without personal interest or prejudice the achievement of McGinness and Fysh, supported by McMaster and others with pioneering vision and patriotism, in the birth and growth of Qantas." That, he wrote, was only eight years ago and "Hudson Fysh has not yet received his knighthood, although honours have been conferred for many less deserving achievements". Fysh was to wait many more years for this honour.

While the subsidized services attempted to digest the government initiative on RAAF participation in their activities, Kingsford Smith and Ulm, on 1 January 1930, launched their new airline, with the inauguration of an intercapital service between Sydney and Brisbane. It was the beginning of the first major unsubsidized airline operation in Australia. Using four eight-passenger Avro X aircraft, powered by three Armstrong Siddeley Lynx engines, the journey took five to six hours for a single fare of £9.13s.0d. Despite the high fare, the service immediately attracted passengers. After six months of operation the company declared an impressive interim dividend of 8 per cent and, in June, began a Sydney–Melbourne service. The response was equally enthusiastic and in its first three months the service carried 676 passengers, with a passenger load factor of 45 per cent which rose, by year's end, to 50 per cent. With good aircraft, Ulm's gift for administration and a team of Australia's finest pilots (among whom were G.U. "Scotty" Allan and P.G. Taylor, both to become nationally recognized aviators) it seemed that Australian commercial aviation had come to maturity in one courageous bound, setting standards for the world in unsubsidized airline flying. As if to further validate the irrelevance of subsidies two more independent airlines began operations that year; Queensland Air Navigation began a Brisbane–Townsville service on Qantas's flank and New England Airways started up at Lismore, in northern New South Wales.

In this year of heady enterprise, Qantas added a mere forty-five miles to its route network, in the remote and sparsely

(POST THIS IN YOUR OFFICE) 4—700—1/7/30

The Queensland & Northern Territory Aerial Services Ltd.
(ESTABLISHED 1920)

Time
Saved
is Money
Saved

VH-UJB

Always
use Air
Trans-
portation

"Q.A.N.T.A.S."
AIR MAIL
Information

Brisbane to Camooweal and Normanton
(LINKING WITH CAMOOWEAL—DALY WATERS SERVICE)

WINTER TIMETABLE:—April 2nd, 1930—September 30th, 1930
COMMENCING 15th JUNE and SUPERSEDING PREVIOUS SCHEDULES.

SUMMER TIMETABLE—October-March, Approximately 1½ Hours Earlier.

Northerly Trip Read Down   Southerly Trip Read Up

		MILES (Inter Town)		MILES (From Brisbane)			
	Depart 6.45 a.m.		BRISBANE		Arrive 4.40 p.m.		
	Arrive 7.35 ..	75	TOOWOOMBA	75	Depart 3.50 ..		
	Depart 7.50 ..				Arrive 3.35 ..		
	Arrive 10.10 ..	212	ROMA	287	Depart 1.15 ..		
	Depart 10.40 ..				Arrive 12.45 ..		
	Arrive 12.25 p.m.	157	CHARLEVILLE	444	Depart 11.05 a.m.		SUNDAYS
	Depart 1.25 ..				Arrive 10.20 ..		
	Arrive 2.35 ..	110	TAMBO	554	Depart 9.10 ..		
	Depart 2.50 ..				Arrive 8.55 ..		
	Arrive 3.25 ..	57½	BLACKALL	611½	Depart 8.20 ..		
	Depart 3.40 ..				Arrive 8.05 ..		
	Arrive 4.45 ..	99	LONGREACH	710½	Depart 7.00 ..		
	Depart 7.00 a.m.				Arrive 3.25 p.m.		
	Arrive 8.20 ..	107	WINTON	817½	Depart 2.05 ..		
	Depart 8.35 ..				Arrive 1.50 ..		
	Arrive 10.15 ..	132½	MACKINLAY	950	Depart 12.15 ..		SATURDAYS
	Depart 10.30 ..				Arrive 12.00 noon		
	Arrive 11.25 ..	71	CLONCURRY	1021	Depart 11.05 a.m.		
	Depart 12.25 p.m.				Arrive 10.20 ..		
	Arrive 1.55 ..	124	MT. ISA	1145	Depart 8.45 ..		
	Depart 2.10 ..				Arrive 8.30 ..		
	Arrive 3.45 ..	124	CAMOOWEAL	1269	Depart 7.00 ..		
	Depart 12.25 p.m.		CLONCURRY		Arrive 9.55 a.m.		FRIDAYS
	Arrive 3.05 ..	215	NORMANTON	1236	Depart 7.15 ..		

(Left margin brackets: TUESDAYS / WEDNESDAYS)

LUGGAGE—One 24in. Suit Case (30lbs.) Free.
LANDINGS MADE FOR PASSENGERS AT DALBY, MITCHELL AND KYNUNA WHEN REQUIRED.

PASSENGERS AND GOODS BY AIR.

Rates and full particulars can be obtained on application to Head Office or any Agency.

THE AIR MAILS.

Rates and full particulars can time for your correspondence. Mark letters "By Air Mail," and post in the usual way. Additional postage required, 3d. per ½ ounce.

AIR TAXI SERVICES.

Machines to carry one to four passengers are available at short notice from Brisbane, Charleville, Longreach, and Cloncurry. Tours arranged to any part of Australia.

BOOKING AGENTS:

Brisbane—BURNS, PHILP & CO. LTD. (Chief Booking Agents)
DALGETY & CO.
GOLDSBROUGH MORT & CO.
GOVT. TOURIST BUREAU.
LUYA, JULIUS LTD.
THOS. COOK & SON.
Toowoomba—R. R. RIVETT.
Dalby—THOS. JACK & CO.
Roma—MARANOA LTD.

Mitchell—MACFARLANE & CO.
Charleville—G. HERRIMAN.
Tambo—A. HAMILTON.
Blackall—SMITH'S GARAGE LTD.
Longreach—" QANTAS " LTD.
Winton—F. W. BODE & CO.
Mackinlay—L. SIMPSON.
Cloncurry—ADAM SCOTT.
Mt. Isa—J. BOYD.

Camooweal—SYNNOTT, MURRAY & SCHOLES LTD.
Normanton—BURNS, PHILP & CO. LTD.
Townsville—BURNS, PHILP & CO. LTD.
Cairns—BURNS, PHILP & CO. LTD.
Rockhampton—WALTER REID & CO. LTD.
Sydney | BURNS, PHILP & CO. LTD.
Melbourne | (Chief Booking Agents)
Adelaide | or any recognised Tourist Agents.

Or Q.A.N.T.A.S. Ltd.—Head Office: The Wool Exchange, Eagle Street, Brisbane

Over One Million Miles flown in 10 years Air Transport, on which is based our Organised Service, and Flight Safety.

JACKSON & O'SULLIVAN, PRINTERS, BRISBANE.

Qantas timetable, winter 1930.

121

populated north, and not even directly connected with its existing ports. Larkin's Australian Aerial Services had, at last, begun operating its Camooweal–Daly Waters route from the Qantas terminal point at Camooweal, but it was deeply in dispute with the Civil Aviation Branch. The government had intended that the railway line from Darwin should extend to Daly Waters and had based the Camooweal link on this premise. In fact, the railway was extended only as far as Birdum Creek, a little less than fifty miles short of Daly Waters. Larkin was asked to extend his operations on to Birdum Creek but refused. His unrealistic tender for the Camooweal–Daly Waters route and the remoteness of the route from his southern operations made it, from the outset, unprofitable. Despite the clear need for the railhead connection, and the embarrassment of the Civil Aviation Branch, he refused to budge and stuck to the terms of his contract. Qantas was invited to fill the gap and, in a spirit of goodwill and political acumen, agreed. Their contract required them to fly the mails between Birdum Creek and Daly Waters for the four-month wet season each year, when mail delivery by road became impossible, an annual mileage of some sixteen hundred miles. The route started four hundred and seventy-five miles from their terminus at Camooweal and some seventeen hundred miles from Brisbane where the de Havilland Moth, used for the job, had its base. The annual mileage just to get the Moth to and from Brisbane was twice this route total. It was an absurd situation that reflected little credit on either Larkin or the Civil Aviation Branch that had installed him on the Daly Waters section. Qantas was asked, on 7 January 1930, to respond within forty-eight hours to Civil Aviation's request to operate Birdum Creek. "As the distance is only forty-five miles," Fysh told McMaster, "the cost per mile is enormous — about ten shillings. Am wiring tomorrow stating we willing to operate service at that figure."[35] Despite the urgency of the telegram, the Defence Department did not conclude their arrangements with Qantas until the following year.

The first Qantas Gazette of 1930 carried a modest announcement in the field of aviation medicine.

> Air sickness [it said] is much less common than sea sickness but during summer afternoons or flights in the far west air sickness is sometimes experienced. It is now generally recognised that chewing gum is of value in minimising the effects of all travel sickness and it has been recommended by the Air Ministry to the leading British Air Transport companies. Supplies of chewing gum, neat-

ly got up in small envelopes, have been provided for the use of
passengers on Qantas planes by Messrs Wrigleys Ltd., and are
now in general use with good results.

For Qantas, 1930 was to see a geographical shift of its operational and managerial centre from country to city that would
reinforce old ambitions, add to its stature and financial
strength, and critically influence its future. On 24 February,
at a meeting at Longreach, the directors resolved "that the
office of the Company be established in the city of Brisbane
. . . on or before 30 June". Tenders were to be called for the
supply and erection of a hangar at Archerfield aerodrome "87
feet by 90 feet with two lean-tos of 30 feet".[36]

Fysh tackled the major reorganization involved with his
customary single-mindedness. The office staff in Brisbane, he
advised, would be the managing director, secretary, accountant, two stenographers, a junior clerk, and an office boy. Flying staff duties were to be reallocated.

"It is necessary for one pilot to do the Brisbane–Longreach
sector," he reported to the board on 8 April 1930, "making
Longreach the central change-over station for the route. Mr
Moody was asked to do this and as he has advised his inability
owing to private reasons, he has been advised that his services
will not be required after July 1st."[37] Fysh appointed Lester
Brain to the Brisbane headquarters in charge of sales,
demonstrations and agency tours, taxi trips and, as chief
pilot, a reserve pilot for the route. Russell Tapp was allocated
to the Brisbane–Longreach route and E.H. Donaldson given
Longreach–Camooweal, with Arthur Affleck operating the
Flying Doctor Scheme. The volatile C.W.A. Scott was
appointed instructor at the Flying School and a new pilot was
required for Cloncurry–Normanton. Both Fysh and Arthur
Baird were set down as reserve pilots, based in Brisbane. The
new company secretary, H.H. "George" Harman joined them
on 27 May, "a man of great integrity, a hard worker and good
company man", wrote Fysh.[38]

George Harman opened the Qantas Brisbane office on 16
June 1930 in the Wool Exchange Building. With him was
Miss Ida Isaacs who had joined the company in Longreach on
28 October 1928. She was to serve Qantas for thirty-six years
as secretary to Hudson Fysh. The airline had just completed
one million miles of flying when Fysh, on 22 June, left his
Longreach home to move to Brisbane.

There were, also, drastic board changes. McMaster, with

some sadness, was aware that the old board was no longer appropriate.

> I sincerely regret that the reorganisation is necessary [he wrote]. But we have to face the position in the best interests of the shareholders and the future of the organisation. The whole position for Qantas appears to me to be serious ... I feel that the stronger the financial interests we get on the Board, the better. No one regrets the breaking up of the old Board more than I do but Qantas has to go ahead. There is no getting away from the fact that her position as premier in aviation in this State is being attacked.[39]

Dr Hope Michod, who had so ably filled the position of chairman from 17 November 1923 to 30 October 1926, resigned from the board in June "owing to pressure of his practice in Brisbane".[40] Maj. Thomas McLeod resigned, to live in England. D.C. Crombie, G. Morgan Reade, and N.F. White agreed to resign on or before the 25 October annual general meeting. Only three members of the old board were to remain — McMaster, Templeton, and Fysh. F.E. Loxton, a director of Burns Philp, became the fourth board member. "We will all feel a pang at parting company ... especially after the anxious times we went through together in the early days", wrote Norman White. "Fortunately some people have made lots of money and it is to be hoped that Loxton's anticipations of contributions from them may be realised. It would be very sad to die in the hole after our change of policy."[41]

The new policy was expressed publicly by McMaster in the *Longreach Leader*.[42] "Qantas must either expand and enter the coastal and interstate services", he said, "or gradually lose the position she now holds as one of the premier and most successful pioneering services in the Commonwealth. The general policy of Qantas must undergo a complete re-survey." Their future was, he said, in the largest centres and it was there that Qantas had to look for expansion.

There were competitors with similar philosophies. Not only had Qantas seen Kingsford Smith and Ulm move massively into Brisbane with their impressive Australian National Airways; within Queensland itself Queensland Air Navigation Ltd., on 1 April, started a service between Brisbane and Townsville and other smaller companies planned new routes.

Only days before the Brisbane office opened, the minister for defence, A.E. Green, had announced on 12 June "sweeping reductions in the rate of subsidy payable in respect of certain airlines", with further annual decreases and "the avowed object of hastening the day when commercial air transport will be self-supporting".[43] For Qantas this meant a reduced consolidated price for the operation of all services, starting at two shillings and ten pence a mile for the first year, a penny less for the second, and a further two pence a mile less for the third year. One threat had dissipated, however. The Air Force, headed by Air Marshall Williams, wanted no part of the proposed integration of personnel with the subsidized airlines. The uncertainty caused by the previous six-month extension of their contract was removed and a new contract, for a three-year period from 10 June, was concluded at the reduced subsidy rates with the Department of Defence.[44]

Despite the effect of the Depression, the managing director's report of 20 October 1930 noted the sale, in a period of six weeks, of four Gipsy Moths, one Hawk Moth, and one Puss Moth, with a net return in commissions of £600. Fysh reminded directors that Qantas was the sole agent for parts for the de Havilland machines. The company took delivery of its own Puss Moth and ordered a second, with the intention of stationing one of them at Longreach on the sale of one DH50. (The DH50, VH-UJS, had burst a tyre on take-off at Cloncurry on 26 September and went to the workshop for a month for repairs.) Somewhat laconically Fysh noted: "The Hawk and Puss Moths make the whole of our present fleet, with the exception of the DH61s, obsolete."[45]

The fleet, with the arrival of the second Puss Moth, now consisted of: two seven-seat DH61s (Jupiter Mark XI, 480-horsepower engine); two four-seat DH50s (Jupiter Mark VI, 460-horsepower engine); four four-seat DH50As (Puma 240-horsepower engine); one single seat Gipsy Moth (Gipsy 100-horsepower engine); two two-seat Puss Moths (Gipsy III 105-horsepower engine). The DH50s in the fleet had been built in the Longreach workshops.

Qantas formally farewelled Longreach at a function there in October 1930. The *Longreach Leader* reported that in its ten years the airline had carried 10,400 passengers, flown more than a million miles, accumulated assets of £57,000, and operated in an area covering half a million square miles. The names of its pilots were household words and, said the *Leader*, its reputation was worldwide.[46] G.A. Taunton, a director from 1926, told the gathering: "Many a man and woman in the western towns has reason to pay homage to the spirit which inspired the founders of Qantas."[47]

There was one sad note from the *Longreach Leader*.

125

Victory, the first DH50 owned by Qantas pictured in operation on the Flying Doctor Service about 1930. Note the position of the patient in the passenger cabin. The doctor, seen here standing on the wheel, could sit at the head of the patient in flight.

"McGinness", it wrote, "is virtually unknown to most of you but . . . it was McGinness who first conceived the idea of Qantas." (Fysh sent a copy of the paper to McGinness in Western Australia.)

The tenth annual report, presented at the annual general meeting in Longreach on 25 October, showed a profit for the year to 30 June 1930 of £5,770 and recommended a record dividend of 7 per cent (a return of 14.6 per cent on capital). All branches of the Qantas operations had shown satisfactory expansion and the loss in subsidy had been compensated by increases in passenger, freight, taxi, and general trade returns. Operating costs on a mileage basis had been reduced.

They were excellent results but the year 1930, despite its major advances and stimulating changes, had revealed a worrying operational development. There had been an increase in the number of forced landings and breakages totally out of balance with the extra mileage flown. The forced landings had been mainly due to the troubles with the Jupiter Mark XI engines but, Fysh told his pilots, the breakages were mostly due to their own errors, and the majority of them "should have been easily avoided".[48] There were, in fact, eighteen forced landings for 1930 with seven "breakages", well over double those for 1929 and more than in any other single year of operations. Fysh set out the figures from 1922 to 1930; a total of eighty forced landings involving two major and seventeen serious accidents, with one "breakage" every 37,140 miles. Of the eighty forced landings, seventy-six were caused by engine failure or mechanical trouble in aircraft or engine.

Such statistics were not, of course, for the general public. The November 1930 *Qantas Gazette* reported: "The carrying out of the regular Brisbane–Camooweal and Cloncurry–Normanton air route schedules is accomplished with such small divergence from timetable and such absence of thrills or unexpected happenings that there is little of interest to *Gazette* readers to read." This tranquil comment is, in many ways, an appropriate one, despite the rash of forced landings. Qantas had indeed mastered the task of operating scheduled airline services across the wide spaces of inland Queensland. It was the last year, though, in which Qantas ambitions and perspectives would be limited to such operations. Developments overseas would, from now onwards, increasingly direct their attention to the rich possibilities of great new air routes that, in the words of Prime Minister Hughes in 1921, would mean that Australia could "in one bound be loosened from the fetters imposed by our remoteness and brought in close touch with the western world".[49]

A mercy dash by Qantas Air Ambulance in early 1930. The DH50 Air Ambulance *Victory* brought the man from Camooweal to Longreach where he was transferred to this DH50, *Iris*, for the flight to Brisbane.

The Imperial Link
1931

8   Hughes had, of course, made that remark when advocating the acquisition by Australia of the seven airships offered "as a free gift" by Winston Churchill, whose policy it had been to abandon airship development in favour of aeroplanes. Now, nine years later, Britain had embarked on a new and dramatic initiative to link London and Karachi with "the largest and most revolutionary airship in the world".[1] It ended dreadfully, in disaster.

Early on Wednesday 1 October 1930 the huge R101 airship was taken out of her shed and readied for a test flight over London prior to departing, three days later, from Cardington for Ismalia and Karachi. She was 777 feet long and could lift a gross weight of 165 tons. The test went well and on the afternoon of Saturday 4 October, clearing after a wet morning, the R101 rode at the head of her mooring tower, a most impressive sight. Her fifty-four passengers and crew, including the air minister, Lord Thompson, and the director of civil aviation, Sir Sefton Brancker, were all on board by seven o'clock and, lights blazing, she slipped her mooring, rose effortlessly into the night, and set course for France.

Some eight hours later, just after 3:00 A.M., R101 was south of Beauvais in rapidly rising wind and heavy rain, flying at fifteen hundred feet — just twice her own length above the ground. Disaster struck swiftly and violently. The nose of the airship was caught in a strong down current of air and she dived steeply, crashing into the ground in a plantation of small shrubs, and bursting into flame.[2] There were only six

128

survivors, but neither Lord Thompson nor Sir Sefton Bran-cker were among them. It was the end of a pioneering flight of great potential significance to Australia, and its air links with England.

Just five days after this tragedy, Kingsford Smith again pro-jected himself into the public eye when he took off from England, on 9 October, in an Avro Avian Special Sports air-craft for a high speed flight to Australia. Amy Johnson, in May, had made her remarkable solo flight from London to Darwin, taking twenty days. Kingsford Smith, arriving in Darwin on 19 October, took ten and a half days. Apart from the time taken, there was another difference between the two solo flights. Kingsford Smith was building up, in the minds of the public and the powerful, a not unwarranted association for himself and Australian National Airways with the air route between England and Australia.

That there would soon be commercial air services along this route was in little doubt. Fergus McMaster emphasized the importance of such a development to Qantas in a letter to directors on 24 February 1931. In the context of possible Qantas reactions to the Townsville service of the Queensland Air Navigation Company, he stressed the immediate need to consider "the position of Qantas as a whole".[3]

"One of the principal questions", wrote McMaster, "is the possibility that Port Darwin will be made the connecting point either by a direct service from England, or by a more immediate connection by the Dutch company."[4] (The "Dutch company" was KLM, headed by Albert Plesman, perhaps the most remarkable single person in the history of commercial airline development. "He ate, drank and slept with KLM and air transport", wrote Roy Allen, "which he saw as a calling of high ideals rather than a money-making business of flying people about.")[5] KLM, on 12 September 1929, had in-augurated a fortnightly proving service to Djakarta from Amsterdam, a distance of 8,540 miles and the longest air route in the world.[6] The obvious next step was to link Djakarta with Australia, either by the shortest crossing of the Timor Sea to Wyndham, in Western Australia, or to Darwin. If the overseas air service was to come from England, then the obvious operator was Imperial Airways whose route to the Middle East had been extended to India in April 1929 and now operated once weekly.[7]

"Whatever the overseas airline that eventually services Port Darwin, the competition for the connecting service to

Advertising poster from the early 1930s.

southern Australian centres will be keen", McMaster wrote.[8] "It must become the principal service in Australia." If Qantas were to make a determined effort to secure this route then, he argued, it should be as free as possible "from any other service that might be a liability". To handle Darwin, a considerable amount of new capital would be required and, he said, "we must make Qantas shares as attractive as possible to new investors. This share capital question has a direct bearing on the Northern Service."

"The immediate future is of vital interest to Qantas", he stressed. "Perhaps the whole future of Qantas as an airline operating company rests with securing the Port Darwin service and the control of the territory north of Brisbane."

It was an important letter, McMaster arguing that only the possible future developments in civil aviation could have any attractions for investors. At its present stage and under current conditions it was not, he said, a commercial proposition depending, as it did, on "subsidy in some shape or form".

As far as the Queensland coastal route north from Brisbane was concerned Qantas, he thought, should find out whether the operator of the route, Queensland Air Navigation Company, wanted to come to an arrangement. However, the company which had begun operations on 31 March 1930 from Brisbane through intermediate ports to Townsville and had been losing some eleven hundred pounds a month, now failed. Despite McMaster's warning about services "that might be a liability", Qantas moved on to the route on 7 May 1931. It was equally unsuccessful, attracted few passengers, and withdrew on 25 September.

Times were tough, and worsening. "The sheep raising districts of the west are in a low financial condition, unprecedented in their history", the *Qantas Gazette* reported in February 1931. Hit by a disastrous three-year drought, it said, station properties were mortgaged to the hilt, well in excess of what they would bring if sold. When the rains came at last "the squatter was met by a slump in the value of wool, putting prices below the cost of production". And, the gazette said, the general financial and business depression had made money scarce just when credit was needed.

For Qantas, surprisingly, the depressed economic conditions did not cut passenger numbers, though fares had to be substantially reduced.[9] The *Gazette* conclusion was that "a full measure of utility is provided, causing people to travel by air at a little extra cost". Nevertheless, with fares squeezed

Return of the Brisbane to Townsville service, Archerfield, 8 May 1931. This route was operated without subsidy and Qantas was forced to abandon the service in September 1931.

and costs under close scrutiny, all salaries, wages, and directors' fees were cut.

On 1 April 1931, in England, the British Post Office announced that two experimental round-trip airmail services would be undertaken between London and Sydney, to leave London on 4 April and 25 April. Planned as extensions of Imperial Airways' London–Delhi service, it was agreed that on arrival at Darwin the mails would be transferred to Qantas for onward passage to Sydney.[10] The first Imperial Airways aircraft, however, did not get as far as Darwin. Mail left Croydon, England, as scheduled on 4 April and was carried on the regular service to Karachi without incident. There it was transferred to the DH66 aircraft *City of Cairo* but, on the last stage of its flight to Darwin, it ran short of fuel and crash-landed near Koepang, Timor, on 19 April. There were no injuries and the mail was undamaged but, for Qantas, it was a setback. With no multi-engined aircraft to fly the over-water sector to Koepang, it had to step aside while Kingsford Smith and G.U. Allan, in the *Southern Cross*, came to the rescue, bringing the mails into Darwin on 25 April. On the same day that the *Southern Cross* arrived in Darwin, return mails for England left Brisbane in the Qantas DH61 *Apollo*. They connected in Darwin with the *Southern Cross*, which then flew the mail on to Akyab for transfer to Imperial Airways. Capt. Russell Tapp commanded *Apollo* on these first airmail flights for Qantas, while the mail to and from the southern cities of Sydney and Melbourne was carried by Australian National Airways. (Tapp flew some four thousand miles in four days on his return trip to Darwin. On the southern journey he flew low to avoid head winds and reported, on his arrival in Brisbane, that he had sighted two cars broken down in the Territory. "One wanted me to stop", he told press. "I couldn't as I was in a bit of a hurry.")[11]

The second experimental airmail service set out on 25 April from London for Akyab and was met there by the *Southern Cross*, which again brought the mail to Darwin for transfer to Qantas and the flight south to Brisbane. Fysh himself flew the second return trip from Brisbane to Darwin on 17 May, in the DH50J *Hippomenes*. This time Imperial Airways flew the mail on from Darwin, in a DH Hercules aircraft purchased from West Australian Airways.

The first onward mail trip from London to Brisbane had taken, because of the Koepang crash, twenty-four days; the second took only eighteen days. The first Brisbane–London return trip was completed in nineteen days; the second in only sixteen days. At the time, the fastest sea mails took a month.

Australian National Airways, with their over-water expertise, were responsible for the successful completion of these grand experiments. With some vigour and considerable expedition, Kingsford Smith and Ulm set out immediately to exploit their achievement. Fysh sent a worried telegram to McMaster on 22 April: "Application made by A.N.A. to operate permanent route Brisbane–Darwin and to India. Receiving considerable support. Position fairly critical to our interest."[12] Australian National Airways had thrown down the gauntlet. Other pressures came from West Australian Airways, who pressed for an immediate mail connection with KLM through Wyndham, while the British saw the Empire link to Darwin as the exclusive role of Imperial Airways. ANA, KLM, and Imperial Airways all had the aircraft, pilots, and experience to fly overseas routes. Qantas, with only single-engined aircraft and inland routes, had so far never seriously looked beyond Darwin in their strategies. The fact that their main services, between Brisbane and Camooweal, lay on the final stages of the world route most likely to be used for a mail link with England was a threat as well as a strength. If another operator were chosen to bring mails right through to Brisbane, Qantas could be pushed off its route and, in Fysh's words, "forced to close its doors".[13]

The application by Ulm and Kingsford Smith for a permanent ANA route from Brisbane through Darwin to India had, however, been made in the shadow of tragedy and rapidly escalating financial difficulties. On Saturday morning, 21 March, at eight-fifteen, one of Australian National Airways' most experienced bad-weather pilots, T.W. Shortridge, took off from Sydney for Melbourne in the three-engined Avro X *Southern Cloud* with six passengers. Shortridge had more than four thousand flying hours to his credit and had made an intensive study of blind flying on the Sydney–Melbourne route.[14] Across his path that day was a cyclonic storm, with heavy cloud and winds that rose to over sixty miles per hour. The aircraft never reached Melbourne and an

The ill-fated *Southern Cloud* airliner of Australian National Airways which disappeared during a flight from Sydney to Melbourne on 21 March 1931.

intensive search did not locate any wreckage; *Aircraft* speculated that the *Southern Cloud* could have been blown out to sea, or could have crashed in dense forest. (The remnants of the Avro X were, in fact, found in the Snowy Mountains of New South Wales in 1958.) The loss of public confidence and the effects on patronage of the airline came at the worst possible time, for the deepening Depression had bitten into ANA's revenue. Its position rapidly worsened. "Mr C.T.P. Ulm . . . made a gallant effort to carry on in the face of tremendous difficulties", wrote *Aircraft*, but at a meeting of ANA directors on 18 June, "it was decided to suspend temporarily present air services as and from Friday 26 June, pending the result of negotiations now proceeding with the Commonwealth Government".[15] No financial assistance from the government ever came and ANA services never resumed. There was, however, plenty of fight left in Charles Ulm.

As this situation was developing, the Dutch showed their capabilities and strength. On 19 May their aircraft *Abel Tasman* landed in Melbourne at the conclusion of an experimental airmail flight from Batavia. The magazine *Aircraft* commented on "the keen interest aroused among the authorities here" and the efficiency and regularity with which the schedule was adhered to. "There seems no real reason why Australia should not adopt as a temporary measure", it wrote, "the suggestion of the Dutch authorities that for the time, until general conditions make it possible to subsidise the Australian end of Imperial Airways' air mail, use should be made of the Dutch line to speed up mails between Europe and Australia."[16]

A Dutch service, whether temporary or prolonged, would have eased the financial pressures on a hard-pressed Australian government. "The two big airways subsidised by the government", wrote *Aircraft*, "are, of course, Qantas — the pioneer aviation company of Australia — and West Australian Airways. There have already been indications from the Federal Government that the subsidies being paid to these two companies are in danger . . ."[17] The public argument intensified. There were even suggestions that the government could save money by abolishing the Royal Australian Navy and that Australia should pay a subsidy to Britain for the use of the British navy for sea protection. "In a national crisis", wrote *Aircraft*, "the Royal Australian Navy would be practically useless in the face of organised invasion", while the organization provided internally by the commercial airlines

Fergus McMaster (left) and Hudson Fysh (right) with a passenger during a stopover at Moscow station, McMasters' property, in early 1931. The aircraft is the Jupiter-engined DH50 *Hippomenes*, the last DH50 built at Longreach.

"would be invaluable as a defence measure".[18] Happily, neither the prime minister, Mr Scullin, nor the defence minister, Mr Chifley agreed. "It would be most unfair", concluded *Aircraft*, "if companies such as Qantas — which has carried on for years under difficult circumstances; which has opened up vast areas of Queensland that would otherwise never have been developed to the extent they are today; which has ushered in a new era for outback man, bringing him medical attention, fresh food, fast mails, and making his life easier and happier — were to be forced out of existence at a time when they most need some financial support from the Government."[19]

It was in this atmosphere that Fergus McMaster set down his view that Qantas should establish formal links with Imperial Airways. The Imperial Service from London to Darwin, he wrote in a letter to Fysh on 15 May 1931 from his property Moscow near Longreach, should be under the one control.

> You might be able to suggest in some way that if Qantas was the operating company from Darwin, Imperial Airways might have representation on the Qantas Board and that a subsidiary company of Qantas would operate the service, keeping all operations of that service separate from its other activities. [If there were] any future interruption such as that caused by the *City of Cairo* [crash], the organisation at Darwin would have suitable

machines and staff to do the work done by Kingsford Smith this time.

If a subsidiary company consisting of Qantas and Imperial Airways interests were formed, it would mean that the Darwin–Brisbane–Sydney–Melbourne service would not only have the advantage of direct Australian management, but would also be in the closest touch and of assistance to the overseas section from Darwin. Suggestion could also be made that this organisation could make contact with a branch service of West Australian Airways at some suitable point, thus allowing the mails to get to Perth and Adelaide by the quickest route.[20]

McMaster also suggested that Qantas would make any connection at any point, permanently, that might be agreed upon, and that it was prepared to form a subsidiary company with Imperial Airways "to operate any section of the Imperial Route".

"The Qantas Board recognises that the Imperial link is not a commercial concern and is prepared to do all possible for Imperial reasons, providing the shareholders are secured against loss", he wrote. "Personally, I am keen upon the Imperial mail for national reasons." He asked Fysh to push "the matter of triple-engined machines as much as possible, and to get in touch with Westland Aircraft and Blackburn, as well as the American people". If de Havillands "have definitely decided to go out of the large machine production", he said, "we must sooner or later break with them for some of our plant." Vickers, he thought, did not appear satisfactory for Australian conditions.[21]

Fysh wrote to George Woods Humphery, managing director of Imperial Airways, on 16 June 1931 suggesting cooperation between them. It was, in Fysh's words, "the first definite approach".[22] (Fysh had, in fact, written to the Commonwealth director-general of posts and telegraphs, H.P. Brown, on 15 April offering a permanent airmail link at Darwin with Imperial Airways, using a Puss Moth. It was an initiative that he himself described as "nothing less than stupid".[23] He wrote again, a week later, expressing Qantas interest in going beyond Darwin, using flying boats. Both were hasty and ill-considered reactions to Ulm's application for the route to India.)

As the battle lines formed for the fight to share in the air routes that would join Australia and the Old World, the individualists in aviation, in 1931, sought to establish faster and faster times for the journey. C.W.A. Scott, tiring of his routine as flying instructor for Qantas at the Brisbane Flying

School, returned to England to attempt to better Kingsford Smith's time of ten and a half days and did so, setting off from Lympne on 1 April and arriving at Darwin in nine days twelve hours. Australian J.A. (Jim) Mollison took over fourteen hours off this time in August, but flying from Australia to England, completing the trip in eight days twenty-one hours and twenty-five minutes. Another Australian, C.A. (Arthur) Butler, on 31 October, departed for Australia from Lympne as Scott had done and beat the Scott record to Darwin by one hour forty-five minutes. Impressive as these speeds were for 1931, they paled against the world air speed record set at Calshot, Southhampton, England on 29 September. Flight Lt. G.H. Stainforth, in a Vickers Supermarine S6B seaplane with a 2,600-horsepower Rolls-Royce engine established a new official world air speed record of 407.5 miles per hour.

As Australian National Airways was closing its doors, Qantas recorded a much reduced net profit of £2,989 for the financial year to 30 June 1931 and recommended a modest dividend of 4 per cent. This profit, said the directors, "which only represents 7.57 per cent return on paid up capital, is hardly an

Archerfield aerodrome in early 1931. Qantas moved from Eagle Farm to Archerfield in January 1931.

adequate return for an aviation company". However, the considerable cost of new buildings and additional plant at Archerfield aerodrome and the transfer of operations from Eagle Farm was met from the year's revenue. Operating costs were reduced by £2,314 though mileage flown increased by 27,077 miles. "Substantial reductions have been made during the year in salaries and wages of all staff", said the directors' report.[24]

While Imperial Airways and KLM were reaching, in the newly conquered element of the air, halfway across a world that had, less than two generations before, been geared solely to the horse for travel on land, the proliferating airlines of the United States concentrated competitively within national boundaries. Juan Trippe's Pan American Airways, now three years in operation, saw the emergence of American Airways and United Air Lines, Braniff and Northwest, Western Air and Transcontinental, the predecessor of Continental (Varney Speed Lines), Boeing Air Transport and, amongst others, Chicago and Southern who would later become known as Delta. They battled not only against each other but against a public that viewed the US industry's high accident rate without enthusiasm and recognized with collective wisdom the poor safety margins and great discomfort of the cold, noisy, and smelly aircraft offered by American manufacturers. They were to wait only a little longer for their aircraft builders to make amends. Boeing's all-metal, ten-passenger 160 mile per hour Boeing 247 would fly in February 1933 and Douglas, five months later, would introduce for TWA the precursor of the world's most enduring airliner, the DC3, with the maiden flight in July of the big, fast, and revolutionary DC1.

The closing months of 1931 saw two developments in Australia that began three years of what Fysh later described as a war of nerves and manoeuvre for the rich overseas airmail contract.[25] Most spectacular was the courageous move by Ulm and Kingsford Smith to mount an all-Australian return Christmas airmail flight to London; most intriguing was the move by West Australian Airway's astute Norman Brearley to float the idea of a merger between ANA, WAA, and Qantas to form a large new company that would operate both within Australia and overseas.

With the backing of the Post Office, ANA's Avro X *Southern Sun* left Melbourne on 21 November under the command of G.U. ("Scotty") Allan with fifty-two thousand items of mail for England. On board there was only one passenger, the controller of civil aviation, Lieutenant-Colonel Brinsmead. But the sheer bad luck that seemed to dog Ulm and Kingsford Smith in their commercial ventures was with them again. The aircraft reached Alor Star in Malaya but, on take-off from a water-logged aerodrome on 25 November, the centre engine failed and the heavily loaded *Southern Sun* crashed. The mail was unharmed and there were no injuries.

Australian National Airways' Avro *Southern Sun* stands near the Qantas hangar at Longreach on 21 November 1931 during a brief stopover en route to England.

For Brinsmead the ANA misfortune turned swiftly to deep personal tragedy. He decided that he would not wait for the arrival of ANA's *Southern Star*, which Kingsford Smith rapidly readied at Sydney to rescue the mails. Brinsmead caught a KLM aircraft from Bangkok to continue his journey. It, too, crashed on take-off. Five people were killed and Brinsmead was so severely injured that he remained incapacitated until his death, in Australia, in 1934.

Qantas had closely followed the ANA mail initiative. When news of the Alor Star accident reached Fysh he telegraphed McMaster: "Southern Star crashed. In event Imperial Airways doing return trip have offered co-operate by doing Darwin–Melbourne section."[26] But Ulm and Kingsford Smith had no intention of abandoning their venture to Qantas and Imperial Airways. Kingsford Smith picked up the mails at Alor Star on 5 December and, with Scotty Allan on board, delivered them to Croydon, England, on 16 December. There was, though, even more bad luck to come. The day before they were due to depart with the return mails the *Southern Star*, after dark and in foggy weather, crashed at Croydon. Repairs delayed the departure until 7 January and the mails arrived in Sydney, after a fast trip, on 21 January 1932.

Hudson Fysh (as he often did on notable airmail flights) sent airmail covers to a number of people on this pioneering Australian venture, including C.G. Grey, editor of the English magazine *The Aeroplane*, and G.E. Woods Humphery, managing director of Imperial Airwarys. Grey acknowledged his with a generous tribute to the courage of Kingsford Smith and Ulm.[26] Woods Humphery had a different perspective. With matchless pomposity he commented: "We are fully alive to the intentions at the backs of the minds of the promoters of the air mail flight to London and back as we have, unfortunately, other experiences of people with little behind them creating nuisances, as we call them."[28]

Norman Brearley had written to Ulm as ANA were preparing for the Christmas mails trusting "that you will reap some benefit in due course from your courage".[29]

"I feel", he continued, "that there is something to be done regarding a regular service, but I realise that the subsidy allotted to the Perth–Adelaide route is the principal stumbling block." That subsidy still had, like the Qantas contract, two years to run but West Australian Airways, ever since those initial inflated mail loadings, had been understandably unpopular in Civil Aviation Branch circles. There was little likelihood of any subsidy renewal and the imminent possibility of change following introduction of a regular England–Australia service posed a major threat to the long-term future of Brearley's airline. To Ulm, however, Brearley put it this way: "I feel that the time has arrived when consideration should be given to the future of air mail services in Australia and the linking up with England."

He proposed the formation of a group consisting of ANA, Qantas, WAA, and the government and "possibly the Commonwealth Railway Commissioner" to draw up a programme of future developments "in order that competition for future contracts be avoided". The group, he wrote,

> would form a large new company which would take over the existing contracts and assets of the three interests and allot shares, and in some cases cash as well as shares, for the items referred to.
>
> Part of the programme would be the cancellation of the East-West (Perth–Adelaide) contract and the application of the subsidy

so saved to the link between, say Broome and Singapore. The new company would then be in a position to standardise equipment where feasible and carry out the operations now conducted by Q.A.N.T.A.S. and ourselves, preferably under the existing management.

The company, he said, would depend on the revenue received from the mail traffic "to supplement a comparatively meagre subsidy and thus make it a paying proposition".

After referring to "the difficulties regarding the Perth-Adelaide contract" and the decline of 10 per cent in mail carriage on the route compared to an increase throughout the world on British services of 45 per cent, he commented: "There may be a certain amount of difficulty with Q.A.N.T.A.S. if this matter is opened up too early with them." He felt sure that "in due course they could be persuaded to fall into line" and avoid the ruinous competition that would face them all "with Larkin still in the field on expiration of existing contracts".

Though Brearley, quite sensibly, was looking to the future of his own company, the proposed amalgamation had much to offer for the hard-pressed Australian National Airways. By mid-November all three parties had exchanged letters and telegrams and the Qantas reaction became clear; in brief, it was to sit tight and await developments.[30]

Qantas director A.N. Templeton did not approve of amalgamation and viewed even "a working arrangement to maintain our position" with caution. "If we merge with Ulm and Brearley, their contribution will be their machines and practically nothing else of advantage to us", he wrote to Fysh on 3 December.[31] "We will contribute our organisation which has proved the only successful one in Australia. We are on good terms with Civil Aviation, we are not broke . . . I cannot see any good reason for going to the rescue of others at this stage." He wanted definite proposals before going into any discussion and thought Qantas would more likely get sympathetic consideration from Civil Aviation for a link-up with Imperial Airways. He was, however, "open to conviction". In a letter to McMaster, also on 3 December, he added, "A.N.A. is certainly on the rocks financially and most probably will fade out of the picture".[32] McMaster replied that he was substantially of the same opinion. "The only thing I wish to stress", he wrote, "is that Qantas keeps the door open for negotiations in case there does eventually become a necessity in Qantas interests to join in an amalgamation."[33]

142

In that same spirit, Fysh replied to Brearley for Qantas on 22 December 1931 saying that "the position is that we are waiting to hear something more definite".[34] He asked for Brearley's views on share allocations in the proposed new company; on the question of ANA being heavily in debt; on membership of the new board; on whereabouts of the company's headquarters; on proposed protection of present staffs and the basis for contracts to be obtained from the government. Not too subtly he concluded: "Things are going ahead nicely for us at present as we have experienced quite a marked revival of business during November and the present month."

As the battle lines were being drawn to resolve these major issues Qantas, on 3 December, began its wet season operation on the forty-five mile route between Daly Waters and Birdum Creek with the little DH Moth VH-UGW. It brought them, if only symbolically, just a little closer to Darwin.

It was an interesting end to a turbulent year in Australian commercial aviation. As it closed, a new and important figure emerged in the Civil Aviation Branch to succeed Brinsmead. Capt. Edgar Johnston, who had joined the branch when it first formed in 1919 and been responsible since then for airfields throughout the Commonwealth, was appointed acting controller of civil aviation. An infantryman at Gallipoli, a member of the 10th Light Horse in Egypt, an artilleryman in France, and, finally, a pilot in the Royal Flying Corps he was to become controller of civil aviation from December 1933 and to remain at or near the centre of events in Australian civil aviation for some thirty years more.

Daly Waters, December 1931. Qantas DH60G VH-UGW during its first "wet season" deployment from Brisbane to operate between Daly Waters and Birdum Creek. This exercise lasted from December to March 1931–32, 1932–33, and 1933–34, using the same aircraft.

Many Proposals
— No Marriages
1932

9   Edgar Johnston found himself, almost at once, with a new
government and a new minister for defence. On 6 January
1932 the government of Joseph Lyons succeeded the short-
lived Labor government of James Scullin. Sir George Pearce,
Johnston's new minister, had held the same post in the
Hughes government from 1918 to 1921 when Johnston had
joined the department. Together they were now to help shape
the future of Australian civil aviation as it reorganized to face
the changes thrust on it by the development of international
air routes.

Johnston had a high opinion of Qantas. In an unofficial
letter to Fysh on 13 January he remarked on "the returned
confidence in the business community which the change of
government is expected to produce" and forecast that though
he did not expect government financial conditions to improve
there was "every reason to hope that there will be funds to
keep the existing services going after termination of present
contracts".[1] He added: "So far as I personally am concerned,
the excellent record of Qantas and its high reputation both
with the public and with those more intimately concerned
with your activities will ensure that its claims for inclusion in
any further development schemes will not be overlooked. I
fully appreciate that your claims to operate to the Northern
Territory have been considerably established by 'right of
conquest'."

The various aviation pressures on the government were considerable. On the day after this letter was written, Charles

Ulm in his capacity as joint managing director of Australian National Airways, wrote directly to the new prime minister, J.A. Lyons, submitting proposals to enable his company to "carry on valuable air services, retain for Australia its large modern aircraft and equipment and continue to employ its highly skilled and specially trained personnel".[2] His company, he pointed out, had "received no help from the Federal Government nor any other government. I am directed to inform you", he wrote, "that unless the company does receive assistance in one of the forms suggested, it cannot carry on." It would have to dispose of the whole of its equipment, "most probably outside Australia". One of Ulm's proposals was an offer to the government "to assume without liability, a one half interest in the capital of the company". The Larkin Aircraft Company, West Australia Airways Limited, and Qantas Ltd. had, he reminded the prime minister, all been "heavily subsidised for the past seven or eight years", and "practically the whole of the Larkin Company's subsidised air services have been discontinued". West Australian Airways, he said, had flown some 300,000 miles a year and Qantas 100,000 miles while Australian National Airways, in 1930, flew 583,700 miles on regular services and "a total of 681,220 miles — more than the combined mileage of the two subsidised companies". Further, he argued, Qantas on a subsidy of two shillings and eight pence a mile, operated only single-engined aircraft with "far less safety and efficiency than the airlines operated by either West Australian Airways (on the east-west route) or by A.N.A.".

Alternative proposals put to the prime minister were for an ANA subsidy of one shilling and sixpence a mile on the Sydney–Brisbane route, or for a discontinuance of ANA's services and application of "its equipment and organisation to the immediate establishment of a regular weekly air mail and passenger service, each way", between Wyndham or Darwin and either Delhi, Rangoon, or Singapore. These services were to link with Imperial Airways routes to London and Europe.[3]

This, then, was the objective of ANA, one of the three companies then talking amalgamation; a quite separate international operation, if it could achieve government blessing.

Meanwhile the initiator of the amalgamation proposals, WAA, was having some second thoughts in which Qantas also had no place. Brearley wrote to Ulm on 25 January 1932 suggesting "with completion of your experimental air mail flight from Australia to London and back, the time appears

145

opportune to approach the Federal Government with a joint proposal".⁴ The two airlines, he wrote, should jointly organize and operate an overseas service (using most of the Perth–Adelaide subsidy for the purpose) that would connect either with Imperial Airways or KLM.

Ulm sent a copy of these Brearley proposals to the prime minister on 1 February and told Brearley he was "glad to support the idea of submitting amalgamated proposals".⁵ He asked the prime minister to consider his suggestion that the government take half the capital in ANA "in conjunction with the present suggestion that the unexpired portion of the Perth–Adelaide air service subsidy be utilised to immediately enable the inauguration of a regular air service linking Australia with India, thus joining up with Imperial Airways present services".⁶ Ulm told the prime minister he was confident that ANA could arrange an amalgamation or part-amalgamation with West Australian Airways.

This two-way amalgamation was something new and exciting to run with; on the same day (1 February) confidential telegrams were exchanged between Ulm and Brearley. Ulm wanted details of annual subsidy amounts for Perth–Adelaide and their expiry dates. Brearley responded immediately: "Minimum thirty-nine thousand yearly expires June 1934. Important that operations [on proposed overseas routes] receive full [mail] surcharge revenue, thus substantially reducing subsidy."⁷

Ulm sent a further telegram that afternoon stating that he was immediately contacting the prime minister to ask for a specific appointment to discuss the amalgamation proposals. He revealed to Brearley that ANA had "separate proposals before Cabinet" but was sure his directors "will agree to scrapping them now in view of my considered opinion amalgamated proposal certain success". The telegram concluded: "This matter biggest move yet [for] sound development [of] Australian aviation therefore consider imperative you immediately come this side [so] that we may finalise detailed proposals for personal presentation to Cabinet. In view Fysh's telegram 30 January glad your agreement my advising Fysh that on account necessity to act urgently regarding Imperial service, that we jointly propose approaching Cabinet leaving question Qantas joining amalgamation proposals later date."⁹

At this stage it is clear that ANA's thoughts of going it alone on an overseas service had been scrapped in favour of

Brearley's suggested ANA–WAA combination; and that
Brearley's original strategy to link WAA direct with a Dutch
service from Batavia at Wyndham in Western Australia was at
least open to modification. Certainly, Qantas, having expressed its "wait and see" attitude to the three-part amalgamation,
was now at best at arm's length from the ANA–WAA moves.
It was not, however, inactive.

Only two days after the flurry of telegrams between Ulm and
Brearley, Hudson Fysh and F.E. Loxton met Sir Walter
Nicholson, the government-appointed director of Imperial
Airways, in Brisbane. Out of this meeting, Fysh wrote later,
came a formula for possible co-operation with Imperial Airways.[9] Referred to as the "Gentleman's Agreement", it
envisaged the formation of a new company ("The Commonwealth and Imperial Airways Ltd.") with necessary capital to
be raised by Imperial Airways and Qantas and board representation to be proportioned to share interests. In calling for
Australian capital, wrote Fysh, the option would be given to
ANA, WAA, Larkin, and others to subscribe; but Imperial
Airways and Qantas were to hold controlling representation.[10]

As all three companies examined alternative courses of
action, Qantas and its chairman, McMaster, did take
Brearley's amalgamation proposals seriously and studied their
implications. The Qantas financial consultant, accountant
Alex Jobson of Sydney, prepared a lucid, analytical brief.[11]
Qantas, he said, had a federal subsidy agreement worth
£20,000 a year, for about eighteen months. "There can,
however, be no certainty that this agreement will be renewed
with Qantas on its expiry", he wrote. If tenders were called,
other existing aviation companies would tender. If a new
company were formed without Qantas it would "undoubtedly
put in a quotation". If it were formed with Qantas, "it is possible that Larkin may be able to rouse some influential opposition to it and may be able to thwart the scheme". In brief,
whatever course Qantas took there were risks.

Jobson looked at the financial implications for shareholders
if Qantas did not join the merger. "As rapid expansion of its
operations is not very probable, the shareholders cannot
reasonably expect any marked growth in earnings. Indeed the
best they can expect for a time is a recovery to the 1930 net
profit of £6,073 out of which a seven per cent dividend was
paid."

If amalgamation did go ahead, he wrote,

the paid up capital of the merger company may, for the sake of argument, be set down at £150,000, comprising W.A.A. £90,000, Qantas £35,000 and A.N.A. £25,000. The profits are estimated at £60,000 subsidy, £27,000 from mails and, say, £4,000 from services on the Qantas route — £91,000 in all, subject to expenditure, depreciation, etc. of say £75,000, leaving a net profit of £16,000 remaining. This would suffice to pay eight per cent of the total capital, distributing £12,000.

In that event, Qantas would receive in dividends £2,800 with which to pay dividends. If its directors decided to return £10,000 of its cash to its shareholders, reducing capital to about £30,000, it would be able to pay a dividend of seven per cent, distributing £2,100 and leaving £700 for reserves.

This, he said, approximated the best rate of dividend (paid in 1930) by Qantas. There was, therefore, "a reasonable prospect of the merger being a benefit to Qantas shareholders from the point of view of dividends", and greater possibilities of expansion.

Jobson pointed out that it would be "inequitable" if the merger were carried out entirely on the basis of the value of assets transferred, for "W.A.A. and Qantas are both to surrender valuable subsidy rights. A.N.A., on the other hand, has no subsidy to surrender."

Of considerable personal interest to Fysh, he commented: "It is essential that the management of the business taken over from Qantas should continue in the same hands. For this reason I think Qantas should insist on an agreement for a term of years for the engagement of Mr. Fysh as manager for Queensland." It was at best a bleak prospect for Fysh. While Brearley could conceivably be expected to concentrate his considerable energies in Western Australia, there was no doubt whatever that Charles Ulm would have emerged as the central and senior figure in Australian commercial aviation.

Ulm acted with scrupulous frankness in all but one of his dealings throughout the merger negotiations. He sent copies of all his telegrams and correspondence with Brearley and the prime minister to Fysh. His hopes were high. In a letter to Fysh he wrote:

I can confidentially advise you that there is an excellent possibility of A.N.A. receiving Government assistance on the first proposals we submitted [for separate and independent ANA overseas services]. I am pretty well informed as to opinions and possibilities in Canberra and, in addition, am informed, of course in the strictest confidence, that any united proposals submitted would have not only the fullest support of the Civil Aviation Branch, but their active interest and boosting help.[12]

Ulm did, however, undertake one confidence that he did not reveal to the other two merger partners. On the same day that he wrote to Fysh, he sent a confidential letter to Edgar Johnston.

> I have not [he told Johnston] asked permission of either Brearley or Fysh to let you peruse correspondence between us. However, I am enclosing copies of this correspondence for your personal information believing, as I most conscientiously do, that it is not only in the interests of the three companies that you should be privately informed, but it is really and sincerely in the best interests of the future development of civil aviation in Australia. For the present I am not advising either Brearley or Fysh that I am taking you so fully into my confidence in this matter and will not do so until the three of us meet, and then only if I consider it wise . . . any suggestion of amalgamation partly or in whole between the three companies or any two of them bristles with difficulties. As far as A.N.A. is concerned, anything for the present and future is better than nothing.[13]

Ulm and ANA were obviously apprehensive about the future; Brearley, though never admitting the inevitability that WAA's subsidy would cease, clearly acted on the assumption that it would; Qantas, as Jobson had pointed out, could not be certain of an independent future. All saw amalgamation as some kind of saviour but none thought of it as other than an essential though bitter medicine.

Fysh was concerned at Brearley's continuing consideration of a KLM link with WAA's northern ports. On 27 February he wrote to him advising that he had had discussion with Mr A.E. Rudder of Rudders Ltd., the Australian agents of Imperial Airways, and had "as a result of this and consideration of the matter of co-operation with Imperial Airways or the Dutch" come to certain conclusions. One was that working with the Dutch could jeopardize the whole amalgamation scheme. Another was that "Imperial Airways and the British Government are going to be for us or against us, and that if it is to be against us, things will be made decidedly awkward". Overseas routes could only be achieved by international negotiation, he wrote, and the Dutch needed British co-operation for their Amsterdam–Batavia service. "The British government and public would be all for an all-Red Route and, personally, I think it an essential for Empire reasons." He pointed out that linking with a British company would "greatly assist with Cabinet and . . . in obtaining that ten-years contract which will be one of the hurdles to get over with our Government".[14]

McMaster summed up the current situation in a long letter to his three fellow directors on 10 March.[15] No agreement had been reached at the Melbourne meeting on 18 February between Brearley, Ulm, and Fysh, he said, other than that each

> would place the proposals before their respective Boards and make an honest endeavour to bring about finality and an amalgamation, if possible.
>
> We are all convinced that it would be to the interests of the capital already invested, and also in the interest of aviation and its future development, if one strong organisation could be formed to develop and operate the main air lines [in] the interests of the Commonwealth.

The proposal, he wrote, was for a company with a capital of £150,000 divided into £1 shares. All assets other than reserves of cash would be pooled. All subsidized services operated by WAA and Qantas would be taken into the pool. Payment to the three merging companies would be in fully paid shares, with WAA getting 80,000 ordinary and 20,000 8 per cent preference shares; Qantas 20,000 ordinary and 5,000 preference shares; and ANA 25,000 ordinary shares. The head office and management would be in Sydney or Melbourne, with local Boards of Advice suggested for the various states. The Commonwealth government would be approached to take shares in the amalgamated company. McMaster outlined matters relating to plant, revenue, and expenditure, subsidy, the form of the proposed directorate, and the manner of valuing plant and goodwill. One feature of the Melbourne discussions that did not appeal to him was the exclusion of Larkin Aircraft, New England Airways, and other airline operators with large capital invested. The government, he thought, would not be justified in subsidizing one group of three interests (Qantas, WAA, and ANA) "without giving due consideration and protection to the others who have pioneered. It appears to me [that] all five airline operators will have to be considered and all given equal consideration in proportion to their assets of value to an amalgamation." It was vintage McMaster; commonsense and fairness. "My principal objections to the proposed amalgamation", he said, "are the constitution of the directorate, the amount of capital required and the method proposed to finance working expenses and additional aircraft and plant. The initial expenses will be heavy. I am definitely opposed to rushing into this service . . . I am also definitely against linking with the Dutch service at Batavia. This Empire link should be all British in every way and should connect with Imperial Airways at Singapore, Wyndham or Darwin."

Aircraft magazine reported the Melbourne meeting of Ulm, Brearley, and Fysh as one of "two events of great importance to the aircraft industry". The other was a report to the Federal government by the auditor-general in which he advocated the discontinuance of all subsidies to airlines.[16] This shock recommendation was followed by a letter to Qantas and ANA from M.L. Shepherd, secretary of the Department of Defence. In response to enquiries from Brearley, he stated that the department was unable to give any assurance to the proposed amalgamated company composed of Qantas, WAA, and ANA, that the continuation of the Queensland (Qantas) and North-West (WAA) services would be assured in conjunction with the ten-year contract which they sought for an overseas connecting service to England. Shepherd also made it clear that the department would not agree to even a temporary connection at Batavia with KLM until the possibilities of linking with an Empire Service had been fully explored.[17]

In a "further memorandum concerning the proposed amalgamation", Qantas consultant Alex Jobson pointed out that in a merged company West Australia Airways "by virtue of its holding as shareholders or as a group, would have a dominating influence". Norman Brearley, meantime, had started horse-trading, with pointed comments favourable to the WAA cause. "I am afraid", he wrote to Fysh, "that your valuation of your service as compared with our North-West service is a little wide of the mark."[18] On the expected termination of his Perth–Adelaide subsidy he argued: "It is not at all definite that this contract will never be renewed." He pointed out the possibility "of any one of our contracts being tendered for by other interests". And, to quash any Qantas ideas on their own worth, he wrote: "I would also again mention that, in the event of an England–Australia service coming about and traversing the Q.A.N.T.A.S. route, it would not necessarily mean that your company would carry the mails, as that section of the route might be sufficiently attractive to others to enable them to beat you to it."[19]

On 29 March, Brearley advised Fysh: "My Board has authorised me to negotiate to finality. We are apparently all agreed that, subject to satisfactory share allocation and the clearing up of minor matters, the amalgamation can proceed."[20] The content of his letter, however, hardly justified this sanguine view. He confirmed his opinion that "there is obviously no need to load the new company with new capital, as this will be supplied by banks without any difficulty and would cover our requirements for working capital and new equipment ...". Neither McMaster nor Jobson accepted such a judgment. Brearley had declared that "to invite Larkin to join in would be the equivalent of introducing poison into the system" and that "New England Airways did not appear to have any substantial claim". McMaster had made it clear that both Larkin and New England should have the opportunity of joining in.[21] On the major issue of linking with Imperial Airways, Brearley remarked that "already it appears that [IAL] have taken on more than they can manage. The many breakdowns on practically all their services in recent months make us feel diffident about their ability to satisfactorily connect with us at Singapore. The comparatively slow speed of their machines and the unsuitable equipment selected by them would be serious drawbacks to our programme." All in all, for the voice of "a dominating influence" in the amalgamated company, these Brearley views were hardly those of McMaster.

McMaster was witheringly contemptuous of Brearley's financial competence. In a wrathful letter to Fysh on 31 March he wrote:

> Brearley is very unsatisfactory both regarding his absurd claims in connection with the hostels, hangars, lighting equipment and excess plant on his Perth–Adelaide section, which would be impossible of sale and of no earthly use to the amalgamation, and also in that he apparently is prepared to go with the Wyndham–Singapore service without giving any consideration as to where finance is to come from or how he intends to meet the many difficulties that must be connected with the operation of such a service. It would appear that he has been so careless in his investigations and proposals that he should not be relied upon in any way and you, yourself, should perhaps take more of the initiative. Brearley appears to me to be hopeless, and finality will be impossible unless he treats the position more seriously.[22]

Charles Ulm took the same view of Brearley's cavalier attitude. By coincidence he also set it down in a letter on 31 March, but to Edgar Johnston, not Fysh.[23] The question of the England–Australia airline was, he wrote, "of really enormous importance" and "Brearley, at least, is treating it far too lightly". Ulm had had a flying accident in Melbourne and spent his convalescence working hard on the amalgamation proposals. He promised to send Edgar Johnston a copy of a "fairly voluminous document". His plan, he said, was for the

air services affected to become entirely self-supporting. Ulm
had, earlier in the month, written to the prime minister on the
attitude to Australian airlines of Imperial Airways.

> You will no doubt remember that I personally advised you that
> the English company, Imperial Airways Ltd., had adopted a
> rather uncompromising and unco-operative attitude towards
> Australian companies operating any section of the route between
> Australia and England. [However] I am happy to report that
> today [8 March 1932] Mr. A.E. Rudder, the Australian represen-
> tative of Imperial Airways, advised that I.A.L. had cabled him
> stating they were delighted to co-operate with the new combina-
> tion of companies if formed and believe they would be able to
> provide a service between Calcutta and Singapore, and possibly
> Batavia, should Australian interests be able to ensure the opera-
> tion of a regular service between Australia and Singapore.[24]

On 6 April Fysh advised McMaster of a new Brearley
bombshell. West Australian Airways now contemplated
cancelling their Perth–Adelaide service and opening up a new
route from Wyndham in the north, direct to Adelaide. He
proposed that WAA would link with KLM at Wyndham and
would start the new service on 1 October.[25]

One day later, Ulm forwarded copies of his own comprehensive amalgamation recommendations on behalf of ANA to
Fysh, Brearley, and Edgar Johnston. It was by far the most
competent and comprehensive document yet to emerge. In
forty-two closely typed foolscap pages he now argued, in
essence, against amalgamation, saw no great economies from
it in operating costs, and thought each of the three companies
should operate those sections of the route most suitable to it.
As he developed these arguments it was clear that his submission was designed to convince Johnston, the minister for
defence, Sir George Pearce, and Prime Minister Lyons that
the section most suitable for Australian National Airways was
the overseas link. None of West Australian Airways flying
equipment, he said, was suitable for the Australian section of
an England–Australia airline. (It was not even necessary to
criticize Qantas aircraft on this score; their single engines
ruled them out.) It would be economically unsound, said Ulm,
for the combined company to take over at Brearley's £75,000
valuation the WAA equipment. "I claim it would be
unreasonable and wrong from every viewpoint to include [this
plant] in any scheme of capitilisation connected with [the
amalgamation]." By contrast, he wrote, all three companies
were agreed that the tri-motor Avro X aircraft operated by
ANA were suitable and safe. He noted that he and Kingsford

153

Smith had made the flight from England to Australia in 1929; that ANA was the first and only company to operate, without any assistance whatever, an all-Australian experimental airmail flight to and from England; that the goodwill built up by ANA was something it "must definitely claim as a valuable asset when considering any question of amalgamation"; and that "it must be considered that Kingsford Smith and — to a lesser extent — Ulm have a definite publicity value to any air service operating company". Their undoubted experience was also, he said, an asset.

He then proposed terms for an amalgamation which he himself frankly acknowledged would be "unfair to W.A.A. shareholders" and would give ANA more shares than either Qantas or WAA. It was, he said, a scheme of capitalization "not likely to be acceptable to Qantas or W.A.A.". There was, he judged, "little prospect or desirability of the three companies amalgamating".

Having argued the exclusion of WAA and Qantas from any overseas operation with both logic and vigour, Ulm took care to demonstrate to the government that he fully understood their financial problems. Any government contribution of moneys should, he said, be repaid. The government should enter into new seven-year term contracts (for both internal and overseas services), subject to annual review and including clauses that would enable reduction of maximum government commitments. The overseas service, he said, "would be entirely self-supporting from mail revenue in a short period". With passengers added it would become "highly profitable within a period of, say, five or six years".

He backed these assertions with detailed figures of expected airmail loads, mail fees, passenger traffic, and air miles projected. "If an average of five passengers were carried per single trip this would total 520 passengers per annum at a charge of, say, £150 per passenger, exclusive of accommodation charges en route. This would give a total revenue from passengers of over one shilling and two pence per mile from passengers alone." He continued: "If an average of 700 pounds of mail and five passengers per single trip [were carried] total revenue would equal four shillings a mile — sufficient to operate without subsidy."

Commenting on air services within Australia, he wrote: "It seems apparent that Qantas have operated their subsidised services to the entire satisfaction of the Civil Aviation Branch, Department of Defence, and also the Auditor General's

Department appear satisfied with progress made towards
these services becoming self-supporting." Qantas, he added
disingenuously, "advise having built up large liquid reserves
during the past eight or ten years whilst it had been operating
under government subsidy".

On West Australia Airlines, Ulm concluded that the east-
west Perth–Adelaide service "is little or no use in the general
scheme for transporting incoming overseas mail". It was
reasonable and economical, he said, for mails for Perth to go
south via West Australian Airways, and for mails for
Brisbane, Sydney, Melbourne, and Adelaide to go south "over
the present Qantas service to Brisbane". The east–west
service, he wrote, "is virtually unnecessary at present and
unlikely ever to become a self-supporting one, at least for
many years to come". It was unfortunate, he said, for the
government that it had to "carry the burden of some £33,500
per annum net subsidy for this service for the next two years"
and any plan to eliminate in whole or part "this unnecessary
expenditure by the Government was desirable".

Ulm then made the comment (unexpected in the light of
ANA's intercapital operations) that it was unnecessary and
undesirable to go to the expense of having an air service
between, Sydney, Melbourne, and Adelaide.

It was agreed he said, "that W.A.A. could not reasonably be
expected to voluntarily relinquish their present [Perth-
Adelaide] contract without compensation in some form" and
he included a comprehensive analysis of government savings
and cash returns to WAA shareholders achievable if the
service were terminated.

Qantas, he concluded, should retain the Camooweal–
Brisbane route in the east and WAA the Wyndham–Perth
route in the west. Not unexpectedly the plum was reserved for
Australian National Airways; ANA should get a seven-year
contract for the overseas service from Rangoon to Wyndham,
plus a contract internally to operate the Brisbane–Sydney
route. It was a confident document and an ambitious conclusion but Charles Ulm believed, on perfectly reasonable
grounds, that he had the prime minister and the government
on his side.[26]

Brearley's first reaction to the Ulm document was a side-
step; a proposal that instead of amalgamation WAA, ANA,
and Qantas should continue their present activities but form a
new and separate company to operate overseas, subscribing
equal portions of shares.[27] A more considered reaction soon

155

followed. "I came to the conclusion", he wrote jointly to Fysh and Ulm, "that it would be impossible for us to arrive at any satisfactory basis for discussion with such an overwhelming swing in the suggested proportionate values of the three companies." He was still convinced that "to make our proposals attractive to the Government" they should be put forward by an amalgamated company and reiterated his idea for a new and separate company financed now by "a cash subscription from each of the three existing concerns". The Ulm proposals were, he said, "far removed from what must be considered as reasonable".[28]

Charles Ulm thought as little of Brearley's proposals as Brearley thought of his. He wrote to Edgar Johnston: "In personal confidence I can tell you I consider some of the suggestions brought up by Norman Brearley to be definitely unsound for everybody but W.A.A. However, I know you are fully awake to all or any 'manoeuvres'."[29] In another letter to Johnston he remarked: "It is becoming increasingly difficult to deal or even negotiate with Norman." He nevertheless thought things could be brought to a satisfactory conclusion, he said, "particularly as, to date, I have found Hudson — although slow — very honest and straight forward in his dealings with me".[30]

Meanwhile, McMaster's distaste for his possible partners and his uncertainty about the correct course of action were growing. "I do not like Brearley's attitude", he told Fysh. "I am satisfied any further correspondence with Brearley will not advance matters." He recognized that "Brearley . . . naturally must be the leader" but had grave qualms. McMaster wanted to "clear up all the apparent differences and difficulties before approaching the Government with a definite proposition" while Brearley, by contrast, wanted to sort out these "domestic difficulties" after they had come to an arrangement with the government. This, McMaster thought, was unsound and "also exposes Qantas to a degree of trickery". Once matters were agreed with the government, Brearley and Ulm would, he said, be able to "force matters" if there was any subsequent difficulty with Qantas.

Uncharacteristically, McMaster wrote: "I quite admit that I am not fully in touch with the atmosphere of the whole position. It is for the Board as a whole to decide and not for you and myself." With evident irritation he asked Fysh to "definitely state what you consider should be done".[31]

Brearley's agile mind produced yet another scheme, just one

week after the proposal for a separate overseas company. In
another joint letter to Ulm and Fysh on 26 April 1932 he now
proposed that Qantas should operate internally from Newcastle Waters to Brisbane, that West Australian Airways
should "divert its existing line between Adelaide and Perth to
a line between Adelaide and Wyndham via Alice Springs",
and that the overseas route between Rangoon or Singapore
and Australia should be left to Australian National Airways.
He also wanted a branch line for WAA through Broken Hill to
Sydney. "This plan safeguards the future to Q.A.N.T.A.S.,
which would certainly be jeopardised under the plans submitted by A.N.A.", said Brearley.[32]

McMaster was not impressed by Brearley's concern for
Qantas. He saw the new proposal as a clear and obvious threat
to the company's future and wrote to Fysh on 8 May: "I sent
you a telegram last Thursday from Devoncourt [station] after
considering your letter dropped by the mail plane. I stressed
the danger of a rival route being established from Wyndham
to Adelaide with a branch service via Broken Hill to Sydney.
Once the route is established via Broken Hill then, if there is
any reduction in routes in the future, I feel that the route via
Brisbane [the Qantas route] will be the one to be cancelled."[33]

With Ulm alerting Edgar Johnston to Brearley
"manoeuvres", McMaster warning Fysh of the possibilities of
"trickery", and Brearley judging Ulm's proposals as "far
removed from reasonable", amalgamation of any kind seemed
an unlikely solution to the problems of Australian commercial
aviation. All three, however, shared a common apprehension
regarding the outsider, Larkin, and none underestimated his
potential as a threat to their individual futures or tentative
collective ambitions. His power base was the state of Victoria
and he now mustered his considerable energies and supporters
to counter the joint proposals of Qantas, WAA, and ANA with
his own plan for the future of Australian air transport.

Lasco was the only company other than West Australian Airways and Qantas to operate a regular route service in the first
ten years of civil aviation in Australia.[34] It tendered successfully in November 1921 for the service between Adelaide and
Sydney, but did not begin operating it until 2 June 1924. On
19 July 1925 Lasco eliminated the final stage to Sydney from
Cootamundra, replacing it with two branch services — from
Broken Hill to Mildura, and from Hay to Melbourne. Lasco
flew over densely populated areas and suffered much more

157

than Qantas or WAA from competition from alternative means of transport. (To 30 June 1928 Larkin's services flew more miles than Qantas but achieved only some 70 per cent of Qantas's passenger-miles.)[35] Larkin's unrealistic tender for the remote North Queensland service between the Qantas terminal at Camooweal and Birdum Creek had proved not only a financial fiasco but a source of bitter conflict with the Civil Aviation Branch. Without access to some of the longer subsidized routes of WAA and Qantas he now faced a bleak future. A boots-and-all fighter, Larkin launched a massive propaganda campaign through two expertly mounted devices. One was a publication called *Wings*, the other a gathering in Melbourne of assorted Australian aviation interests in what was grandly called the "First Annual Air Convention". His main targets were West Australian Airways (which he attacked savagely) and the Civil Aviation Branch but, as the administration of government subsidies was his main theme, Qantas also received a blast or two. (When Hudson Fysh responded to one pin-prick, *Wings* commented "Fysh Bites".) "*Wings*", proclaimed the publication, "stands for Honest Expenditure of the Aviation Vote, now over £100,000 per annum."[36] The inference was obvious.

Despite all this public antagonism from Larkin. Fysh followed through on the McMaster policy that attempts should be made to bring Larkin interests into the amalgamation discussions. On 17 May he wrote to the chairman of Lasco, L.M. Macpherson: "So far as Qantas is concerned, we are out to do our best to assist in the formation of an organisation which, by its stability and standing, will be able to take over the major air routes of the Commonwealth, and also fly overseas. Such an organisation should if possible include the Larkin companies." An agreement, he said "at first sight appears almost insurmountable" but might be effected if all pulled together.[37] The following day he followed up with a second letter saying he could also speak for ANA and WAA, and that their efforts to bring in the Larkin interests were genuine. On 19 May, however, a blunt telegram followed these conciliatory letters, asking Macpherson to "refrain from independent negotiation" with the authorities "as promised".[38]

Meanwhile arrangements for the Larkin-inspired Air Convention, to be held on 25 May, went ahead. On 23 May Fysh telegraphed the minister for defence: "Regret have no confidence whatever in gathering and question qualifications of convenors as operators. Feel convention engineered [by] one interest which hostile practically all other companies."[39] The convention opened on 25 May but was boycotted by WAA, ANA, Qantas, and the aero clubs. On 26 May the attempt to bring in the Larkin interests on amalgamation proposals ended. Fysh wired Macpherson: "Consider you have broken off negotiations by breaking your personal promise to me, Ulm and Brearley not to proceed [with] your independent negotiations until possibility inclusion Lasco interests in proposed combined settled one way or other." He accused Macpherson of inaccurate press disclosures and disclosure of confidential details of negotiations.[40] Correspondence followed in which Macpherson protested both his innocence and good intentions, but it was all over. Fysh wrote to the secretary of the Defence Department on 13 June that Larkin interests had pushed on with the convention and their other representations "at a time when they were negotiating with the three companies".[41] The Larkin scheme for reorganization of air services — "obviously a counter-proposal to that of A.N.A., W.A.A. and Qantas" — was "an impractical and retrograde suggestion", he said. Larkin, in the context of retrenchment in the civil aviation industry, had put forward proposals for co-ordinating air routes with rail services "at a substantial reduction in subsidy cost" estimated at forty thousand pounds "if tenders are called".[42] Fysh told the secretary that Qantas had built up its own business and did not think it should "have to tender against others for the very right to carry on that business". He reminded him of the results of tendering on the Daly Waters connection.[43]

Brearley told Fysh in a letter on 1 June that he had had an interview with the minister (Pearce) and that "the Government is definitely on our side and definitely against Larkin. I think we must in future completely ignore the Larkin organisation."[44] He stressed the importance of lodging their own proposals "with a unanimous voice". Without this there would not, he said, be any prospect of securing long-dated extensions of the north-west and the Qantas routes unless by open tenders, "Say, every three years". (The Air Convention met again in Melbourne at the end of June but this time Ulm was there with proxy votes from all those who opposed it. They were disallowed. The non-Larkin forces then broke away from the convention, held their own meeting on 28 June, and formed a separate body, the Association of Australian Aviation Industries.)

159

Seeming agreement between WAA, ANA, and Qantas now followed swiftly. McMaster and Ulm met in Sydney and by 13 June 1932 were able to exchange letters that promised finality to the protracted negotiations and manoeuvrings of the past months. "We have come to agreement on all the essential conditions attaching to the proposed co-operation of the three companies, A.N.A., W.A.A. and Qantas", McMaster wrote to Ulm, "in the proposal to be placed before the Government by you on behalf of the three companies."[45] He then set out the principal conditions agreed. There was to be co-operation without any financial liability, directly or indirectly; each company was to retain its own identity; co-operation would include interchange of plant, aircraft, and personnel and, where practicable, shared ground organization; ANA would operate Wyndham–Calcutta, WAA would operate Wyndham–Perth and Wyndham–Adelaide, Qantas would operate Newcastle Waters–Brisbane, while ANA and/or Qantas would operate Brisbane–Sydney. Among other conditions were those governing compensation to WAA for the cancellation of its Perth–Adelaide service. McMaster was not certain that the lettergram sent to Brearley on this subject was "sufficiently clear". He then, with clarity and some emphasis, outlined the somewhat complex details of the compensation arrangements and his understanding of the limits of the Qantas liability.

Ulm's letter to McMaster on that same day, Sunday, 13 June, recapitulated the lettergram they had jointly sent to Brearley on 11 June which began "Qantas and A.N.A. [have] reached finality on all points". He then set out details of the arrangements for WAA's compensation. Ulm next quoted telegrams of reply from WAA expressing their acceptance. It did look very much like unanimity. But Brearley had been a continent away, in Perth; and McMaster had been uncertain that the lettergram, on which Brearley's acceptance had been based, had been sufficiently clear. That McMaster did not want to rush ahead is clearly stated in his 13 June letter to Ulm. "There must be considerable delay yet in finalising the proposal placed before the Commonwealth Government, setting out in detail the many conditions attaching to the proposed re-organisation of the air services", he wrote. Ulm, evidently, saw no reason at all to delay. A second letter to McMaster on 13 June, acknowledging receipt of McMaster's, simply said: "The way seems now clear to finalise and immediately present the combined proposal to the Government." He meant what he said. Again on that same day, 13

June 1932, he wrote to Sir George Pearce: "On behalf of Australian National Airways Limited, West Australia Airways Limited and Queensland and Northern Territory Aerial Services Limited, I now hand you herewith a Proposal covering the establishment of the Australian section of the England to Australia Air Service, and the re-organisation of Australian Internal Air Services."[46]

His letter to the minister pointed out that their plan would "enable all Australian Air Services in which the Government is financially interested to become entirely self-supporting within a comparatively short period". It also urged that, though it had been government policy in the past to call open tenders for air services, this time it should, instead, invite interested organizations to submit their own proposals for the reorganization of internal air services and the establishment of the Australian section of the England–Australia route.[47]

While the uneasy and prolonged negotiations of the three major Australian companies had been dragging on, the Australian government had set up an interdepartmental committee under Edgar Johnston's chairmanship. Representing the departments of the Treasury, the Postmaster-General, Defence, and the Interior, its prime task was to assess the competing claims of the British, Dutch, and Australian companies to operate an overseas airmail service.[48] The Dutch had a proven record of reliability and efficiency on their long route from Amsterdam to Batavia inaugurated, after their proving flights, in October 1930. To continue it, by the shortest Timor Sea crossing to Wyndham in the north of Western Australia, would have given Australia an immediate and inexpensive air route to Europe. A connection by West Australian Airways at Wyndham through Alice Springs to Adelaide (and possibly also to Sydney via Broken Hill) would have linked the service with the eastern capitals. On financial considerations alone, it was an attractive option for a government hard-pressed for funds.

The second possibility was the extension of Imperial Airways Far East service to Australia. Though a longer route and a slower service than the Dutch one, it too had financial attractions, as Commonwealth subsidies would be limited to £37,500 a year. The British secretary of state for dominion affairs had sent a cablegram from London to the Prime Minister's Department on 30 July 1932 expressing H.M. government's gratification on learning "from your telegram of

8 June that there is a prospect of early extension of the air service between England and India to Australia by means of co-operation between Imperial Airways and a combination of Australian companies". The cable suggested carriage of mails by IAL as far as Singapore.[49] Australia responded that "although the proposition of an England–Australia service is being studied, the Government is unable to commit itself in any way until the report of the inter-departmental committee is received".[50] (This was a conciliatory stance for the British, Sir George Pearce told Parliament, "wanted to control the England–Australia service as far as Darwin, and . . . strongly pressed that proposal upon the Commonwealth Government".[51] Even within the Australian government there was some support for this British view.)

The third possibility before the committee was for an Australian company to provide an overseas service to a point such as Singapore or Rangoon, where it would link up with the Imperial Airways' service to London. This was what Charles Ulm was hoping for but it soon became clear that any possible acceptance of his 13 June proposals to Sir George Pearce would have to wait until the government had received and considered the report of the interdepartmental committee. Edgar Johnston, in a personal letter to Ulm on 15 August, assured him that "the Committee is doing its best to finalise deliberations and submit its report at the earliest possible moment". The subject, he said with commendable understatement, was complex. "Our report may", he added, "have a very serious effect upon the whole future of civil aviation in this country."[52]

Delay was far more critical for Ulm and Australian National Airways than for West Australian Airways or Qantas, as ANA's financial position was rapidly deteriorating. Brearley, as McMaster with his usual perspicacity had anticipated when he had urged caution on 13 June, was soon backing away from the apparent accord reached in Sydney. He now wanted financial guarantees from Qantas that would ensure payment to WAA of interest on whatever of the agreed annual compensation payments (in respect of the cancelled Perth–Adelaide service) might remain unpaid. "West Australian Airways were endeavouring to depart from the spirit of the agreement reached between Mr McMaster and Mr Ulm in Sydney, and generally accepted at that time", recorded the minutes of a Qantas directors' meeting held in Brisbane on 15 August.[53]

By mid-September there was still no decision from the

government nor any finality with Brearley. "If Brearley is
going to continue in the spirit that he has adopted towards the
Sydney agreement," McMaster wrote to Fysh, "then both he
and Ulm should be advised that Q.A.N.T.A.S. will seriously
consider negotiating with other organisations."[54] One option
that McMaster thought had considerable possibilities was "an
amalgamation of interests with de Havilland and Imperial Airways, the objective being the service from Calcutta to Sydney,
and the construction of all aircraft used in commercial and
defence aviation by the one organisation". The construction
of defence aircraft, he wrote, was "to be under the closest co-
operation and co-ordination with the Imperial
Government".[55]

By October it was clear that Qantas disillusionment was
deepening. Board minutes for 11 October recorded that cables
had been exchanged with Imperial Airways "on the question
of the re-opening of original negotiations for an England–
Australia connection, in the event of the failure of the present
proposition".[56] The twelfth Qantas annual report, submitted
at the annual general meeting in Brisbane on 11 October 1932,
recorded: "Commercial aviation is passing through a critical
period, and this is particularly so with Q.A.N.T.A.S. in that
present contracts expire during the present financial year, and
must come up for consideration by the Government." In the
past, said the report, contracts had been renewed after
necessary adjustments, but if the proposed policy of calling
open tenders and contracting with the lowest tender was
adopted, it would not only be an unsound policy for aviation
but unfair to organizations such as Qantas which had expend-
ed considerable capital and built up highly efficient staffs and
organizations. Such a policy, the report concluded, could easily force organizations such as Qantas out of airline operations.

The report showed a net profit for the year to 30 June 1932
of only £1,468 and recommended a 4 per cent dividend. Profit
for the year, it said, "represents only 3.72 per cent on capital".

Included in the modest profit was a net profit of £42.10s.0d
from the Australian Inland Air Ambulance contract (the Flying Doctor Service). "This contract", said the report, "is not
operating primarily as a commercial undertaking but more in
the form of a service."[57]

As the year drew to a close the situation, far from clearing,
grew even more confused. On 12 December, in a paper to the
board, McMaster canvassed not only the possibility of the
amalgamation with WAA and ANA, but a combination with

163

ANA only and a four-way amalgamation that would include the three Australian companies and Imperial Airways.[58]

On the Qantas–ANA option he commented to the board that Qantas would have to discharge in cash the ANA liabilities of £15,250. Further, while ANA valued their assets at £15,250 cash plus £15,360 in deferred shares (in a merger) "the Receiver, who should be in a position to estimate values and who is controlling the position, is apparently prepared to accept £15,250 cash only". That meant, he said, that Qantas would be paying £15,360 to ANA in the form of deferred shares for goodwill value only. "This arrangement", he wrote, "would be a difficult one for directors of Qantas to justify to their shareholders." There were other financial aspects of such an amalgamation that concerned him; the new capital required would "completely deplete reserves"; Qantas directors "under present difficult financial circumstances" would not give personal guarantees to secure bank accommodation for further finance, while the position of Mr Ulm and his directors, and their capacity to give personal guarantees, should be ascertained.

These doubts were communicated formally to Ulm by Fysh, who wrote then to McMaster: "Your report must have been a great shock to him and one simply does not know what move he is taking now. I should say he is either trying to clear off his debt himself, or trying for an amalgamation with Brearley, or both."[59]

In fact, all was not well between Ulm and Brearley at this time. In a joint letter to Ulm and Qantas on 17 December Brearley wrote: "The directors of this company are very much disturbed to note that A.N.A. are reported as having made an offer to the Government to operate the overseas section of the route temporarily." WAA, he pointed out, was also "in a position to make a similar offer . . . and presumably obtain the first leg-in on the overseas sector from Australia to India". Mutual trust was hardly high.[60]

It was a confused and exhausting end to a year of tension and uncertainty. Fysh was worried about McMaster's health. He wrote wishing him and Mrs McMaster "all of the best for Christmas" and hoped that "the very pressing difficulties through which the pastoral industry is passing will show up in a more hopeful light in 1933. I hope you don't mind me saying that you need a good holiday, that it is your duty to take this in the interests of your family and your pastoral company. A holiday will cause less of a dislocation than an inevitable breakdown."[61]

164

One of McMaster's last letters of the year, from his Longreach property, Moscow, was to A.E. Rudder, Imperial Airways representative in Australia. "Not having anything definite of a business matter to place before you, and not being blessed with a secretary — and unblessed with a lot of office work — I have put off writing to this late hour", he wrote. He wished Rudder and his wife a most happy Christmas, then continued:

> Aviation matters are still very mixed and it is hard to see how matters are going to turn out for such organisations as Imperial Airways and Q.A.N.T.A.S. The whole position is very complicated, and is made more so by the political pressures of such people as Ulm and Brearley — and even Larkin is well in the mix-up.
>
> I have heard from Fysh that you expect the Imperial people to do something of a definite nature about the middle of January. Personally, I do not think anything will come out of the Q.A.N.T.A.S., A.N.A. and W.A.A. negotiations, but they have to be gone on with until a definite decision is reached. I think negotiations will break down, and if definitely broken down we should then be in a position to definitely place something before your people, or they could do so with us. I think the position will eventually result in either an organisation including Imperial Airways, or Q.A.N.T.A.S. will have to stand alone. Personally, I wish for the Imperial Combination.
>
> Well, old man, I will say goodbye with a wish that Imperial Airways and Q.A.N.T.A.S. will yet be closely associated in the development of aviation.[62]

At year's end, there were at least no longer any uncertainties regarding government intentions. The report of the inter-departmental committee went to the minister in November. Its two main recommendations were that an air service should be established linking Australia and the United Kingdom and that the Commonwealth government should accept responsibility for providing the service between Singapore and Darwin. Internally, from the inception of that service, there should be mainland air transport systems linking Darwin–Cootamundra (NSW); Katherine–Perth (WA); Charleville–Roma (Queensland, with Johnston as chairman advocating Charleville–Brisbane); Cloncurry–Normanton (Queensland); and Ord River–Wyndham (WA). The committee also recommended that an air transport service should be established between Melbourne and Hobart, via King Island and Launceston (Tasmania).[63] A Cabinet subcommittee, in December, accepted in substance the committee's proposals. The overseas link to Singapore, the government agreed, was to be an Australian operation.

Tender Competition
1933 to 1934

10 Qantas began 1933 knowing that final decisions had to be taken soon, for time was running out. Their contracts with the government terminated on 9 June 1933. Acceptance by the government of the recommendations of the interdepartmental committee for the establishment of an Australian service to Singapore and a reorganization of internal services (that did not include Brearley's Perth–Adelaide route) meant imminent government decisions of major importance to West Australian Airways, Qantas, and ANA. Fysh went to Sydney and Melbourne in search of solutions and in the week beginning 27 January had meetings with Charles Ulm, A.E. Rudder, Edgar Johnston, M.L. Shepherd (secretary of the Defence Department), Sir George Pearce, minister for defence, the assistant minister, J. Francis, and the minister for customs. The meetings concluded with a long session alone with Brearley, a joint conference with Ulm and Brearley, and finally, a second discussion with Rudder.[1] From Melbourne he wired McMaster on 2 February his view that Brearley "will stress immediate settlement inclusive Qantas and reconstructed A.N.A., or warfare", adding: "Brearley undoubtedly out [to] trick us." He asked if McMaster was "willing agree settlement giving Brearley or Brearley and Ulm control personally" which, he said, he himself was definitely against.[2] He knew, of course, that McMaster would not agree. Then, on 3 February, Fysh wired that Brearley, Ulm, and he had all agreed that amalgamation was impossible. They wished only for "a strong working agreement" with Qantas.

166

Imperial Airways, said the Fysh wire, was "anxious co-operate Qantas".[3] The concept of a joint ANA, WAA, Qantas operation was finally dead. Fysh advised that Ulm and Brearley both opposed any co-operation with Imperial Airways but all three agreed to continue to try for a working agreement.[4]

On Wednesday 22 February 1933, the Qantas board met at 7:30 P.M. in the Wool Exchange Building, Eagle Street, Brisbane. Fysh, in his report to the board, said that Qantas had two options: an agreement with ANA and WAA or the formation of a new company with Imperial Airways. He made no recommendation but commented that Qantas, ANA, and WAA "can never become happy bedfellows".[5] A.E. Rudder, the Australian representative of Imperial Airways was, after discussion of other business, invited to be present, the minutes of that board meeting recorded.

> Mr Rudder conveyed to the board the contents of a cable which had just been received by him from Imperial Airways intimating their desire that Qantas should be associated with them in a new company recently formed by them in Australia known as "Australia Empire Airways Limited", and outlining their suggested terms and conditions of such association. The matter was discussed very fully by the board. Thereafter, Mr Rudder withdrew from the meeting.
>
> It was moved by Mr Campbell [substitute director for A.N. Templeton who was unable to attend the meeting], seconded by Mr Loxton and carried unanimously that Qantas should associate themselves with Imperial Airways in connection with the proposed new service to England on the basis of the terms and conditions submitted by them, but subject to certain modifications to be arranged with Imperial Airways.[6]

It was the most important and far-reaching decision taken to date by the company and was to have a profound effect on the structure and future of civil aviation in Australia.

Fysh wrote to Sir George Pearce on 28 February:

> We wish to advise that the long attempt which has been made to combine the interests of Qantas, West Australian Airways and Australian National Airways, and in which we joined enthusiastically, is apparently at an end.
>
> As a final effort to bind the negotiating companies we attempted to include Imperial Airways in the proposed merger, but the way was definitely closed when Major Brearley, on behalf of his company, refused to give consideration on the project.
>
> At the last conference, the firm demand of Major Brearley to operate from Perth to Darwin and Darwin to Camooweal finally made us realise that no agreement was possible that would be in the fair interests of Qantas.

In joining forces with Imperial Airways this company is assured of a connection based on confidence and strength, and which will make for efficient operations in the future. It is with the sincere regret of the directors of this company that an agreement between the Australian companies has failed, but it has been their duty to face facts.[7]

From the Qantas viewpoint, the failure of the amalgamation proposals was in essence caused by their mistrust of Brearley. Though the financial position of Australian National Airways was a substantial contributing factor there was, throughout the long negotiations, a continuous and mounting unease and apprehension towards the man who, as McMaster and his advisers had judged, would by the proportion of his contribution to a joint company, have been its leader and dominating influence. Qantas acted throughout with openness and honesty, as Charles Ulm had acknowledged. An all-Australian solution was always accepted by McMaster and Fysh as the one they should work towards and, despite qualms about what they saw as differences in ideals and practices between Qantas and West Australian Airways, they had sought to achieve agreement. McMaster, even in his private and confidential correspondence with A.E. Rudder as late as December 1934, made it clear that despite his own long-standing preference for "the Imperial combination", the Australian negotiations had to continue. And Fysh, in his own words, "was still sitting on the fence" when the actual board meeting began which decided that Qantas should associate itself with Imperial Airways.[8]

This decision by no means secured the future for Qantas. The IAL–Qantas combination not only had to be formalized on terms agreeable to both, but faced open tendering against competitors; and it was widely known that the operating costs of Imperial Airways were high. Further, the government's attitude to a tender combining British and Australian capital was in doubt. (Fysh had cabled McMaster's friend, Sir Donald Cameron, in London before the board decision, that Qantas faced the position of deciding between Imperial Airways or Brearley and Ulm. Qantas, he said, "trust Imperial but doubtful if together can secure Singapore–Brisbane contract owing high cost Imperial and strong opposition [from] passed-over Australian interests".)[9] Qantas had to show "the fullest possible Australian control and influence", Fysh told A.E. Rudder, if it was to influence the final government attitude to an Imperial Airways–Qantas tender. "We feel the danger to be very real, but to finally weigh up its exact extent is, of course, an impossible matter." The combine, he said, "must play for safety and make the [Qantas] control amply secure".[10]

Brearley himself put the political position clearly, in a bulletin from West Australian Airways:

> With Federal Government subsidies for the Darwin–Singapore route, Australian operators very rightly regard the whole of these routes as being Australian territory for the purpose of aviation development. Imperial Airways has formed a branch company in Australia for the purpose of tendering but the Australian Government are not likely to be misled by propaganda that was intended to secure any of these contracts for a company whose headquarters are outside Australia.[11]

The "branch company" was the Australian Empire Airways Limited mentioned by Rudder which IAL had previously registered to handle its Australian operations. Qantas, however, refused to recognize this company and insisted on a direct relationship with Imperial Airways.[12]

The chief opposition to the IAL–Qantas combination, Fysh wrote on 21 March in a letter to F.A. de V. Robertson, of *Flight* magazine in London, were West Australian Airways, Larkin, and Australian National Airways — "or rather," he corrected himself, "Ulm's new company, because A.N.A. are in liquidation". Larkin, he said, was still "the thorn in the side of Australian aviation that he has been since the first commencement of the subsidised services". Fysh added that the Dutch, too, were "trying to move heaven and earth to get a leg in, and may even go as far as to refuse permission for landings in Java should they not be allowed to land in Australia". The Qantas association with IAL, he concluded, would be "kept thoroughly Australian and definitely not swallowed up by Imperial Airways".[13]

Neither the demise of ANA nor the final breakdown of the amalgamation proposals had checked the energies of Charles Ulm. In a long "private and confidential" letter to Edgar Johnston on 8 April 1933 he now set out his plans to build "aircraft of the Fokker type" in Australia, and to sell them "at a profit, at a price below the cost of importing them". He was, he said, "financing the whole of my present plans out of my own pocket", purchasing parts of an Avro X from the liquidator of ANA and "retaining Wackett's services for engine matters". His plans included a quick trip "home to England and back", taking "Scotty Allan and Bill Taylor with me".[14] In a later letter, he amplified the plans for his flight: "After reaching England we shall carry on from Ireland to

New York, across the U.S.A. to Oakland, and thence on to Australia via Honolulu, Suva and New Zealand."

"Flights across the Atlantic and Pacific Oceans", he said, "will rivet the public's attention more than ever on the performance of an Australian-built aircraft, under the most exacting conditions — with the result that when tenders are called for the operation of the Darwin–Singapore service, the Australian public will insist that wholly Australian organisations and personnel must do the job . . . or it will be the death knell of Australian aviation."[15]

Qantas now had to hurry their new IAL partner along. "As time passes and the time for tendering for the new routes becomes closer," Fysh wrote to Rudder on 5 May, "my directors feel that an effort should be made to go beyond the very loose and open terms of the Gentleman's Agreement between Imperial Airways and Qantas, with the object of reaching finality on such points as are capable of being cleared up at the present stage." Until all points could be settled, he said, "it will be necessary to carry on under the guiding principle of mutual confidence". The biggest chance of disagreement and misunderstanding in the future would, he added, come from an attitude of silence now, each party having its own ideas. "I feel you must recognize this danger."[16]

Imperial Airways had, of course, other things than Australia on its mind. In the previous October, they had had to cope with political difficulties in the Persian Gulf and transfer their route to India from the Persian to the Arabian side of the Gulf; in January they introduced the Armstrong Whitworth XV four-engined monoplane aircraft on the England–Cape Town service (a service begun the previous April); in February they replaced the Alexandria–Cairo train journey on the England–India service and England–Africa service with an air sector; and on 18 February they celebrated the completion of their first ten million miles of flying.[17] For Australia, IAL preparations were nearing completion for the departure from England on 29 May of the IAL Armstrong Whitworth XV *Astraea* on a survey flight to Darwin and on, by intermediate ports, to Brisbane, Sydney, Canberra, and Melbourne. That the flight and the modern new airliner were to prove of great public relations value was not entirely accidental.

Fysh was invited to join the *Astraea* on its return flight to England. He thought it, though, too big an airliner for the Darwin–Singapore service and told McMaster so in a letter on 22 May.

The new four-Gypsy-engined de Havilland machine now being designed is the obvious job. The machine will carry 2,500 pounds payload at a cruising speed of 110 miles per hour and will cost in Australia about £10,500 — as against the Atalanta's [the Armstrong Whitworth XVs] 4000 pounds payload at 120 miles per hour and its cost, in Australia, of £25,000. I am trying to induce de Havillands to get a little more speed into the machine even at a sacrifice in payload. For purposes of comparison, our DH61 machines carry a payload of 1900 pounds at 100 miles per hour and ... cost about £8,000. Tying ourselves up to such a large type [as the Atalanta] at the outset, before requirements are known, is a big business risk.[18]

While Charles Ulm pressed rapidly forward with his plans to win public support by an epic flight in an Australian-made aircraft, the resourceful Larkin proclaimed a cost-free solution of the overseas airmail problem to the government. Lasco offered to start an unsubsidized service from Darwin to Koepang in the East Indies, using three-engined aircraft. No guaranteed maximum mail loading was sought and any load offering would be carried on a poundage basis for eight shillings a pound. The service, said Larkin, would be weekly in each direction and would, under co-operative arrangement made with KNILM (the KLM Netherlands East Indies service), distribute the mails throughout Java, Sumatra, and the Malay States as well as exchange airmails to and from Europe.[19]

Both this Larkin request and KLM's long-standing offer (first made to Prime Minister Scullin in 1930) to extend their Batavia service to Darwin were refused by the government.[20] Departmental involvement in such decisions meant, of course, a hectic time for the new controller of aviation, Edgar Johnston. The records in the "Tenders" file of the Civil Aviation Branch show that, in addition to the information on operators and their proposals, he was at the same time keeping track of the detailed performance and loadings of no less than eighty-two different types of aircraft, all of them British-made. He found time, however, to write a personal note to Charles Kingsford Smith saying: "I understand that your Pilot's Licence is expiring or has done so. For the Lord's sake attend to it, as I would hate to have to prosecute Sir Charles Kingsford Smith for a breach of the regulations."[21] Kingsford Smith, like Ulm, also planned a flight to England. His proposal was a unique one for his aim was a trip with paying passengers in the old Southern Cross. There were no takers. Aircraft reported: "The fact that Sir Charles Kingsford Smith

171

Archerfield about 1933. An Avro of New England Airways is parked in the foreground.

failed to get passengers for his proposed trip to England in the *Southern Cross* suggests that the demand for seats on a regular service would be too small to justify the Government subsidising big passenger aircraft."[22]

In the battle for public attention, the flight to Australia of the "big passenger aircraft" of Imperial Airways, the *Astraea*, dominated the press. The first stories were not exactly helpful. The aircraft left Croydon on 29 May ("a fortnight late", commented Larkin's *Wings*)[23] but on the last leg to Darwin was forced down at Bathurst Island because of fuel shortage. "Owing to strong headwinds," the Brisbane *Telegraph* reported, "it was decided not to risk the full trip [Koepang–Darwin] and the officers in charge made a landing at Bathurst Island, half an hour's flying time from Darwin. Here further fuel supplies were taken aboard . . ."[24]

All this was forgotten when the *Astraea* landed at Brisbane on 23 June. "The presence of so many thousands of people at Archerfield over the weekend", said the *Telegraph*, "proves beyond all shadow of a doubt that the advent of Imperial Airways's wonder liner has stirred the imagination of the populace to a remarkable degree."[25] The paper estimated that ten thousand people gathered on the aerodrome next day, despite a bitterly cold wind, and "swarmed around the aeroplane so that it was impossible to move it".

Its very size was breathtaking. Much larger than any aircraft yet seen in Australia, it had a wingspan of ninety feet — "too great to allow entrance to any commercial hangar in the country" said the Qantas *Gazette*.[26] Its four Armstrong Siddeley

Serval engines each provided 340 horsepower, giving it a top speed of 150 miles per hour. It could carry either seventeen passengers or a mix of nine passengers and a ton of mails and freight, plus its crew of captain, first officer, wireless operator, and engineer. "Grace, beauty and efficiency in flight — the *Astraea*", was the summary of the *Telegraph*. The purpose of the flight to Australia, said Maj. H.G. Brackley, air superintendent of Imperial Airways, was to survey the proposed England–Australia route. "We have come to Australia", he said, "as ambassadors of commercial aviation and not as poachers on existing services."

A triumphant tour of Sydney, Canberra, and Melbourne followed with, everywhere, the same tumultuous welcome and press attention. "The mighty aeroplane, impressive in the air, where she dwarfed local machines which escorted her into Mascot, was even more impressive in her bulk and wingspread on the ground", said the *Sydney Morning Herald*. "Her arrival opens a new chapter in flying in the Commonwealth."[27]

The *Astraea* taxies to a halt at Archerfield, 23 June 1933. The commander on this survey flight, Capt. A.R. Prendergast of Imperial Airways, died in the crash of QEA's second DH86 near Longreach on 15 November 1934.

The *Astraea* undergoes a mechanical check in the Qantas hangar at Archerfield, 23 June 1933, after the official welcome to its crew. The largest aircraft seen in Australia up to that time, the *Astraea* shows in this photograph why the editor of the Qantas Gazette reported that it was "too great to allow entrance to any commercial hangar in the country".

So alarmed were the Larkin interests at this tidal wave of acclamation and its ensuing effects that a telegram was sent on behalf of the Air Convention to the proprietors of all the major newspapers, urging press restraint:

> By clever propaganda and methods beyond reach of Australian aircraft operators, Imperial Airways' monopoly is endeavouring to stampede government, press and public into pre-supposing that company will secure subsidy contract for Singapore–Australia air link. As tenders not yet called, and as several Australian companies propose tendering, appeal to you to place fair limit on space devoted to Imperial Airways, and make it clear to public that tenders have yet to be called, and the Government has stated its intention [of] giving preference [to] Australian companies.[28]

While the *Astraea* was in Brisbane, Charles Ulm arrived in Singapore with Scotty Allan and P.G. Taylor, on their way to England in Ulm's new aircraft, *Faith in Australia*. Fergus McMaster, meanwhile, was "rather hurriedly" drafting material to "form a guide for Mr Fysh in negotiations in London" with Imperial Airways.[29] Fysh was to be a passenger in the *Astraea* on its return flight to England, charged with producing a draft agreement from what Imperial Airways described as "a concordat [with Qantas] for the formation of a joint company to tender for and, if successful, operate the

Singapore–Darwin–Brisbane section of the England–Australia service".[30] The *Astraea* left Darwin on 7 July for Karachi where Fysh transferred on 16 July to the *Hannibal*, an even bigger airliner, for the five-day journey to Croydon. That he was somewhat overwhelmed by the experience is evident in *The Log of the Astraea*, which he compiled en route. "One is simply wafted on a magic carpet from the land of Australia", he wrote. It was "a galaxy of changing effect . . . a perfect kaleidoscope".[31]

Though the visit of the *Astraea* to Australia had certainly helped the cause of the Qantas–Imperial Airways partnership, it had also stirred up those who opposed it. A.E. Rudder was sensitive to their accusations of dominance by Imperial Airways and wrote to McMaster on 28 August: "It seems to me that a little more Australian character might be added if the tenders are submitted in the name of Qantas."[32] Brearley, in his WAA *Bulletin*, continued to attack Imperial Airways' efficiency and accident record, provoking an uncharacteristically bitter comment from Fysh, in London, to McMaster: "He has forgotten the opening of his own north-west route, [referring to the fatal WAA crash that occurred] and the fact that surplus subsidy revenue has not gone into his service but to enrich himself and his shareholders."[33]

By 6 September, McMaster was able to wire A.E. Rudder that Fysh had advised by cable from London agreement with

Charles Ulm and a group of associates purchased *Southern Moon*, one of ANA's Avro airliners when that company ceased regular services in June 1931. It was overhauled and modified to emerge as the *Faith in Australia* in early 1933. Ulm, Scotty Allan, and P.G. Taylor left Australia in June 1933 in an attempt to fly around the world through both hemispheres. This attempt was terminated following a take-off accident in Ireland and the trio returned to Australia in October. Ulm subsequently made several flights between Australia and New Zealand in VH-UXX in 1933 and 1934.

175

Imperial Airways on share interests "and other vital factors". That McMaster wanted everything out in the open is clear from the comment that followed: "Personally against any make-believe regarding share interests." Like Rudder he preferred, he said, "for political reasons [that] Qantas lodge tenders for [the] combined interests".[34]

The political debate was certainly hotting up. Senator Dunn (Labor, New South Wales), on 1 September, in an urgency debate on the Singapore service in the Senate, praised the achievements of Kingsford Smith and Ulm and other Australian airmen and declared:

> Apparently these men are to be left on the beach, while this profitable contract goes to Imperial Airways, to be run on British capital, manned by British airmen, and paid for with good Australian cash. What chance has Smith or Ulm, or any other Australian without money, to compete with this wealthy monopoly in open tenders? They will be frozen out and the Government, by its encouragement of the propaganda stunt of the *Astraea*, is already preparing the public mind to see them frozen out.

The auditor-general, the senator continued, had for three years in succession "condemned the proposal for an Australian–British air mail service". His 1931 report had stated, the senator quoted:

> Although it is perfectly clear that the Australian financial position is such that it cannot afford the huge subsidy which would be necessary to maintain such a service, endeavours are being made by certain commercial interests to influence the Commonwealth Government with a view to establishing the service. No real justification for an English–Australian air mail service has been established.

The senator then made it plain that he considered those vested interests — "the nigger in the woodpile" — to be Imperial Airways. "Australia", he said, "is not the first to feel the imperial tentacles of this octopus." Referring to associations "with Australian directorates that are interlocked with British concerns" he linked Imperial Airways with "the mammoth Dunlop interest", and the "powerful British–Australian financial Baillieu group". The Melbourne *Herald*, he said enthused about the *Astraea*'s visit "because British financiers, through the Baillieu group, control that newspaper and, through it, nearly one-half of the newspapers of the Commonwealth". He accused the *Sydney Morning Herald* and the Melbourne *Argus* saying that they "have already joined in the chase on behalf of this British company".[35] This opposition view was to be elaborated and repeated in both Houses in the weeks ahead.

A handwritten letter from Fysh to McMaster on 17 September, from the Grosvenor Hotel, London, expressed a different perspective. "There is not the slightest doubt but that control would remain in Australia", he wrote. Though the effects of his initial welcomes and impressions had worn off and there had since been differences of opinion and discussions, he was, he said, "only more settled in my opinion that Woods Humphery is a great leader and that his executives are excellent. Their policy is our policy to an extraordinary extent. Their principles of operation are right, and they are not out to make points." It was a quiet and personal letter, not meant for an audience. "In the early days," he wrote, "you had your dreams for Qantas. Now all lies at our feet if we get Singapore–Brisbane. It will be no monopoly, however, as we have not yet done with Brearley and the Dutch."[36]

Apart from the controversy about who should operate the Singapore service, there was wide public debate about the route it should follow in Australia. It was the firm government policy that, from Darwin, the service should follow the established route down to Charleville in Queensland and then terminate, further south, in the New South Wales country town of Cootamundra, the half-way point in the rail-link between Sydney and Melbourne. Brisbane was to retain its branch route by air with Charleville, but there were to be no air connections by the new service with Sydney or Melbourne. The alternative route, publicly argued by McMaster, was that the England–Australia service should operate through Brisbane to Sydney. The *Sydney Morning Herald* commented:

> It is understood that the management of the Qantas service in Queensland, whose experience surely entitles it to be heard, fully shares the disappointment of Imperial Airways with the Federal Government's reluctance to consider a route through Brisbane to a Sydney terminal as an alternative to a country route to a Cootamundra terminal . . . [The Government policy] illustrates too narrow a vision of the new epoch about to open in Australian overseas communications.[37]

In Brisbane, the *Courier-Mail* reported that "European airmen ridicule the idea of terminating the world's longest air service at Cootamundra, instead of Sydney, via Brisbane. Nowhere in Europe is the influence of railways allowed to retard air development."[38] Fysh had put the Qantas view direct to Sir George Pearce, arguing that a Darwin–Cootamundra trunk line "operating wholly through the back country, passing by the city of Brisbane and having no city terminal, will result in . . . an airways system neglecting many basic operating principles, and not in conformity with world development".[39]

The government was unmoved. The tender forms, with conditions of tender and contract, were issued on 22 September and specified Cootamundra as the Australian terminus for the England–Australia service. The terminus in England was London.

The tender forms set out three "divisions" which could be tendered for: the overseas division (Singapore–Darwin); the eastern division (Darwin–Brisbane–Cootamundra, with subsections listed as Darwin–Mt.Isa–Longreach, Longreach–Brisbane, Charleville–Cootamundra); the western division (Katherine–Perth, with subsections Katherine–Broome, Broome–Carnarvon, Carnarvon–Perth).

Aeroplanes, said the conditions of tender, shall have a cruising speed of not less than 110 miles per hour and a cruising range of not less than 600 miles (against a head wind of 30 miles per hour) for the overseas division (and not less than a 300-mile range for the other divisions). For the first two years of a five-year contract tenderers could use aircraft with a cruising speed of not less than 95 miles per hour.

The tender conditions were immediately criticized by the two authoritative British aviation magazines, *The Aeroplane* and *Flight*, and the Australian magazine *Aircraft*. C.G. Grey, editor of *The Aeroplane* and perhaps the most respected aviation commentator of his day, described the minimum speeds required as ridiculous. "Five years hence", he said, "cruising speeds ought to be 200 miles an hour."[40] The magazine *Flight*, the organ of the Royal Aero Club, said it did not see any signs that air transport was ruining the railways in Australia or anywhere else. "Therefore it seems a pity to send an airway into the wilderness [Cootamundra] in order to subordinate it to the interests of the railways."[41] *Aircraft*, in Australia, pointed out that with Cootamundra "as the absolute terminal point", passengers arriving there would have to catch their train to Sydney or Melbourne at three in the morning. "It appears that the only possible reason the Government had in entertaining this farcical proposal was to necessitate the final transport of mail and passengers over Government Railways."[42]

Sir Charles Kingsford Smith and Charles Ulm both lent substance to C.G. Grey's remarks by making separate high

speed flights from England to Australia within weeks of the
issue of the conditions of contract. Kingsford Smith flew a
Percival Gull (the *Miss Southern Cross*) from Lympne
(London) to Australia in seven days four hours forty-three
minutes, and went on to receive an extraordinary welcome
from a crowd estimated at some hundred thousand on his
arrival in Melbourne on 15 October. He had cut forty hours
off the record set by C.W.A. Scott. Charles Ulm left London
three days before Kingsford Smith's Melbourne arrival and
(with Scotty Allan and P.G. Taylor) in his aircraft *Faith in
Australia*, bettered the time of the Gull and set a new record
by flying from England to Australia in less than a week (six
days seventeen hours fifty-six minutes).

Ulm had temporarily abandoned his plans for trans-Atlantic
and trans-Pacific flights. "When he returns to Australia," said
a press report from London, "he will devote his attention to
preparing tenders for the air mail contracts for the service to
Australia next year."[43]

Kingsford Smith announced his own intention to tender for
the Australia–Singapore contract, when he passed through
Sydney on 15 October. "I told Mr Ulm in London", he said,
"that if his company, which will also tender, was successful in
getting the contract, I would join his board of directors in an
advisory capacity. In the meantime, I am preparing . . . for my
own tender for the aerial mail contract."[44] The England–Australia service, he said, could be operated "on a basis of ten
days". His company would also, he said, undertake the
building and sale of aeroplanes. He had a licence for the
building of the Percival Gulls in Sydney.

Commenting on the Ulm and Kingsford Smith flights, the
Brisbane *Telegraph* said: "One notable effect of two new
records within a few days of one another has been to focus
criticism upon the terms of the proposed aerial mail service
contracts between England and Australia. The schedule proposed was absurdly generous."[45] In London the *Evening
Standard* also referred to the two flights and the minimum
speeds specified for the airmail contracts. "Britain is standing
still so far as the main air routes are concerned", it wrote. "We
shall be condemned to the operation of the Australian route at
speeds other countries are now leaving behind."[46] The Air
League, in England, cabled Ulm: "Well done. Your flight is
almost an insult to the Anglo-Australian air mail schedule."[47]

In the House of Representatives on 25 October, Mr J.A.
Beasley (Lang Labor) moved the adjournment of the House to

discuss the conditions of tender and alleged that the tenders had been rigged to benefit Imperial Airways. He repeated charges of undue influence by Baillieu interests. Mr C.L. Baillieu, he said, through the *Melbourne Herald* chain of Australian newspapers, "is the recognised Cabinet maker. His servant, Sir Keith Murdoch, has been knighted by the Government."[48] The government, through the assistant minister for defence, J. Francis, replied vigorously. The allegations, he said, were based on information gleaned from "a small, disgruntled coterie known as the Air Convention, which had been bombarding members of Parliament for months with all sorts of documents and dodgers. This small coterie had at last found a spokesman in the House, but it had no authority to speak for Australia. it had an axe to grind."[49]

The Air Convention had included the prime minister, J.A. Lyons, in its bombardment. Its chairman, H.T. Shaw, had written a strong letter on 19 October to the prime minister requesting a Royal Commission on aviation expenditure. "You claim", he said, "that the Government has satisfied itself that there was no foundation whatsoever for accusations of favouritism, malpractice, etc." and that departmental officers had been instructed to "ignore the baseless and harassing criticism and innuendos of the Air Convention. Well informed people", the letter continued, "could only conclude that it is your desire to further the tyrannical administration of the Civil Aviation Branch" ensuring that "the flow of political favours will continue to those self-seeking monopolies".[50]

Shaw received a withering reply.

> I am directed by the Prime Minister to reply to your letter of 19 October. The pressing of personal grievances by publicity methods and the imputation of dishonest motives to all who do not happen to agree with you are not likely to impress . . . emanating from a body which makes pretensions of a representative character which are obviously not warranted by facts. The self-styled Australian Air Convention is representative only of a limited group of persons in Victoria . . . pursuing personal vendettas . . . The determination of policy is a matter for the Government, subject to the direction of Parliament.[51]

The Qantas annual general meeting that year was held with Hudson Fysh still overseas. The thirteenth annual report, referring to the Australia–England service, recorded that " a basis of agreement has been reached between Q.A.N.T.A.S. and Messrs Imperial Airways Ltd. for the formation of an Australian Company to tender for, and if successful, operate

the Singapore–Port Darwin–Cootamundra–Brisbane Sections
of the proposed service, in addition to the other activities at
present carried out by Q.A.N.T.A.S. In associating with
Imperial Airways Ltd. your Directors have been influenced by
the National aspect involved in this Empire Service."[52] The
directors reported a net profit for the year to 30 June 1933 of
£1,063 and recommended a dividend of 4 per cent.

Fysh, his work finished in London, returned to Australia
through the United States and flew in the fast, all-metal
Boeing 247 aircraft of United Airlines on their night beacon
service between Chicago and San Francisco. He was vastly
impressed. "All these high speed machines here make
everything look out of date in England, except the Handley 42
— which is supreme in its class", he wrote to Woods Humphery at Imperial Airways. There were, he said, forty-two services in and out of Chicago every twenty-four hours. On the
night route, he wrote: "There is a landing ground every twenty miles, all lit up for landing, and every ten miles a revolving
beacon."[53] Fysh also had a preview of the Douglas DC2 and
DC3 which, he wrote, "was to revolutionise all our previous
ideas of air transport aircraft".[54] It "was, of course, only a
twin engined type and primarily designed for service on the
transcontinental routes of the U.S.". Qantas and Imperial, he
added, considered four engines essential for long Empire
routes. "The U.S.A. in 1933 had not lifted its sights much
above the horizon of its own country and no aircraft had yet
been produced capable of operating regularly with a
reasonable payload over the Atlantic", he wrote later.[55]

From the US West Coast, Fysh continued his return
journey by ship. An apologetic letter from a hard-pressed
McMaster at his Devoncourt property awaited him. "I am
sorry I can't be in Brisbane to welcome you home after your
very successful negotiations with Imperial Airways", wrote
McMaster on 29 October. "Unfortunately at present I am tied
up with shearing here." McMaster added that he had gone
carefully through the agreements with Imperial Airways.
"There are some provisions with which I am not in full
accord", he said, "but taken as a whole the agreements are
satisfactory, and I wish to congratulate both yourself and the
representatives of Imperial Airways for the fairness and
soundness of the decisions."[56]

One of the decisions was the choice of a four-engined de
Havilland aircraft (sponsored by Imperial Airways in its
development) for the Singapore–Darwin route. To be called

the DH86, it offered either the Gipsy IV engine as powerplant or the new and more powerful Gipsy VI. Qantas and IAL chose the latter, but left the final decision open in case the less expensive, though lower-powered Gipsy IV gave them a better chance of securing the contract with a lower tender price.[57]

Fysh had prepared a final report for the board on his overseas journey while still at sea on the SS *Monterey* between New Zealand and Australia. Earnest, and somewhat stilted, there is no doubting its sincerity.

> Imperial Airways are thoroughly national; their work constitutes one of the greatest Empire movements — there is no thought of pecuniary gain. Qantas started off in 1920 strongly national and with expansive ideals, as reference to Mr Fergus McMaster's early speeches and prospectuses will reveal. I would like to stress that this early spirit be not allowed to die, and that our expansion be thoroughly Empire, and that we go forward with strong confidence in the future and with optimism, without which any pioneering venture, such as the one to which we have set our hands, is useless.
>
> The position, as I see it, is that we have the chance now to engage in a part of one of the greatest Empire transport developments in history. If we are beaten out of the contracts, Australian and Empire air development [will] suffer, which means we have a strong duty to perform — besides the saving of the Qantas company from virtual extinction. The whole outcome of affairs hinges around the next few months.[58]

Fysh read his report to the directors at a board meeting on 14 November, a week after his return. McMaster moved a resolution of appreciation of his efforts and "a hearty welcome back to Brisbane". That board meeting also discussed the agreement with Imperial Airways, suggested amendments relating to subscribed capital, and decided to leave matters for final negotiation with S.A. Dismore, secretary of Imperial Airways, who was expected in late December. The minutes record:

> Clause 28 of the conditions of contract applicable to the new Services being called by the Australian Government make it necessary for tenders to be submitted in the name of the Contracting Company. In these circumstances it was proposed by Mr Campbell, seconded by Mr Loxton, and carried that a cable in the following form be sent to Imperial Airways: Clause 28 makes imperative register Qantas Empire as tendering company. Subject to your approval propose drafting Articles of Association conjunction Rudder for submission Dismore [on] his arrival."[59]

And so "Qantas Empire" it was. McMaster formally instructed Messrs Cannan and Peterson, solicitors, in a letter on 28 November to draft the Memorandum and Articles of Association. "It has been agreed between Messrs Imperial Airways Ltd and Q.A.N.T.A.S. to register a company in Queensland under the name 'Qantas Empire Airways Ltd.' to tender for the Australia–Singapore Air Mail Service", he wrote.[60]

The *Qantas Gazette* said that the company

> is quietly confident in evolving its plans for submission to the Commonwealth Government ... It has been mentioned that the contracts should be so Australian as to even exclude British capital. This is a strange theme indeed, when it is remembered that right from the inception of the occupation of Australia by whites, British capital has been instrumental in developing the various industries. We live on British loan money, and British capital is today flowing into manufacturing, pastoral and mining pursuits — they just can't get enough of it. Why should aviation be excluded?[61]

Meanwhile, the first passenger ever to travel on Qantas scheduled services, and its link as aviation pioneer with a more remote Australian pioneering past, Alexander Kennedy, had celebrated his ninety-sixth birthday in Brisbane with a flight to Mt. Isa to see his family. The *Courier-Mail* recalled his sixty years in Queensland and his birth in Perthshire, Scotland. "He founded many station properties", it said, "which today are household words." The old man himself recalled: "When I first went west I travelled by bullock team, because I could not afford to buy a pack horse. If we covered ten miles in a day it would be good going." Now, he said, he always flew. "I leave Brisbane on Tuesday morning and have lunch in Mt. Isa, 1,200 miles away, on Wednesday."[62]

Qantas Empire Airways Limited was registered in Brisbane on 18 January 1934. On 22 January a meeting of four men was held at the Wool Exchange Building, Eagle Street at 5:45 P.M. They were A.E. Rudder and S.A. Dismore, representing Imperial Airways Ltd, and Fergus McMaster and Hudson Fysh representing Qantas Ltd. At this first meeting of Qantas Empire Airways, the full board of directors, as agreed with Imperial Airways and Qantas, was appointed. They were: F. McMaster, chairman; A.E. Rudder, vice-chairman; H. Fysh, managing director; W.A. Watt, P.C., director; F.E. Loxton, director; F.J. Smith, director; H.H. Harman, secretary.

The meeting concluded formal business and recorded the submission of "the proposed tenders for the air mail contracts

Hudson Fysh and S.A. Dismore, secretary of Imperial Airways, photographed on the roof of the Wool Exchange Building in Eagle Street on 24 January 1934. They are sitting on the metal box containing Qantas Empire Airways' tenders for the overseas air services which they lodged with the federal government in Melbourne on 31 January 1934.

with a list of the proposed tender prices". It was resolved that they "be and are hereby approved subject to such additions and/or amendments deemed necessary" by Fysh and Dismore "in the light of later information".[63] Dismore, in his four weeks in Australia, had not only laboured to finalize the Qantas agreement, but had worked arduously with Fysh both in England and Australia to prepare the tender documents. They were due for submission by 31 January.

The agreement leading to the formation of Qantas Empire Airways provided for a capital of £200,000 of which Qantas and Imperial Airways were each to hold 49 per cent. The remaining 2 per cent was held by an umpire, Sir George Julius. He was, Fysh later wrote, "an umpire who never had to blow his whistle".[64] One clause, proposed by IAL, expressed the basis of their association. "It is the intention of both parties that each shall have a 'square deal' in the sense that that expression is understood by fair and reasonably minded men."[65]

Two days after the first Qantas Empire Airways meeting in Brisbane, Fysh and Dismore set off for Melbourne by train. With them was a black tin box containing the tenders — twenty-two submissions in all for the various routes and variations for each route. There were spaces left for price, to be completed at the last moment.[66]

"In our sleeper from Sydney to Melbourne," wrote Fysh, "we had that precious box on the floor, always within sight. Then who should come in but Ulm and Brearley, on their way to Melbourne to lodge their tenders. They sat down for a yarn and rested their feet on that box . . ."[67]

The tenders were lodged at 4:15 P.M. on 31 January 1934 with fifty-one minutes in hand; official closing time for their receipt was six minutes past five.[68]

Qantas Empire Airways Inaugural 1934 to 1935

11 "The great surprise", Fysh wrote to McMaster on 9 February, "is that Larkin did not tender. It is surmised that he could not raise the capital. Our opposition appears to be Brearley and Ulm, who will jointly form a company to be called Commonwealth Airways — if successful."[2]

New England Airways (started by G.A. Robinson from Lismore, New South Wales, in 1930) seemed, said Fysh, to be the other opposition. "Our chances now appear better than ever but, of course, we do not know what is in the tenders."

Qantas Empire Airways had tendered with five of the new DH86 cabin biplanes, powered with four Gipsy VI engines. In construction its forty-six-foot fuselage was, technically, an unobstructed plywood box with spruce stiffening and fabric outer covering. Its wings had a span of sixty-four feet six inches and were of two-spar wooden construction with the engines mounted on the lower wing. Empty weight was 6,000 pounds and it could carry ten passengers plus a crew of two at a cruising speed of 145 miles per hour.

The tender price submitted for the Singapore–Brisbane main trunk service and the Charleville–Cootamundra terminator was two shillings and eleven pence a mile, reducing in the fifth year by six pence a mile, requiring for the five-year term of the contract a total subsidy of £339,486. (A tender was also submitted for the short, northern branch line between Cloncurry and Normanton at two shillings and four pence a mile, reducing to two shillings and two pence.)

Edgar Johnston, as controller of civil aviation, was a

186

member of the committee charged with reporting on the tenders. (The others were the finance secretary, T.J. Thomas, as chairman; the assistant secretary, Department of Defence, M.M. Maguire; and the secretary of the Contract Board, A.S.V. Smith.) Johnston advised Fysh that the committee expected to complete their consideration of the tenders in a month, with the final decision resting with a Cabinet subcommittee.

In the period of waiting, there were strident attacks on almost everybody by the Air Convention interests. "A large section of the Australian Press", they charged, "was continuing to provide space and prominence to overseas propaganda calculated to enhance the prospects of the Imperial Airways–Qantas combine securing the new air mail contracts, regardless of the lowest tenderer." Officialdom, it said, had prepared tender forms "giving tremendous advantage to de Havilland aeroplanes — whose payloads, speeds and ranges fit some of the sections like a glove".[2] The de Havilland Aircraft Company was accused of withholding prices and particulars of their aircraft "from at least one prospective tenderer", indicating "collusion".

Under the heading "Symptoms of Graft", the Air Convention *Bulletin* charged that there were rigged tender forms and contracts by negotiation; deputations and requests for public inquiries were ignored. "How, in the face of these and other unmentionable facts can we refrain from being suspicious of graft? We must assume the worst", it wrote.[3]

There was a more subtle, if quite proper, approach to the application of persuasion by Sir Charles Kingsford Smith. In a "personal" letter to Edgar Johnston on 20 February he wrote advising "definitely that I am associated with Robinson in his tender for the mail subsidy, and anything that can be done to help him will also help me. Naturally, old man, I am not suggesting you do not consider each tender on its merits." Then with even further disingenuousness he advised: "The *Southern Cross* will, incidentally, become a possible standby in the event of a shortage of Avro Xs on this section."[4]

McMaster, though by no means sure of the outcome of QEA, had no high opinion of the opposition and was scathing in a letter to Fysh on 2 March, about the motives behind the use of the *Southern Cross*.

There is no telling what will be done about the tenders, but it could hardly be imagined that the Ulm and Brearley lot would be considered for the Singapore–Brisbane section, or that the loose

187

arrangement between Robinson [New England Airways] and Kingsford Smith would be seriously considered — with three old machines and the old *Southern Cross*. There is no doubt they were hard pushed, to make use of loose sentiment when they included the *Southern Cross*.[5]

Charles Ulm, now under severe financial pressures, at once turned his energies, with characteristic realism, to possibilities quite unconnected with the airmail tenders. His old colleague, Kingsford Smith, was in better financial shape. He had not only won a knighthood but, in October, received a personal telephone call from Prime Minister Lyons advising him that the government had decided to make him a grant of £3,000 — free of income tax. Further, Kingsford Smith had accepted in the same month an appointment with the Vacuum Oil Company "in an advisory capacity on all matters pertaining to civil aviation". The salary, said press reports, "is believed to be considerable".[6] He had other irons in the fire. The aircraft built for him at Cockatoo Docks, Sydney, the *Codock*, had flown successfully and in March 1934, he visited New Zealand "for the flotation of a company to purchase this machine and place an order for three more", with the object of starting a trans-Tasman "Dominion Air Service".[7] By contrast Ulm, in a letter to Edgar Johnston on 6 March, wrote: "I have now to set about earning some cash and, quite frankly, could do with a job — for if I don't get it [he had lodged a tender for carrying out upper air meteorological flights] I shall probably have to start a barnstorming job." Just three days later he wrote again: "I am having a particularly rough spin."[8] Edgar Johnston, who regarded Ulm as the outstanding business mind and administrator in commercial aviation of his day, could not help him and had to advise that his tender for the meteorological flights was unsuccessful.[9] He noted, he said, Ulm's interest in the Bourke–Adelaide service, for which tenders were expected shortly, and that "Ulm was going into the possibility of other overseas services". Ulm had completed, in February, his fourth flight across the Tasman in *Faith in Australia*. He contemplated a new Sydney–Brisbane service (and wrote to Fysh on 12 March thanking him for his offer of co-operation if this service commenced) and, with those "other overseas services in mind", he publicly expressed his opinion that a regular service across the Tasman was possible and that the right type of aircraft for it would soon be available.[10] His immediate interest, however, he told the *Sydney Morning Herald* on 19

February 1934, was "the tender for the air mail contract from Singapore to Brisbane and Cootamundra".

Despite all his financial pressures and business preoccupations, Ulm, with his wife, found time to comfort Brinsmead in the last days of his long semiparalysis and decline. They went out of their way, wrote Fysh, to give him friendship, care, and attention and to ease his sad condition. Brinsmead died on 11 March.[11]

The minister for defence, Sir George Pearce, had announced publicly that he was not going to accept personal responsibility for the letting of the airmail contracts. The onus would, he said, be on Cabinet as a whole. ("I do not altogether blame him", Harman wrote to Fysh. "There will be a lot of mud-slinging when the contracts are let.")[12] The necessity to get Cabinet together, however, had caused delays while the recent return of the prime minister from England raised possibilities of new influences and doubts in Fysh's mind. It was his main worry that Lyons might be under the impression that QEA would be swallowed up by Imperial Airways. In a letter on 23 March to director W.A. Watt he wrote that if the prime minister expressed such an opinion "the outcome may be most damaging to our cause". He thought the prime minister would be likely to advise Cabinet on the matter, and possibly attend Cabinet meetings that considered the tenders. "Unless the issue is more or less clear cut in our favour," wrote Fysh, "his attitude will mark the turning point as to which way things will swing."[13]

On 19 April 1934 it was the prime minister himself, J.A. Lyons, who announced the outcome. Qantas Empire Airways was awarded the Singapore–Brisbane service. The departmental technical committee report, made public, revealed that there had been only one other tenderer for the overseas route — the Brearley and Ulm combination. (Both tenderers had proposed the DH86 aircraft.)

Qantas, said the report, had submitted four alternative tenders for the Singapore–Darwin section, Ulm and Brearley six. The lowest of all these tenders came from Qantas (£207,248) but offered the use of aeroplanes capable of cruising at only 119 miles per hour and was rejected. Analysis of the remaining tenders for Singapore–Darwin also favoured Qantas, who tendered £228,478 using aircraft with a cruising speed of 145 miles per hour. This compared with a tender £44,483 higher from Ulm and Brearley for this sector, said the report.

Analysis of tenders for the eastern division (Darwin–Brisbane–Cootamundra) also favoured Qantas Empire Airways, who quoted £180,764 for the five years. Tenders were also received for this division from New England Airways and from Ulm and Brearley.

For the southern Charleville–Cootamundra section alone, tenders were received from New England Airways and Aircraft Pty. Ltd. (Butler Air Transport).

There was, however, a surprise in the report of the technical committee. No request, it said, had been made in the conditions of tendering for a combination of the Singapore–Darwin and Darwin–Brisbane–Cootamundra services; but both QEA and Ulm–Brearley had submitted combined tenders. Examination of the combined tenders, said the committee report, at once disclosed that the acceptance of a combined tender would be of the utmost advantage to the Commonwealth.

The lowest tender for the combined sections came from Qantas Empire Airways (£315,700) but was rejected because of the 119 mile per hour cruising speed offered. However, the next lowest tender, using aircraft cruising at 145 miles per hour, also came from QEA (£339,486). The lowest tender submitted by Ulm and Brearley for the combined section was for £351,379. (The highest of all the QEA alternative tenders for the two sections was £596,804; the highest from Brearley and Ulm was £821,687.)

Qantas, then, won with its combined tender for Singapore–Darwin–Brisbane–Cootamundra of £339,486 over five years. The committee pointed out that if it had not considered the combined tenders submitted, it would have recommended acceptance of the four separate Qantas Empire Airways tenders.

If, said the committee report, it had disregarded the important factors of speed and service of aircraft and had recommended acceptance of the two lowest tenders received for the separate sections of the route, the combined amount would have totalled £340,806. By accepting the combined tender there had been the benefit of high speed, high efficiency aircraft as well as a saving of £1,320.

The committee's recommendations were not, in fact, adopted fully by Cabinet. The QEA combined tender for Singapore–Darwin–Brisbane was accepted, but the southern section from Charleville to Cootamundra was awarded to C.A. Butler. The cost was some two thousand pounds higher using Butler but, said the prime minister, was justified because it introduced a second operator.[14] (Butler tendered with DH84 Dragon aircraft. He was well known for his one-man flying operations in country districts and for his record solo flight from England to Australia.)

The aircraft specified in the winning QEA tender, the DH86, was the fastest British airliner in existence and the fastest four-engined airliner in the world. It was also, of course, the first four-engined aircraft to be used in Australian aviation. Compared with the twin-engined American DC3, however, it was slow.

For Norman Brearley the government announcement was doubly disastrous. West Australian Airways not only failed in its overseas bid but also lost its Perth–Katherine service to MacRobertson Miller Aviation Company (headed by the oldest living Australian aviation pioneer, H.C. Miller and founded, in 1927, in partnership with Sir MacPherson Robertson). Further, WAA's Perth–Adelaide subsidy contract had expired on 1 April 1934 (though WAA continued to operate it by contracting with the PMG Department to carry mails, and by its reasonable passenger traffic revenue).

Neither Ulm nor Kingsford Smith won anything from the government decisions. Kingsford Smith told the press they were a serious injustice; the Australian airmen "who have been primarily responsible for the development of aviation in Australia have been overlooked", he said. "Apparently my tender was not even considered."[15] Ulm, in a personal letter to Edgar Johnston, said he wished the new service every success. "I trust the public will support it generously." He thanked Johnston for his sympathy at his own failure to get one or more of the contracts. He did not, he said, think the government meant to reflect on the ability of Australian airmen.[16] In a press statement he said: "Probably cost was the most important factor considered."[17]

The contract for the short Melbourne–Hobart sector was awarded to Tasmanian Aerial Services, formed in 1932 by the Holyman brothers, Ivan and Victor (grandsons of the founder of the Tasmanian shipping company, William Holyman & Sons Pty. Ltd.). They were, in combination with four other major shipping interests, soon to emerge as the biggest single force in Australia's internal air services.

For the new Qantas Empire Airways it was a heady moment. "I have been simply inundated with messages of congratulations", Rudder wrote to Fysh. "The win seems popular and so far the press is entirely friendly."[18] From the

191

other side of the continent, on his farm in Western Australia, came a simple telegram from Paul McGinness, "Congratulations your success in securing the contract. Best wishes future."[19]

Both the prime minister and the minister for defence expressed government satisfaction at the tender prices. Sir George stated that under the new system, route mileage would increase by some 46 per cent (from 5,529 to 8,070 miles) and annual mileage by 95 per cent (from 551,216 to 1,078,480 miles a year) while annual subsidy would rise by only 9 per cent (to £102,263 from £93,361). With anticipated airmail revenues taken into account, average net annual cost would, he said, reduce by nearly 30 per cent.[20]

The first full board meeting of Qantas Empire Airways Ltd. was held in Challis House, Martin Place, Sydney on 1 May.[21] Present were McMaster, Rudder, Loxton, Fysh, and Watt, with F.J. Smith "represented by proxy in favour of W.E. Johnson". Dismore, secretary of Imperial Airways, was present by invitation. It was moved that the formal contract for the carrying out of the new service be signed and sealed on behalf of the company. Hudson Fysh "intimated that tentative dates had been agreed with the Controller of Aviation for commencement of the overseas service from Brisbane on 11 December and from Singapore on 17 December".[22]

On 19 May 1934 a circular letter to shareholders of the Queensland and Northern Territory Aerial Services Limited informed them that Qantas Empire Airways Limited had been formed with a nominal capital of £200,000 and a paid-up capital of £120,000 "which is being subscribed equally by the Queensland and Northern Territory Aerial Services Limited and Imperial Airways Limited. Our shareholders will remain as shareholders in the Queensland and Northern Territory Aerial Services Limited and they will participate in any profits that may accrue to 'Q.A.N.T.A.S.' from the operations of Qantas Empire Airways Limited."[23] The paid-up capital of Q.A.N.T.A.S., the letter concluded, was then £39,430.17s.11d.

Qantas senior pilot Lester Brain left for England on 23 May to visit de Havillands and, on its completion and test, fly out the first of the QEA DH86 aircraft. Brain stood high in the estimation of the company. "Your work", Fysh had written to him only the month before, "has contributed greatly to the high standards maintained by Qantas. It is this all round standard that has placed us in our present position."[24] (Those standards were sometimes maintained under severe pressures. Fysh paid tribute to pilot Russell Tapp at much the same time noting that Tapp had flown 123 hours 30 minutes during the past month, "the highest number of hours flown during any one month by a Qantas pilot".[25]) Fysh himself departed for Singapore on 14 June, flying by Moth up the route to Darwin to inspect all landing grounds and facilities. He took the

steamer to Sourabaya and the KLM air service on to Singapore where, he told the press, he would "investigate the progress being made in providing facilities for inaugurating the Singapore–Australia service".[26]

The Qantas Puss Moth at Fergus McMaster's property, Moscow, near Winton, on 15 June 1934. McMaster can be seen on the right. Hudson Fysh and Arthur Baird were making a survey of landing grounds in the Northern Territory to determine any necessary changes before the overseas services began in December.

As these preparations for the new airmail service gathered momentum, the Dutch service KLM foreshadowed the competition that Fysh had anticipated. Albert Plesman, KLM head, announced in London on 2 July that his company intended to compete in the air service to Australia and "would seek an equitable division of traffic with Imperial Airways".[27] KLM aircraft were fully loaded on the run to Batavia, he said, and "there was plenty of traffic for two services to Australia". The Australian government was quick to respond. Extension of the Royal Dutch Air Mail service from the East Indies to Darwin, said the postmaster-general (Parkhill), would be a matter of arrangement between governments.[28]

Lester Brain had his first flight in England in the new DH86 type on 3 July and reported that he expected to take delivery of the first QEA aircraft on 1 September. Hudson Fysh, returning from his inspection of landing grounds between Singapore and Brisbane, reported that "everything is going smoothly so far as ground organisation is concerned. There is nothing sensational or new I can say."[29] To his directors, Fysh was able to report good results for the financial year to 30 June 1934 — a profit of £4,616, the third highest in the history of the company, representing 11.7 per cent on paid-up capital.

The public appetite for excitement and achievement in aviation matters had, for the decade since Cobham's first flight from England, been well served and increasingly stimulated. *Aircraft* magazine had described 1933 as a golden year in aviation.[30] An Italian Air Force pilot, Warrant Officer Agello, in five sprints across a measured mile, had achieved an average speed of 423.76 miles per hour in a Macchi seaplane. Two French pilots, Maurice Rossi and Paul Codos, extended the nonstop distance record by flying from New York to Rayak, Syria, covering the 5,657 miles in just under fifty-five hours. Kingsford Smith had broken C.W.A. Scott's record from England to Australia in his Percival Gull, taking seven days four hours forty-three minutes. Ulm, in *Faith in Australia*, lowered this time a week later, to six days seventeen hours fifty-six minutes (though Kingsford Smith retained the record for a solo flight). The US airman, one-eyed Wiley Post, had cut the record for an around the world flight, via the Atlantic and Europe, to seven days eighteen hours forty-nine minutes. Public fascination with every kind of aviation achievement seemed endless, and was matched by men equally fascinated with the risks and challenges that the new element of the air offered. Jim Mollison crossed the South Atlantic in a Puss Moth in a solo record of eighteen hours from Senegal to Brazil. The Frenchman Jean Mermoz, made the same crossing but with a crew of six in a twelve-ton trimotor aircraft in fourteen hours and two minutes. Speeds and distances conquered were not the only criteria to compel public attention. Gustav Lemoine, of France, set a new altitude record of 44,817 feet. Soviet pilot Euseyev claimed a record for a parachute jump, falling from 23,400 feet to 500 feet before pulling the rip-cord. The Marquess of Clydesdale and Flight Lt. D.F. McIntyre circled the peak of Mount Everest and, reported *Aircraft*, Flight Lieutenant Boscola of Italy raised his own record for upside down flying to five hours fifty-one minutes.

In Australia, the battle for the contract to initiate the nation's first regular overseas air links had provided media and public with aviation drama spiced with personal and political conflicts. There was now, in the wake of government decisions, a temporary lull. It was filled by preparations for what Sir Keith Smith, second in command of the first-ever flight from England to Australia in the Vimy, described as the most important air race ever organized — the Centenary Air Race from Mildenhall, Suffolk, England, to Melbourne.[31] Arranged as part of the centenary celebrations of Victoria, the prize money was provided by Sir MacPherson Robertson (who also donated £100,000 as a centenary gift to the City of Melbourne).

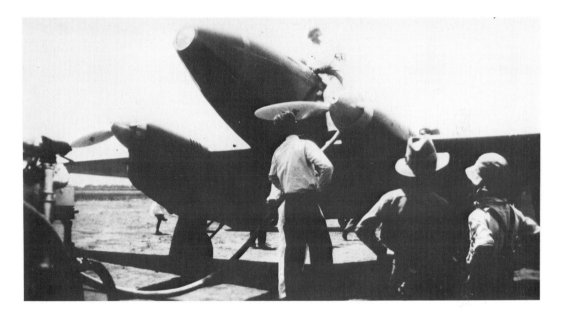

The Centenary Air Race attracted world interest. It not only challenged its entrants with the necessity for high and sustained speed in competition with one another, but with the conquest under these pressures, of immense distances. As a race to the other side of the world, it concentrated international attention on Australia, and on the new air route that would link it to England.

The risks to the lives of the many aviators who had, with varying motives, pioneered the new air routes and tackled each new aviation record as it was broken, were well recognized. Though risk was central to the public drama of their exploits, it was also of deep concern to many commentators and administrators. Yet for some of those whose careers were irrevocably committed to aviation, and whose public reputa-

The DH88 Comet racing aircraft, G-AOSS *Grosvenor House* which won the speed section of the 1934 Centenary Air Race, being refuelled at Longreach on 22 October 1934. The English pilot was C.W.A. Scott, who had flown for Qantas from 1927 to 1930.

The KLM Douglas DC2, winner of the handicap section of the 1934 Centenary Air Race from England to Melbourne at Darwin on 5 November 1934. The aircraft was returning to Europe.

tions required regular reinforcement from their admirers, there seemed no alternative to the pursuit of recognition and the acceptance of living with risk. For some who were already heroes, and who had already made the flights that would ennoble their memories there was, in this need to maintain the stature they had won, something of the inevitability of tragedy. Both Charles Ulm and Kingsford Smith were to fall victims to these forces.

Ulm, busy with other enterprises, was not involved in the Air Race. A new company, Great Pacific Airways, had been registered in Sydney with E.T. Fisk, head of Amalgamated Wireless Ltd. as its chairman; Ulm was the only initial co-director.[32] He had also renewed his plans for trans-Atlantic and trans-Pacific flights and wrote to Edgar Johnston on 24 August that he had placed an order in England for an Airspeed Envoy aircraft powered by two Lynx engines. "I am leaving for England next Thursday, the 30th," he wrote, "and hope to make the flight early in November." He told Johnston that he was making arrangements to sell the broadcasting rights of the flight and asked him for letters of introduction "to the effect that I am a decent bloke in good standing in the aviation industry out here". Johnston willingly complied.[33] Kingsford Smith had entered for the race, with a Lockheed Altair aircraft, but withdrew before it began. (Edgar Johnston had advised him that only aircraft certified under the requirements of the Paris Convention could enter for the race and the Altair, which had not been, was ineligible.) He, too, planned a trans-Pacific flight (for October–November), but in a west to east direction, departing from Brisbane.

It was in the atmosphere of prerace excitement that Qantas suffered the first of two major disasters. On 3 October, the DH50J *Atalanta* took off from Longreach at 5:40 A.M. on the scheduled mail flight to Winton with two passengers. The pilot, N. Chapman, had joined Qantas in May and had been selected as one of those to fly the DH86 aircraft on the Singapore route. He circled the homestead of Fergus McMaster's property, Moscow, dropped a parcel of papers, and continued towards Winton, flying low; he never arrived, and a search was instituted. The burnt-out remains were later sighted from the air by pilot Eric Donaldson; there was no sign of life. Donaldson returned to Winton, where he picked up Fergus McMaster and flew back to the site of the crash, landing near the wreckage. "I did not want to see the bodies," he wrote in his report, "so Mr McMaster offered to provide an exact description of their position for Civil Aviation before their removal."[34] The cause of the crash was a mystery.[35]

Arthur Baird, in his report after carefully examining the burnt-out wreckage, said he did not consider it the result of an attempted landing; the engine, he noted, was running at the time of the crash. (Fysh later wrote to Chapman's widow: "There is no authentic evidence whatever which throws any blame on Norman. We mourn the loss of a good officer."[36]) It was a severe and public setback.

On 13 October, after a leisurely flight of nineteen days from England, Lester Brain landed the first of the QEA DH86 aircraft at Brisbane. With less than two months before the start of the Singapore service, there were now problems with pilot

The remains of Qantas's DH50J *Atalanta* which crashed on 3 October 1934 at Vindex station, south of Winton, on a regular flight from Longreach.

A large crowd gathers at Archerfield on 13 October 1934 to see Qantas Empire Airways' first DH86 at the conclusion of its delivery flight from England.

numbers, following the loss of Chapman. "Having extreme difficulty procure experienced DH50 pilot. Required [for] two months. Appreciate urgent assistance", Fysh wired the Civil Aviation Branch on 10 October.[37] On the same day G.U. "Scotty" Allan accepted a position as pilot for the Singapore route on the big DH86 aircraft. Far more experienced in long overseas flights than the other Qantas pilots, he was a strong and valuable addition to the team. His contract with the New South Wales Aero Club expired on 26 October, and he was offered an initial salary of £650 a year and required to fly as required on the Queensland routes until the start of the overseas service. It was the beginning of a long association in which Scotty Allan would rise to the position of assistant general manager of Qantas.

The requirement for a DH50 pilot was filled on a temporary basis by W.H. (Bill) Crowther, an instructor from the

Queensland Aero Club who had been taught to fly by Lester Brain. A former jackeroo, whose interest in aviation had been stirred when he had galloped his horse to the railway line near Charleville to sight Ross and Keith Smith fly south in the Vimy from Darwin in 1919, Crowther stayed to become one of the best known and most senior of QEA pilots.[38]

Lester Brain, as chief pilot of QEA, had by now accumulated 6,694 flying hours. Not far behind in flying time was Russell Tapp, with 5,435 hours. Scotty Allan had logged 4,000 hours. These were the men who were to command the four-engined DH86 aircraft on the Singapore service. Eric Donaldson, in charge at Cloncurry and flying the Aerial Medical Service, had flown over 4,000 hours while Arthur Baird, though appointed works manager to the new QEA, had 2,563 flying hours to his credit.[39] Hudson Fysh, with five minutes short of 1,700 hours logged, was nearing the end of

The passenger cabin of Qantas's DH83 Fox Moth looking from the right-hand side, taken at Archerfield in February 1934. Doors on both sides of the cabin permitted air ambulance staff to lift patients into the aircraft on a stretcher. This was an improvement on the DH50 where a stretcher had to be placed in the cabin first and the patient then lifted in by hand.

199

The last new aircraft type to be introduced by Qantas before Qantas Empire Airways took over all flying operations was the DH83 Fox Moth. VH-URI was placed in service in February 1934, replacing the DH50 on the Flying Doctor service based at Cloncurry.

his career as a pilot (and would fly less than 3 hours in 1935).[40]

Another pilot of great distinction, P.G. Taylor (later to be knighted), had agreed to join the Qantas Empire Airways team. He was then preparing, with Sir Charles Kingsford Smith, for their great flight across the Pacific in the single-engined *Lady Southern Cross* (which left Brisbane on 22 October and arrived in San Francisco on 4 November). Taylor had agreed to return to Australia from England either as pilot or accompanying the third DH86.[41]

To allow for staff expansion and increased traffic, Qantas moved from its offices at the Wool Exchange Building to bigger premises at 43 Creek Street, Brisbane. Amongst its less glamorous preparations for the expansion of business was the appointment of a chief accountant. Selected by Imperial Airways in London, after a request from Qantas, he was an Australian from Dubbo, New South Wales. He had worked in London, Paris, and Rotterdam and was in Berlin adding to his international experience with a finance firm when chosen by Imperial Airways. He spent some months with them gaining experience of airline matters and was regarded by his peers as able but abrasively Australian. When he left England by sea for Australia, Imperial Airways were uncertain of his intentions and in some doubt that he would actually take up his appointment with QEA.[42] His name was Cedric Oban Turner, and he was to have more direct effect and influence on the emergence of Qantas as a major world airline than any other single person.

On 18 October, five days after the arrival in Brisbane of the

first DH86 airliner, the Centenary Air Race started. Amid great public excitement and attention, the speed section was won by C.W.A. Scott and T. Campbell Black in their de Havilland Comet. Their time from England to Melbourne was seventy hours fifty-four minutes. To Darwin, it was a mere fifty-two hours thirty-four minutes. There was immediate comparison with the twelve-day schedule for the England–Australia airmail service and a flood of public criticism. "With exquisite if unconscious humour," wrote *The Bulletin*, "this [schedule] was published while Scott's Comet was flying from Mildenhall to Darwin."[43] The Dutch airliner (a DC2) that took part in the race, *The Bulletin* continued, flew out to Melbourne in three days eighteen hours, which included nineteen stops and a ten-hour delay caused by storm. "This achievement", it concluded, "has made the Commonwealth's twelve day schedule look ridiculous, and even the bureaucracy admits that something will have to be done about it." In London, *The Times* called for Britain to do better.[44] "The Empire Airmails", said an editorial, "should observe schedules comparable with America's most prominent

Capt. W.H. Crowther, about 1935 (left).

Capt. R.B. Tapp, about 1935.

201

airlines, but at least two million pounds must be spent to equip routes to enable night flying." The London *Daily Telegraph* commented: "It is all a question of cost. The British subsidies are very low compared with the Dutch and American. Imperial Airway's twelve-and-a-half day service to Brisbane will not satisfy public opinion for a moment longer than the time required for its replacement."[45] Sir Eric Geddes, chairman of Imperial Airways, responded that the company did have plans for a seven-day service to Australia. "Imperial Airways", he said, "is not going to be frightened off its policy of steady and efficient progress by any air race performance."[46] Speed in itself was not, in fact, the basis of Imperial Airway's policy. Britain's international air services were operated primarily to maintain air communications between parts of the British Commonwealth. Circuitous routes and short, uneconomic stage lengths with numerous stops were often deliberately operated to implement government policy for meeting "the needs of the people of the sparsely settled portions of the Commonwealth to whom air transport has proved such a blessing".[47]

There was, of course, no possibility of any immediate change to the airmail schedule. Though critics persistently pointed to the 200 mile per hour speed of the Douglas aircraft, Geddes countered that in actual airline operation between New York and Chicago it averaged 164 miles per hour. The DH86, by contrast, cruised at 145 miles per hour but had four engines compared with the twin-engined Douglas. For over-water operations both Imperial Airways and Qantas insisted on four engines. There was, wrote Fysh, no other aircraft in the world at the time to rival the DH86 for its planned role.

Qantas and Imperial Airways had agreed that de Havilland could sell the DH86 type to the winner of the Australian government contract for the over-water route between Melbourne and Tasmania, the Holymans. The first of two DH86s ordered by them, and named *Miss Hobart*, had been shipped out from England and assembled at Point Cook, Victoria. It made its first flight on the route across Bass Strait linking Hobart, Launceston, and Melbourne, on 1 October 1934. The Holyman DH86 aircraft was similar to those of QEA but had only one pilot's seat and one set of controls. (The QEA aircraft, with a different nose, had two pilot's seats and two sets of controls.) On 19 October, on the sea crossing between Launceston and Melbourne with G.E.M. Jenkins as pilot and nine passengers onboard, the *Miss Hobart* disap-

peared. On board also was Captain V.V. Holyman, the company's chief pilot and traffic manager. Air and sea searches found no trace of wreckage, though later a seat was washed up at Waratah Bay, some ten miles from the last position report transmitted from the aircraft.

For Qantas, the tragedy and the consequent public apprehension and concern had come at a critical time in their preparations to introduce the DH86 on the Darwin–Singapore route. The Timor Sea crossing of 512 miles was then the longest regular over-water route in the world and, though their contract with the government specified that no passengers were to be carried for the first three months on this section, the blow to confidence from the *Miss Hobart* mystery was severe. The Commonwealth Air Accidents Investigation Committee met in public sessions to hear evidence on the disaster.

The committee was actually in session in Sydney when even more devastating news came through. The second Qantas DH86, on the very last leg of its delivery flight from London, had crashed with total loss of life after leaving Longreach for Brisbane in the early morning of 15 November.

Again there was shock, bewilderment, and mystery. In both cases it was obvious that weather had played no part. It seemed reasonable, with four-engined machines, to doubt that

Miss Hobart, the first DH86 of Holyman Airways at Point Cook RAAF station, Victoria in late September 1934. VH-URN was the second DH86 to be built; the initial four were single-pilot aircraft but all subsequent DH86s were completed with side-by-side seating for captain and first officer. The *Miss Hobart* was sent to Australia by sea, and crashed into Bass Strait on 19 October 1934.

203

engine failure had caused either crash. In each case, the pilot in command was highly experienced. Indeed, the Qantas DH86 had been flown from England by R.A. Prendergast, who had commanded the *Astraea* on its Australian trip.

The Air Accidents Investigation Committee suspended their inquiry into the loss of the *Miss Hobart* to concentrate on the Longreach crash, and then report on both. The DH86 was at once withdrawn from flying in Australia pending the committee's recommendations.[48]

The wreckage of VH-USG, QEA's second DH86, which crashed soon after take-off from Longreach on 15 November 1934 on the last sector of its delivery flight from England. A spare engine which was being carried in the passenger cabin can be seen alongside the fuselage. Note the position of the tail fin — the forward section of the vertical tail — which has pivoted ninety degrees to the right. Failure of the forward attachment on the tail fin was suspected to have caused the crash.

Two kangaroo shooters, breakfasting a few miles from Longreach, had seen the last moments of the Qantas DH86. As it had flown towards them in the early sunlight, it began a slow flat turn to the right. The turn tightened and the speed fell off as the aircraft went into a flat spin, rotating rapidly and losing height. It hit the dry ground some two hundred yards from their camp. Prendergast, his co-pilot and wireless operator W.V. Creetes and engineer F.R. Charlton were killed immediately. A passenger, Mr "Bunny" Broadfoot, Shell Company representative, died soon afterwards.[49] The news was telephoned to Longreach from nearby Barsdale sheep station. Scotty Allan and Qantas engineer Jack Avery were on the scene soon after the police and ambulance. Lester Brain and Arthur Baird arrived from Brisbane in the afternoon. Officials from the Civil Aviation Branch began immediately an intense and protracted inquiry.[50]

All plans for the start of the new airmail service on 10 December were, on that clear morning, thrown into confusion. The starting date, however, was important to the government, as well as to Qantas and Imperial Airways. Not only was it the anniversary of the first England–Australia flight by Ross and Keith Smith, but also, elaborate plans had been made for the opening of the service by HRH, the Duke of Gloucester, then on a royal visit to Australia. On the day following the crash, after a telephone conversation between Fysh and Imperial Airways' air superintendent in London, H.G. Brackley, it was pointed out that Imperial Airways had sufficient resources in aircraft to adhere to the planned schedules, even if all DH86 machines remained temporarily unavailable.[51] A few days later the minister for defence, R.A. Parkhill (who had taken over from Sir George Pearce on 12 October) announced that 10 December remained the date for the official commencement of the England–Australia airmail service.[52] Imperial Airways had agreed to operate the section from Singapore to Darwin using their four-engined Armstrong Whitworth *Atalanta*-type aircraft, while Qantas Empire Airways would carry the mail between Darwin and Brisbane using DH61 and DH50J aircraft from the old Qantas fleet.[53]

On 19 November, the Brisbane *Courier-Mail* reported an interview with Capt. P.G. Taylor, still at the time engaged to join the new Qantas service. "I read with deepest regret", said Taylor, "of the double tragedy in which two planes crashed in reasonably good weather for no apparent reason. I arrived in England today in furtherance of an arrangement to leave for Singapore immediately to enter the Qantas Empire service. Now I have no plans." In the same interview he praised US aircraft. "The American planes are far ahead of the British in speed and safety although in comfort they are inferior."[54]

To Hudson Fysh on 21 November Taylor cabled that he regarded the second DH86 accident as sufficient proof of the unsoundness of the aircraft. The government, he said, should suspend the service and eliminate the type. "Respectfully advise will not on principle fly DH86 under any circumstances."[55] His telegram, wrote Fysh, was about the last straw.

"From Tasmania to Longreach in Central Queensland and now, back to Brisbane, the members of the Air Accidents Investigations Committee have been rushed by train and aeroplane", reported the Brisbane *Courier-Mail*.[56] The crash site at Longreach and the remains of the airliner there were exhaustively analyzed. The DH86 that Lester Brain had flown out from England was examined on the ground and tested vigorously in the air. "The machine was put through abrupt manoeuvres", said the *Courier-Mail*.[57] "It was throttled back to two engines, the port and starboard engines being cut off alternatively, and corrections were made with the rudder and the variable fin to counteract the torque occasioned by this." It was this fin post and the controls and surfaces attached to it that were most under suspicion. The whole of the fin (to which the rudder was attached) could itself be moved to assist directional stability. Arthur Baird believed that fin post and fin had failed. Lester Brain and Scotty Allan concluded that the main factor had been loss of directional stability following a load distribution in the aircraft which placed the centre of gravity aft of the normal position. In the DH86 remaining, the fin post fittings were strengthened, the rudder trim tab adjusted, and the centre of gravity position carefully monitored when loading the aircraft.[58]

Hard on this second DH86 disaster, and with continuing newspaper coverage of the evidence given to the committee, came news on 4 December of the disappearance of Charles Ulm in his Airspeed Envoy aircraft, *Stella Australis*, between the United States and Honolulu. Though the loss of the air-

Charles Ulm — second from left — with two American business associates and his co-pilot, G. Littlejohn (right) pose beside their Airspeed Envoy before take-off for Honolulu from San Francisco in December 1934. This was the last known photograph of Ulm.

craft itself was certain, the confirmation of Ulm's death followed a long and painful period of uncertainty. "A charter vessel was dispatched to search the islands between Honolulu and Midway for at least a month", Edgar Johnston was advised in a letter from Ulm's Sydney office. "Mr Ulm", it said, "must have known for at least an hour before that it would be necessary to force land in the sea. The manufacturers of the Envoy have cabled that it will float indefinitely. We are hopeful that we will receive ... good news before very long."[59]

That news never came and, after the long wait, Edgar Johnston had to write to Mrs Ulm: "I am afraid . . . that the time has now arrived when we must abandon all hope ... Charles' interests were wholeheartedly in flying and all of us had grown to regard him as a leader who would have done greater things for aviation in the future. To me he was a very dear friend."[60] Mrs Ulm replied: "I simply cannot contemplate the future without him. Still, the thought that his life was worthwhile may be a big consolation to me."[61] Kingsford Smith expressed the perplexity of all those who knew Ulm at the possible cause of his old colleague's death. He wrote to Johnston:

Poor old Charles Ulm came to a tragic end. It is impossible from the scarcity of information available to form any very definite opinion of how it all happened, but it looks as though they were somewhat uncertain of their position throughout the flight, and were relying on picking up the wireless beam at Honolulu. Whether their uncertainty of position was due to bad weather conditions or to laxity or inefficiency in navigation I do not know, but it seems almost inconceivable that with Charles in charge the latter could be the cause.[62]

Charles Ulm had played a sustained and constructive role throughout the long negotiations for amalgamation of Australian National Airways, West Australian Airways, and Qantas. Without the dominance, both in size and manner, of WAA and the uncertainty felt by Ulm, Fysh, and McMaster towards Brearley, that merger, which at one stage seemed certain, may have succeeded. For Hudson Fysh it would have meant, as he acknowledged, his own rapid and certain elimination. For Ulm it would as certainly have meant a senior and central position in Australian commercial aviation and, with challenges sufficient even for Ulm, no necessity for the final flight that ended his life.

Archerfield, on 10 December 1934, Hudson Fysh escorts His Royal Highness, Prince Henry, Duke of Gloucester on an inspection of the DH61 which operated the first service by Qantas Empire Airways. A.E. Rudder, vice-chairman of QEA, is behind the duke and Sir Leslie Wilson, the governor of Queensland, is visible in the background between Mr Rudder and Capt. Lester Brain who flew *Diana* on the inaugural service.

On 10 December 1934, two years after the report of the inter-departmental committee on Australian air routes, His Royal Highness, Prince Henry, Duke of Gloucester inaugurated the first airmail service between Australia and England. At a ceremony at Archerfield aerodrome, Brisbane, the duke, with a pair of gold scissors, formally cut a length of ribbon linking the QEA airliner, *Diana*, with the official stand. It was a ceremony first proposed by Edgar Johnston, with some lightness of heart, in a letter to Hudson Fysh six months before. The original date for the start of the service had been 11 December. Johnston had written: "I learn that the Prince is probably leaving Brisbane [at the conclusion of his Australian tour] on 10 December, the day before that fixed for the opening of the service. Appreciating, however, the wonderful advertisement it would be and what a fine gesture . . . for the Prince to despatch the first mail . . . I think we could, if necessary, arrange for the first trip to run a day earlier." He did not know, he said, what form the function would take, but added: "One idea would be to get him to, say, cut a ribbon, releasing the first plane for her journey. It seems a bit

208

ridiculous but I cannot think of anything better on the spur of the moment."[63] His suggestion prevailed. The prime minister, Joseph Lyons, and the minister for defence, Archdale Parkhill, made appropriate speeches. The duke cut the ribbon and remarked, with royal wit: "Mr Brain is kindly doing duty for us as Father Christmas."[64]

Some minutes later at 10:00 A.M., the DH61 *Diana*, flown by Brain, and DH50 *Hippomenes*, with Russell Tapp, took off. They carried 1,267 pounds, 4.75 ounces of air mail in fifty bags on QEA flight number W1. Just 209 miles on they landed at Roma, where they met the *Apollo* on the last inward air-mail service of the old Qantas from Camooweal. They also met Fergus McMaster, who had missed the Brisbane ceremony. The *Apollo*, flown by Scotty Allan, had been due in Brisbane the day before but heavy dust storms had held it up at Longreach. It left for Charleville on the morning of 10 December reached there at noon and then went on to Roma to await the arrival of the overseas mail. At Roma, Scotty Allan changed aircraft and took over the onward flight to Darwin of *Hippomenes* from Russell Tapp, who was ill. Tapp, however,

Lester Brain places a symbolic mail bag in the mail locker of *Diana*, at Archerfield on 10 December 1934. In reality the two aircraft were loaded to capacity, with fifty bags of mail between them.

209

Passengers and crew of the last service by Queensland and Northern Territory Aerial Services at Roma on 10 December 1934. Fergus McMaster is third from right with pilot Scotty Allan to his right. Bill Crowther who joined Qantas as a pilot on 15 October 1934 is second from the left.

This unique photograph shows the two aircraft (left and centre) operating the first Qantas Empire Airways service and the *Apollo* (right) which was making the last scheduled flight of Queensland and Northern Territory Aerial Services. *Apollo* with Fergus McMaster among its passengers had been due in Brisbane on 9 December but was delayed in Longreach by heavy dust storms.

took command of the inward flight to Brisbane by *Apollo*, and the last service of Queensland and Northern Territory Aerial Services Ltd., with McMaster on board, ended at Brisbane at ten minutes past five on 10 December 1934.

Q.A.N.T.A.S. had completed twelve years of continuous airline contracts and, from 10 December, now transferred these airline operations and its general activities to Qantas Empire Airways Ltd., in which it had equal partnership with Imperial Airways. The old Queensland and Northern Territory Aerial Services Ltd. was, from now on, a holding company in QEA. (This holding company will now be referred to as Q.A.N.T.A.S. to distinguish it from Qantas Empire Airways.)

Diana and *Hippomenes* flew on to pick up the southern mail at Charleville, where Butler had brought it from the New South Wales terminus at Cootamundra. Collecting more mail on their way north along the old Qantas route, they arrived at Darwin with a total of 55,967 items for transfer to the Imperial Airways aircraft, *Arethusa*. The mail reached Croydon airport, London, just after midday on 24 December 1934, fourteen days after its departure from Brisbane.

The DH84 carrying the first overseas airmails from the southern states arriving at Charleville on 10 December 1934. C.A. Butler, founder of Butler Air Transport piloted this first service which departed from Cootamundra, NSW earlier in the day.

For Fergus McMaster the missed ceremony was a small matter compared to a grave issue of confidence, involving both Imperial Airways and his own managing director Hudson Fysh, that now erupted. It brought forth the full force of his toughness and anger. Hudson Fysh, he learned, had for some time been corresponding on a personal basis with the managing director of Imperial Airways, Woods Humphery, on matters of fundamental importance to the future of QEA and to the interests of the shareholders and directors of Q.A.N.T.A.S. without advising his chairman about the issues involved.

Fysh had been admitted to the counsels of the great and had, with some innocence, fallen in with the conditions that were, implicitly, made the price of such confidentiality; he was enjoined to secrecy. That such secretiveness was a way of life with Imperial Airways was, paradoxically, no secret. From 1928 the company had deliberately pursued it as policy, main-

211

At Fanny Bay aerodrome, 10 December 1934, Australian officials meet the crew of the *Arethusa* who took the first Australian overseas airmails from Darwin to Singapore. Several of these Armstrong Whitworth AW15 airliners were chartered from Imperial by QEA while the DH86 aircraft bought by QEA for the Brisbane-Singapore service were grounded.

ly to protect itself from the competitive pressures of KLM.[65] Lord Brabazon (then Lt.Col. J.T.C. Moore) and others had attacked the airline's attitude in Parliament in the early thirties; Balfour had blamed its related high-handedness in India with so offending the Indians that no British service was able to operate there.

It had become evident that high mail surcharges had limited the volume of mail sent by air, and that this barrier would make impracticable the planned extension of the airline. So within this citadel of secrecy a bold plan was devised in 1932 by airline staff for the carriage, without surcharge, of all first class mail by air throughout the Empire. Woods Humphery put the proposal to his chairman, Sir Eric Geddes, who accepted it. Detailed estimates were drawn up and, in March 1933, Geddes submitted the scheme to Cabinet. It was imaginative, far reaching, costly, politically complex, and, through 1934, still secret. It also presupposed the financial support of the Dominions (excluding Canada) and, through the British government, their early acquiescence. Further, it was formulated and eventually submitted to the Dominions concerned without any prior consultation in the form of a British Government Blue Paper.[66] Edgar Johnston, when he read the proposals, saw the British intention as a pooling of resources in equipment and personnel that would put the supreme operational control of the through service to Australia under one company (Imperial Airways). The Indian and Australian companies, he said with sarcasm, would be "privileged to display their names and national registration marks on certain aircraft of the service's fleet".[67] The British proposal, in addition, involved the replacement of the new DH86 airliners so recently ordered by QEA by flying boats, whose operation over the considerable stretches of inaccessible country between Darwin and Townsville Edgar Johnston saw as "definitely undesirable".

These matters were the subject of the "personal" correspondence between Woods Humphery and Hudson Fysh.

On 26 September 1934, in a long letter of fourteen typed pages, marked "Strictly Personal and Confidential", Woods Humphery told Fysh of the background to Imperial Airways' plan to carry all first class Empire mail by air without surcharge.

> We have come to the conclusion that the surcharge air mail system has been a failure and could, in fact, never succeed. [The only way was] to obtain a sufficient volume to enable air transport operators to carry it at a cheap rate, and to carry the whole of the first class [letter mail] by air.

The first regular airmails from Britain are handed over by QEA Capt. Eric Donaldson to Toowoomba Post Office official, Mr E.J. Fallon (right), 21 December 1934.

213

It is necessary in this air service business to plan one's programme a long way ahead because planes take a long time to
build, particularly the large planes; and Government negotiations
. . . also take a very long time. With a change of Government
policy of such magnitude as this, it was necesary to plan a
thoroughly intensive propaganda campaign.

There are several reasons why we decided last winter to go all
out to try to convert the Government. First of all, our large fleet
— that is, our large aeroplanes — are coming nearer to their
obsolescence life and it is now necessary for us to think of their
replacement. As our present contract with the Government ends
in 1937, in respect of the Africa route, and in 1939 in respect of
the India and Singapore route, it seemed to us last year highly
desirable that we should ask the Government to make up its mind
as a matter of policy whether it wishes to carry on with the surcharge airmail system.

I will not bother you with all the moves and details . . . but
towards the end of last year the Cabinet set up a Cabinet Committee to enquire into this question. The Committee authorised the
Post Office and the Air Ministry to go into negotiations with us.
These were very complicated and very changeable. In fact they
were so changeable and uncertain that it was not only useless but
almost impossible to have kept you fully informed. The whole
matter was, and is still, strictly secret.

I must therefore bind you to the strictest secrecy in the matter
yourself, and would ask you at this stage not to communicate it
even to your Board, although I of course appreciate that you
would probably wish to mention it to your chairman — but I
would like to please impress upon him also the necessity for strict
secrecy.[68]

Woods Humphery next summarized the arguments
Imperial Airways had put to the British government for combining mail and passenger services, rather than providing
separate mail services by air. A combined service would,
Imperial Airways submitted, correct the imbalance of mails
from and to the United Kingdom and would provide a higher
frequency. "The Government," he told Fysh, "particularly
the Post Office, regard frequency of service as . . . definitely of
greater importance than speed. In order of importance the
Government places regularity first, frequency second and
speed third."

Imperial Airways had first, he continued, to determine the
actual amount of mail to be carried on the Australian, New
Zealand, and African routes.

The total quantity amounts to 1,650 tons outwards and 950 tons
homeward to the British Isles, including Canada and smaller
parts of the Empire not served by the Australia and Africa routes.
[In terms of ton-miles, and only including those parts of the

Empire served by the two main trunk routes we arrive at a total of
fourteen million ton-miles of mails to be carried per year.] From
these figures we have to arrive at the best compromise between
the size of the aircraft and the frequency of the service.

Frequency gave me one limiting factor . . . [There] must be at
least two services per week in each direction.

Altogether we worked out thirteen different schemes and had
seventeen different aeroplanes designed. Finally we came down to
an aircraft having a payload of about three and a half tons, and
having a total weight of 40,000 to 42,000 pounds. With this class
of aircraft there would be a frequency of five services a week each
way to India, three of which would extend to Singapore and two
of these would go on to Australia. We worked on Sydney being
the terminal.

Throughout our studies and talks with the Post Office and Air
Ministry . . . cheapness of operations was a factor of paramount
importance. Therefore we set down the hypothesis that the whole
fleet must circulate regularly back to the British Isles for major
repairs.

There would be a total of about twenty-four million ton-miles
per year of which fourteen million would be required for the carriage of letter mail. We came to the conclusion that the flying boat
had substantial advantages over the landplane for our purposes.
Therefore, our basic scheme allowed for the use of flying boats all
the way to Sydney.

I call it our basic scheme because there may be many modifications. It may be quite impractical to operate flying boats between
Darwin and Sydney, or the Commonwealth Government may
prefer that between Darwin and Sydney the service should be
operated by land planes.

Woods Humphery now turned to the position that Qantas
would, as Imperial Airways saw it, hold in this still-secret
scheme, with all its potential to affect the vital interests of the
new-born QEA.

If you accept the Singapore–Brisbane service mileage . . . as
being fair and reasonable participation by Q.E.A., then it
amounts to 993,000 miles per year, out of a total of seven and a
half million miles per year to be operated. We have estimated that
to work the seven and a half million miles per year will necessitate
about thirty-seven aircraft, so that Q.E.A.'s proportion of that
number would be five.

Woods Humphery now advanced for the first time the
Imperial Airways argument on fleet control that was to pro-
voke such bitter opposition from Edgar Johnston.

The next question is how would you operate? If you base those
five aircraft in Australia and work them between Sydney and
Singapore it rather cramps the flexibility of the fleet as a whole.
In addition, it must increase the cost. If, on the other hand, you

work those Australian boats all the way back to England and work the Imperial boats all the way to Sydney, you will obtain much greater flexibility — and to obtain the economy it would be advantageous to permit Imperial to carry out the major repairs and maintenance of your boats while they are in England. The division of receipts under this arrangement could be provided for by a pool.

I appreciate that there may be serious objections to not having the main repair base in Australia.

(This was to prove an accurate assumption. The issue of a major repair base for Australia was to be pushed vigorously by Fysh and prove of critical importance when war came.)

Woods Humphery, having so far put forward radical plans for the acquisition of large flying boats by QEA in specific numbers, before even the first overseas flight of their new DH86 aircraft, now proceeded to suggest radical changes to the company's route structure, and even to provide for a future role for the old Q.A.N.T.A.S. They were, in McMaster's eyes, hardly matters to keep secret from the Qantas board, or to be treated as worthy of possible mention to the chairman of Qantas only at Fysh's discretion.

Woods Humphery continued:

You may think that if it is practicable to work the flying boats all the way to Sydney. Q.E.A. should confine its activities to the main trunk route, and that such internal services between Darwin and Brisbane as are required by the Government should be operated by Q.A.N.T.A.S., which would restart as an operating company.

It would be necessary for QEA, said Woods Humphery, to undertake responsibility for the entire ground organization between Malaya and Australia, as well as the fleet operation organization.

As the fleet passes east of Singapore, they come under the entire control of Q.E.A., whether the fleet belongs to IAL or Q.E.A. Similarly, west of Singapore, the entire fleet . . . would come under the control of Imperials.

[There was] among the many other problems to be faced, the provision of the necessary capital. I am assuming that Q.A.N.T.A.S. would wish to continue to be equal partners with us in Q.E.A.

I know you will not let the fact that the scheme is beyond Q.A.N.T.A.S. resources influence your mind because, of course, the scheme is far beyond our present resources also. We shall have to obtain a very large amount of additional capital, and you should stand the same chances of obtaining your share in Australia as I hope we shall [at] this end.

No scheme of this magnitude, he wrote, could possibly be put out to competitive tenders. "It can only succeed if it is backed by the whole Empire."

Woods Humphery concluded this first outline of Imperial Airways' revolutionary vision of future Empire communications by again impressing on Fysh the need for secrecy.

> Obviously, if any inkling of the idea got from you or your company to Johnston or one of the Government people they might easily feel very hurt that a communication from the Government here was not the first they heard about the proposal, and it might easily make them hostile to it. Please, therefore, keep this letter in your personal file.

In a second "Strictly Private and Confidential" letter, Woods Humphery told Fysh that the British government had chosen, from the schemes submitted to them by Imperial Airways, an aircraft speed of 130 miles per hour "for reasons of cost alone".[69]

"I can assure you", he wrote, "that speeds of 160–180 miles per hour or more are absolutely out of the question. An increase of speed of twenty miles per hour adds about £500,000 a year to cost." For the Dutch, he said, or anyone else operating a relatively small capacity service, the bill for extra speed would not be so excessive.

"The Dutch", he wrote, "are bound to make a gigantic effort now to obtain a proportion of the British mail because it is their only chance of expanding their service, and Plesman is an ambitious man. This scheme which we have tentatively agreed with the Government for carrying the whole of the Empire first class mail completely kills Plesman's chances — if the Dominions and Colonies will all play in with our proposal." In the meantime, he added, Imperial Airways would increase its frequency "so as to drive a first blow at the Dutch".

"I can assure you and anybody else that there is no conceivable chance of the Dutch or any foreign company getting one ounce of the British mail from here", he said, adding that it would be a great blow if the Australian government gave the Dutch any part of the Australian airmails.

Hudson Fysh at first responded to these considerable confidences with gratitude.

> When I have first hand knowledge of what you are working for it is of enormous assistance here. One is working for a goal if the facts are known.

217

I would continue to urge the highest speed which you can induce your Government to pay for. The constant form of criticism of Imperial Airways here has been on the speed question.

I am sure you will forgive me when I say that Shorts, in all their productions, never looked like producing a fast machine. A cruising speed of 135 miles per hour will never be tolerated, and something like 200 miles per hour is required. It is not at all a question of being stampeded by Douglas, but of recognising facts.[70]

Fysh did not question Woods Humphery's suggestion that there be a change to the QEA route structure. "I agree also", he wrote, "that Q.E.A. as part of the England–Australia organisation has got to part company with its local aspect in serving the outback residents of Australia, and it may be that Q.A.N.T.A.S. will come into the picture again."

On the central question of keeping these matters of high policy secret from his board, and the suggestion from Woods Humphery that it would be at Fysh's discretion whether or not they be mentioned to McMaster, Fysh appeared to raise no objection. He wrote:

I am glad you gave me a loophole to inform our chairman, Mr Fergus McMaster, on your correspondence as he has a deep interest in the affairs of Q.A.N.T.A.S. and Q.E.A. and can be entirely relied on as regards secrecy. Mr McMaster has been more than an ordinary chairman to Qantas and, besides being a founder, has been heart and soul in every move that has been made. On his support much of our success depended, and his views would be valuable as regards the future.

That Fergus McMaster responded with wrath to his relegation by Woods Humphery to a secondary role (and this itself left to the discretion of Fysh), and to the insistence on secrecy in relation to the QEA board, is dramatically evident in the abrupt change of tone by Fysh in his next letter to Woods Humphery.

Our chairman [wrote Fysh on 24 November 1934] took the strongest exception to your letter to me. The outline of the scheme certainly should not have come through me without some suitable preliminary . . . It could be likened to my writing to you and saying you can show it to Sir Eric [Geddes] if you like, but please ask him to keep his mouth shut.[71]

The policy of secrecy by Imperial Airways had by now, in a more general way, begun to poison relationships on the QEA board. Fysh told Woods Humphery:

The feeling between the Q.A.N.T.A.S. directors on the Q.E.A. Board, including myself and Mr Rudder [the Imperial Airways member] has reached a stage at which the business of the Board is being seriously interfered with. [It has been fairly well established] that for some months Mr Rudder has been receiving information from you reference future plans which must affect Q.E.A., and has been privately negotiating with Ministers . . . while our Chairman knows absolutely nothing of what your plans are, even in broad outline.

[Rudder] is an extremely difficult man for a practical man to get on with. There is no doubt but he has a most irritating manner in discussing matters, and particularly with our Chairman he has at times become almost insulting when matters were not agreed or actions taken as suggested by him.

Mr Rudder's methods have also irritated Sir George Pearce, our Controller of Civil Aviation [Edgar Johnston] and Mr Critchley, the representative of the British Government in Australia. There is also a great suspicion of self interest in some of Mr Rudder's actions, and definite evidence that he wants to retain all the control possible in Sydney. I can see no hope of matters righting themselves till some alteration is made.

Woods Humphery made conciliatory noises. On 5 December, in a letter to Fysh, he expressed his embarrassment. The Air Ministry, he explained, had forbidden him to communicate their negotiations to any of the Imperial Airways subsidiary or associated company boards because of their fear of a leakage.

"I have communicated our negotiations to you, and in turn to Mr McMaster, solely on my own authority. I felt it quite impossible for me to go on discussing these matters with the Air Ministry without telling you and your Chairman."[72] On the same day as he wrote, he telegraphed: "Appreciate your difficulty but please also realise that for tactical reasons the scheme is officially a Government one and it is essential that we allow Government Departments to take full credit, thus allowing ourselves to be relegated to the position of consultants. No commitments have been made or will be made before full consideration and agreement with your company."[73]

By letter he also told Fysh that "the procedure to which your Chairman objects is perfectly normal procedure here — and the transposed possibility would also be quite normal".[74] (The "transposed possibility" was, of course, Fysh's less elegant analogy that Sir Eric Geddes could be asked, in similar but reversed circumstances, to "keep his mouth shut".)[75]

Fysh (also on 5 December) wrote to Woods Humphery: "I

feel sure the position has not been quite realised by you in England. The facts are . . . the Q.A.N.T.A.S. side of the Board has not been advised in any proper way of your schemes for the future and certain negotiations have been going ahead, which affect the future of Q.E.A., without their knowledge."[76]

At this point Fergus McMaster himself directly attacked Woods Humphery. With the new Darwin service barely one week old, he wrote with barely concealed anger to the Qantas Imperial partner.

"I understand", he began his letter to Woods Humphery, "that negotiations are proceeding with the Commonwealth Government and the Imperial Government — a result of pressure by Imperial Airways — with the express object of bringing about a material alteration to, or possibly a cancellation of, a vital section of the present Q.E.A. contract, and without any reference to Q.A.N.T.A.S."[77]

There were also, McMaster said, "both inferences and definite statements in your letter [to Fysh] and in several cable messages . . . that I, as Chairman of Qantas, might be justified in taking as a personal reflection on myself and other members of the Qantas Board". The situation, he said, would make it impossible for the QEA board to function. Tension had become so pronounced that a board meeting had been cancelled.

McMaster then accused Woods Humphery of "going over the head of Qantas and Q.E.A. on matters of policy of a very vital character.".

"These matters", he wrote, "should have been communicated by your company to me, as Chairman of Qantas." If, said McMaster, Imperial Airways was free to negotiate secretly on such vital matters as the suggested cancellation of the present contract held by QEA (the land section from Darwin to Brisbane) and the substitution of the coastal service in lieu, then Qantas would be similarly entitled to negotiate, unknown to Imperial Airways, for things that might well conflict with the interests of Imperial. Such a position, said McMaster, would be intolerable.

The bitter schism in the QEA board, the now-explicit conflict between McMaster and Woods Humphery, and the ambivalent position in which Hudson Fysh now appeared made Fysh concerned for his own position. He wrote, in private, to Woods Humphery:

It is no exaggeration to say that, as things are, Board meetings are impossible at present . . . Such a state of affairs, if it goes on, is crippling to the proper conduct of the whole business, and on top of the ordinary worries has just been somewhat of a last straw.

I also realise, of course, that the present state of affairs, if it goes on, will result in a loss of confidence in myself by some or all interested parties. At present I enjoy the full confidence of the Board, at least in regard to the Q.A.N.T.A.S. side, but I must say, while the present position prevails, I am not anxious to receive any letters from anyone marked "Private" or "Confidential", and I am not anxious to write any letters under these headings . . . If things go further it may be considered that this is improper, or that one has been working for one's own ends which, of course, would be ridiculous because, whatever one's own failings, I do have certain principles which have been far above consideration of position or money, and my only objective is to carry out my job as managing director of Q.E.A.

The Board is miserably situated. Firstly, it consists of Imperial Airways interests and Q.A.N.T.A.S. interests, with the Imperial interests on the Board served by one man, Mr Rudder. Then McMaster is away on his properties and only comes down to Brisbane for meetings once a month, which means I am often left here to effect important decisions without his assistance. We cannot carry on properly in this way.

If McMaster was to retire, Mr Loxton would not take the chairmanship and I consider matters would go from bad to worse. [Mr McMaster's] retirement would cause great resentment. I would also say that Mr McMaster is the only one of the directors who has any knowledge of the aircraft operations side of the business, which is a great help because, through the years with Qantas, I have found him sympathetic but not interfering.

For many years I have urged Mr McMaster to settle in Brisbane where, from time to time, he has had important positions offered him. He has always been unable to consider the move but now, I believe, he would be willing to do so . . . but would, of course, have to receive adequate remuneration as Chairman. I honestly know of no more capable or energetic man who would give the necessary time or push the company so strongly as Mr McMaster.

I very much regret having to write a personal letter such as this, and I do trust that this is my last — but the position is very acute. I feel it my duty to write, no matter what the ultimate effect on myself may be.[78]

That McMaster was himself well aware of the problems caused by his absences from Brisbane, and that he had also faced the possibility that he should retire from the chairmanship, was made explicit in a letter to Fysh on 26 December 1934.[79] He wrote that his present position, living at Longreach, was unsound.

I am too much away from my own office work. Some other

arrangement will have to be made. I cannot contemplate going on as we are indefinitely and I feel that the present arrangement is not fair to yourself nor sound for Qantas or Q.E.A. I must go right out of the whole organisation and allow someone else a free hand, or the position be so adjusted that I would be compensated for the difference of my living costs here and the cost of living in Brisbane.

I cannot keep in proper touch with the position under present conditions. There are big developments ahead in which Qantas will not be able to sit on the rail.

I wish it to be understood that although it might be somewhat of a wrench to break away from the Qantas associations, and the possible larger developments ahead, the best possible arrangements should be made in the interests of both companies, and personal interests or desires should not be considered.

Fysh, though accepting Woods Humphery's requirement for secrecy in relation to the Qantas board had, in fact, disclosed his understanding of Imperial Airways' plans to the minister, Parkhill, and sent a copy of his letter to Edgar Johnston, "The proposal to carry all first class mail by air is, of course, a matter of high policy and high finance, particularly the latter", Johnston had responded, "It seems to me it would certainly mean scrapping the DH86 for the overseas and eastern trunk route, and they might conceivably be too small for the western division."[80]

A.E. Rudder, as Imperial Airways representative in Australia, tried to defuse the secrecy issue in a letter to McMaster on 14 December, only four days after the inauguration of the service to England from Brisbane. "I am anxious to take the quickest means of clearing up what I believe is purely a misunderstanding, caused in the main by uncertainty as to the nature of the developments at Home and the difficulties of communication." Mr Woods Humphery, he said, "will be greatly distressed that the position had not been so fully explained to you personally as it might have been".[81]

McMaster's answer, on 18 December, was cold and blunt.

I regret that it is difficult for me to accept your views that the misunderstanding has been caused in the main by the nature of the developments in London and the difficulties of communication, nor can I accept as satisfactory your assurance that Mr Woods Humphery will be greatly disturbed that the position was not so fully explained to me personally as it might have been. This is not a personal matter when I or any other individual, as a personal favour, should expect an explanation.[82]

Qantas, not QEA, McMaster said, should have been consulted and general agreement arrived at before any action was

undertaken that might alter the contract for the Brisbane–
Singapore service. Unless that basis was accepted, he wrote,

> Qantas naturally would be forced to protect its interests and
> would be justified in acting independently with the Australian
> Government. I feel that you will agree with me that Qantas would
> have a greater political influence in Australia than Imperial
> Airways.
>
> It is disturbing that Imperial Airways should write privately to
> the Managing Director and enjoin secrecy. I would suggest that as
> far as possible personal correspondence should be avoided.

He ended: "With kind regards, and wishing you the compli-
ments of the Season."

McMaster's letter crossed with another letter to him from
Rudder, also written on 18 December. Woods Humphery had
cabled Fysh, said Rudder, that no commitment would be
made without consultation "and asking Fysh to discuss all his
relative correspondence with you"[83] Woods Humphery had
also indicated that Sir Eric Geddes was writing fully by the
next mail. Government concern for secrecy, he said in this
cable, had tied their hands.

Two days later, in London in the House of Commons, the
veil of secrecy was lifted. The under-secretary of state for air,
Sir Phillip Sassoon, on behalf of the government, revealed that
the Empire Air Mail scheme was in process of being submitted to other Commonwealth governments. It had, he said,
three main features — a material improvement in schedules, a
substantial increase in frequency of service, and the carriage of
all first class mail to the Empire countries concerned by air.
He could give no date for the inauguration of the scheme, but
stated: "The provision of the necessary fleet, ground organization etc. will require a period of something like two years
before a project of this magnitude, constituting as it does, the
largest step forward which has yet been taken in the development of Empire air communications, could be brought into
full operation."[8]

Sir Eric Geddes cabled McMaster immediately:

> Important statement regarding Government plans for develop-
> ment Empire air mail services made in House of Commons today.
> Although we have assisted and advised in consultations we were
> required by Government to keep matter secret and not permitted
> disclose their plans to anyone. You may rest assured we have not
> committed you in any way. If plans discussed mature, I believe
> effect cannot fail to be attractive to Q.E.A.[85]

He followed his cable with a long, explanatory letter on 28

December outlining the reasons for the emergence of the radical new scheme that was, in the years ahead, profoundly to affect the operations of both Imperial Airways and Qantas.[86]

> I can only hope that you will understand fully that my hands have been tied. Indeed, I have several times raised the matter specifically with the Government.
> Last year, 1933, the time had arrived for the Board of Imperial Airways to consider the question of fleet replacement for the India and Malaya line. The agreement with our Government for this line runs until 1939, but there is an understanding that we should be due to bring in a new generation of aircraft next year, 1935.

A study of the service, said Sir Eric, revealed

> that not only would it be impossible for us to get the line on to a self-supporting basis by the end of the ten years agreement, but that it was extremely likely, if not certain, that the last few years would turn out to be the most serious financial loss for us.
> [The cause was that] the air mail had not grown in accordance with the estimates agreed with the Government when the subsidy rates were fixed — in other words, the surcharge air mail system had failed. Briefly, it failed because at any surcharge at all — no matter how small — the volume was too small to carry economically.

It was useless, he continued, to consider a major fleet replacement. The matter was further complicated because the Africa service, also, was showing signs of failure in regard to airmails. "It was inevitable that the future of the Empire air mail services as a whole, as far as our Government is concerned, had to be reviewed." The failure of the surcharge system to produce the necessary volume also, he said, "has the very serious disadvantage of being a bait for foreign competition, as is shown by the efforts of the Dutch to extend their service to Australia".

"You will see, therefore, that the whole of the future of our Company was vitally at stake", he wrote. The board, he said, made its representations to the government, and a Cabinet committee was formed which eventually "accepted and passed a scheme which it felt able to put before the Dominion and Colonial Governments". The scheme, said Sir Eric, was left as elastic and flexible as possible "because we, naturally, in the absence of consultation, could not know the wishes of our partners on the routes".

> The sudden mania for speed, apparently without consideration of cost, volume or traffic, or effect on time schedules, resulting from

the London–Melbourne air race . . . caused the Government to review the whole of their previous considerations.

I have been wondering, and I have discussed with Humphery, how we can bring Qantas Empire Airways into the next stage. I am sure you will see that it is absolutely essential that Q.E.A. should come in when the proper time arrives.

First of all we must ascertain the attitude of the Australian Government to this vast proposal.

Sir Eric then suggested that at the appropriate time one or possibly two QEA directors should "come over and discuss the matter with us here". It would, he said, "be a good thing if we could meet and get to know each other, which is the best way of avoiding any misunderstanding".

> May I conclude [he wrote] by expressing the hope that in this very complicated matter, whatever may happen, you will at all times believe that in the talks which I am obliged to have with my own Government, Qantas Empire interests and Qantas Empire point of view is always before me.

Fysh, formally released from his undertaking to treat the Woods Humphery correspondence as private and confidential, submitted it to McMaster on 2 January 1935. In a covering letter he wrote: "I still feel, with you, that the directors of Q.E.A. should have been informed . . . Anything otherwise is only making the company out here the merest puppet of Imperial Airways."[87]

McMaster's anger had, it now proved, provoked what was to be a constructive and critical exchange of views between the chairman of the vast Imperial Airways organization and the chairman of Qantas. Responding to the Geddes letter, McMaster, on 22 January, wrote:

> I have read your letter very carefully. I realise that you had to protect your main interests in the London–Singapore section, and it would be unreasonable for us to expect that Q.A.N.T.A.S. interests in the Q.E.A. contracts could escape being involved to some extent. We must realise that any major development on the London–Singapore section must involve the Singapore–Australia section.

McMaster then began to develop an argument for fundamental change in the relationship involving Imperial Airways, Q.A.N.T.A.S., and QEA.

> The unfortunate position is that the interests of the Q.A.N.T.A.S. shareholders are not altogether identical with the interests of Imperial Airways in the Q.E.A. contracts. Certain developments which would be desirable and possible for Imperial Airways could be quite the opposite for Q.A.N.T.A.S.

As a result of your cable message and letter, I am satisfied that you did not neglect Q.A.N.T.A.S. interests.

I have been wondering if it might be possible to more fully merge the interests of Imperial Airways and Q.A.N.T.A.S., in proportion to their shareholdings, so that, whatever development took place, the results would be common to both interests. The present position is not a happy one for Q.A.N.T.A.S., and appears to me to be unsound for Imperial Airways — for both companies have to consider their major interests to a great extent individually.

Under the present arrangement Imperial Airways, with its 100 per cent interest in the London–Singapore section of 8,000 miles and only a 50 per cent interest in the 4,000 miles from Singapore to Australia, is in quite a different position to Q.A.N.T.A.S., dependent for its bread and butter on its 50 per cent interest in the 4,000 miles section. For instance, Imperial Airways could contemplate without anxiety the replacement of the whole of the Q.E.A. aircraft — without provision for obsolescence — whereas Q.A.N.T.A.S. is not in a position to do so.

If some basis could be secured whereby the two interests could be made common for the whole of the England–Australia service, in proportion to the shareholdings, it would help in what will always be more or less difficult adjustments.

The letter ended with his agreement to visit England for discussions.[88]

Sir Eric Geddes responded quickly. "I agree with you", he replied on 15 February 1935, "that it would simplify matters enormously if some arrangement could be arrived at whereby the two interests could be more closely woven into the Australian route as a whole. In fact, some such arrangement will, I think, be essential for the smooth working of the Government's new plans."

Geddes reminded McMaster that the existing division of the route arose from "the desire of the Commonwealth Government to segregate completely and control alone the Singapore–Darwin sector of the line". To any student of transport, he commented somewhat tartly, it had been obvious all along that each section was so dependent on the other that the isolation of one was not readily workable.[89]

This brief exchange between the two chairman was to lay the basis for both future understandings and future misunderstandings. Its immediate effect was to calm the wrathful McMaster and to restore reasonable accord.

Geddes concluded his letter with a reference to the first operational crisis of the provisional service, which had very nearly ended as a major disaster. Just after midnight on 16 January, the Imperial Airways aircraft *Athena* had taken off

from Koepang in fine weather for the crossing of the Timor
Sea to Darwin. It had left Singapore a day behind schedule
and the pilot, V.G. Wilson, was attempting to make up time
by flying, without rest, through the night. There were no
proper facilities for night flying on the route and it was, in
fact, prohibited.[90]

"Half way across the Timor Sea," Wilson later told the
press, "we encountered a terrific storm of thunder and lightning."[91] They reached the coast, after a four and a half hour
crossing, just before dawn. "I was unable to see any beacon
lamp or lights, or the aerodrome or the town," said Wilson,
"so I followed the coast eastward. The direction-finding
equipment was out of order because of static. We dared not even
put out the aerials because we picked up fireworks from
lightning. Petrol was getting very low. I have never met conditions like them."

He decided to make a forced landing. "I flew on to the
north-western side of Point Stuart, to a ridge surrounded by a
swamp, and put the machine down there", he said. Then a
group of Aboriginals arrived on the scene and told them their
position. On the emergency radio they passed it to Darwin.

The *Athena* was found soon afterwards by Qantas pilot,
Captain Hussey, flying from Darwin in a DH61. He landed
safely alongside, checked that passengers and crew were unin-
jured, then took off for Darwin to bring back petrol supplies.
On take-off, the DH61 struck a bog at high speed and the propeller, hitting the mud, disintegrated.

"Immediately," reported the press, "eleven native boys, six
lubras and one half-caste began to dig out the Qantas plane
and transfer 100 gallons of fuel to *Athena*. This coloured help
came from Mr. Max Freer's buffalo shooting camp, ten miles
away."[92]

Athena chose a take-off path to avoid the bog and, taking
Hussey and his crew, arrived safely in Darwin. The mails
went south the following day and the DH61, *Diana*, was later
fitted with a new propeller and flown out.

Apart from damaging publicity, the accident provoked
internal argument and accusations. Fysh cabled Imperial Airways, with minimum diplomacy, if accurate judgment: "Consider method of operating *Athena* last trip and possibly your
other trips courting certain disaster." He was asked by
Imperial Airways to withdraw the cable.[93] The press criticized
the Commonwealth government for inadequate ground
facilities on the route. The controller of civil aviation ex-

pressed displeasure with Imperial Airways for what he believed was their initiative in provoking the press criticism. Edgar Johnston wrote to Fysh:

> It does seem that he [Wilson] undertook his flight by night without any weather report and apparently knowing that Darwin radio was not aware of his coming, and knowing also that Koepang radio . . . had closed down. If this is accurate, it is a very serious matter commanding drastic action.
>
> It is rather annoying to us to be publicly blamed for installing unsatisfactory equipment which apparently was never given a fair chance to work on this occasion. If the pilots wish to do foolish things they should at least refrain from blaming the Department publicly for the consequence of their stupid actions.[94]

In a second letter he said he did not blame Fysh for the adverse publicity, "I do think, however," he said, "that it has been more or less deliberate on Imperial Airways part."[95]

Geddes denied these accusations but in a letter to McMaster made his position plain: "Ground organisation on this sector is a matter between Qantas and the governments of Australia and the Netherlands Indies."[96]

Qantas, so close now to achievement of that dreamtime vision of spanning oceans, was still held back by the problems of the DH86. They had not themselves yet flown their route between Darwin and Singapore. Lester Brain and Scotty Allan, however, after Qantas workshop alterations to the DH86 rudder tab, had carried out tests which, to them and to Fysh, appeared to solve the problem of directional instability. "All of Qantas now have confidence in the machine and we are anxious to commence operations", Fysh told Johnston.[97] "To us, of course, almost overwhelming evidence points to the fin giving way in the air as the cause of the accident."

Johnston replied: "All our people here are wholly unconvinced that the fin was the cause of the accident." Referring to the Qantas tests, he wrote: "I feel it almost too good to be true that the sealing of the rudder flap can make so great a difference."[98] He sent his own officer to Brisbane to assess the Qantas optimism.

When the board of Qantas Empire Airways assembled in Brisbane on 25 January 1935, they heard the verdict. The Civil Aviation Branch's pilot had carried out independent tests of the aircraft's directional stability and now declared himself satisfied. Release of the DH86 for service was at last assured.[99]

Almost immediately there was another crisis and the whole

Capt. Lester J. Brain, QEA
flight superintendent, about
1935.

issue of the safety of the aircraft was again reopened. The first
of two additional DH86 aircraft (VH-USF) for QEA had been
flown out from England. On its arrival in Darwin it was found
that the fin bias gear was defective. Its certificate of airworthiness was suspended. Again, that elusive overseas inaugural
day receded. Permission was given by the Civil Aviation
authorities for the aircraft to be flown back to Singapore for
inspection and there, QEA service engineer George Boehm,
found a serious malfunction of the bias gear.[100]

Imperial Airways attacked the Australian decision to suspend the aircraft. "The action of the Australian Civil Aviation
Department in declining to certify the airworthiness of the
DH86 machine just flown to Darwin from Croydon has astonished Imperial Airways", reported the London representative
of the Brisbane *Telegraph* on 28 January. The continuing
Australian ban on the DH86 was, Imperial said, a serious
embarrassment. The Civil Aviation Department responded,

229

with some anger, that only the defective aircraft itself was affected. There was no ban on the DH86 as a type.[101] Johnston wrote to Fysh: "Official advices indicated that Imperials rushed into their criticisms without any knowledge of the facts at all. I have told them pretty plainly what I think of it."[102]

Publicity photograph taken at Archerfield in early 1935 showing embarkation for a flight on a QEA DH86.

Then the second of the two new DH86s (VH-USG) which had arrived by sea in Brisbane was found, in the QEA workshops, to be faulty; there was incorrect location of the fin bias traverse screw. Qantas modified both aircraft. In Singapore, a new fin post was made and fitted to VH-USF. Its certificate of airworthiness was restored and, in Brisbane, the fault on VH-USG was corrected. They were, at last, ready to begin operations with the new airliner.

The first of the DH86 aircraft to enter scheduled QEA service, RMA *Canberra*, left Brisbane on 29 January 1935, with Lester Brain in command, carrying mails for transfer to Imperial Airways at Darwin. On board were First Officer

Publicity photograph taken
inside a QEA DH86 at
Archerfield in early 1935.

Passenger cabin of a DH86
looking forward.

L.R. Ambrose, Engineer A. Williams, and pilot W.H.
Crowther, travelling as passenger to Darwin. (Bill Crowther
had been taken on to replace P.G. Taylor.) It was the beginning of multi-engined operations for Qantas and of a new,
two-day service with the DH86s between Brisbane and their
stepping-off point for the rest of the world, Darwin. The new
service cut a day off the old schedule. It was also the last big
step necessary before the start of these overseas operations.
Though there were still operational details to be clarified,

Fysh, weary and unwell, felt that he could now take a short holiday. Edgar Johnston wrote to him on both matters.[103]

"I am sorry to hear that the strain we have been through recently has affected you physically", Johnston said, advising him to get away and forget all about flying; but, with his solicitude, came a last departmental point. The range of the DH86 specified in the tender documents for the Darwin–Singapore section of 600 miles against a 30 mile per hour headwind was, he reminded Fysh, a minimum. "I discovered that Brain was under the impression that, if a wind in excess of 30 m.p.h. were blowing, the Company would be doing everything required of it under the contract by sitting down and waiting for the wind to drop." This, said Johnston, was not the case. There was every need to have arrangements to carry additional petrol when circumstances demanded. "The Department expects trips to be undertaken and completed to schedule under all reasonable conditions, and I should hesitate to agree", he said, "that a wind in excess of 30 m.p.h. constituted unreasonable conditions."

More than reasonable conditions prevailed at Darwin on 26 February 1935 as Qantas prepared, for the first time, to meet those departmental expectations. At Fanny Bay aerodrome, where Hudson Fysh had welcomed Ross and Keith Smith after their flight from England in the Vickers Vimy in 1919, Captain Scotty Allan lined up RMA *Canberra* for take-off in the early morning light. The four engines wound up to full power and the DH86 accelerated down the grass. Moments later, it lifted off on the first overseas departure from Australia of a Qantas flight.

Refuelling a DH86 at a Queensland aerodrome, 1935.

The Imperial Imperative
1935

Though the problems with the DH86 aircraft and the misunderstandings between the two partners of Qantas Empire Airways had been substantially resolved by the time of the inaugural Qantas overseas flight from Darwin in February 1935, McMaster and Fysh were now to face, in the four years leading up to World War II, a period of unparalleled complexity and pressures. As well as the considerable challenge of operating as an overseas airline, there lay ahead a sometimes stormy, and much extended, political environment that involved the Australian, British, New Zealand, and Dutch governments, the looming uncertainties of war itself, and a dramatic collapse in McMaster's health. It was in this period that they, and the small group of able people under them, transformed the local, inland operator into an international airline that, with a fleet of great flying boats, laid the basis of a world reputation for safety and technical excellence.

In those first weeks of February 1935 there were two as yet unrelated initiatives that were closely to involve Qantas. One marked the beginnings of Australian government involvement in the concept of a trans-Tasman air service, the other the arrival in Australia of a high-level British delegation to urge the merits of the proposed revolutionary Empire Air Mail Scheme and the adoption, for its implementation, of large and untried flying boats.

Edgar Johnston advised the secretary of the Ministry of Defence that the Postmaster-General's Department had received a letter from the New Zealand authorities. "This

233

administration", said the letter, "is keenly interested in a weekly trans-Tasman air mail service link up with the service now operating between England and Australia." Johnston added his comments: the project, he said, had been well in mind for many years but was beset with difficulties, mainly the operational one of spanning some twelve hundred miles of the Tasman Sea. "It is comparable", he said, "in some respects to the spanning of the Atlantic, something not yet attempted for a regular service to North America." Three types of aircraft could, he said, make the direct crossing with a small commercial load — the little DH *Comet*, in some nine hours with a load of 400 pounds; the Douglas DC2, of 18,000 pounds gross weight, in just over ten hours with 600 pounds payload, and the Sikorsky S42 flying boat, of 38,000 pounds gross weight, in just under eleven hours with a payload of 3,700 pounds.[1]

The British delegation arrived in Brisbane by QEA DH86 on 22 February, having had special dispensation to travel from Singapore on the new service. It lost no time in urging, through the press, the advantages of flying boats for the long distances flown across the oceans on Empire routes. The delegation leader, British director of postal services Sir Frederick Williamson, said modestly: "We are not here to dictate to the Commonwealth Government."[2] He stressed, however, that it was necessary for Australia to obtain the right perspective on the rapidly expanding airmail services, and on the critical issue of costs.

An integral part of that perspective was the requirement for an Empire view of world affairs. It was not lacking in Australia. Although the Statute of Westminster 1931 had given legal authority for the transfer to Australia and other Dominions of full sovereignty over their own affairs (a sovereignty that had been recognized in principle by the Balfour Declaration of 1926), Australia had not yet adopted the statute (and was not to do so until 1943). The attitude of Qantas itself was proclaimed as a slogan on a Staff News circular of 7 November 1934 and read: "Let Us Think And Act Imperially." In practical terms it meant maximum possible co-operation with Imperial Airways on the through route from England to Australia. It also meant maximum possible resistance to Dutch intrusion into Australia.

By mid-1934, Fysh had already been suspicious of Dutch intentions. "I really am very worried indeed about the Dutch proposals [to link Batavia and Darwin]", he wrote to Edgar

Johnston. "You may have to fight to see that QEA don't receive a heavy blow in loss of overseas passenger traffic. I refuse to swallow that the Dutch simply wish to come to Darwin. Undoubtedly they will want to come on to Sydney and Melbourne. The next step would be pressure to receive a portion of the mails."[3] Fysh thought the Dutch "wonderful people to meet socially, or when no actual business is being conducted". But, he said, "they are very tough, I can assure you, when it gets down to a matter of price".[4]

Two days after making this comment, on 21 July 1934, Fysh received a letter from KNILM on agency agreements for the Netherlands East Indies. They quoted a fixed annual payment of 10,000 francs as "the very lowest figure at which we can render the services required . . . a large reduction of the original amount of 22,870 francs". They had, they said, made this reduction in the sincere wish to co-operate with QEA and were now offering their services at below cost price.[5] Fysh replied promptly that the QEA board, at its meeting on 1 August, had felt unable to agree to this price which was, he wrote, more than double that which was contemplated.[6] To Edgar Johnston he commented with feeling: "I am beginning to despair of an agreement with KNILM owing to their unrelenting attitude and inclination to lay down the law. Apart from price, which includes not one item of out-of-pocket expenses, they wish to say exactly what they will do, not what we require. If KNILM don't agree, I expect Imperial Airways will consider putting the screws on KLM."[7] By the end of August, however, there were slight signs of compromise. Johnston wrote to Fysh: "I agree with you it might be politic to go some little distance to secure the fullest co-operation from the KNILM."[8]

The right to operate through the Netherlands East Indies was, of course, essential to QEA for their Darwin–Singapore service and their negotiations with the Dutch were the first of many tough encounters with other countries in that specialized form of airline horse-trading involving traffic rights.

Edgar Johnston wrote to Fysh on 10 September 1934 that the prospect of Dutch expansion to Australia was

a very real danger, and having in mind our dependence on Dutch goodwill for the successful operation of our own service to Singapore, I would be very loath to recommend a direct refusal to a Dutch application to come on to Australia.

I do believe that if we run a fast service to Singapore we can make it very difficult for the Dutch to compete against us. If the

British through service will stand comparison with the Dutch service, then the fear of Dutch competition is not very great as the Australian and British public would stand firmly behind us. [But] if the Dutch can and do run a much faster service, then I think the public would force our hand into giving permission to the Dutch.

Johnston thought it should be possible to fly the Darwin–Brisbane section in one day and two nights, making a three-day schedule. For Darwin–Singapore he thought a four-day schedule "about as fast as the trip could be run without consistent night flying. But I contemplate a three-day schedule with regular night flying."[9] Replying, Fysh reminded him of the difficulties on the Brisbane–Darwin sector. "What a tall order it is going to be", he wrote, "to operate a modern, high performance type from grounds in Australia largely only suitable for our present local types." Between Brisbane and Darwin, he pointed out, "there are no less than seventeen scheduled stops in a distance of 2,028 miles, while on the Darwin–Singapore section of 2,331 miles there are only four regular stops".[10] Each place, said Fysh, had to be "regularly landed at in all weathers according to timetable".

On the issue of Dutch charges in the Netherlands East Indies, Woods Humphery did indeed attempt, as forecast by Fysh, "to put the screws on KLM". He sent Fysh copies of his correspondence with Plesman in which he had concluded that, as they had failed to make satisfactory arrangements, QEA would now appoint their own local agents. As far as traffic was concerned, he told Plesman, QEA was a transit company and not primarily interested in local traffic. "That, my dear Plesman, is your province", he wrote, "and we have no wish to compete in any way with traffic from your Eastern Colony to your Mother Country. Similarly, traffic to and from Australia and India we regard as being our proper province, but on this I am sorry to say, there does not seem to be reciprocal thought."[11]

To Fysh, Woods Humphery was somewhat blunter. "I think there is no possibility of avoiding a war with those people," he wrote, "and therefore, whilst doing nothing in any way to precipitate it, we should prepare ourselves to stand entirely on our own. I hope you will agree."[12] Fysh responded that he did.[13]

The glamour weapon of the Dutch, for any war of airline operations, had been dramatically demonstrated to Australia in the Melbourne Centenary Air Race. Their Douglas airliner had captured the public imagination. Fysh wrote to Dismore at Imperial Airways on 22 December 1934 that "Johnston has thoroughly caught Douglasitis". So, he said, had everyone else, including the whole of Qantas.

> I have had it [wrote Fysh] since my visit to Clover Fields outside Los Angeles, and my present prayer is that your manufacturers will catch the disease good and hearty. The American manufacturer has got far away ahead in the present period of development of commercial aircraft. I do not refer by any means to speed alone, but to methods of construction and general engine features. Here in Australia at the present moment there is quite a revulsion against British commercial aircraft. This is not altogether unwarranted.[14]

The new Empire air route between London and Brisbane which for the first time provided a fast and regular means of communication for the two countries, was by far the longest air service in the world. Covering 12,754 miles it was operated by three organizations: Imperial Airways flew from London to Paris and from Brindisi, Italy, to Karachi via Cairo (the Paris–Brindisi link was by rail); Indian Trans-Continental Airways flew the service from Karachi across India to Rangoon and on to Singapore; Qantas Empire Airways linked Singapore and Brisbane. (Indian Trans-Continental Airways was 51 per cent owned by IAL and 49 per cent by the Indian Government, with IAL exercising control. It was, wrote Fysh, "to all intents and purposes an IAL affair . . . except that their *Atalantas* had Indian registration marks".[15])

A variety of aircraft types were used. The Handley Page 42W *Heracles* type, carrying in comfort thirty-eight passengers at 100 miles per hour and providing meal services and stewards, operated London–Paris. From Brindisi to Alexandria, across the Mediterranean, the four-engined Short S17 *Kent* class flying boat was used. It carried sixteen passengers at 105 miles per hour and had often to stop for refuelling at Mirabella, Crete. From Cairo to Karachi, IAL used the Handley Page 42E *Hannibal* type, which resembled the *Heracles* but had greater range, in exchange for a smaller passenger capacity of twenty-four. The route was Cairo–Baghdad and on to Sharjah in the Persian Gulf where, wrote Fysh, "a landing was made on the desert and the Handley Page taxied in alongside the IAL Resthouse through an opening in barbed wire entanglements, which were closed tight for the night".[16]

The *Hannibals* terminated at Karachi, where the smaller Armstrong Whitworth *Atalantas* took over. With a capacity of nine passengers, they called at Jodhpur, India, for a night stop, then Rangoon and on to Singapore, connecting with the DH86s of QEA. The basic weakness of all the IAL aircraft was in their range, which was sacrificed in exchange for payload. The Handley Page *Hannibal* and Armstrong Whitworth *Atalanta* had a range, without extra tanks, of some 400 miles; the Short S17 *Kent* was little better at 450 miles.[17] By contrast, the *Commonwealth* class DH86, though limited to a maximum of ten passengers, had a range of 750 miles, a speed of 145 miles per hour, and superior economics.[18] (As a comparison, the Douglas DC3 could carry twenty-one passengers at a cruising speed of some 190 miles per hour. The first Douglas aircraft to be used by Australia, a DC2, commenced operations with Holyman Airways in June 1936, and the first DC3 entered service with Australian National Airways in the following year. Their importation into Australia became legally possible after the government sent Edgar Johnston abroad in 1935 to investigate civil aviation matters. "I took technical experts with me," said Johnston, "and as a result I recommended that we accept the American certificate of airworthiness in Australia."[19] Between 1 July 1936 and 30 June 1939, forty-nine American aircraft were imported[20].) On the new Empire route from Brisbane to London the first class air fare was £244.

The final managing director's report of the old Q.A.N.T.A.S. by Fysh was submitted to the board on 24 January 1935 and noted that the company had ceased to operate when Qantas Empire Airways had taken over on 10 December 1934. The period dealt with by the report, from 1 July to 9 December 1934, had been on a yearly basis by far the most profitable in the company's history. Records had been broken in passenger bookings but the principal reason for the profit of £4,977 disclosed had been the very low depreciation for the period of only £1,219. The fleet had been "written down to a bedrock value, at which QEA had agreed to take it over".[21]

The birth of Qantas Empire Airways and the opening of Australia's first regular international air service had stimulating consequences for the controller of civil aviation, Edgar Johnston. Fysh advised Woods Humphery on 8 February that Johnston would leave shortly on a world tour.

> He is going via America and Canada and will be about six weeks there, I believe. He will then go on to London and tour the Continent before flying out to Australia on the Empire Service. It is

vital for Johnston to be carefully cultivated, as he leaves here definitely hostile to IAL, de Havilland and all British aircraft. I know Johnston very well personally. He is absolutely straight and, at times, pig-headed. This trip will improve him enormously, but it is essential that he gets the British angle.

What he will appreciate most from you, and what will have the most effect, will be candour, and no secrecy and mystery. If you can get him to really see your big [Empire air mail] scheme and back it, the position out here in regard to the future will be enormously eased, as he will be the Government's authority on his return.[22]

In fact, the initial response to the Empire Air Mail Scheme by the departments of the Postmaster-General and Civil Aviation varied. The former was, in general, supportive; the latter (incorporating Johnston's views set down before his departure overseas) was cautious and full of reasoned doubt. In a confidential memorandum to Cabinet on 4 March 1935, the Postmaster-General's Department summarized the main features of the scheme and the proposal for a fifteen-year contract commencing in 1937. The estimated cost of the scheme annually, they wrote, was £2,650,000. Earnings from passenger and freight revenue were put at £1,150,000 and collections annually from foreign countries for carrying their mail put at £30,000. Estimated earnings from surcharges on Empire mail to foreign destinations were £45,000. This total revenue still left a net annual contribution from governments of £1,425,000. Its proposed apportionment was: mail payment by the United Kingdom £525,000, plus subsidy of £313,000; mail payment by the Dominions, £300,000 plus subsidy of £287,000. The Australian share of the total Dominions apportionment was put at £44,000 for mail and £90,000 in subsidy — a total of £134,000 sterling (or £A167,500). Heavy capital expenditure would be involved for ground organization between Sydney and Singapore, said the memorandum, and there would be annual maintenance costs at least £5,000 in excess of the existing landplane service. "The proponents of the scheme", wrote the PMG Department, "stress the desirability of maintaining the existing mail contract subsidies with the various shipping companies, the Orient Line being that affected by the Australian aspect." The main disadvantages seen by the PMG were the considerable increase in the financial obligations of the Commonwealth and the diminished measure of control of the Australia–Singapore section. The advantages were that "the projected air service will occupy nine days at the outset and seven days in the near future" as against thirty-two days for the existing sea-mail route. Frequency of mail service would double to twice a week. The prestige of the Empire would be enhanced and, said the memorandum, the service would "be of special benefit to highly placed public men, officials and others concerned with important commercial interests". The report concluded that there was much to be said in the scheme's favour, with the primary consideration being one of finance.[23]

In contrast to the Postmaster-General's Department, the acting controller of civil aviation, A.R. McComb, expressed misgivings in a paper to the secretary of the Defence Department on 6 March 1935. He questioned

> the wisdom of accepting the admittedly revolutionary United Kingdom scheme and abandoning the earlier view of the Commonwealth that development and improvement of the England–Australia air connection should proceed by evolutionary stages with increase in frequency, reduction in through transit time [by recourse to night flying, faster aircraft etc.] and gradual reduction in the air mail surcharge fee. [The British Delegation's scheme would] compel the general taxpayer to bear an additional burden, whereas under the Commonwealth plan the users of the airmail would themselves have to pay . . . by way of surcharge fees on their mails.

Broadly speaking, he argued, the anticipated difficulties and problems arose from the basic feature of the United Kingdom scheme — the proposal to carry all first class mail by air without special surcharge fee. "This would involve very large mail loads, difficulties of operating aircraft of sufficiently large carrying capacity and result in the Commonwealth receiving no appreciable revenue as a set-off against the very considerable disbursements in subsidy." The machines contemplated were, he wrote, expensive in first cost and in operation and maintenance. The British Delegation had said it would be uneconomical to write off such large aircraft in less than seven years. Thus, commencing in 1937, they must operate the same aircraft until 1944. The view was held, he said, that "if the United Kingdom scheme did in fact represent an outstanding development in air mail transport in 1937, it must almost certainly be obsolete by 1944".

The British proposal, he observed, seemed to involve an annual Australian grant towards an Imperial Airways service. If adopted it was "difficult to see how Civil Aviation in this country will be fostered". All available Commonwealth funds would go to finance the new scheme. Its introduction would necessitate the termination or drastic revision of many existing airmail contracts.[24]

Five days after the preparation of these submissions by the postmaster-general and acting controller of civil aviation, a secret paper was put to Cabinet by the Defence Department. It recapitulated the genesis of the UK scheme "formulated and submitted to the Dominions concerned without any prior consultation", and the despatch of the British Delegation to India and Australia early in 1935 with the apparent desire of "securing the Dominions' early acquiscence". A conference had been held in Sydney from 25–28 February 1935 with the Commonwealth represented by the minister for defence (Archdale Parkhill); the postmaster-general (Senator A.J. McLachlan); the director-general of posts and telegraphs (Mr H.P. Brown); the secretary, Department of Defence (Mr M.L. Shepherd); the controller of Postal Services (Mr M.B. Harry); and the chief clerk, Civil Aviation Branch (Mr S.H. Crawford). The British Delegation consisted of the director of postal services (Sir Frederick Williamson), the deputy director of civil aviation (Mr Francis Bertram), and the parliamentary private secretary to the British under-secretary for air (Mr Thomas Loel Guinness MP).

The Cabinet paper reaffirmed that "from the civil aviation standpoint in Australia it preferred to proceed in progressive stages" but it was appreciated that this would need the co-operation of the Indian and United Kingdom governments "who, however, have apparently agreed to adopt the more far-reaching Empire all-mails scheme". This patent lack of enthusiasm continued. On the question of control, the paper noted: "It is extremely difficult to appreciate in what manner or to what extent the Commonwealth could expect to exercise any effective measure of control over the operation of its national Company (apart from . . . airworthiness certificates, licensing of crews etc.)". Johnston's sarcastic comment that QEA would merely be privileged to display its Australian registration markings was then included. "Based on the meagre information available," the report went on, "the additional expenditure would be not less than (a) additional capital costs of £140,00 (b) additional recurring costs of £116,500 annually", exclusive of costs for improved facilities (landing grounds, night lighting, wireless, etc.) and establishment of additional air distribution services from Sydney. "It seems that participation in the Empire Scheme at the outset would involve the Commonwealth in net additional cost of not less than £200,000", the report concluded. In addition, in the opinion of the acting controller of civil aviation, "the flying boat stopping bases from Darwin to Sydney had been laid down on paper apparently without any serious consideration at all".[25]

Woods Humphery wrote a "Strictly Personal" letter to Fysh on 2 April that would, had its contents been known to Edgar Johnston, have confirmed his worst fears on the British attitude to control of the Australian section of the proposed flying boat service.

> One thing worrying me a little is the idea that QEA would have a separate contract with the Australian Government in regard to their participation in the service . . . We have made it quite clear that it was our idea that there should be one contract only, and that would be between the Home Government and Imperial Airways, and in it would be provided in specific terms the participation by QEA and Indian Trans-Continental Airways. I fear that there might be some obstacle from Johnston, who might feel that the most important air mail service that Australia was interested in was not, partly at any rate, under his control.[26]

A week later he told Fysh:

> I understand from the Delegation that the principal anxiety in Australia is the suggested abandonment of the internal landplane route as the main trunk route. It could be a pity to allow a local consideration, important as it is, to affect adversely the service as a whole.[27]

Hudson Fysh, meanwhile, had been assessing some of the physical realities of the proposed flying boat route between Darwin and Sydney. He described the difficulties and expense of establishing depots on the remote Gulf of Carpentaria in a letter to Woods Humphery on 9 April. "I have been", he wrote, "to the Roper River, Booraloola on the McArthur River, and to Normanton and Karumba at the mouth of the Norman River, and these form about the only regular points of white habitation along the shores of the Gulf, except for the missionaries on Mornington Island." Fysh pointed out that Roper River had sea communication only, by lugger, with Darwin, and had foreshores of mangrove and mud; that McArthur River was similar, with the white population of Booraloola fluctuating "from about three to six, with a public house, a store and a police station". A small steamer or lugger from Darwin called intermittently. Karumba, on the mouth of the Norman River, "consists of a pilot station, where live a

242

white man and his wife", wrote Fysh, adding: "To establish a depot at Roper River would be as difficult as establishing ourselves on a desert island."[28]

Though the issue of flying boats and the ambitious Empire airmail scheme dominated high policy, there were plenty of other more pressing matters that faced Fysh. In a draft of the chairman's address for the annual meeting, Fysh wrote that the heavy volume of overseas mail between Darwin and Singapore was "a very serious question for the Company, although a very gratifying position for the Government. The revenue being received by the Government through the surcharged air mail approximately pays the cost of the service to the Government. In other words, the service is practically self-supporting."[29]

The popular response to the new airmail service had, in fact, far exceeded official expectations. The Inter-Departmental Committee, in its estimates, had allowed an average weekly mail loading from Australia of 191 pounds and an inwards average of 201 pounds. In less than three months, however, the outward average was 450 pounds and the inward average 400 to 500 pounds per week (mail volumes not anticipated for some six years by the committee). As QEA was obliged under its contract to give priority to mail over passengers it now found that the high mail loadings would deprive it of revenue from passengers. (Ministerial permission to carry passengers was given on 31 March 1935, commencing from Brisbane on 17 April and from Singapore on 22 April.)

The service across the Timor Sea, wrote Fysh, "is ridiculously cramped owing to the unexpected volume of mails carried". Without doubling of frequency ("duplication" was the term in use) at an early date, QEA would not, he said, be able "to fulfil the intentions of the Government in providing an adequate mail, passenger and freight service". The service, said Fysh, "has already lost the greater portion of its value to the people of the interior, owing to lack of space available for passengers and urgent freight".[30]

To Woods Humphery, Fysh wrote: "Our whole immediate policy seems to be bound up with whether the Brisbane–Singapore service is to be duplicated or not in the near future. Our authorities are not likely to duplicate or push till the matter is rather forced from your end. They will give way, I think, to pressure. The Government are receiving almost three times the revenue they expected from air mail surcharges ... Our contract is recognised as inequitable."[31]

QEA and Imperial Airways had reached agreement to pool, in proportion to mileage, the revenue from passengers and freight which, because of their overwhelming success as carriers of mail, was now being denied them. It had been decided that IAL would account to Qantas in sterling for the proportion of revenue due to them from traffic travelling from places west of Singapore to destinations east of Singapore. QEA was to account to IAL in Australian currency in a similar manner for traffic from east of Singapore continuing westward. Both companies agreed to keep their intercompany accounts with dual currency columns. "Ticket butts", said the QEA Organisation Notes setting out these arrangements, "will be collected by the pilot and returned to Head Office at the end of the flight. Ticket butts will be checked with the passenger list and with the ticket register."[32]

The first overseas passenger to travel on a QEA service, following official approval for scheduled passenger flights on 31 March, was Maj. A. Philips, a reserve officer of HM Coldstream Guards. He boarded the DH86 RMA *Melbourne* at Archerfield aerodrome, Brisbane, on 17 April, with Capt. H.B. Hussey in command. At Charleville he was reunited with Lady Mountbatten, the second QEA overseas passenger, now on her way to join her husband, Lord Louis, in Malta. Major Philips and Lady Mountbatten had completed a voyage by schooner from Tahiti to Sydney, where the major had caused Rudders Limited, QEA agents in Sydney, some embarrassment and Hudson Fysh some irritation by his attempts to conceal his identity. On 11 April, Rudders telegraphed Fysh: "Papers publish Sydney message stating Major Philips accompanying Lady Mountbatten. Presume this is incorrect as we have a Mister Wilson booked."[33] Fysh replied: "We are sure you will realise with us the many unsatisfactory features connected with the booking of Lady Mountbatten and Major Philips, alias Wilson. It is quite understood that this class of passenger will be in many instances very difficult to deal with and wish to alter their minds quite a bit. We would point out, however that we cannot book passengers under assumed names."[34] (The first passengers for QEA in the opposite direction, from Singapore to Sydney, were not as illustrious or as troublesome. They were writer Richard Coke and rubber broker J.B. Usher, who left Singapore on 22 April.)[35]

It was the grand plan of Imperial Airways that this fledgling service to Australia should, with the introduction of flying boats and adoption of the Empire airmail scheme, continue on to New Zealand. In Australia, however, aviation interests led by the immensely popular Sir Charles Kingsford Smith began to oppose the British master plan with increasing vigour. In Wellington, Kingsford Smith put his own plan to the New Zealand government for a trans-Tasman air service using Douglas aircraft. He hoped, reported the Melbourne *Argus* on 27 March, for a company with a capital of £125,000, and proposed that the New Zealand and Australian governments would guarantee the company a weekly revenue of £1,200. He also proposed "that a remuneration of £5,000 be paid to him for supervising the inauguration of the service and proceeding abroad to purchase equipment". The *Argus* commented that the Commonwealth was unlikely to adopt his proposal "owing to its being interested in the British proposal for a comprehensive service in 1937".

The Tasman Sea had been flown nine times from Australia between 1928 and 1934, and six times from New Zealand. Kingsford Smith, Charles Ulm, and P.G. Taylor were its recognized conquerors and, with some justification and public support, saw it as an area for local development. The death of Ulm had deprived the trio of any true business and administrative ability, though Kingsford Smith's commercial ambitions hardly faltered. While deeply involved in plans for the Tasman, he wrote to Edgar Johnston on 19 February 1935 about

> ideas for trans-continental air services . . . though not necessarily to the exclusion of all others. I am genuinely interested in the promotion of faster air services and am busily attempting to interest capital in the flotation of a company to exploit the manufacture of American aircraft under licence in this country. You know my views are that the Americans undoubtedly build a better class of aircraft for Australian operation than the English, regrettable though this may be . . .

In the same letter he commented at some length on the likely circumstances of Ulm's death.

> It was indeed a tragedy about poor old Charles Ulm and I am absolutely at a loss to understand why he did not check up more carefully on poor Skilling's [the navigator's] ability, for I am convinced that although he probably was an excellent marine navigator, he could not use a bubble sextant with any accuracy. Also, he had only just learned the morse code, which comprised his total knowledge of radio. Needless to say, I would not dream of expressing these views publicly, but unfortunately they are the facts. I checked up carefully every detail of their preparations at

245

Oakland airport and, as far as I can understand them, they did not even carry any demolition tools to cut their motors adrift in the event of a forced landing in the sea, nor did they carry fuel in their blowlamp to operate their water-distilling process. I am afraid the poor lads were in too much of a hurry to get going, with consequent sacrifice of the usual care which generally distinguished Charles Ulm's efforts.[36]

Kingsford Smith's reference to faster services touched on an issue that concerned Johnston, worried Fysh, and irritated Woods Humphery. Speed, wrote Woods Humphery to Fysh on 23 April 1935

is purely a question of what can be done for the money. The British Government has stated the limit it is prepared to go to under the new scheme. If you can find a means whereby this extra speed can be got without additional power, I shall be very pleased to hear of it. As it is, the new planes that are to be built for us by Armstrongs, Shorts and Handley Page are the cleanest things that you can possibly imagine. Douglas, which you so much admire, is a rough blacksmith's job compared with the finish that has been shown to us by sample as proposed for our new planes . . . The cruising speeds of all the planes now being built for us — that is, the landplanes and flying boats — are between 150 and 155 miles an hour, but please keep this confidential.[37]

Edgar Johnston also wrote from abroad to Fysh on the issue of speed. "On the last set of internationally operated airlines schedules I received," he conceded, "the Brisbane–Singapore service is the fastest international air service operating in the world." But, he went on, "The Dutch will, of course, completely scotch this when they start their fast service in June".[38] Fysh responded at once: "Our show is going like a piece of well-oiled clockwork. Our passenger bookings are quite good and the mail just goes on growing in a most alarming manner." Duplication, he said, was now a pressing necessity. "The Government continue to make vast sums of uncontemplated money while we see our payload vanishing and are, on our side of the bargain, losing money." He described the QEA contract as iniquitous. "I do hope, in any alteration or renewal, that we will receive a little more latitude and trust." The two outstanding disabilities on the ground were, said Fysh, the lack of a good direction-finding station at Darwin and Koepang and the want of wireless stations at Cloncurry and Longreach.[39]

The QEA overseas airmail service left Brisbane each Wednesday morning at five minutes past seven, summer timetable. Its main intermediate ports (there were six in all on the

246

first day) were Charleville (where the southern mail from Butler's service was collected) and Longreach, with a night stop at Cloncurry. Passengers were accommodated at the Post Office Hotel, where McGinness and McMaster had had the meeting that led to the beginnings of Qantas. On the second day, the service flew on to Camooweal and Daly Waters, where the mail from Western Australia was loaded. Darwin was sighted in late afternoon and passengers taken for the night to the cottage on the cliff at Vesty's meatworks, leased and renovated by the airline. The rent was two pounds a week, which Fysh considered too high.[40]

Heading out over the sea from Darwin, new techniques of navigation were used. An observation of Cape Fourcroy, a hundred miles from Darwin, gave a good position check, and the extremity of the continental shelf was, wrote Scotty Allan, easily observable as it rose to within six or eight feet at low water, some 140 miles from Koepang. "Immediately after leaving this strip of cheerful light green," he wrote, "the bottom of the sea falls vertically to an awe-inspiring black depth of around six thousand feet."[41] To allow for the effect of wind on the aircraft's track when out of sight of land, drift sights were taken. Lester Brain issued a memo to pilots outlining the technique. "In flying over the sea, a sight may be taken on the froth from a wave that has spilled, but not on a 'white horse' that is still running. Where there is no chop on the water a sight can almost invariably be taken on floating debris, discolouration or submerged reefs." Brain also insisted on pilots obtaining the following wind or headwind component of the upper winds from their driftsights to verify the data supplied by the Darwin Meteorology Station.[42] The station, using upper air balloons, found that the strong south-east winds that helped the aircraft from Darwin to Koepang often became calm or changed to light westerlies above eight thousand feet, so that at this height a tail wind was also possible in the other direction. (On clear nights the station attached Chinese paper lanterns to the balloons, which were bought in Singapore by QEA pilots for fifteen shillings a gross.) "In the monsoon period," wrote Allan, "the crossing was often flown at 1,000 feet, owing to the heavy build up of monsoonal cloud, skirting the worst downpours." Scotty Allan always worked hard at minimizing fuel consumption on his own flights so that, he wrote, "each trip was endlessly interesting and never boring; consequently, also, never fatiguing. Present day pilots' fatigue", he commented many years later, "is doubtless nine-tenths boredom."[43]

A.E. Rudder, QEA vice-chairman, set down his comments as a passenger on the return Singapore–Brisbane journey in a letter to Fysh.

> The change from such luxurious accommodation at Singapore to almost native jungle simplicity at Rambang is startling, and the unusual and romantic side may not be fully appreciated by some travellers, especially women. The rest house is really very well arranged and comfortable. One of the main difficulties is that the native servants do not understand a word of English. The food is somewhat mysterious and not attractive to English taste. As the lighting is by kerosene lamps, some difficulty is experienced in reaching lavatory accommodation, no commodes being provided in the rooms.

Rudder judged the Darwin Rest House a success. "The place is beautifully situated, well furnished and very comfortable. The food and attention leave nothing to be desired." For the refreshments at places of call to Longreach he had nothing but praise, except that there could be "more adequate provision for covering the food from flies". He also remarked that "kerosene cases may be in keeping with the rough conditions [as seats] but nails are apt to tear clothing and cause annoyance". He suggested cane chairs or camp stools. There were, he said, "complaints, loud and sustained, and rightly so, regarding the quality and inadequacy of transport arrangements between aerodrome and hotel" at Longreach but he praised the attention, food, and accommodation. "Our ground staff suffer by comparison in smartness and deportment with similar people on the other side", he observed. "In my experience, men live up to their dress — especially uniforms." In the air, Rudder observed his own physical reactions and found his heart pumping just a little above normal at ten thousand feet, while he had a slight tendency to headache. He noted: "There is room in this direction for medical and scientific research, as the results of high flying might be very serious to people suffering from acute blood pressure."[44]

To help pilots maintain schedules on the route there were, on the Cloncurry–Longreach sector of 311 miles, six revolving beacons set 60 miles apart so that night flying was possible when services were running late. However, commented A.R. McComb to Edgar Johnston on 31 May 1935

> Qantas were very sticky about commencing night flying on this section with the facilities and arrangements made. Frankly, I feel they were apprehensive about night flying due to their not having had experience of it and, from Fysh's letters, we gathered he was

rather nervy about it. I might mention that we have arranged for the Australian Inland Mission at Cloncurry, and Hegarty, the postal employee at Longreach, to keep in touch with the plane by wireless during the night flying section.[45]

Rudder's comments had resulted from a visit to England with McMaster to discuss the proposed Empire Air Mail Scheme and the use of flying boats. Before leaving, on 1 May 1935, they had met with the minister for defence for a briefing on the official government view. Archdale Parkhill made four

main points: first, Australia would much have preferred to be left alone to improve and perfect the existing scheme, with reduction of expenses; second, Australia strongly desired to control the route from Singapore to Sydney (and certainly from Darwin to Sydney); third, the question of flying boats would be subject to further information; and fourth, the fact that the Imperial Airways proposal was an Empire scheme was the main and paramount reason why consideration was

A.E. Rudder and Fergus McMaster at Batavia aerodrome in May 1935, en route to London for discussions with Imperial Airways board of directors.

being given to it. At their meeting, McMaster reminded the minister that though he was a member of the QEA board, he retained responsibilities for the original Q.A.N.T.A.S. company. If, he said, Imperial Airways wanted a company to be formed in Australia — to be known as Qantas Imperial Airways — this would "require the Qantas people to put up something like £150,000". Assuming they were unable to find this amount, and the capital was supplied by Imperial Airways, would the Commonwealth government accept a local company obviously controlled by British capital? Or would the government come forward and find the full amount or portion of it? Archdale Parkhill gave a half answer. The government, he said, would decide when the full facts were known. It would, he said, be most reluctant to put public money into a company with private enterprise where the latter was a dominant factor.[46]

As these pressures from England for great change on the Empire air route grew, the Australian government was made aware of United States ambitions for a Pan American Airways route across the Pacific. The air attache at the British Embassy in Washington, Group Capt. G.R. Macfarlane Reid, wrote to Edgar Johnston that "the United States seem to be nosing out a route to Australia already". Reid enclosed a cutting from the *New York Times* on 22 May 1935 describing the activities of the Coast Guard cutter *Ithaca* and reporting that "its recent 7,500 miles cruise to strategic islands south and south-west of Hawaii will further strengthen the already established American domination of Pacific aviation routes." These islands, said the paper, will be important "when and if Pan America's air line, now being established from Alameda, California, through Honolulu, Midway, Wake, Guam and the Philippines to the Orient, is extended from Honolulu to Australia".[47]

These matters of state were far from Fysh's mind when he wrote to Woods Humphery on 10 May. The swelling volume of mail and difficulty of accommodating passengers on the QEA route to Singapore was being compounded by shortage of seats on the IAL service beyond Singapore. "The turning away of one passenger", he wrote, "is a serious thing for us. It represents a quarter of our total possible passenger load westbound on the overseas section, and one third eastbound."[48] Qantas had already made representations to the government for a variation of its contract in relation to excess mail loadings, to compensate it for passenger revenue loss. The minister for defence, Parkhill, rejected the suggestion but was not entirely unsympathetic.

> The contract has been in operaton for only five and a half months and the service open for the carriage of overseas passengers for only a little more than a month. It has not yet been definitely established that your company has sustained actual financial loss attributable to the unexpected growth in air mail traffic. It has been decided to defer further consideration of your representations until the contract has been in operation for twelve months.

He softened the blow by adding:

> The Government realise it may be found necessary to review the position at an earlier stage should mails increase to such an extent as seriously to interfere with the Government intention that the service provide reasonable facilities for passengers and freight as well as mails. The solution may lie in the introduction of a more frequent service.[49]

Increased frequency was, of course, exactly what Qantas wanted. The airline promptly took up the ministerial hint and set out its case for duplication in a letter on 6 June 1935. Average mail loadings for the first year, based on mail loadings to date, would be three times that estimated by the government, said Qantas. An excess revenue of £45,000 annually above that estimated by the government was being recovered from mails. This excess, Qantas concluded, should pay for duplication.

The existing Singapore–Brisbane service, Qantas submitted, was inadequate because the excess mails resulted in insufficient passenger space across the Timor Sea, which was a bottleneck. Passengers and freight were being refused in both directions. Additionally, the usefulness of the service to the people of the interior from Brisbane to Darwin was almost eliminated in comparison with the original service, and it was impractical to call at all necessary outback centres because of delay to mails for southern capitals.

Qantas added two further points of substance, the first dear to its own heart, the second designed to appeal to the keeper of the public purse. An additional frequency would, said Qantas, provide further reason why a Dutch extension to Australia was unnecessary; and, finally, the increased mileage "would be flown at a contract rate of approximately two shillings a mile as against three shillings and one penny for the present mileage, thus greatly reducing the average cost per mile to the Commonwealth Government". Duplication, said Qantas, would cost approximately £46,000 per year.[50]

251

Meanwhile, in London, McMaster had been meeting with Imperial Airways to discuss their revolutionary plans for Empire civil aviation. He was welcomed in true British fashion by a luncheon with the board of directors of Imperial Airways comprising the Right Hon. Sir Eric Geddes GCB GBE, chairman; Sir George Beharrel DSO, vice-chairman; Sir Samuel Instone DL; Sir Hardiman Lever KCB; Sir Walter Nicholson KCB; the Hon. Esmond Harmsworth (son of Lord Northcliffe); and G.E. Woods Humphery, managing director. Only two directors were unable to attend — Marshal of the Royal Air Force Sir John Salmond and H. Scott Paine.[51] McMaster was dined at the House of Commons on 3 June and had discussions with S.M. Bruce, Australian high commissioner, next day. Meantime, he had sampled the famous IAL Night Service to Paris, leaving Croydon at six and dining on board with hors d'oeuvres, consomme jardiniere, a cold selection of chicken, York ham, lamb, and veal-and-ham pie with salad, all topped off with trifle and coffee. From Paris he visited the old battlegrounds of World War I and he paused in the cathedral at Amiens to note (on his IAL menu card) an inscription from one of the tablets: "In this Diocese lie the dead of the Battles of the Somme 1918." It was a solemn interlude for him.[52]

McMaster outlined the results of his London visit in a letter to Edgar Johnston on 6 June 1935. The objective, he said, had been to establish the position of QEA assuming "that the Australian Government decided to co-operate with the United Kingdom and other Dominions and Colonial governments on the scheme for carrying by air all the first class letter mail within the Empire". He enclosed a draft outlining the proposed method for QEA and IAL co-operation in which, he said, "although provision has been made for the full operation of the fleet as a complete unit, the constitution forming the present Qantas Empire Airways is unaltered". He added: "After having flown the whole route from Australia I feel that the development should be by flying boat as against landplane." If Australia joined in fully, wrote McMaster, "the move will lift Empire air transport from its present restricted use, whereby it is confined to carrying small loads of highly surcharged mail, to a more definite form of development in a truly commercial sense". It would also, he said, encourage inter-Empire travel by air. "One has only to use the [present] service to realise that it is quite inadequate and cannot be satisfactory to the Government or ourselves as contractors" he concluded.[53]

Neither Johnston, at the head of civil aviation, nor Air Vice Marshall Williams, at the head of the RAAF, shared McMaster's view of flying boats, or the likely outcome of IAL pressures to control the service between Australia and Singapore. In a letter to Fysh on 10 June, Air Vice Marshal Williams remarked cheerfully: "Where does this flying boat to Sydney idea come from? Whoever put that up is either dotty or has an idea to take your part of the service from you."[54]

In purely operational terms, the new DH86 service to Singapore had proved highly successful. Lester Brain and his pilots had mastered the new techniques necessary for long flights over the ocean, while Baird and his engineers kept the aircraft flying. "Things are going nicely on the route", Fysh was able to tell McComb on 12 June though, he said, he expected the first real test of landing grounds and navigational aids, as well as of flying personnel, in the next monsoon season from December or early January. "One of our nightmares", he wrote, "is the possibility of being held up, for perhaps days, through not being able to get off some boggy ground." Qantas was not by any means, he said, out of its financial worries "but if overseas passengers keep up as they are at present, we won't be unduly worried for the first year. I am more worried about the second year as subsidy comes down by threepence a mile and we have budgeted for an average of two overseas passengers a trip each way. As this on present mail loadings represents sixty-six per cent of available passenger seats I don't see how we can realise it unless there is a tremendous rush of passengers."[55]

McMaster arrived back in Brisbane on 20 June 1935 and at once expressed his full and public support for the Empire Mail Scheme. He told the Brisbane *Telegraph*: "Britain is resolved to use flying boats on all Empire trunk lines. They will place Britain in the forefront of the world's race for air supremacy." The scheme, he said, was colossal in conception. "Australia should have no hesitation in playing her part, enabling flying boats to come all the way to Australia, down the eastern seaboard to Brisbane and Sydney, and eventually on to New Zealand." There would, however, he added, "be cogent reasons for the continuance of the existing overland route to Darwin because of the vital service it supplies to the outback".[56]

The link with New Zealand mentioned by McMaster was also in Edgar Johnston's mind. From London on 26 June 1935 he wrote to the secretary of the Department of Defence about

253

Pacific air services. While in the United States, he said, he found that "Pan American made no secret of their interest in an Australian connection". They were "not so anxious to operate the connection themselves as obtain a connection to Australia to increase the traffic on their other routes", and were "prepared to find the capital to help establish a connecting service if that were necessary and welcome". He concluded: "A matter of perhaps a more urgent nature is the establishment of British claims to any islands in the Pacific to which title is not very definite."[57]

To his acting controller, McComb, Johnston expressed his suspicions about British reticence on IAL's plans for flying boats.

> Although the United Kingdom Director-General of Civil Aviation was at some pains to assure me that only two of these machines had been ordered, Scott Paine of the Power Boat Company, who is also a director Imperial Airways, let fall to me that Imperials had just placed an order for a million pounds worth of new equipment. This sum would be involved in ordering the complete fleet of flying boats [approximately twenty to twenty-five units]. It seems likely, therefore, that Imperials and the British Government are anticipating the Dominions' acceptance of the Empire Scheme.

Johnston sent McComb data on the flying boats which were under construction, estimating that the cost of the two completed prototypes was £45,000 to £50,000 each.[58]

Only three days later, a much annoyed Johnston wrote privately to McComb. "Dear Mac," he began, "They are all at me here to support the Scheme full out. Rudder was the first; Woods Humphery and Dismore have all been tackling me, mostly over lunches. I am fairly satisfied that the whole Scheme is designed to destroy our national aspirations for our own service. Whether this is deliberate or not I am not prepared to say". While IAL had good propaganda methods, he said, he found it "exceedingly difficult to get any information about the flying boats". He damned the "colossal inefficiency" of the Air Ministry. "Each man", said Johnston, "seems to keep himself in a very watertight compartment, and know about a quarter of what he should to do the job properly ... I rather fancy they regard me as a wild Colonial when I speak my views and ask them what they are going to do to meet them. One invariably gets that soft answer which means nothing — and annoys me."[59] It was apparent that Hudson Fysh's plea to Woods Humphery for candour had gone unheeded.

254

In stark contrast to Johnston, McMaster was now publicly and vigorously supporting the plans of Imperial Airways. Only a few days after Johnston set down his criticism to McComb, McMaster told the Brisbane *Telegraph* that on his visit to London to discuss the development of the England–Australia service and its possible extension to New Zealand, the basis for full co-operation had been reached with Imperial Airways and Indian Trans-Continental Airways. He had, he said, inspected a full-scale mock-up of the new and revolutionary type of flying boat being built for IAL and was impressed. Flying boats would, said McMaster, provide sounder commercial results than any system operated by land-planes.[60] McMaster's statement was taken up in Sydney by the *Sydney Morning Herald*, which declared in a leader on 9 July:

> Australian officials in England, who have been thrashing out details of the plans recently submitted to the Federal Government by a British delegation, have so far advanced the discussions that large flying boats will definitely enter the Australian service in 1937, and probably continue to New Zealand . . . It seems from the statements by the chairman of Qantas, Mr McMaster, who returned recently from a special conference . . . in London, that Australian ministers have recognized the need for both larger aircraft on this end of the service and the inevitable resort to flying boats. The Commonwealth Government for a time resisted the proposal to use flying boats from Darwin southward . . .[61]

Controlling Interests
1935

13 While Qantas had been preoccupied with the London talks and the capacity problems on the DH86 service across the Timor Sea, Kingsford Smith and P.G. Taylor had pressed their Tasman ambitions on both public and government. These two great airmen sought public attention in the way they knew best — a flight across the Tasman from Sydney in the now legendary *Southern Cross*. It almost cost them their lives but resulted in an adventure and an escape from disaster that thrilled the people of Australia and England. Taylor emerged from the episode as a hero, with his coolness and courage part of a story that would be passed on to future generations of Australian children. On 16 May 1935, with Taylor as navigator, Kingsford Smith took off from Sydney and set course for New Zealand. The flight was billed by them as the King's Jubilee Service. When the eight-year-old *Southern Cross* was in mid-Tasman, some six hundred miles from Sydney, an exhaust pipe broke on the centre engine and a piece of metal splintered the starboard propeller and put the starboard engine out of action. Smithy turned back for Sydney. Then one of the remaining two engines began to give trouble. Taylor climbed out of the small window of the cockpit. Clinging to a narrow strut with one hand, he removed one of the plates of the engine cowling, to reach the oil drain pipe. In the pocket of his flying coat he had placed a thermos flask, while a kit bag was clamped under his arm. Painstakingly he drained the oil from the starboard engine and, using thermos flask and kit bag, transferred the oil to the port engine

256

to keep it functioning. They limped back to Mascot where, reported the *Sydney Morning Herald*, the waiting crowd greeted them "with cries of 'Good old Smithy' ". Sir Charles, said the report, "looked tired and haggard. He was stone deaf but assumed his usual nonchalant air as he waved to the crowd." P.G. Taylor told the *Herald* that the object of the flight had been to raise public interest in Australia and New Zealand "so that people of the two Dominions would ensure that the trans-Tasman air mail service would be owned and operated by their own people. Quite frankly, we do not want the English company, Imperial Airways, to operate a service which is our own by right of the pioneering development which has been done."[1] In London, the *Daily Mail* declared that Sir Charles's struggle over the Tasman Sea had thrilled the Empire.

Kingsford Smith at once followed up the nationwide interest in their adventure. On 6 June 1935 he announced in Melbourne that he, P.G. Taylor, and Flying Officer B. Shield had registered a new company whose object was eventually to start a regular air service between Australia and New Zealand. It was named the Trans-Tasman Development Company Ltd., with Mr John Stannage as company secretary. That very day, the Melbourne *Argus* reported a London statement by Imperial Airways "contesting P.G. Taylor's view that the Tasman Sea air route should be the prerogative of Australian and New Zealand operators". The route, said the IAL statement, "was certain to be included among the trunk lines of the great Imperial system".[2]

Kingsford Smith, however, was convinced that his popular support would sway the government. On 20 June he submitted proposals for the establishment of an experimental air service to New Zealand for a period of at least six months. No suitable British aircraft were available, he said. He proposed either the American Sikorsky S42 or the Martin flying boat. The Sikorsky, he said, had a range of 2,000 miles at 160 miles per hour, and cost £72,000. The press report of his submission said: "At present the object of Sir Charles and Captain Taylor is to get the Federal Government to take an active interest in a trans-Tasman aerial service and invite the financial and active co-operation of the New Zealand Government."[3] On 24 June Kingsford Smith wrote to the minister for defence, Archdale Parkhill, saying that as Cabinet, although impressed with his proposals, was reluctant to provide the entire capital, he was prepared to provide the capital and operate the service, either for a £44,000 annual subsidy with one trip each way a week, using a Sikorsky flying boat, or two flying boats and a double frequency for a subsidy of £80,000 a year. He suggested, however, a 50 per cent capital participation by the Commonwealth.[4] Parkill was not impressed and told McComb that the government was not "likely to be stampeded on Smithy's proposal".[5] Reporting this to Edgar Johnston, McComb added: "Incidentally, the Commonwealth Government has given Smithy £3,000 for his *Southern Cross*. It is proposed, we understand, to keep it at Canberra as a museum relic. I was asked to say what I thought [its] commerical value, and advised £1,500 was the outside value."[6]

McComb, in the same letter, advised Johnston that the PMG scheme for the carriage of mails within Australia had been accepted generally in principle though not yet approved by Cabinet. "I feel with you that if the PMG scheme were approved by Cabinet on the basis of no surcharge for air mails, then it would be much more difficult to fight against the proposed Empire Air Mail Scheme." A letter to McComb from Johnston, in London, crossed with McComb's letter. Johnston reported that he had seen a statement in *The Times* of 11 July saying that the minister agreed with Kingsford Smith's contention that the Tasman service was entirely a matter for Australia and New Zealand. The statement, said Johnston, was causing some consternation in London but, he added, "I trust and hope it is the view of the Minister and the Government".[7]

To Fysh, on 12 July 1935, Johnston wrote, in a personal letter:

> I can see no other result but the complete swallowing up by Imperial Airways of Qantas, who would cease to have any responsibility to anyone except Imperials . . . Certainly Qantas could have no contract with the Commonwealth Government. I feel that the main requirement today is an acceleration of the Empire Service, particularly on the section between Singapore and London. We have comparatively fast aircraft on our section and, with the provision of reasonable night flying facilities, could operate by the end of this year as fast as is proposed under the Empire Scheme for 1944 . . . I think we should endeavour to retain an Australian service from Singapore to Australian terminals.[8]

Johnston wrote a confidential letter to the secretary of the Department of Defence the next day, saying that a conference had been arranged for 17 July between Mr R.G. Menzies, attorney-general, himself, and the United Kingdom government representatives to discuss informally Australia's draft reply to the United Kingdom government on the Empire Scheme. This draft, Johnston thought, did not dispose of serious objections to the Scheme from Australia's point of view. These were the virtual merging of the three existing companies of the United Kingdom, India, and Australia and a sacrifice of Australian control on the Singapore–Australia section, plus departure from the "Australian practice of close control over the contractor's operations and the arrangement of a fifteen-year contract by negotiation instead of tender".[9]

That all these aviation matters were becoming issues of wide public interest is evident from a letter by A.E. Rudder to Woods Humphery on 16 July. "On my return," he wrote, "I was startled to find that this country seems to have gone crazy over air developments. Much of this is due to Kingsford Smith's and Taylor's activities in regard to New Zealand, the new proposals to carry air mail within Australia without a surcharge . . . and the desire of the shipping companies to take some part in local air services." Rudder reported that he had had an hour with the minister for defence. "Parkhill states", he said, "that if you do not get a move on, the Commonwealth Government will act independently and make their own arrangements, not only for the improvement of the Singapore service but also the extension to New Zealand." Australia, however, definitely favoured an Empire and not a local service, said Rudder. "As a matter of fact there is no love lost politically between Australia and New Zealand, and Australia does not care very much whether there is an Australian–New Zealand service or not. On the other hand, New Zealand is intensely Imperialistic and more dependent on the Mother Country."[10]

The London meeting for 17 July advised by Johnston took place at Australia House, with R.G. Menzies as chairman. Present were Sir Christopher Bullock, United Kingdom permanent secretary of the Air Ministry; Colonel Shelmerdine, director of civil aviation; Mr Francis Bertram, deputy director; Sir Donald Banks, Post Office; and Edgar Johnston, controller of civil aviation, Australia. Menzies opened the discussions urbanely, saying that he was there to listen and report. "I know extremely little about it", he said. "It is not my department." It was Edgar Johnston who bore the brunt of the arguing and, while Menzies displayed his equanimity and wit, suffered some measured disdain from the British.

Johnston first pressed Australia's objections to the additional cost that would flow from the Empire Scheme, such as feeder services beyond the terminating ports. The United Kingdom thought these should not be admitted. "On the mail side," announced Sir Donald Banks with a ring of finality, "we have discharged our function when we land our mails in the country." That, responded Johnston bluntly, was perfectly sound if the United Kingdom was going to run a service to take just their own mails to Australia. "But this is an Empire service," he pointed out, "supposed to be drawn up in collaboration with the lot of us to serve the Empire."

Menzies interposed: "I can quite see that the trunk system for the airmail service is one which starts at every provincial centre in England and ends at every capital in Australia." Johnston, thus encouraged, then pressed for a surcharge on the airmails to bring in revenue, and Menzies gave philosophical support. "We are too inclined", he observed, "to encourage people to believe that they can always have the latest and best without paying for it. A surcharge system does seem to me to make the man who gets the benefit pay for it."

Johnston argued that a surcharge would reduce loads and enable a smaller and faster aircraft to be used. The Douglas, he reminded them, had flown the route in four days. It could provide a regular service to Australia in seven days and still allow ten hours every night on the ground. That, he said, "is the best we can give seven years from now with the flying boat". He urged a service that would cruise at 200 miles per hour and give an average journey time of four days.

Sir Christopher Bullock: "Captain Johnston is suggesting that the whole Empire service be reorganized to meet the Australian position."

Johnston: "I feel that if you try to convince me, I can try to convince you."

Menzies, mediating: "Are there any other questions that require discussing?"

They turned to the question of control, with Johnston pointing out that Australia wished to retain adequate power over its own national company.

Sir Christopher Bullock: "You lose control of your machines west of Singapore. We should lose control of our machines east of Singapore."

Johnston: "If the Australia–Singapore operations would be entirely under the control of the Commonwealth Government, to whom the operators would be solely responsible for their operations within that section . . . I think that would cover our points entirely."

Sir Christopher Bullock: "That . . . would certainly need straightening out."

It was not straightened out at that particular meeting. A diplomatic Menzies chided Johnston: "I do not see how you can say that on one side of Singapore machines are going to run once a week and on the other side twice a week." The meeting closed, but Johnston was optimistic.[11] He reported in a confidential and personal letter to McComb on 20 July: "I tackled them on the proposal to carry all mails by air, not because I was opposed to that in principle but mainly because the United Kingdom claimed that, carrying all mail, it was impossible to provide high speed at a cost within the means of the Government. I expressed the alternative of carrying less mail but at a speed that would put us in the foremost position of air services in the world. This idea appealed to Menzies." Johnston said that he believed the United Kingdom conclusions had already been determined.[12] (However, both he and McComb continued to press their views in Australia.)

McComb told the secretary of the Defence Department that Imperial Airways' plans for through control of the service to Sydney were not unbiassed. They wanted this, he said, "to strengthen their claim that they are the only people to run the trans-Tasman service".[13] Johnston, in a move to thwart Imperial Airways, wrote to McComb on 20 July about Kingsford Smith's proposal for an experimental service across the Tasman. "It might be advisable", he said, "not to oppose the proposal, as long as we are not required to take responsibility for recommending a contract by negotiation. My reason is that the early institution of even an experimental service will greatly strengthen our position in any arguments on the Empire Scheme."[14]

Woods Humphery was well aware that Johnston opposed the plans of Imperial Airways. He told Fysh by letter on 23 July 1935 that though the case for the flying boat was conclusive they had not, in Johnston's various talks with them and with government officials, convinced him. Johnston wanted mails to Australia to be dealt with separately from the all-up scheme, and carried with a surcharge in aircraft with similar characteristics to the Douglas. "He has seen nothing of British transport", said Woods Humphery, "and evidently does not appreciate the special requirements of the Empire services. Your Controller is straight and honest, even if he is a stubborn rather than a strong man."[16]

261

At chairman-to-chairman level, McMaster described the Australian attitude to Sir Eric Geddes at the end of July. There was now, he said, "a definite swing towards the use of land aircraft. A lot will depend upon the attitude of Mr Menzies and Captain Johnston. The press reports are to the effect that Mr Menzies is behind the proposals. Much will depend on what push he can give, for definitely there will be considerable opposition and apathy. I do not expect that Captain Johnston will give very much assistance". Both the Defence and Postal departments, said McMaster, now pressed for fast landplanes. "Naturally, every weakness in the flying boat proposal is exaggerated." In discussions with the minister and secretary for the Defence Department, he said, he had stressed that the British proposals were merely a basis for co-operation, but he sensed that "the feeling appears to have been that the proposals were submitted in a 'stand and deliver' atmosphere, to be taken or rejected".[16] (McMaster was also occupied at the time with seasonal difficulties on his properties. He told A.E. Rudder on 22 July: "I am afraid our losses have been severe with the cold rain, but no heavier than they would be had the drought continued into the storm season. Cold rain losses are usually severe, but they are swift and inexpensive compared with droughts. Anyway, it is all in the game, and why worry . . .")[17]

Fysh described the Australian attitude more forcefully in a letter to Woods Humphery:

> Shepherd, the Secretary of the Defence Department, is most antagonistic to IAL and to the Scheme, and the Minister for Defence and Air Vice Marshal Williams are right against the boat scheme as taking the control out of the hands of Australia. This attitude is followed by Johnston and lesser officials. The only man I found in favour of boats is H.P. Brown, Director of Postal Services, who is a man of vision. [There is] great dissatisfaction at what is termed the "take it or leave it" attitude of the British Government. The only chance of real success is to immediately amend the proposals, giving the Sydney–Singapore section the same Australian flavour as it has now.

Fysh pointed out that the government currently had four major aviation issues to consider: duplication of the present overseas service; the 1937 Empire Mail Plan with flying boats; reorganization of internal Australian air routes; and the expansion of air services from Australia to New Zealand.[18]

The government was moving, if slowly, towards duplication of the QEA service to Singapore. The minister for defence announced on 26 July 1935 that the Air Contracts Committee would be asked to review the mail contracts with a view to the adoption of a twice weekly service. Cost was the overriding Government concern. A departmental memorandum of 2 August calculated that average mail loadings per trip between mid-May and mid-June had earned revenue of £585 inward and £526 outward, results that were some 25 per cent above those estimated for the sixth year of the service. Annual revenue from overseas mail on this unexpected scale was calculated at £65,000. Internal airmail revenue on the QEA route was put at £11,000 per year, providing gross revenue from all airmail of £75,000. The department estimated that the net cost of duplicating the QEA service, taking this revenue into account, would be a further £75,000. This, it said, closely approximated the net loss estimated for the once weekly service at the time the government approved the scheme. It was certain, said the department, that weekly loadings with a duplicated service would exceed these current loadings, thus reducing net cost. An increase of 25 per cent would lower net cost to £54,000 a year, while a 50 per cent increase in loadings was not beyond the bounds of possibility.[19]

Qantas had submitted its full proposals for duplication to the minister. Commenting on them in a letter to Johnston, Fysh said the only alternative was a review of QEA's present contract conditions "owing to the unprecedented growth in the air mails . . . anticipated at 800 pounds weight per trip each way by the end of the year".[20] Johnston thought the QEA charges for providing a doubled frequency unduly high, but in a letter to McComb on 14 August, rejected the suggestion that the books of QEA should be investigated, saying: "Surely it is not proposed to make this an excuse for a virtual review of the Qantas contract. To do so would be most unwise, as the contract was only recently let on tender. Anything approaching revision . . . at this stage is much too dangerous for my liking."[21] (The Q.A.N.T.A.S. profit for the year ending 30 June 1935 was £4,821 on a paid capital of £44,431, and a dividend of 4 per cent was declared.)

On the issue of the Tasman service to New Zealand, McComb told Johnston on 30 July: "The New Zealand Government is not taking kindly to Kingsford Smith's proposal . . . Its view is not too comforting to us as far as our proposal to consider an Australia–New Zealand service independently of the British Empire Scheme is concerned."[22]

Kingsford Smith's colleague in the venture, Capt. P.G. Taylor, paid a surprise visit to Fysh, who told Woods Humphery:

> I had no wish to see him and gave him no information. I expect his mission was to spy out the land. He and Kingsford Smith are straining every nerve to get in on the Sydney–New Zealand service and he told me that the worst thing we could do would be to combine with Imperial Airways in running the service. At the same time, Taylor ran down Imperial Airways and de Havillands in a most bitter and unrelenting manner — and, in fact, everything British. I have never heard so much pure hate for a long time. It is obvious that he and Kingsford Smith are unbusinesslike and incapable when it comes to organising and operating a service like that between Sydney and New Zealand. But they have a certain following in Parliament and among the public which it is not wise to ignore. I think the Australian Government and public should be told without delay of the broad plans for the service, and that you have a type [of aircraft] building.[23]

Woods Humphery was, however, bringing the considerable apparatus of British power and influence to bear on the battling Kingsford Smith and Taylor. "On the subject of Kingsford Smith's activities," he told Fysh on 30 July 1935, "I have arranged with the Air Ministry and the Dominion's Office for them to telegraph the New Zealand Government, asking them not to commit themselves to anything before consulting with the Government here. In the meantime, we are preparing a scheme ... to put to the United Kingdom Government."[24] In Australia, the acting prime minister, Dr Earl Page, received a cable from the New Zealand government on 5 August saying: "Kingsford Smith stated here that he considered the Australian Government favoured his scheme and would prefer him to be the contractor." The cable pointed out that New Zealand thought such a separate scheme very expensive and that any discussions about the Tasman service were premature pending development of the London–Sydney first class mail service.[25] Unaware of these developments, Kingsford Smith told the minister for defence, Parkhill, that his Trans-Tasman Development Company had completed negotiations with a British aircraft manufacturer to build Sikorsky flying boats in England for the Tasman service.[26] In London, the *Daily Express* charged that "Sir Charles Kingsford Smith is today planning a pirate air route with American aircraft over the 1,200 miles between Australia and New Zealand. It will compete with the general Empire air mail speed-up and extension scheduled to begin in 1937."[27] The *Express* quoted the New Zealand acting prime minister, Sir Ethelbert Ransom, as critical of the venture. "It would scarcely be keeping faith with Britain and would certainly be an embarrassment," said Sir Ethelbert, "were New Zealand at this stage to become prematurely committed to a separate proposal. The Tasman service must be considered part of a comprehensive Empire scheme."[28] In the battle between the Empire and Sir Charles Kingsford Smith, it was evident that the big battalions were with the Empire.

Fysh set out the offical QEA view on IAL's plans for Edgar Johnston and sent him a copy, on 8 August, of the *Qantas Gazette*. The issue had the significant title "Empire Airways". "It contains", wrote Fysh, "a declaration of policy which I am certain must be on the right lines." New Zealand, said the *Gazette* article, is vitally interested in joining the Empire chain but "the route can only be considered logically as the final link of the Empire Main Trunk Service. Economically, the Service is one, and any break of gauge would prove decidedly detrimental. As peoples of the world are drawn closer together [by aviation] the need of a greater measure of co-operation becomes more obvious. For Britishers, the first consideration must be Empire co-operation."[29] Fysh's parliamentary friend, J.V. Fairbairn, read the article and wrote to Fysh expressing his concern about the Kingsford Smith pressures and the attempts by his supporters to find employment for him.

> Although I consider the extension . . . to New Zealand desirable, from the Australian and Empire point of view, I consider the value of an Australia–New Zealand service would be five to six times greater to New Zealand than to Australia. The suggestion that the two countries share the cost of such a service equally — just to create a position for a certain person — seems to me preposterous. I will discuss the matter as soon as possible with members of Cabinet.[30]

McMaster prepared a formal resolution for the Q.A.N.T.A.S. board on the Tasman issue: "That we as representatives of the Queensland and Northern Territory Aerial Services Limited support in general principle the proposed extension of the Empire Air Mail Service from Australia to New Zealand and will use our influence for the full participation of Q.A.N.T.A.S. on a basis to be agreed, should such action be desired by the Governments concerned." His fellow directors accepted the resolution.[31]

It was a stance that the controller of civil aviation opposed.

On 14 August, Johnston wrote to McComb: "I am still hopeful of bringing about an Australia–New Zealand show." He had, he said, been rushing around England seeing factories and new machines and designs. "They certainly seem to be seized with the importance of speed now", he wrote. "All except Imperials, who are quite happy to potter along at about 140 miles an hour." On the Empire Mail Scheme his views had not changed. "I am still as adamant as ever in my opposition to the Empire Scheme", he wrote. "In fact, more so. I am certainly very definitely opposed to handing over control of the operations and I believe we should fight for Singapore."[32] He reported that he had dined with Woods Humphery and found he would not be greatly upset if Australia did not accept the Empire Scheme. Woods Humphery had said he felt sure the United Kingdom government would find the money to run the service to Australia and New Zealand and "would carry the British and New Zealand mails, and make such charges as they considered reasonable for conveyance of Australian mail to Europe and New Zealand". His inference, Johnston commented, "was that these British charges would have to come out of Australian consolidated revenue, as it would be impossible politically for Australia to demand a high surcharge from its letter-posting public."[33]

Hudson Fysh had to apportion his energies, as usual, between matters of high policy and internal Qantas housekeeping. Appropriate salary levels for pilots occupied him and he wrote seeking Dismore's advice. (Dismore had been promoted in March to the position of assistant general manager of IAL.)

> I find in making estimates for Captains under duplication that Brain is quoting that your Captains realise £1,400 per annum, and that in order to ensure smooth working, now that our Captains have proved themselves, and if more flying eventuates, they should be paid a higher remuneration. At present our Captains average about £885 per annum plus living allowance. With three extra Captains, under duplication, they will average £1,010 per annum for 952 hours [flying] each per year. The Flight Superintendent [Brain] would do six only return trips to Singapore per year as against fourteen by each Captain. Personally, I think — considering present Captains will get a rise of twenty-five pounds per annum as from December next — they are paid well enough. It seems, however, that we will have to increase Brain's salary to allow him to draw more than the Captains; say £850 salary plus £250 flying pay. What do you consider our policy should be?

It was now becoming apparent, at the highest levels in Imperial Airways, that their initial sanguine expectations for swift Australian acquiescence in the plan which they had developed in such secrecy was not to be forthcoming. Their vision of Empire was certainly shared, but the exercise of power was in dispute. Control by Australia of the Australian overseas airline was the central issue. It was a new and significant manifestation of Dominion independence and a novel projection, geographically, of Australia's perceived national rights in the air. The chairman of Imperial Airways, Sir Eric Geddes, wrote at some length to Fergus McMaster on 2 September 1935 setting out both the grand perspectives of the British scheme and the unwelcome obscurity now overshadowing them. For Geddes, Australian independence, seen from England, was Australian parochialism.

> After our talks in London, I expect it seems to you, as it does to me, that the Home Government and some of the Australian ministers and officials are viewing the Scheme through very different spectacles. As you know, the scheme of sending all letter mails to the Empire by air was born of a higher thought than fulfilling purely local requirements. It was part of a far wider plan to bring into closer association the various units which together form the British Empire, and to give to those territories the most rapid and frequent intercommunications possible at the lowest economic cost. The plan involved the fullest possible co-operation between the Dominions and Colonies, which was justified on the grounds that the plan would be for the ultimate benefit of all, even though it did not necessarily meet each separate local requirement. That was, and is, the essence of the Scheme as you and I know it.

It would seem, he said, that Mr Parkhill was particularly exercised over the local disadvantages of the Scheme so far as they affected Australia. (Parkhill thought flying boats of little use for defence purposes.) Sir Eric continued loftily:

> In the opinion of those best qualified to judge, military requirements and those of commercial transport are incompatible. Similarly the requirements of the inland service . . . are incompatible with those of the main route.

Sir Eric firmly denied the charge that Britain had adopted a "stand and deliver" attitude.

> Surely the main question for decision by Australia is whether or not it wishes to participate . . . The ways and means should surely be capable of solution between the two Governments. If Australia does not wish Australian-registered aircraft to fly through to England and so achieve the system of throughworking — an essential feature of our plan — then the alternative would be to end the throughworking of the fleet at Singapore or Darwin, leaving the onward transmission of the mails to the capital cities to be the responsibility of the Australian Government.

267

Sir Eric said he was not quite sure what was intended by "Australian control", nor had Australia yet indicated how it would propose to exercise control. Edgar Johnston, said Sir Eric in his perplexity, had given as an instance of control the right of Australia to fine carriers if mails were late. He observed that if the Australian subsidy were paid direct to QEA it would not be sufficient to enable QEA "to carry out profitably as large a proportion of the operations as you and I agreed. That might entail going back to one of your original suggestions, that the junction of the two companies' services would be Darwin instead of Singapore." On what he saw as another instance of Australian sensitivity Sir Eric said: "As you know, we do not intend that Indian aircraft should operate through to Australia, and as the colour question is rather delicate in your country it would be as well to correct Parkhill's impression." His letter concluded with a reference to the Tasman service. "New proposals are being studied which will come before our Board in the near future, when I can inform my colleagues that your company would now wish to be associated with us in the projected service to New Zealand."[35]

A.E. Rudder, QEA vice chairman and representative of Imperial Airways in Australia, returned from meetings in New Zealand on 9 September 1935. He appeared to be not only well satisfied with himself, but more pleased with his accomplishments for IAL than for Qantas Empire airways. He wrote to McMaster:

> My mission was a complete success. Both the Union Steamship Company and the New Zealand Government are perfectly satisfied with my proposals — reflected in the enclosed copy of Heads of Agreement. You will notice one important condition — that Imperial Airways shall be the principal company in operating the trans-Tasman service. It means that the New Zealand Government insist upon Imperial Airways holding directly or indirectly a fifty per cent financial interest. This aspect was very fully discussed by Cabinet at a meeting which I attended at the request of the Government, and is a condition paramount.
> Time is the essence of the contract as there is a general election in New Zealand on 5 November and the Government would like definite action quickly. Besides, there is the possibility of a Labor Government getting in which might upset everything, unless we dig in while we have the opportunity.[36]

Rudder, obviously excited and full of his own importance, now picked a fight with McMaster, accusing him of pushing for a Qantas majority interest on the Tasman. Fysh became involved and was upset. He wrote to McMaster on 25 September:

> It was with exceeding regret that I was drawn into the unfortunate controversy between yourself and Mr Rudder on the 19th and 20th, during which a serious difference of opinion was disclosed, and which resulted in friction. I supported your arguments on the question of Qantas participation in the New Zealand project — that you never demanded a two thirds or even half interest for Qantas. [Mr Rudder] obviously keenly resented my statements that he was mistaken in his reading of your previous attitude. It places me in a position I feel keenly. From time to time there has been a good deal of friction between Mr Rudder and other members of the Board, though there has been no friction between Mr Rudder and myself in recent months. This friction is certainly a disturbing element and may easily cause serious disruption.[37]

The disagreement with Rudder, and McMaster's anger, had repercussions in London. Sir Eric Geddes was concerned, and wrote to McMaster on 22 October: "At no time have I felt less in your confidence." Mr Rudder, he said, had both cabled and written his regrets that he has unintentionally misquoted you. "As to financial participation of QEA in a New Zealand service, you left this to me, and I am still without any fixed or even settled ideas on the subject." He referred to other misunderstandings. "You may take it", wrote Sir Eric, "that we had not contemplated having two flying boat bases at Sydney; still less is it conceivable that we should be interested in both and that QEA should be interested in one." He promised QEA help "in any reasonable way, to safeguard your interests and prevent new capital, [for the expansion into flying boats] and particularly new capital held in one large block, dominating the position".[38] (The wealthy British Pacific Trust had been reported in the Brisbane *Courier Mail* of 25 September as offering to back Kingsford Smith "to the extent of more than £100,000 in his proposed trans-Tasman service". The Brisbane *Telegraph* of 1 October reported that the trust was forming a company, Airlines of Australia Limited, to acquire the main assets of New England Airways Ltd. and the main plant, hangar, and aerodrome of the Larkin Aircraft Co., Melbourne.)

In the midst of this bout of friction and misunderstanding, there was a major disaster that threatened the future of the DH86 fleet. On 2 October 1935, the Holyman Airways DH86 *Loina* disappeared in Bass Strait, on a flight from Melbourne south to Launceston, with three passengers and two crew. A radio message was received at Flinders Island, where the airliner was due to land en route: then nothing. Floating wreckage was found later.

Qantas had by now flown some 316,000 miles with their DH86 fleet. Timetable observance had been good and there had been no accidents. Fearing suspension of the type's certificate of airworthiness, Fysh cabled the Civil Aviation Department that QEA had complete confidence in the DH86. "However," he wrote, "the witch hunt was on again with a vengeance. Under orders, almost at once, we were busy ripping open our aircraft wings, tail planes etc. in search of structural trouble. Of course nothing was found."[39] A committee of enquiry was set up but, at least for the time being, the DH86s were not grounded.

Fysh, coping with the disruption caused by the mandatory examination of the QEA fleet, was at the same time pressing Edgar Johnston to expedite duplication of the Singapore service, and resist pressure to let the Dutch come to Australia.

> The worst thing that could happen would be to let them in in any shape or form and not to duplicate [he argued]. It would be nothing short of disastrous and would lead to all sorts of trouble with the press and public, who would clamour for a Dutch air mail connection. Competition, Dutch or any other, is a big question. It does appear that you will eventually have to give some measure of protection to your selected airlines . . . In the final count, we are partners with the Commonwealth, and it is not in the interests of the Government to see us in difficulties.[40]

The approbation, or otherwise, of press and public mentioned by Fysh remained a powerful influence on both established aviation companies and those attempting to influence the government in starting new ventures. If most of the great pioneering flights had had their motivation in the pursuit of sheer adventure and achievement, with prize money and glory a mere gamble, many of the flights that followed were undertaken to generate public acclaim or political support. It was not necessarily an ignoble motive, nor were such enterprises possible for men lacking skill and courage. Charles Ulm had lost his life in such a venture. P.G. Taylor had openly acknowledged that his near-disastrous flight with Kingsford Smith in the *Southern Cross* had been "to raise public interest" in their plans for the Tasman.[41] Now, Australia was to lose its most accomplished and illustrious airman to this same elusive cause. Sir Charles Kingsford Smith left London early in November with Tommy Pethybridge in *Lady Southern Cross* in an attempt to break the record time for a flight to Australia. On a night crossing of the Bay of Bengal, on the way to Singapore, they vanished. The whole nation mourned. In the intense search that followed, Scotty Allan assisted in a Qantas DH86; but no trace of *Lady Southern Cross* was found. (It was not until 16 March 1936 that leave was granted in the Probate Court in Sydney for Lady Kingsford Smith to swear to the death of her husband. "From today," said a press report, "Sir Charles Kingsford Smith is legally dead.")[42]

Fergus McMaster, in his role as chairman of Q.A.N.T.A.S., the partner of Imperial Airways in Qantas Empire Airways, was still deeply preoccupied with what seemed to him the insincerity of A.E. Rudder and the possible duplicity of Imperial Airways in their attitude to the trans-Tasman service. "The whole of these negotiations have been somewhat peculiar", he told Sir Eric Geddes. "The understanding in London was that, should IAL decide to offer an invitation to the Q.A.N.T.A.S. interests to participate in the New Zealand extension, that invitation would come direct from yourself." There was, said McMaster, no indication in Geddes's letters that he had made a definite decision on the matter, yet Rudder "had been pressing for some considerable time for Q.A.N.T.A.S. to join in". The inference from Rudder, however, had been for the smallest possible participation by Q.A.N.T.A.S.

> The objective [said McMaster] has been to associate Q.A.N.T.A.S. interests for political reasons only, and not out of any loyalty . . . Under the circumstances, our association in the New Zealand extension carries no value whatsoever. I made it clear [in London] that Q.A.N.T.A.S. would be prepared to come in or stand out, and had it been put to us openly that the association was only wanted for political reasons, I feel sure that neither myself nor my co-directors would have hesitated to come in. But it is quite a different thing when it is realised that full or reasonable confidence has not been extended . . . We seem to get at cross purposes, and it would appear to me owing to an air of mystery and lack of openness.[43]

McMaster said that, on behalf of Q.A.N.T.A.S., he now formally applied for a 15 per cent interest in the Tasman extension.

Sir Eric Geddes replied:

> We would like to have the closest association with you operationally and will work strenuously to that end, but we would prefer to leave the question of financial participation open for the present. To avoid any misunderstanding I will in future deal with this

271

matter personally and solely. The delay in finalising the Empire Mail Scheme with Australia naturally makes it difficult for our Government to go forward with the New Zealand extension.[44]

The delay in finalizing the Empire mail scheme centred around the Australian government's strong reaction to the proposal that Australia should relinquish "that section of the route along which QEA", wrote Hocking and Cave, "had built such a reputation for regularity and safety". It was pointed out in press and Parliament that of twenty-four delays of one day or more on the London–Brisbane service to 31 December 1935, twenty had been due to IAL; and, also, the Australian section was conducted at a lower cost per mile.[45] Fysh told Edgar Johnston that lack of sufficient aircraft had accentuated the IAL difficulties and that "from what I know of the actual causes of delay, these in the main result from aircraft becoming bogged in Burma and India, engine trouble with the *Atalantas* and weather in the Mediterranean". Unfortunately, wrote Fysh, "we never hear of KLM delays. They are an awfully good show." Fysh thought that IAL "must be trying to operate their duplicated service from Karachi to Singapore with three *Atalantas* which, for a distance of 3,600 miles, is pretty thin considering engine and landing ground troubles".[46]

The *Sydney Morning Herald*, however, was strongly critical of the Australian government. In a leader on 6 December 1935, the *Herald* commented:

> The existing service is becoming so overburdened with mail freights that it may not be able to accept passengers. Yet passengers are its best paying traffic . . . Six months ago, the Government was warned that the service must be duplicated to cope with the traffic offering and in prospect. Meanwhile the outer Pacific is beginning to sing with the winging of flying boats. Pan American Airways has flown the first giant flying boat from the Golden Gate via Honolulu to the Philippines in one week, or sixty hours of actual flying time. That craft, the *China Clipper*, has opened another chapter of romance in the Pacific. The same organisation has made an agreement with the New Zealand Government to run a branch service from Honolulu to Auckland . . .

The *Herald* criticized the Australian government for holding to the concept of landplanes for the Singapore–Australia route and said:

> Would it not be better for the Australian Government, holding the views it apparently does, to relinquish the Singapore–Darwin route to Imperial Airways? . . . Nothing is so patent about the

official administration of air services in Australia as its lack of imagination. Because Defence wants a landplane service from the Sydney–Brisbane region to Darwin, the Government resists the flying boat scheme.[47]

(Pan American had inaugurated their service to the Orient on 22 November 1935 using the four-engined Martin *China Clipper* flying boat. The agreement between Pan American and the New Zealand government for a service between Honolulu and Auckland was announced in December 1935.)

Fysh took time off from his major concerns on 11 December to compliment Scotty Allan. "As Captain in charge of aircraft for the last twelve months it is not too much to say that you have had a brilliant record of service, the punctuality and freedom from accident observed speaking strongly for yourself and all other captains."[48] Two days later came news that shattered this hard-won rhythm of regularity. A Holyman Airways DH86, the *Lepena*, flying from Launceston to Melbourne with two pilots and eight passengers, sent out a dramatic radio signal: "Port lower wing crumpling. Making for Hunter Island [off north-west Tasmania]." The aircraft made a forced landing on the island, with no injuries to crew or passengers. Immediately, the minister for defence announced that the airworthiness certificates of all DH86 aircraft in Australia had been cancelled. A temporary exception was given to enable two Qantas aircraft carrying Christmas mail to continue on to Singapore, but without passengers.

Arrangements were made at once by Fysh with Imperial Airways to keep open a service between Singapore and Darwin using *Atalantas* and IAL crews. From Darwin to Brisbane small de Havilland *Rapides* were organized. But the crisis was over within three days and airworthiness certificates restored to the DH86s. An interim report of the *Lepena* mishap said that a loosening of an aluminium strip on a wing strut fairing, plus crew caution, had led to the emergency landing. Other damage had resulted from the landing itself, on rough ground, and not from any structural defect. QEA resumed normal operations.

The 1935 year drew to its close with some clarification of views by the various parties, but no resolution of issues. Geddes wrote a calming letter to McMaster on the "apparent air of mystery and lack of openness" that had so upset McMaster, pointing out: "I am also working in the dark in some matters and do not yet know how the New Zealand proposals are viewed by the interested Governments."[49] Hudson

Fysh wrote a far from calming letter to Edgar Johnston on Christmas Eve. "I think I can say that we were all astonished not to receive any word of congratulations from you or the Government on the completion of our first year's contract, during which a very great measure of success has been achieved and many difficulties overcome. I can assure you, Edgar, we feel very discouraged at the moment in regard to relations in general."[50] To Sir Donald Cameron MP, Fysh wrote:

> The official attitude to QEA is extraordinary. The last thing we want to do is tread too hard on the corns of the Minister and, personally, I think it is mostly his advisers who are at fault. But I often wonder if we don't take things lying down too much. We are expected to meet any and every eventuality satisfactorily and form the backbone of Australian operations with a difficult route . . . but so far as I can see, without any thanks whatsoever — in fact, the opposite. Because our operating staff are mainly responsible, I can say that our first year's operations were really a magnificent effort, and the schedule efficiency was as good as anything put up in any other part of the world. Yet we got no message of congratulations. Perhaps it is because of IAL participation. We are regarded as half-breed foreigners.[51]

In much calmer vein he set down a year-end statement for Fergus McMaster of his views on both flying boats and the controversy over control of the Singapore route. From a purely economic standpoint, he wrote, the England–Australia route should be operated by one government and one company, but there were several extraneous factors. "The governing factor is the desire of Australia to control the Singapore–Brisbane section of the route. In a lesser sense, there is the desire of Q.A.N.T.A.S. to retain control of the destinies of the route through QEA and in partnership with IAL." Members of the Australian government and Department of Defence had repeatedly expressed this desire for Australian control which "is one of the stumbling blocks in securing a settlement of the 1937 Scheme in a manner reasonably satisfactory to both parties". If, wrote Fysh, Australian control were lost, the Australian government would greatly lose interest in the Empire service and "would regard it as an outside project which has swallowed a promising Australian activity . . . In fact, operations would be almost exactly akin to that of the Orient and P. & O. shipping companies." Fysh then stated clearly his views on actual operational control of the planned service. "I maintain that free interchange of crews and aircraft must result in the operational control passing to Imperial Airways, as the larger concern, and that any QEA control would not be much more than a blind. QEA would in reality become managers for IAL in Australia . . . What I do wish to say emphatically is that if the Scheme goes through as put up by the British Government, Australian control and with it Qantas control will have been given away."[52]

As chairman, Fergus McMaster reviewed the QEA stance for the minister, Archdale Parkhill, in a personal letter on 27 December 1935, enclosing a copy of a draft agreement between Qantas and IAL which, he said, "establishes the basis for the operation of QEA in the 1937 Empire Air Mail Scheme, should your Government decide to participate therein". McMaster recalled Parkhill's apprehension, expressed in a recent conversation in Sydney on 19 December, that Qantas would be absorbed by Imperial Airways, and would lose control of the Australia–Singapore section.

> Under the protection of the Agreement, [wrote McMaster] I am convinced that QEA could operate the larger Australian interests in the 1937 Scheme just as competently and completely as the Company is doing under existing controls . . . There is no reason whatever why Australia should not make Singapore the Australia terminal overseas and confine the Australian portion of the fleet to the Australian section only. Provided the costs can be met by the Australian Government, there is no reason why it should not be able to control this section of the route as at the present moment.

McMaster then turned to the issue of aircraft type. "Flying boats appeal to me as the most sound basis for development of Empire air services", he wrote. "Sound commercial results will be possible to a greater extent on a route such as that from England to Australia with a large commercial type of flying boat than would any system of land aircraft." The objection to the fleet being allowed to operate freely between London and Australia might be overcome, he said, by changeover of crews at Singapore, "thus keeping Australian control". If this were done, he concluded, he could not see any great objection to the aircraft being allowed to operate freely between London and Australia. In common with others he was, he said, disturbed at the possible cost to Australia of the all-letter airmail proposal. If, however, Australia could meet the cost, then the fullest co-operation was warranted. "At no time, perhaps," wrote McMaster, "has there been greater reason to minimise the isolation of Australia, or to have a more closely welded Empire."[53]

McMaster had, in fact, recognized the operational pattern that was to prevail: Australian crews to remain on the Australian section but all flying boats to operate over the whole route between Australia and England. What could not be clear as 1935 ended was that the Australian government, in its determination to preserve control of the Australia–Singapore route for Qantas Empire Airways, was taking the first step towards the emergence of Qantas as Australia's first "chosen instrument" as an international airline. Australia was also, in its attitude towards this first international air route, beginning to recognize and declare a clear national interest separate from the emotional and traditional bonds of Empire.

Calling a Spade a Spade
1936

Edgar Johnston began his correspondence with Hudson Fysh for 1936 on 3 January somewhat testily. He was sorry, he said, that no telegram of congratulations had been sent on completion of QEA's first year under contract; there had been a great rush of work; he had himself worked right through a good many weekends; half his staff had been refused leave.

14

Though the letter was a personal one, Johnston told Fysh:

> Frankly, I must say the price asked by you [for duplication of the Singapore service] astonished me. There is a considerable probability of duplication not being approved unless the cost can be reduced substantially. I would like you to understand, Hudson, that it is not my desire to question expenditures that are essential to operate the extra service with reasonable regularity and without undue risk. Any proposals which seem to me to be furthering the interests of Australian civil aviation and prompting its growth have my wholehearted support and very active co-operation.[1]

Johnston's minister, Archdale Parkhill, wrote a personal letter to McMaster on the same day, but in more friendly vein. He saw no objection, he said, to Qantas submitting an account to the government for the costs incurred by the company as a result of the grounding of the DH86s. "I fully realise the seriousness of suspending the certificates of airworthiness of the DH86 machines, but I felt that there was no other course open to me in view of the loss of life and danger to lives that were taking place in Australia as a result of accidents to these machines."[2] Overall, however, the official attitude to Qantas of both the minister and the controller of civil aviation now grew increasingly chilly. On 31 January, the press carried headlines that the Empire Flying Boat Scheme had been rejected by Cabinet.[3] "I think it will be conceded", said Archdale Parkhill to the press, "that the Commonwealth is the proper judge of what is best for Australia. The problem of a flat rate for air mails within the Empire is not the most important aspect. The control of the specific route from Darwin to Singapore, the future of aviation in Australia, and the relation of both these matters to Australia's defence are much more important to Australia."[4] The press did not agree with him. "Only Parkhill could argue against control by a single organisation under joint British-Dominion supervision", wrote *The Bulletin*.[5] "The Lyons Government has made a grave mistake. The Scheme had great Empire significance", commented the Brisbane *Telegraph*.[6]

Fysh told Dismore at Imperial Airways on February 4:

> Our authorities have turned the [flying boat] project down flat, and all I can say in their defence is that your Air Ministry did not take reasonable steps to prevent this. Things might have turned out differently and the Controller of Civil Aviation put in a good word, but his attitude is flatly hostile and uncomprising. The fear of British control is overshadowing his judgment, and through this aspect is growing up a certain official coldness towards us as not being a purely Australian enterprise. We can give you no more support on the 1937 Scheme until we are able to push some modified plan. Anything else is quite futile.[7]

Woods Humphery was upset. "I am most disturbed by the news that your Government has decided against coming into the Empire Mail Scheme", he wrote to Fysh. "The British Government is committed up to the hilt. It looks to me very much as though there is going to be a devil of a muddle for some time ahead."[8] Fysh put the blame on Edgar Johnston.

> I think the present indecision and apparent muddle on the part of the Government in regard to all Australia's advancement in commercial aviation at the present moment is due to the undoubted incompetence of Johnston, and to the fact that the Government has had thrust on it the duty of making decisions on a whole bagful of projects for which it was totally unprepared . . . One must confess to a certain amount of sympathy for their difficulties.[9]

Woods Humphery was not slow to join in this denigration of Edgar Johnston, and went on to voice his concern over American initiatives.

> I am sorry Johnston is so pro-American. He would not perhaps be if he knew what the responsible American authorities in aviation think of him. I confess I felt very irritated in America at the

278

voluntary adverse comments that were made to me — which in loyalty I was bound to defend. I have no doubt that you share my anxiety over the tremendous thrust that America is making to obtain a paramount position on world airways. I suppose you have heard that Pan American's Pacific service was suspended after the last two or three flights for over a month, and is still not working regularly owing to troubles in leaking petrol tanks, controllable pitch propellers, engine mountings and engines. So thank God we are not alone in our troubles. In America, these big corporations seem to get the press so well behind them, and they are not subjected to the gunfire which we get.[10]

In the midst of these demanding problems, Edgar Johnston received a sad request. It came as a personal, handwritten letter asking for help from the man who had provided the initial impetus for the creation of Qantas. Paul McGinness was in financial trouble. McGinness, it was evident, had applied to Johnston in the previous month asking for a position with the department. This second letter, written from Mount Lawley, Perth, gave some details of his predicament.

Dear Jonno, [it began] I received your letter of 23rd December and note it is impossible at this junction [*sic*] to place me in the Department. Yes, I am prepared to take any job that is offering . . . Later on, when a chance arrives, you might be able to slip me up to a reasonable position. I have left the farm and am at present in Perth. I have assigned the farm to my creditors, lock, stock and barrel. It will pay them about two shillings in the pound. I walk out of it after ten years with a clean sheet and an empty pocket. I was a fool to have ever left aviation, but we live and learn.

There was an anxious postcript which said simply: "Resources limited. Try and get me in as soon as possible."[11] Johnston, who had himself joined the Civil Aviation Branch in 1919, had known McGinness from the beginning. He was upset, but was unable to find McGinness an opening. Funds were tight in the department, and there had been many other aviators thrown out of work during the Depression who had asked for help.[12]

Edgar Johnston had a similar letter in the same week from someone else. The secretary of Kingsford Smith's company, John Stannage, wrote asking if he could join the department. "Now it seems certain that we have lost dear old Smithy," he said, "and I have almost completed the finalising of his affairs, I shall have to look for another position." Smithy's plans for the Tasman, he wrote a few days later, were completed in almost every detail before he left on his last tragic venture, and the Trans-Tasman Air Service Development Company was, said Stannage, certainly going to carry on with those plans. "We are hoping for positive Government support from either New Zealand or Australia . . . to thereby warrant the commencement of a service that was Smithy's great ambition." Kingsford Smith's widow, Mary, said Stannage, was supplying them with funds. The service would be a continuous livelihood for her and for her son. Despite his hopeful sentiments, Stannage told Johnston he thought the company's prospects were dismal.[13]

Meanwhile Fysh, responding with irritation to Johnston's own testiness, rejected the controller's criticism of QEA costs for duplicating the Singapore service. "If our price is not understood," he wrote, "I feel it is your job as Controller to explain it and get it across. The queer thing is, we badly want duplication and have gone through and through our price with no further result than our final quote." He summarized mounting cost pressures. "An enormous amount will have to be done in training and equipment. We should now be commencing to train people for tighter schedules and instrument flying. It means heavy expense for us. I can see that one of these days I must withdraw Brain from regular flying on the route, which means employment of another Captain."[14]

Lester Brain, on whom so much had depended for the operational success of the QEA service, had other plans for his future which had been maturing for a considerable time. They were not linked to the projected QEA expansion. On 11 February 1936, Brain wrote to Edgar Johnston:

As I indicated to you a year or so ago, I should be quite interested in any position in the administration and executive side of aviation, and would be willing to drop quite a bit in gross income to this end. I have no particular wish to drop active flying, but am more interested in civil aviation than in the actual flying of aeroplanes. I was very pleased that you should remember and phone today. I would accept a position as number two to you, but not a position as one of several, unless as senior and definitely your deputy. The commencing salary would need to be not less than seven hundred pounds. The salaries of the four senior people in your Department can do with a good lift if they are to get and hold good men. Your position and that of your immediate assistants are underpaid compared with the necessary experience and responsibilities, and with comparable positions elsewhere in aviation. In my present position I earn over one thousand pounds, my work being partly executive and part flying. I am in a written understanding with the company of three months notice either way . . .[15]

(Nothing came of this exchange; Lester Brain did not leave Qantas until World War II ended, when he became the first general manager of the government-owned domestic operator, Trans-Australia Airlines. Interestingly, R.M. Ansett, who was to become TAA's national competitor as head of Ansett Airlines of Australia, commenced his first scheduled air service between Hamilton, Victoria, and Melbourne on 17 February 1936, a few days after Brain wrote his letter to Johnston.)

Lester Brain had, as an airman, expressed his view on flying boats in a confidential memo to Fysh.

> After twelve months experience on the route between Singapore and Darwin, I am greatly impressed with the suitability of conditions for flying boat operations, particularly on the safety aspect. On the section from Singapore to Koepang, one is always near comparatively sheltered waters. Gales are almost unknown in the Timor Sea, and a boat could land and float around for weeks in the doldrums. Over the greater portion of the year, the open sea is calm enough to allow a machine to take off. Around the shores of the islands of the Indies there is no surf, the water usually lapping quietly on the coast where native fishermen walk about pushing their nets before them. In view of the oft-repeated phrase, "the dreaded Timor Sea", I feel sure that the real conditions would be a revelation to most people.[167]

Fysh told Woods Humphery that QEA pilots, knowing of KLM operations at Sourabaya, had no desire to fly Douglas aircraft on the route. "In fact, under our conditions, they would be quite unsuitable", he wrote. "I might say here that Johnston's ideal machine for the Singapore–Brisbane route is the new Douglas sleeper transport." For certain routes, such as across America, Fysh conceded that the Douglas was a very fine machine indeed. "Many lessons can be learned from American operations, for which I confess to entertaining the highest regard", he wrote.[17] To Edgar Johnston, he was more critical. Responding to comments from Johnston about repeated late arrivals by Imperial Airways at Singapore, Fysh argued that KLM had done no better, and in some months had been worse. "The Douglas is not proving the success first expected, under weather and other conditions experienced on the Amsterdam–Batavia route. Operating across America over a highly organised system of radio, meteorology and landing ground aids is just about as different as chalk to cheese."[18]

The long-awaited government approval for duplication of the QEA service to Singapore was at last announced, on 27 February 1936, by the prime minister though, Fysh complained to Woods Humphery, official advice from the Defence Department was not forthcoming until 3 March. "We have been offered two shillings a mile, and our final price of two shillings and twopence was stated in a letter to the Air Contracts Board . . . All we can think of is that Cabinet passed duplication not knowing that a disagreement on price still existed."[19] Edgar Johnston wrote to Fysh: "It has been a long time coming and all the time I have been frightened that the Dutch would get in first. However, I do not think we can ignore the possibility of the Dutch extending to Australia also."[20] On the day the welcome news of approval for duplication arrived, Parkhill wrote to McMaster criticizing Fysh for statements attributed to him in the press that complained of a shortage of experienced pilots for the coming duplication of service. These were views, said the minister, which need not have been put forward at all. He called it "the futility of newspaper controversy"[21]. McMaster replied at once expressing his own annoyance. The press reports, he said, had placed the company in a false position with the "somewhat alarmist statement about possible difficulty in securing pilots and engineers". Fysh was very annoyed with the headlining he had received in the Melbourne and Sydney papers, said McMaster. "He is convinced that it will be better in future to directly refuse [to make a statement] or make the statement in writing only. You are the last person that either Mr Fysh or myself would wish to worry."[22]

The minister told McMaster that he had mentioned to Cabinet that the rate of two shillings per mile for the duplicated service, recommended as fair and reasonable by the department, was not agreed by QEA. "I hope I shall not have to go back to Cabinet on the matter", he wrote to McMaster on 25 March. "I dislike doing this because of the difficulties I previously experienced . . . I know it will mean further and perhaps protracted delay, if not abandonment of the project pending a settlement of the British Mail Scheme."[23] QEA, however, reached agreement with the department. On 2 April, Fysh wrote to Johnston: "Yesterday has seen the culmination of consideration of duplication proposals after nearly ten months of negotiation and investigation, though we honestly don't feel too happy about the financial aspect. If our greatest hopes are realised, I don't see how we can possibly realise more than a net six per cent on capital."[24] Meanwhile McMaster had, undeterred, pressed the minister for compensation for the pre-Christmas interruption to DH86 services.

"A claim for three hundred and twelve pounds one shilling and sixpence, being out-of-pocket expenses only, and occasioned as a direct result of the cancellation of the [DH86] certificates has been made to the Department and refused . . . By the action taken, we were penalised for the unfortunate operational conditions pertaining to a service in no way connected with our own", he wrote.[25]

Woods Humphery was both astonished and heartened by the support given the Empire Mail Scheme in the Australian press.

> The attitude taken up by the Australian press re Australia turning down the Imperial proposals, in my opinion, came as a complete surprise to the Australian Government. Personally I would never have forecast such a solid attitude ranged behind the proposals. It has been a complete surprise to everyone. This attitude must have a considerable effect on the politicians . . . and makes prospects of a settlement favourable to the Empire Scheme much [better].[26]

He urged that Fysh draw attention to the strenuous efforts being made by the governments of the major powers to gain the best possible footing on the airways of the world.

> German, Dutch, French and, last but not least, American interests are concentrating on this. The flood of propaganda which has emanated from the USA during the past year or so is part of a well organised plan. It has for its objective mastery of the world's trunk airways. America has entrusted the development of its overseas services to one vast and wealthy company, Pan American Airways. For many years it has operated air services in, to and around South America. It is established in Alaska and China. It is steadily completing its plans for a trans-Pacific service and had obtained permission to operate a service to New Zealand. Plans for a trans-Atlantic service are well advanced. The United States Government has evidently realised that mastery of the world's airways could never be achieved by a small, unimportant organisation.[27]

This line of argument was, of course, central to the IAL vision of a matching, vast, and centrally controlled Empire air route system; moves for independent Australian control were, in this context, manifestations of Australian parochialism. The support of the Australian press reinforced this interpretation and so, sometimes, did the attitude of IAL's Australian partner. The trouble with the Defence Department, the Department of Civil Aviation and many of the Government, Fysh wrote to Dismore on 17 March 1936

> is that they think in terms of Australia, and can't grasp yet how aviation, wireless etc. and the unsettled state of things in the

world must make a full recognition of the word "Empire" a necessity. The history of Great Britain is that of bungling through to bigger things, and all progress seems chaotic and unorderly, but arrives in the end. Whatever faults the Australian people have, and whatever their lack of understanding, they have a quality of calling a spade a spade, and wishing for the full facts of a thing. It is quite impossible to convince them, for instance, that they have got any control over a flying boat crossing the Mediterranean because it flies an Australian flag and has an Australian crew. The flag is no more than a symbol.

In less philosophic manner he wrote:

Mr McMaster's opinion [on the Empire Mail Scheme] is that at present this matter of control is not the chief stumbling block to a settlement from the Australian side, but that the flat [payment] rate [for mails] is the bugbear. I think he is right as far as Cabinet goes, and they are the real people who are settling the matter. However, the Defence people, through Parkhill, are harping on loss of control. I have never been able to give a really effective answer, when directly tackled, to show how Australia will have the same control as she has now . . . if the contract is to be let through the British Government.[28]

Though the government had rejected the Empire Air Mail Scheme, the suitability of flying boats for the section from Singapore was investigated further when Squadron Leader A.E. Hempel, RAAF, was asked officially in March to carry out a survey of proposed bases along the Australian coast in a Southampton flying boat. The results, Fysh wrote, were disastrous.[29]

Hempel condemned the flying boat concept and defended his conclusions in a letter to Fysh on 6 April. "The requirements [Imperial Airways' 'Specification for a Flying Boat Airway'] are such that no place in Australia conforms to the specification. I had to report in terms of this specification. I believe that the flying boat under construction for the Empire routes requires such a run of smooth, deep water into wind to take off, and so flat an approach to alight, that the rivers and most other places are out of the question."[30] (The "Outline Specification" for the alighting and take-off area, allowing for a wind from any direction, called for a length of two thousand yards, a width of two hundred and fifty yards, and a water depth at the lowest tide of at least ten feet. The approaches had to be clear of all obstructions for a distance of at least a thousand yards. The specification said: "To ascertain whether an object constitutes an obstruction, an imaginary line should be drawn at an angle of four degrees to the horizontal from the perimeter of this area. Any objects extending above this imaginary line should be considered obstructions."[31])

On 12 April 1936, the first passenger ever carried by Qantas, Alexander Kennedy, died in Brisbane at the age of ninety-eight. The man who, in 1922, had shouted "Damn the doubters" as his aircraft taxied out for take-off, had almost every year since, made two air trips each way between Brisbane and Cloncurry or Brisbane and Mount Isa. "He was", wrote McMaster, "deeply interested in the development of the [Mount Isa] mines [which were on country owned by Kennedy in the early days]. He knew that the ore deposits were there, but did not realise their great quantity and value. A well for water put down by Kennedy on the bank of the Leichhardt River [Logan Creek well, nine miles on the Cloncurry side of Mount Isa and required by Kennedy when shifting his cattle between his two properties, Devoncourt and Calton Hills] was the only water available for early development of the area."[32]

The result of the Hempel flying boat survey presented QEA with a dilemma. While press support gave the company political advantage in a general way, deliberate airing of Qantas views in the press brought the danger of a powerful and specific overreaction from an antagonized government. Fysh wrote to A.E. Rudder on 20 April:

> As you know, there is practically a deadlock at present. IAL and ourselves say that the route is, or can be made, practicable. The Australian Government says it is not suitable. It should, perhaps, be decided by the Board how much further publicity QEA should indulge in while matters stand as at present. In view of the possibility of the Boat Scheme failing, QEA cannot afford to put themselves in a position with the Australian Government which might well jeopardise their future.[33]

As Hempel's condemnation of the Darwin–Sydney flying boat route was based on the specification drawn up by the Air Ministry and provided by Imperial Airways, the only acceptable means of contesting it was to conduct a further survey using British experts, and to hope that their findings would prove the route's suitability. Arrangements were made for the air superintendent of Imperial Airways, Maj. H.G. Brackley, to make a flight from Singapore to Sydney in a Short *Singapore* III flying boat, lent by 205 Squadron, RAF. Powered by four Rolls-Royce *Kestrel* engines in tandem in pairs, it had a low cruising speed of barely one hundred miles per hour and a poor rate of climb. Hudson Fysh arranged to accompany the survey from Singapore, with A.R. McComb, controller of ground services for the Civil Aviation Department, and Squadron Leader Hempel joining them at Darwin. Brackley, an aviation pioneer and airman of great experience (called "Brackles" by all who knew him) knew that his task had political implications. "At Darwin," he wrote, "we pick up two Australian Government representatives and I can see that I am in for a rather delicate task. The Australian Government don't want the flying boat route, nor do they want the Empire Air Mail Scheme. Until I have been over the route, I cannot state what my reactions will be, but it is not going to be easy."[34]

After a false start on 6 May, when an engine failed and forced a return to Singapore and an overnight stop, Brackley flew down via Banka Island, Sourabaya, Bima, and Koepang to Darwin without incident. With McComb and Hempel joining them, they next flew across Arnhem Land to the Roper River and landed in lonely surroundings where the river ran through flat plains, in thirty feet of water. Their route then took them down the shore of the Gulf of Carpentaria to Mornington Island, then on to the Albert River (where a flying boat base was eventually established). The flying boat next had to make a crossing over land across the broad base of Cape York Peninsula to Townsville, on Queensland's eastern coast. It then followed the coast south, with stops at Bowen and Brisbane, before the final landing in Sydney. Brackley found in favour of the route, and though his report was not enough in itself to settle the issue, it led to further investigations and final acceptance. McComb did not oppose Brackley or condemn the route but Hempel continued to insist that no site in Australia met the official specification for flying boat operation. Both Hempel and McComb went over the route again on Brackley's return flight to Singapore (and were joined by Arthur Baird). Yet another survey was then carried out by the Australian government and, finally, a route was chosen.[35]

A ceremony was held at Brisbane's Archerfield aerodrome on 16 May when the minister for defence, Parkhill, formally inaugurated the duplicated QEA service to Singapore by DH86 and some two hundred people watched Lester Brain set off in RMA *Canberra*. Duplication was, at last, one battle that Qantas could put behind it, though the doubled frequency of the DH86 service was now considered an interim phase by both QEA and Imperial Airways pending the introduction of flying boats. Lester Brain, as flight superintendent, reported to Fysh on the progress of some of his captains on the route. Russell Tapp (to become one of Qantas's finest captains) was under a cloud, following accidents at Singapore and Sourabaya. "Tapp's flying has not reached that standard of excellence and confidence that it should have after 6,000 hours commercial flying . . . For the next three months he should consider himself on probation", wrote Brain. Orme Denny, Brain thought, "was exceptional material to work on. Adair is much slower and not so keen and quick to grasp things." Both Fysh and Brain had great admiration for Scotty Allan. "Like most of the good old pilots he has some queer points", Brain noted. "He would think nothing of sitting down to dinner in the little Rest House at Rambang in pyjamas, or of dining in an old Panama hat at some hot point on the route. He is a good member of a team, co-operates well with whoever is in charge, but he has never exhibited any tendency to leadership himself, and prefers to remain personally efficient and popular." Brain nevertheless recommended that Allan be promoted to senior route pilot, that he wear three half bands on his uniform to indicate his rank, and that his base salary be increased from £450 to £525 a year. "Amongst our [other] captains," wrote Brain, "Crowther promises to be the most adaptable to other work in the long run." Brain was later able to report that comments along the line on Russell Tapp had been very encouraging. "At Singapore he led a cheery, active life of golf and avoided the social whirl. So far so good", he wrote.[36]

Fysh reported to his directors that the Brackley flight from Singapore to Sydney had established beyond doubt that the route was a practicable proposition for flying boat operation. Brackley had advised, he said, that the route was a normal one for development. It was also a shorter route than the existing landplane route (4,841 miles from Singapore to Sydney by landplane, 4,517 miles by flying boat route). However, Fysh reported on 2 June to Woods Humphery, Edgar Johnston and Air Vice Marshal Williams were still irrevocably opposed to the idea of flying boats. "Johnston is flatly not interested and is more difficult to deal with than ever", wrote Fysh.[37]

Fysh put the QEA position to the air vice marshal in a personal letter on 11 June.

In regard to the hopes and aspirations of Qantas, the position, I think, is really this. We have quietly recognised for some years that commercial aviation was destined to become a really big thing, with necessary capital and connections beyond the scope of

Qantas. We have been waiting for years for the shipping companies to get moving and have not understood why they have been so long about it. They have evidently been waiting for others to do the pioneering. A year or so ago, we went in with Imperial Airways, after failure to participate in an amalgamation of the principal airlines of Australia. Want of confidence prevented that amalgamation. We hope we are honest, straight people, and now our whole effort has been in trying to secure Empire aviation co-operation on our section of the route, as befits our connections. I might say also that, although Imperial Airways has stood in the background all the time (and has no control over us except by our own free will) their advice and assistance has been of inestimable value in all sorts of ways . . .

All our big things in Australia, or practically all, are financed in whole or in part from England, and aviation can be no exception. A position which amuses me immensely is all the fuss and bother about British capital, overseas staffs, overseas control etc. which went on when we went in with Imperial Airways. Here we are now, a few years later, and the two principal commercial aviation companies in the eastern states have been grabbed by overseas interests and actually must have more overseas control in the final count that we ourselves. Australian National Airways is obviously controlled by the shipping companies. Airlines of Australia is owned by the British Pacific Trust. We feel our choice has been a wise one. We will always have in view Empire co-operation, even if we are too visionary and only a voice crying in the wilderness. All we can hope is that the outcome of this 1937 Scheme does not go violently one way or another, which is what it looks like at present.[38]

Williams replied setting out his own views at length in a personal and confidential letter to Fysh on 17 June 1936.

You seem to have got quite a wrong impression of my view of the proposed flying boat scheme. Nothing I have ever thought or said has been in the direction of lessening the contact you now have with Imperial Airways. I believe the present arrangement is the ideal one, that is to say, Imperial Airways are financially interested in your operations to the extent that they will always be full out to help and assist you. At the same time, the control of operations and of maintenance is in your hands, and you deal directly with the Commonwealth Government on all matters of subsidy and on all those questions affecting work you do. My opposition to the suggested flying boat scheme (apart altogether from the question of type of equipment used) is that the new proposal would place the control in London. You would become local representative for IAL, nothing more nor less, and your operations in future would be dependent entirely on the decisions of IAL.

Williams then questioned the IAL argument for centralized control and uniform equipment to enable the service to function efficiently.

I say it functions efficiently now, without that centralised control. As to the change of route and type of aircraft employed, I say that given a certain horsepower and a definite load to be carried, the job can be done more economically not only in first cost but also in subsequent operation by a landplane than a flying boat. The proposed flying boat route on the Australian coast would serve nobody and would achieve nothing. A landplane route is already operating and must be developed for defence purposes anyway. Why should it be changed now, and the Commonwealth Government put to the expense of providing the ground organisation for a flying boat service? For what?

You should certainly expand on the lines you have already established yourself. You should expand as the managing director of a company extending its operations not only within but beyond the limits of the Commonwealth, not merely as the local area representative for Imperial Airways, but as one who can deal direct with the Commonwealth Government and make decisions and agreements with them for your own company without reference to London. I want to see the development of an Australian concern, at least a concern definitely under Australian control . . . It doesn't matter much to me where the capital comes from.[39]

It was a cool and balanced appraisal of the separate Australian national interest; there were no references to the emotional bonds of Empire that shaped the outlook of many Australians, from Menzies to McMaster and Fysh.

Fysh let off some steam in a letter to C.G. Grey, editor of *The Aeroplane* magazine in London.

The truth of the whole matter is, of course, that the Australian Government don't want the flying boats on the 1937 Scheme but apparently can't get out of it. They don't want them because (i) they are making a very nice profit out of the present surcharge rates on our route, which helps pay for internal commercial aviation activities (ii) the Defence Department, under which comes commercial aviation in this country, would just hate to lose control of the Sydney–Singapore section of the Empire route, the organisation of which it regards as a potential weapon in war. Also it is not in favour of large [flying boat] units at all, but wants a lot of small ones, very fast . . . which it can turn into bombers. What we [QEA] are striving for is a route sufficiently unified to take care of competition in the future.[40]

As these problems of growth and change pressed on Qantas, one of its past competitors in tendering for the original Singapore service went out of business. The Brisbane *Courier Mail* reported on 26 June that Norman Brearley's Western Australian Airways had been wound up. Adelaide Airways had reached agreement to take over the business for a purchase price of £25,000, which excluded WAA's cash reserves. Major

Brearley announced that the airline's original shareholders had received an average of 30 per cent per annum on their investment for fifteen years and that the 1928 subscribers (when capital was increased) had averaged more than 12.5 per cent and return of all their capital.[41] (Forty-five years later, at the age of ninety-one, an alert and good-humoured Sir Norman Brearley recalled that the Australian government approval for the importation of Douglas aircraft in 1935 had influenced him to sell. He told *Transit*, the magazine of Qantas flight attendants: "I said — 'This is going to cost many thousands of pounds . . . Do I need at my old age of forty-six to still stay in the airline business? I thought I could leave the table with my winnings.' ")[42]

The staff strength of Qantas Empire Airways rose from sixty-four to seventy-six with duplication of the Singapore service. Fysh sent Brain a house-keeping memorandum. "Expenses at Darwin Cottage, now that duplication conditions are operative, are assuming somewhat alarming proportions when taken on a per head basis. Apparently it costs in excess of twenty-five shillings to put up a passenger or member of the crew for one night, which includes dinner and breakfast with the night's board." He commented that the cottage staff had not been included in the company's bonus payments "as my impression is they collect a respectable sum in tips and washing".[43] In an earlier memo about the service he passed on to Brain a suggestion "that a notice be placed in cabins of our aircraft requesting passengers to remain seated while the machine is approaching and landing. I am inclined to think that we should have such a notice to apply to both taking off and landing, and I am not sure that we should not adopt the standard American practice which insists that passengers must have their safety belts on whilst landing or taking off."[44] Lester Brain, on his part, passed back from the route intelligence on some KLM problems. "The [KLM] Douglas avoids flying in bad weather", he wrote. "This week's service flew from Calcutta to Akyab at 18,000 feet. God help the passengers. They all complain of the sudden dashing up and down to altitudes over 10,000 feet, below which the engines give too much trouble. Incidentally, they are again changing engines — from Wright *Cyclones* to Pratt & Whitney *Hornets*. A Douglas had one engine fail and tried to carry on to Basra on the other but had to land in the desert."[45] This was cheery gossip but Brain also had some comments to make on the proposed office space set aside for him by Fysh as flight superintendent. "The basement is unsuitable. Light, ventilation, noise and street smells are all against it, while the approach down a back stairway past the garbage tins and lavatories is most embarrassing. I should feel any suggestion to be dumped there very keenly . . ."[46]

In general, however, the fleet of five DH86 aircraft and their crews continued to operate with safety, regularity, and economy. In the twelve months to 31 March 1936 there had been a net profit of £8,598, permitting a 4 per cent dividend. (QEA had altered their financial year to end on 31 March and coincide with IAL's.) The QEA problems, conflicts, and challenges remained external. Fysh confessed to Woods Humphery that he could not get used to the IAL proposal that QEA and IAL captains should, on the flying boats, interchange over the whole route from Brisbane to London, with its varying conditions. "I feel that a very high standard indeed will be necessary", he wrote.[47] With Major Brackley, Fysh discussed the flying boat route battle. "That wretched specification has a lot to answer for and whoever got it out ought to have their necks wrung." He had, he said, tried to get Hempel to condemn the route as per specification but state that in his opinion it was suitable for flying boats. "A funny chap and I don't know what to make of him", Fysh observed. "I told him that if he damned the route for the use of flying boats he was going to look a very silly sort of person in a few years time." In terms of the route specification, he said, Brisbane would be hopeless and so even would Sydney Harbour, because of high surroundings.[48]

Brackley cheered him with details of

the excellent performance the first Empire Boat has put up during its initial Maker's trials. Its top speed is over two hundred miles per hour, and its take-off is positively marvellous. Through the gate — i.e. using the superchargers — it took off in twelve seconds, with an all-up load of 38,000 pounds. Short Bros. are going to do tests with an overload up to 45,000 pounds but we shall not require to fly the aircraft at a load exceeding 41,500 pounds. All the trials have been carried out on the small River Medway, in front of Messrs Short's Works.[49]

From Woods Humphery came advice that it was essential for future flying boat captains to take up sailing. "I am sure sailing must be awfully good fun", Fysh told Lester Brain. "Cannot we do something definite about it?"[50] His flight superintendent looked at the budget implications and replied that it would cost sixteen pounds for a twelve-foot sailing boat.

Imperial Airways' first Empire flying boat, *Canopus*. Built by Short Bros. at Rochester in Kent, *Canopus* made its first flight on 4 July 1936.

An instructor and other costs would add twelve pounds ten shillings. However, Brain noted, the boat could finally be resold for ten pounds, giving the entire sailing programme a net cost of eighteen pounds ten shillings. "This", concluded Brain, "seems a very reasonable cost."[51] Hudson Fysh agreed.

Meantime new threats linked with the proposals for a flying boat service down Australia's east coast began to concern him. If flying boats operated from Singapore to Sydney, he told Woods Humphery, then the Australian government might re-tender for the Darwin–Brisbane land service, which would entail severe competition in tendering. If Qantas lost the route, he said, an opposition service might then form a link with the Dutch at Darwin.[52]

Though discussions had continued between the British and Australian governments on alternative proposals for the Empire Mail Scheme, there had been no official Australian response to London. On 24 August 1936, Woods Humphery informed McMaster that the British government had offered Australia three alternatives. The first was complete participation in the scheme as originally envisaged. The second involved Qantas participation as originally envisaged but with a surcharge on mail carried from Australia. The third was non-participation by Australia, but use of an IAL service from Australia on a surcharge basis (with Australia merely using the British service as a customer). Woods Humphery had set out the current situation for his director of civil aviation, noting that Q.A.N.T.A.S. had sold out their whole business to the Qantas Empire Airways partnership. He explained to Fysh:

> I said that under these circumstances I was sure that my Board would not contemplate for a moment throwing over our partners simply because the Australian Government did not see fit to come into the new Empire Mail Scheme in which our partners had whole-heartedly supported us all the way through. Some modifications of the partnership might be required as a result of the Australian Government non-participation. First, QEA might wish to restrict that part of the route operated by them to between Darwin and Sydney instead of between Singapore and Sydney. Second, Q.A.N.T.A.S., now a holding company, might be resuscitated as a purely Australian operating company to operate internal services within Australia (other than the main through route . . .

If Australia did not participate financially, he said, steps would have to be taken to protect the operation of the service against any panic action which might be taken by the Civil Aviation Department, such as suddenly withdrawing the air-worthiness certificates of QEA's aircraft — as had been done in the past. It could all be difficult, said Woods Humphery, but "it would not affect the principle that we wish to continue our partnership with Q.A.N.T.A.S."[53]

Having thus summarized three IAL suggestions for the Australian government, none of which in any way addressed the Australian objection to loss of control on the Singapore route, Woods Humphery next put forward his views on the operations of Qantas Empire Airways in any planned Tasman extension. He sketched the Imperial view of the Pacific, and the necessary extension of the Empire route across the Tasman to New Zealand. The United Kingdom deputy director of civil aviation, Mr Bertram, he said, was to go to New Zealand in connection with the authorization that had been given by the New Zealand government to Pan American for a Honolulu-Auckland service, and also to discuss the trans-Tasman service. He had prepared notes for Bertram at the request of the director-general, Sir Francis Shelmerdine, and enclosed a copy of these notes for Hudson Fysh. As far as Pan

American was concerned, said Woods Humphery, it was Imperial Airways' view that they had no immediate project for operating a service across the Pacific to New Zealand but, in accordance with their general policy, Pan American wished to stake their claim and so avoid the nuisance value that could be caused if other American companies made similar moves — as well as avoid the necessity to buy out such companies. The New Zealand authorization, he said, contained no reciprocity but as Pan American had subsequently requested modifications to their project, the New Zealand government "now seems to be inclined to endeavour to obtain some reciprocity". He added:

> I hoped that it would be possible to obtain the use of the United States airports in the Pacific, such as Hawaii, for a British service. Shelmerdine asked me whether we had thoughts of operating across the Pacific, and I said that we definitely had. It will be remembered that at our suggestion the Air Ministry had arranged for the Navy to survey a number of islands and atolls in the Pacific, with a view to establishing British suzerainty.
>
> Shelmerdine asked if we had considered New Zealand or other Empire participation. I told him we had not got so far as formulating any policy . . . but we had certainly discussed within our own councils the possibility of Canadian participation, probably through the Canadian Pacific Railway, in view of their shipping interests in the Pacific — and that I should imagine we would be willing to accept New Zealand participation for the same reason. But we should want to have the controlling interest.

On the specific matter of the trans-Tasman route, he said, IAL was

> committed to take in the Union Steamship Company as partners in the trans-Tasman extension of the Empire line, as representing the New Zealand interest. The arrangement was made that we were to have a controlling interest in the line, and that the Union Steamship Company would have the remaining [capital] unless there were to be some Australian participation, in which case the Union participation would be reduced by the amount of the Australian participation.

Woods Humphery now set out his understanding of the Qantas position.

> The arrangement we made with QEA in this matter was that we should have a controlling interest in the service, and that all negotiations were to be conducted by us; that is to say, QEA would take no active steps whatever in regard to the trans-Tasman service. McMaster had told us that if we wanted Qantas in as partners after we had decided on our policy and our plan of operation, they would be pleased to receive an invitation from us, and

would then consider whether they would, or were able, to participate. Shelmerdine asked me how the new Australian combine, Australian National Airways, stood in regard to this matter. I said that although QEA had placed us under no obligation to offer them participation, we should naturally make them, as our partners, the first offer.

He added that the other Australian combine, Airlines of Australia, would — with its American and other financial interests — "eliminate any desire on our part to have them as partners".[54]

McMaster answered tersely. If Australia did not participate in the Empire Mail Scheme (the number three alternative offered to the Australian government) he could not, said McMaster, see how this would conflict with existing partnership arrangements. "You suggest that your Board might", he wrote, "be faced with carrying QEA on purely as a gracious act if a contract was arranged under alternative number three." McMaster rejected this attitude, saying that the partnership was meant to operate fully irrespective of adjustments between respective governments. On the suggestion that Q.A.N.T.A.S. might again operate internally, McMaster was equally blunt. "The whole of the Q.A.N.T.A.S. interests are in QEA," he said, "and the main trunk service must be the principal development. Any internal services that have not been staked or earmarked for other combinations are very pinched and doubtful propositions."[55] McMaster was, however, in accord with Woods Humphery on his trans-Tasman service views.

The outline of the British position as seen by Woods Humphery was the basis of the brief for F.G.L. Bertram, deputy director of civil aviation, when representatives of the United Kingdom, Australia, and New Zealand met in Wellington in September 1936 to attempt to establish, at government level, the foundations for a trans-Tasman service. The Australian government team was a powerful one — Sir Archdale Parkhill, minister for defence; M.L. Shepherd, secretary, Defence Department; H.P. Brown, director of postal services; and Edgar Johnston, controller of civil aviation. The prime minister of New Zealand, M.J. Savage, led the New Zealand delegation. However, despite these discussions at the highest level, many more were to follow over a long period before binding agreements were made for the Tasman.

On the central issue of the Empire Air Mail Scheme there

was, at last, the possibility of progress. The British government conceded that Australia was free to impose a surcharge on all mails from Australia and, further, that if flying boats proved unsatisfactory within a period of two years, the agreement between the two governments could, in that respect, be reviewed. QEA, it was agreed, could contract with the Australian government and not rely on an Imperial Airways contract with the United Kingdom government. "It would appear", wrote Woods Humphery to McMaster on 9 October 1936, "that the crux of the position is the agreement between the Commonwealth Government and QEA, which might be anything between a perfectly harmless and reasonable document and one which could wreck the Scheme."[56] His information was better than QEA's. McMaster replied on 26 October that QEA "has not been consulted or approached officially in any way, so we do not know what is in the mind of the Government regarding either the Empire Flying Boat Scheme or the Brisbane–Darwin section when the flying boat scheme is adopted and in operation". He wanted to hold on to the inland connection to Darwin "to make the position secure against a Dutch connection there with a rival organisation".[57]

Qantas was, as Fysh expressed it to Woods Humphery, "waiting for something to happen". Fysh used the lull to let his IAL colleague know "in general, just how our organisation is getting along". Before duplication of the DH86 service, wrote Fysh,

> we were still not large enough to enable really adequate organisation in all departments. For instance, publicity and advertising were in the main done by myself. Duplication was our chance to alter this. The position at the moment is that we are fully departmentalised, have ample staff (with the exception of ground engineers) and are sitting waiting for something to happen . . . QEA owes its success to the old Qantas grounding; the influence of IAL; the fact that we have the pick of Australia as regards staff; and that we are still small and concentrated enough to enable the closest supervision to be exercised.

Fysh listed and commented on his senior people.

> *Secretary*: Harman is an able man with long experience with Qantas, and often acts as assistant manager. He has excellent traffic experience and before he came to us was doing Tour and Travel work in Australia and Paris with the American Express Company. He is an old war observer. *Accountant*: In sending Turner you made a very wise shot, and we regard him as a brilliant man, quite able to handle any accounting work. His nearly two years with us have rounded the rough edges which he

displayed at the start, and he has a full realisation of requirements. *Flight Superintendent*: Brain has gone from strength to strength and he stands quite alone in Australia. Brain also has administrative ability. Like Turner he was too young for war service. *Works Manager*: Baird is also quite outstanding in Australia, and as a practical engineer in charge of operations I know of no better man anywhere. Baird was a flight sergeant during the war and won a Military Medal. *Publicity Officer*: Potts is a new addition and has extensive newspaper and advertising experience. Potts is only a low salaried man at present. *Traffic*: We have a young man named Neilsen on this job under Harman. Neilsen is the right type and can handle any traffic requirement. *Captains and First Officers*: Not counting Brain, we have seven Captains and seven First Officers. In addition, we have Captain Donaldson in charge of Cloncurry–Normanton operations. Allan is the senior Captain and is quite the best we know in Australia. With our small size, and considering that we pay much higher than any other organisation in Australia, we have been able to hand pick Captains, with the result that we have an outstanding team. We are now a well-organised air transport unit (the only one in Australia) and fit and ready to undertake new work and responsibilities with knowledge and confidence. Our decentralisation from London has not only relieved you of the undoubted worry of the Australian end, but has enabled us to control in a real way our section. As regards the future, there are so many influences and opinions to be considered that I feel one must continue to rest with hands tied by circumstance until things are settled, and the time for action comes.[56]

Hudson Fysh was not nearly as satisfied with the operational standards of Imperial Airways. He reported to Dismore:

Jimmy Fairbairn [MHR] arrived in Brisbane. He is pro-Imperial Airways but he tells me that it is going to take years to live down the name IAL has in India, Malaya etc. and that people are travelling KLM whenever they can get seats. This is understandable when so many of them [IAL passengers] arrive late and have experienced engine trouble somewhere on the route. Leaving out your bad luck, the phenomenal loss of aircraft from one cause or another has had its effect and is producing a lack of confidence. Believe me, despite that wretched bad luck and the handicap of operating obsolete machines, there is something wrong somewhere.

His letter, he added, was written "in the spirit of absolute helpfulness".[59]

By mid-October 1936, Fysh was able to write to Squadron Leader A.H. Cobby, Civil Aviation Board, that "from reports, it looks as if flying boats are certain, and that a final agreement on all points is not far away". He told Cobby that QEA captains were, as a preliminary, flying the Singapore Flying

297

Club's Moth on floats, and that captains and first officers would shortly be put through a course of instruction in sailing. Fysh asked if Qantas could obtain on loan from the RAAF a Southampton flying boat for three months, with a crew and an instructor in Brisbane.[60] Cobby replied: "There is no chance of the RAAF sending a flying boat to Brisbane. The Chief of Air Staff thinks Point Cook [in Victoria] is the obvious place to carry out training of this sort. In this he will help to the utmost."[61] Fysh reported to McMaster that he had stressed to the chief of the air staff (Williams) that training at Brisbane was needed because QEA was unable to send crews south to Victoria off the route. He had, he said, received an option on a flying boat, the *Cutty Sark*, but Baird thought its hull was unsound and the boat too small for training QEA riggers for water work.[62]

Edgar Johnston praised QEA in a letter to Fysh on 22 October 1936. "We are highly gratified with the excellent operational success of the service this side of Singapore", he wrote. "I only wish that IAL could do as well on the other side." The conference in New Zealand, said Johnston, should result in a workable arrangement, placing control of the trans-Tasman service in the hands of Australia and New Zealand. As for the England–Australia service, he commented: "The Federal House holds strong views on the [Empire Mail Scheme] matter and it remains to be seen whether the House will agree to the Empire Boat Scheme, even with the modifications envisaged to meet the Government requirements in regard to Australian control."[63] There were other problems, which Johnston put to McMaster. Neither QEA nor Q.A.N.T.A.S., he said, would have any claim on the Brisbane–Darwin land section once the contract was finalized for the Empire Flying Boat Scheme. Further, the whole of the plant and aircraft being used by QEA would have to be taken care of by the company, and was no concern of the government. It had been agreed with the United Kingdom government that the flying boat service was a sufficient recompense, without any further compensation for the rupture of the present QEA contracts.[64]

To McMaster, that position was patently unfair and to be fought. He wrote to Woods Humphery on 10 December 1936 that he had inferred from conversations that QEA would just have to accept "any conditions, both regarding the flying boat service and, also, the present QEA contracts resulting from the negotiations between the two Governments". He intimated "that the Board here might find it very difficult to come to an agreement if this attitude is taken up by our Government."[65]

Impossible and Childish Conditions 1937

15 The year 1937 opened with more Dutch pressure to fly to Australia. On 11 January, Sir Archdale Parkhill announced that the Dutch government, through the British government, had renewed its request for the extension of KNILM services to Australia from Batavia. A Dutch Douglas airliner, chartered to a British shipping magnate Sir Laurence Philipps at a reported cost of seven thousand pounds, to bring him with his wife and daughter Gwenthian to Australia on a holiday, showed its paces by crossing the Timor Sea from Koepang to Darwin in two hours and thirty-eight minutes, at an average speed of 190 miles per hour. The performance of both the aircraft and the Philipps family attracted press coverage. Sir Laurence had come, he said, to see horse racing and breeding methods in Australia. Lady Philipps "stressed the necessity of women living a home life". She told the Brisbane *Courier Mail*: "I am not interested in politics and have not taken an active part in social life. I have spent my life rearing a large family."[1]

McMaster reported to Woods Humphery that the year had begun with "a definite political bitterness growing up here, which is dangerous. The press is continually criticising the Minister for Defence, and he is not without a following both inside and outside the Government. The Minister has to defend himself in the House and through the press, and the result is that neither Imperial Airways nor Qantas are any the better off politically."[2] (The Sydney *Sun* wrote: "The proposal to take away from the Australian Government the control of its own air routes and to hand over those routes lock, stock and barrel for fifteen years to Imperial Airways without any guarantee that they would not be operated by obsolete or obsolescent machines" would make the Commonwealth "guilty of gross negligence if agreed to without careful examination".[3] It was a press view that had changed diametrically since *The Bulletin* had mocked Parkhill for not welcoming the original British proposals.) McMaster told Woods Humphery on 21 January that he had been assured that finality had been reached "regarding surcharge, the use of the flying boats and the control of the Australian section, and the only question to be finalised now is the bases along the Queensland coast. You are in a position to know whether this is correct or otherwise, but certainly the position is not improving for either your interests or QEA's by this continuous pin-pricking which is going on through the press, and which is becoming more and more personal and bitter . . ."[4]

McMaster had only one more week of uncertainty to endure. On 28 January 1937, the prime minister, J.A. Lyons, announced that agreement had been reached at government-to-government level on the Empire Flying Boat and Air Mail Scheme. A seven-day, twice weekly service would operate between London and Sydney from January 1938. In a later statement, issued to the press, the prime minister gave more details. It said that the outline proposals for the Empire Air Mail Scheme had first been received by the Commonwealth government from the United Kingdom government by cable in October 1934 and that details were not known until some time later. These first details proposed that flying boats would operate with a useful load of three and a half tons, under a proposed fifteen-year contract between Imperial Airways (and associated companies) and the United Kingdom government. Australia had been asked to contribute to capital and recurring costs of the Scheme on the basis of (i) a fixed annual subsidy of £90,000 sterling (£A112,500) towards operational costs, which amount was substantially reduced by the United Kingdom government to £50,000 sterling (ii) a fixed annual payment of £52,000 sterling (£A65,000) for conveyance of mails of the service. Against this there would be a credit from surcharged mails to and from non-Empire countries estimated at £8,000 sterling per annum.

The Commonwealth, under these initial proposals, said the statement, was to accept responsibility for providing and maintaining the Singapore–Sydney ground organization, and to continue its present subsidy to the Orient (shipping) company despite withdrawal of first class Empire mails from that service. The initial scheme contemplated, as an essential feature, the pooling of resources (equipment and personnel) of IAL and associated companies over the whole route, all major repairs and overhauls being carried out in England.

Before the Commonwealth government had had an opportunity to study and comment on these initial proposals, said the prime minister, it was officially announced in the House of Commons on 20 December 1934 that the United Kingdom government had adopted these proposals in principle. The Commonwealth government, on examination of the scheme had, however, found features open to serious objection. These objections, he said, were not dispelled by the conference with United Kingdom officials in Sydney in February 1935. The Commonwealth counterproposals, in broad terms, were retention of the mail surcharge principle, but with substantially decreased rates, and continuance of present co-operative arrangements under which Australia assumed full responsibility for the Singapore service. The Commonwealth government had, said the prime minister, decided to retain a surcharge of fivepence per half ounce and had agreed to the use of Empire flying boats (subject to the proviso that within two years the agreement in that respect could be reviewed with the right of Australia to terminate it should a satisfactory arrangement not be made). The United Kingdom government had accepted the principle of Australian control of the Singapore section which, he said, the Commonwealth government regarded as being of the greatest importance. This control, it was the government's view, should be absolute and real.

Other matters of substance agreed by the Commonwealth government and set out in the prime minister's statement were:

• All major repairs and overhauls would be effected in England, subject to the Commonwealth's right to make representations for major repairs to be effected in Australia.

• The Commonwealth government would bear costs up to £30,000 sterling per annum in respect of charges and maintenance expenses involved by an agreed schedule of ground organization. The United Kingdom government would bear any excess above that sum.

• The working of the agreements should be supervised and periodically reported upon by a committee to be set up in London representing the governments concerned.

• The new flying boat service would commence on 1 January 1938, provided the Commonwealth government was relieved of any liability for compensation to QEA for termination of the existing contract for the Brisbane–Singapore service (which did not expire until December 1939).

• The financial contributions proposed by the United Kingdom government were accepted, viz: on mail payments, a minimum of £32,000 sterling per annum and a maximum of £52,000, representing sixteen shillings per pound weight for mail originating from Australia.

• Subsidy would rise from a minimum of £40,000 sterling per annum to a maximum of £50,000 at a rate proportional to the growth in mail payments.

The prime minister's statement said that these Australian decisions were acceptable to the United Kingdom government. "The Government believes", he said, "that Australian active responsibility over a definite section of the through service, on which the Government had been most insistent, makes the service more truly an Empire arrangement than that originally proposed, in which Australia's part was little beyond that of a financial contributor." On the second major issue of surcharges for mail, the prime minister observed that the government did not feel justified in giving free air conveyance to overseas correspondence while continuing to demand an extra payment for air conveyance of local correspondence.[5]

The concessions made by the United Kingdom were major ones. They had won agreement for the use of flying boats, but had yielded on the issues of mail surcharges from Australia and Australian control of the Singapore route. This resolution of the basic question of control by Australia of its own overseas airline marked a fundamental turning point in the history of Qantas, identifying it unequivocally both within Australia and abroad with Australian national aspirations and Commonwealth government support.

The financial terms of the agreement marked the first major departure by the Civil Aviation Board from the principle of fixed annual payment for mail based on route mileage.[6] The minimum amount that QEA could receive from the Commonwealth annually (for mail plus subsidy) was £72,000 sterling, the maximum £102,000. Qantas could, in addition, retain revenues from passenger fares and freight charges, but air mail was to be given priority.

McMaster announced that, to implement the flying boat

service, some £480,000 of new capital would have to be raised privately, half of it in Australia. Qantas, he said, would operate a fleet of five flying boats which could each, in addition to mail and freight, carry twenty-four passengers, with sleeping accommodation for sixteen of them.[7] The achievement of agreement between the two governments had now made it possible for QEA to begin negotiations on its contract with Imperial Airways at company-to-company level, and on its contract directly with the Australian government. Edgar Johnston advised Fysh that doubt about future operation by Qantas of the existing Singapore–Darwin service need not hold up the QEA negotiations with IAL. "Of course," he added, "it might affect the adjustments between yourselves and IAL if you should receive the contract for the Brisbane–Darwin [land] service."[8]

While the future Qantas hold on their overland service to Darwin was made uncertain as a result of the flying boat plans, Qantas undertook a new initiative in a bid to operate a service to New Guinea. Following talks in Adelaide between Ivan Holyman of Australian National Airways and Hudson Fysh, agreement was reached that QEA and Airlines of Australia (60 per cent owned by ANA) should form a new company to tender for the service between Sydney, Salamaua, and Rabual. The new company, Australian New Guinea Airlines Proprietary Limited, was incorporated on 23 March 1937 and McMaster was appointed chairman. It seemed a wise and promising initiative. Airlines of Australia was already operating between Sydney and Townsville; Qantas had proven over-water experience; both were organizations of substance. The plan was that Airlines of Australia would operate the Sydney–Townsville section of the New Guinea route while QEA would operate from Townsville to Rabaul. The venture, however, came to nothing. The Airlines of Australia–Qantas tender price was too high and the contract was won by Carpenter Airlines, with DH86 aircraft.[9]

The reduction in subsidy rates accepted by QEA with the duplication of the Singapore DH86 service had, despite Fysh's fears, proved satisfactory. Profits rose from £8,599 in 1935–36 to £16,042 for 1936–37 (year ending 31 March). Every expenditure item of importance had been kept within budget estimates. In a report to the board, Fysh praised both Turner and Neilsen. "Our estimates, general figures and statistics come from the Accounts Department under Mr Turner," he wrote, "and have been excellently handled during the year, proving of the greatest assistance," Neilsen, he said, had been understudying Harman on the traffic side, was gradually assuming more responsibility, and had done good work.[10] Passenger-miles flown for 1936–37 were 2,248,298, up 114 per cent on the previous year; 140, 664 pounds weight of mails had been carried (up 48 per cent) and 51,952 pounds of freight (up 87 per cent). Amongst the famous passengers carried since inauguration of the service, QEA now included Mr Noel Coward and Mr Charlie Chaplin with Lady Louis Mountbatten.[11]

On 24 April, Lester Brain, with Capt. W.H. Crowther and C.R. Gurney, left for England to undertake flying boat training. Competition on the planned flying boat route was, however, looming. In April, formal permission was given by the Australian government for the Dutch, through KLM, to extend their service from Batavia to Australia. It was, because of QEA reliance on facilities across the Netherlands East Indies, an inevitable concession, though the government imposed important conditions. No local passengers or freight could be carried by KNILM between any places in Australia or Australian territories; reciprocal rights of passage and landing were to be granted to Australian airline companies operating to or through Netherlands territory; and Australian mails were not to be available to the Dutch company. The Dutch service, said Australia, could begin simultaneously with the Empire flying boat service, a necessary constraint stressed by McMaster in talks with the acting prime minister, Dr Earl Page.[12]

In England, June saw the coronation of King George VI and, two weeks later, the resignation of Baldwin as prime minister and the appointment of Neville Chamberlain. In the aviation world, Sir Francis Shelmerdine's title of director was upgraded to director-general of civil aviation, in acknowledgment of a general upgrading of civil aviation itself. On 11 June, R.J. Mitchell, designer of the *Spitfire*, died of cancer. Then came a shock for McMaster and Fysh. On 22 June, after a short illness, Sir Eric Geddes died. Imperial Airways lost the man who had been its chairman since its inception in 1924. He had had a remarkable career. In World War I, Geddes was sent to France to organize army communications and by 1917 had provided a system of military roads and railways in the north, holding the honorary rank of major-general. In the same year, he was appointed controller, Royal Navy, and

given the honorary rank of vice-admiral, later succeeding Lord
Carson as First Lord of the Admiralty. After the Armistice, he
wielded the feared and long-remembered "Geddes Axe", cutting the huge expense of government departments created in
wartime. In 1921, he became Britain's first minister of
transport. "His assertive manner and his reputation as a high-
powered businessman made a powerful impression upon
subordinates", said one press comment.[13] Though intensely
admired for his ability and foresight, he was more feared than
loved by those who worked closely with him.[14] His successor
was a financial expert, Sir George Beharrell.

June 1937 also saw the first regular flying boat service by
Imperial Airways to Durban, as the initial arm of the new
Empire Air Mail Scheme, and some justifiable duchessing of
Australian prime minister J.A. Lyons, in England with the
Australian Delegation to the 1937 Imperial Conference,
which began in May.[15] Lyons wrote to Woods Humphery
from Paris to thank him for a trip from Rochester to Amsterdam on 21 June in the Empire flying boat *Challenger*. "Not
only did I save a great deal of time," said the Australian prime
minister, "but I was able to make the crossing in the utmost
comfort. The roominess of the boat was a revelation, and with
it went a sense of perfect security."[16] At the Imperial Conference itself, questions concerning civil aviation were referred to a committee under the chairmanship of Sir Archdale
Parkhill. The committee discussed prospects for the establishment of a British chain of air communications interconnecting
all parts of the Empire, and adopted a number of resolutions
including agreement that whenever an application was received by one member for facilities for foreign air services likely to
affect another member, there should be consultation between
the governments involved. The conference noted with approval "the practice followed by nations of the Commonwealth whereby when operating rights are granted to a
foreign airline, the concession expressly provides for
reciprocal rights as and when desired".[17]

A significant step in the advancement of civil air routes was
taken on the Atlantic in July. After months of planning by
Woods Humphery, at Imperial Airways, and by Juan Trippe
at Pan American, simultaneous experimental trans-Atlantic
flights were made by both airlines in opposite directions. The
Short Empire flying boat *Caledonia* left its base at Foynes on
the River Shannon at 7:55 P.M. on 6 July westbound for Botwood, Newfoundland. The Pan American *Clipper* III flying

boat left Botwood on the eastbound crossing. In mid-Atlantic, they communicated by radio then went on to complete their 1993-mile flights without incident. (It was not until 5 August 1939, however, that regular services started across the Atlantic.)

In Australia, on the day before these Atlantic flights, Fergus McMaster blasted the government for their decisions on the proposed airmail contract with QEA and created uproar in Cabinet.[18] In a letter to J.A. Hunter, assistant minister, on 5 July, he wrote: "You will realise, and I feel sure that every member of your Cabinet will, that it would be impossible for us to undertake a capital outlay . . . on the basis of the contract offered and further, it would be impossible to raise the capital in Australia either by share issue or bank accommodation."[19] Qantas had received the draft agreement from the government for the operation of the Australian section of the Empire Air Mail Scheme which, though not final, expressed substantially the arrangements and decisions reached between the United Kingdom and Commonwealth governments.

> The draft sets out in effect [wrote McMaster] that the present Brisbane–Singapore contract now operated by Qantas must be cancelled as and when the Government may determine, without any obligation on the part of the Government. The unamortised capital involved on 31 December next will be approximately £50,000. The Minister is to have the rights at any time, and even during the first six months of operation of the Empire contract to prohibit the use of flying boats and compel their replacement with landplanes, without recourse against the Government. On failure to comply with such directions, without any breach of contract or misdemeanour on the part of the Company, he has the sole right in the event of the Commonwealth Government terminating its arrangements with the United Kingdom Government, to cancel its contract with the Company at any time, and without any protection for the capital involved.

McMaster estimated that for three services a week each way between Sydney and Singapore, the capital outlay by QEA would be £579,865, and that additional liability attaching to the current Brisbane–Singapore contract would bring the total capital involved to £626,865.

> The contract as drawn up [wrote McMaster scornfully] can only mean one of two things: either it is a clumsy political move to defeat the Empire Scheme, or the Department responsible is incompetent to draft an agreement fully protective of the Government and, at the same time, fair and reasonable for the Company to undertake. Whatever grounds for caution your Government might have had two years ago, when these negotiations were com-

menced, to hedge itself round with these impossible and childish conditions, surely those grounds do not obtain today.[20]

McMaster pointed out that the Empire flying boats had been operating the Mediterranean section for several months in the ordinary routine of service. They had satisfactorily complied with all tests and had been fully accepted by the Air Ministry. "Your Government", he said, "must surely be in a position to decide whether these aircraft should or should not be used on the Australian section, and should come out openly and act accordingly."[21] For the government, said McMaster, to go to the heavy expense of establishing flying boat bases and to expect the company to involve itself in a capital outlay of £600,000, and still insist that the minister, on his sole right, could if he so desired cancel the whole service and demand a landplane service in its place, was an impossible policy, and an impossible contract. The question, he said, appeared to be more political than departmental, and no good purpose would be served by himself or QEA attempting to negotiate an agreement until the position had been considered by Cabinet. "If the Government is determined to force the position, it will mean a complete breakdown of the Empire Scheme — and I cannot see how the Government would escape a political repercussion which would be damaging to its interests at the coming elections . . . Until the agreements are finalised, we cannot approach the public for capital," he wrote, "nor can we contemplate further involving the Company, faced with such impossible contract proposals." It was hard and brave language to use with a government. To Woods Humphery, McMaster wrote: "The Government is in a very unsound and impossible position, more particularly in view of the outstandingly successful flight of the Empire boat on the experimental Atlantic service."[22]

Fysh in a formal report on the draft agreement between the Commonwealth and QEA pointed out that the history of negotiations between the United Kingdom and Commonwealth governments showed that the Commonwealth never wanted the flying boat service and

> had the Scheme forced on them against their wishes. The heads of both Australian Aviation Departments, that of Civil Aviation and the RAAF, have fought the Scheme and are still not in favour of using flying boats. The most objectionable clauses in the draft agreement are those which attempt to express and ensure the idea of Australian control of the service and the general protection of Australian interests as opposed to those of the United Kingdom.

Undoubtedly every possible effort has been made to try and prevent any drift of control away from Australia. These clauses have,
however, been made so drastic or been so clumsily drafted, as to
make the draft unacceptable as a contract.

Fysh said that the main point for dissatisfaction was the Commonwealth right to withdraw, which he thought unworkable.
"It should be remembered", he wrote, "that the Commonwealth's Air Service Contracts have always been most
stringent, placing the operating company greatly at the mercy
of the Minister of Defence. Never have we seen such a
stringent and impossible agreement as the one now put before
us . . ."[23]

McMaster's letter had its effect. The attorney-general, R.G.
Menzies, arranged to discuss privately with McMaster in
Brisbane some of the principal clauses in the draft agreement.
McMaster pointed out to Menzies by letter on 15 July 1937
that the drastic provisions proposed would give the company
no protection and make it impossible for the United Kingdom
government to place any confidence in the association. "The
amount of capital involved, including that of Government
expenditure on the route", he reminded Menzies, "will
exceed a million pounds." No thought had been given to this,
he said. The agreement had apparently been drafted with a
view to meeting local political considerations only. "Particular
attention has been given to impress that Australia is to have
control without any responsibility." There had been no consideration given to co-operation to help British air transport
on the Empire trunk route meet foreign pressure for
supremacy, he said. "Many of the machinery clauses are
irksome and impossible."[24] (Ironically, McMaster was not
only tackling Menzies as attorney-general and distinguished
lawyer on the technical clumsiness of the machinery clauses;
he was also criticizing an over-robust, pro-Australian
approach that Menzies by no means supported. Edgar Johnston's view was that Menzies wanted to hand over civil aviation in its entirety to the British.)[25] McMaster stressed to
Menzies that it was of the utmost importance that the contract
between QEA and the Commonwealth be finalized as early as
possible and that the ground organization be in place to allow
the service to begin as nearly as possible to the contemplated
date of 1 January 1938. QEA, he said, had already made
progress payments on the flying boats from May and was
committed to a total amount of £225,000 on the boats alone
by January 1938.[26]

The British initiative for the international carriage of Empire mails in flying boats, conceived in secrecy, announced without consultation with Australia to the British Parliament, and elaborated amidst controversy and delay was now, with its planned introduction, to extend its effect on Australian aviation to the continent's inland services. Edgar Johnston submitted a report to his minister on 5 August 1937 for the "Reorganisation of Internal Service Consequent Upon the Introduction of the Empire Air Mail Scheme". The three existing domestic services (Singapore–Brisbane; Charleville–Cootamundra; Daly Waters–Perth) would not be suitable for the changed conditions, he wrote, and the landplane service between Darwin and Singapore would become unnecessary. The contracts for these services, he pointed out, did not expire until some two years after the proposed date for commencing the flying boat service. "Mutual agreement to vary existing contracts has much to commend it, if it can be achieved", wrote Johnston. Any proposals, he said, would have to take

Capt. Edgar Johnston, Controller-General of the Civil Aviation Board, in 1937.

into account the existing aircraft held by the three companies: five DH86s by QEA; two DH84 Dragons by Butler Air Transport Co. (Charleville–Cootamundra); five DH84 Dragons by MacRobertson Miller Aviation Co. (Daly Waters–Perth).

On postal matters, Johnston wrote: "Despite the fact that the United Kingdom and certain Dominions had decided to convey all first class Empire mail by flying boat service without surcharge the Commonwealth Government, after weighty consideration, had decided to retain the surcharge, though at a greatly reduced rate, for Australian correspondence sent by the service." It was therefore presumed, said Johnston, that the government would retain the principle of surcharge for mail carried by local air services.

His report then set down its recommendations. The Singapore–Brisbane and Charleville–Cootamundra services would be discontinued; a service from Brisbane through western Queensland and the Northern Territory should be retained, but on a smaller scale; the Perth–Daly Waters service should be improved and should terminate at Darwin. (Qantas, said the report, would have to retain two of its DH86s, with three of them to go to the Western Australian service.) Existing air services operating between the capital cities should, said the report, "be placed on a proper basis, under a considered plan and under definite subsidy contracts, to enable enforcement of timetable and other conditions".[27]

In more dramatic terms, the newspaper *Smith's Weekly* described the situation on 7 August 1937 under the heading "Battle for the Air Routes". Most involved, it said, were "the big three": QEA, with capital increasing to a million pounds; Australian National Airways (capital half a million pounds), whose five equal shareholders were Holyman Bros., Orient Steam Navigation Co., Huddart Parker, Union Steamship, and Adelaide Steamship Co.; and Airlines of Australia (capital one million pounds), 60 per cent owned by ANA. Other contenders in the forthcoming battle were listed as: Guinea Airways (on the Adelaide–Darwin route); Carpenter Airlines (Sydney–Rabaul); Ansett Airways (with orders placed for four Lockheeds and out "to get more than the minor country services they operate"); plus the Dutch KLM and KNILM with the announced intention to extend to Sydney.

"Aviation circles know", said *Smith's Weekly*, "that the establishment of the Empire Flying Boat Service next year will bring about drastic alterations in major airline routes . . .

311

So far as the outlook is concerned, the company most happily situated seems to be Qantas Empire Airways." The newspaper added, however, that "ANA also throws a formidable shadow across the future. With four Douglases and a flock of other aircraft, and nearly two score pilots, and big shipping companies behind it, ANA is the biggest enterprise in the history of Australian aviation."[28]

Hudson Fysh flew to England in August, in company with A.R. McComb, for discussions with the secretary of state for air, Lord Swinton, and the director-general of civil aviation, Sir Francis Shelmerdine. War preparations were now to begin overshadowing even the complexities of the new flying boat service.[29] (Fysh wrote to McMaster, en route, from Singapore on the possibility of an air connection with Dili, in Portuguese Timor "in regard to possible Japanese aggression". His Britannic Majesty's consul-general in Batavia, H. Fitzmaurice, had advised that the new governor of Portuguese Timor, Major Neves da Fontoura, wanted to gain a connection with the outer world by air. Fysh told McMaster that he had explained to Fitzmaurice how the mountains behind Dili would make it a difficult place to use, though it might be made an additional stop.)[30] In that same month of August, HMS *Achilles* raised the British flag on Canton Island, in the Pacific, and landed a representative to study weather conditions. (The island was to become a United Kingdom–United States condominium and a stopping point on the trans-Pacific route between Honolulu and Australia.)

On 20 August 1937, McMaster was able to cable Woods Humphery that Cabinet had agreed to the Commonwealth-QEA contract, but that bases and ground organization had been further delayed. "Cannot contemplate commencement service before August 1938", said his message. "Urge you to restrict avoidable expenditure on flying boats, engines and spares otherwise QEA paying heavy interest considerably in advance of use of plant. Urge costs kept lowest."[31] Both Woods Humphery and Dismore had been greatly impressed by the vigour and clarity of McMaster in his dealings with the Australian government. "I would like to congratulate you", wrote Woods Humphery, "on the extremely clear and forceful way in which you have put your views before the various Ministers." Dismore had relished the McMaster spirit and wrote: "I particularly enjoyed reading your very frank letter . . . in which you referred to the original and quite impossible draft as being a clumsy political attempt to wreck the Scheme.

You have had a very strenuous fight over the agreement but it
certainly seems ... as though you have steered the Government towards wiser counsels."[32]

McMaster advised Woods Humphery by cable on 3 September that the Commonwealth Parliament would dissolve on 9
September for a general election. "We unable sign contract for
ratification by Parliament until we receive your approval",
said McMaster. "Please treat position as urgent."[33] That ratification did not come before Parliament rose on 9 September,
with election day set for 23 October 1937. "There is little
hope of anything being done before the elections are over",
McMaster advised Woods Humphery on 1 October. He was
worried and angered by the delays. In a letter to solicitor
Clifford Minter on 2 October, he wrote:

> We are paying out a lot of money in connection with the [aircraft]
> construction programme and the training of pilots and crews,
> which must go on otherwise it would be impossible to commence
> the service before the end of next year. We have already paid out
> £88,471 and completed arrangements yesterday for bank accom-
> modation for a further £136,000 to carry on the construction pro-
> gramme up to 26 January next, and pending the securing of new
> capital from the public ... The attitude of the Government
> towards the Company has been most unfair ... The Company
> will be faced not only with a heavy interest charge, but will also
> have heavy depreciation and obsolescence costs owing to the long
> delay in the commencement of the service.[34]

Mc Master sent Woods Humphery a copy of the long-delayed
agreement with the Commonwealth commenting: "I am satisfied that the contract as submitted is a reasonably sound one
... Provided the Lyons Government is returned, we can
expect the agreement to be ratified immediately Parliament
assembles, somewhere about the end of November."[35]

Hudson Fysh, meanwhile, had had his first sight in England
of the big new flying boats and described it to Edgar Johnston
as a relevation. He had already seen one briefly at Basra, on
his way to England, and wrote: "The boat makes that important departure from the old idea — one passenger one seat.
Passengers can walk about, mix and use the promenade
deck."[36] His conversations in England with Imperial Airways
on maintenance, repair, and engine overhaul had convinced
him that it was necessary for QEA to carry out some overhaul
of engines in Australia, something not provided for in the
agreements and for which no financial allocation had been
made. "Under the present system," he told Johnston, "even
breakdowns would go to London for overhaul — by ship." No

engine overhauls, he said, meant no engineers capable of carrying out overhauls. It was, he said, a serious matter and would leave QEA without the control and responsibility visualized in the Commonwealth-QEA agreement. We should, said Fysh, imagine the position during a serious European war.[37]

As the date for the Australian general election grew close, McMaster wrote in gentler vein than previously to Sir Archdale Parkhill and R.G. Menzies, looking forward to their personal success and that of their government in the elections. "There is very little life in the Labour organisation meetings", he commented. He told Parkhill that the draft agreement between QEA and the Commonwealth was now "one which I feel my Company can sign, and I wish to thank you for the courtesy and help given in the negotiations".[38]

The government was returned on 23 October 1937, though with its vote reduced. Menzies wrote to McMaster on 25 October: "I was lucky enough to retain my seat. However, though the Lyons Government can now look forward to another term of office, the increased Labor figures in so many electorates was a factor I found to be somewhat disquieting."[39] Parkhill was not so fortunate, and lost his seat. "The result is disappointing," he told McMaster, "but doubtless I shall find some congenial outlet for my future activities."[40]

The break in the parliamentary process had not only compounded the delay in ratification of the Qantas contract but had prolonged the seeming paralysis in the provision of flying boat facilities. McMaster told Woods Humphery on 16 November that no material advance had been made on the establishment of bases and ground organization generally.[41] Lester Brain reported that although the Civil Aviation Department realized the necessity for a slipway and hangar at Rose Bay, on the southern shore of Sydney Harbour, and although the government had at last agreed that the harbour could be used for landing and moorings, Cabinet had refused permission for the slipway and hangar, "no doubt influenced by political pressure". It had been agreed, Brain reported to McMaster, "that passengers and mail may be disembarked into motor boats and put ashore at a jetty. In a real emergency, we could beach the flying boats at Rose Bay between tides."[42] An absurd situation had arisen; Qantas faced delivery of a fleet of flying boats, with pilots and engineers ready to operate them, but it could not make use of them. An earlier suggestion from Imperial Airways that some of the Qantas boats could be

used temporarily on IAL services had met with political difficulties in Australia. The Australian boats would have had to
be placed on the British register and, with the possibility that
these IAL-registered Australian boats would operate east of
Singapore into Sydney, the old spectre of British dominance
and control had again arisen. A polite but perplexed Woods
Humphery wrote to McMaster: "There will shortly be six
Qantas boats which will not apparently be used for several
months and which neither Short Bros nor ourselves can store.
Our suggestion was to circulate some of these boats temporarily on our service before commencement of the Singapore–
Sydney extension. The boat service east of Singapore would
not be started until the QEA boats had been re-registered in
Australia. Our proposals were made with the object of mutual
help." He had, he said, explained the proposals in London to
Hudson Fysh, who favoured them.[43] The IAL proposal was
modified, opposition withdrawn, and on 29 November Woods
Humphery cabled: "First boat now delivered and propose
circulating first two boats on our service under Australian
registration, consequently no change in ownership involved.
Agree leave decision other aircraft in abeyance pending your
discussion with Fysh and settlement of definite starting date
for your services."[44] Woods Humphery, wrote Fysh, was up
to his eyes in problems and tending to become short on
tolerance.[45]

McMaster bluntly defended QEA in the press as the starting
date for the flying boat service receded. Qantas, he told the
Sydney Morning Herald, had kept strictly to the terms of its
contract with the government. Pilots and engineers had been
trained. The airline was ready to commence services on the
contract date in January or as soon as the bases were prepared
and the agreement ratified by Parliament.[46] An editorial in the
Herald said:

> The Rose Bay terminal base exists only on paper; not a tap of
> work has been done there to prepare for the reception, housing
> and overhaul of the new air fleet. The contract for the service has
> still to be ratified by the Federal Parliament and, when it meets
> next week, it will have to listen to a new Defence Minister telling
> a now wearisome story of air mail negotiations . . . Meanwhile the
> Qantas company has performed its part. It has, or by January will
> have, the six flying boats for the Singapore–Sydney run ready in
> England . . . They represent £300,000 of capital lying idle.[47]

Unintentional public emphasis for all this confusion was
provided by Imperial Airways C-class flying boat RMA *Cen-*

taurus, which set out from England on 3 December on the first commercial flying boat survey to Australia and New Zealand.[48] Though it put flying boats, literally, before the public, the delays continued. "We have been pressing as hard as we can for progress to be made on the Singapore–Sydney alighting areas and aids to navigation," wrote Woods Humphery on 3 December, "but the negotiations between our respective Governments seem almost interminable. The delay and misunderstanding occurs in spite of the presence in London of Mr McComb, who has done his utmost to speed up negotiations."[49] A further embarrassment was the success and public impact in Australia of the Douglas DC3. "Unfortunately," wrote McMaster to Woods Humphery, "the advances being made in Australian air services on the introduction of the large Douglas machines is having a very bad effect upon the Empire Scheme because it is felt that the Empire aircraft will be completely obsolete before the service commences."[50] Even the QEA contract with the Commonwealth had not been absolutely settled in detail. The new minister for defence, H.V.C. Thorby, told J.A. Hunter on 3 December: "In regard to the agreement with the Company [QEA], the Civil Aviation Branch, the Attorney-General's Department and the Postal Department are at present examining the amendments sought by the Company, and it is anticipated that they will shortly come before the Government for consideration."[51]

Hudson Fysh, back in Australia, thought that his visit to England "to clean up the Agreement and other arrangements for opening the flying boat service to Sydney" had not proved much of a success. "Air Ministry support of the Scheme was wanting and muddled owing to pre-war military activity and other causes", he wrote. "A number of vital details remained unresolved . . ."[52] On his arrival at Darwin he had handed a prepared statement to the press which unrestrainedly attacked the government delays. "Not a tap has been done in the Netherlands Indies [to prepare bases]," he said, "and I believe the same applies in Australia. If someone does not hurry, the boats will be out of date before a start is made. A start is certainly impossible by 1 January." Fysh said he thought mid-1938 more likely. "The Scheme", he said, "is one of the most important Empire developments of the century. There is provision even in the early stages of no less than thirty seats per week in and out of Australia, as against seven by the present Qantas service. Yet it is being lauded in a hesitant way."[53]

To Edgar Johnston on 15 December he wrote: "I am sure I have thrown a great bombshell into the camp. What I intended to do was attack Government delays. The papers took it I meant the Commonwealth Government. I hoped and expected that my stuff would assist in getting a move on and that your Minister could say that England, not Australia, was mainly responsible."[54]

The Imperial Airways flying boat *Centaurus* arrived in Brisbane on 21 December. Lester Brain, who was on board, reported on the Australian sector of the flying boat route. Darwin Harbour, he said, had good alighting areas but a twenty-seven-foot rise and fall of tide made disembarking facilities expensive. "One of the great needs of Darwin is a modern, first class hotel", he commented. The route from Darwin across Arnhem Land to Princess Elizabeth Bay on Groote Eylandt, at the western side of the Gulf of Carpentaria was, he said, almost entirely across low, rocky plateau and offered no difficulties to air navigation. Princess Elizabeth Bay was "made to order for flying boats, virtually a big lagoon with a narrow entrance to the sea", but uninhabited. "The direct crossing from the Gulf to Townsville is mostly over flat timber country

The first Empire flying boat to come to Australia, Imperial Airways' *Centaurus*, at its moorings on the Brisbane River on 21 December 1937. The aircraft was making a survey of the route to Australia and New Zealand prior to the opening of the flying boat service in 1938.

and keeps well south of the rainy areas between Cardwell and Cairns", he reported.[55] The *Centaurus* flew on to Gladstone, Brisbane, and Sydney. When it returned again to Sydney on 10 January after a flight to Auckland, New Zealand, some fifty thousand people turned out to see it. No one was allowed on board and the visit, like all other matters connected with flying boats as 1937 ended, left a sour taste. There was still to be a considerable wait before flying boats, on a regular basis, were to bring grace and spectacle to Sydney Harbour.

The Most Air-Minded Nation
1938

"We have had no advice as to a starting date", Fysh wrote to Johnston as the new year began. "As such a date could cover a wide range of many months, you will realise that we are unable to proceed on many urgent matters." Qantas, he said, had had to put a brake on operations to avoid a large staff lying idle. "Several months notification will be necessary before the service could be commenced", he told Johnston. "A total of fifty-five flying staff is required to man the flying boats and it is only possible to get these together for training when working to a date. The engineering staff is also another item of great importance, and an organisation has to be set up in Sydney . . . for maintenance of flying boats and engines."[1] Edgar Johnston responded that proposals for the Darwin base had still not been agreed by the United Kingdom government, "neither have we got their agreement to barracks in lieu of cottages at Groote and Karumba. We are asking Works to push on with matters at Townsville, Gladstone and Brisbane. We are pressing on with Rose Bay as fast as possible and expect tenders to be invited for the control building and slipways and jetties very shortly. The design of the hangar is proceeding . . ."[2]

Britain and Australia were not alone in their aviation troubles. Pan American, who had made such giant strides with their route across the northern Pacific to Manila and Hong Kong, had a major setback on their newly inaugurated New Zealand service. On 11 January, the second Pan American flight from Honolulu to Auckland ended in disaster. An oil

16

319

S.A. Dismore, now the assistant general manager of Imperial Airways talking with QEA senior management at Archerfield during a visit to Australia in early 1938 for discussions on the forthcoming Empire flying boat service. From left: Dismore, Arthur Baird, Hudson Fysh, and QEA chief accountant, C.O. Turner.

leak developed in one engine of the flying boat, *Samoan Clipper*. It turned back and began to jettison fuel, in preparation for a landing at Pago Pago in the Samoan Islands. There was a mid-air explosion, all onboard were killed, and the service was withdrawn.

The minister for defence, H.V.C. Thorby, told McMaster on 9 February that the Dutch would be allowed to begin their service to Australia on 1 July 1938 "or at such an earlier date as the Empire Flying Boat Service may be inaugurated". Conscious that this decision imposed further pressures on Qantas, he added: "Everything possible is being done to expedite completion of the main organisation at Rose Bay. I have received the approval of the New South Wales Government and the Woollahra Council to the general layout."[3] The decision to allow the Dutch to start meant that their service to Sydney would be in place before the Empire service unless the delays by governments were curtailed. With a start to the service at least in sight, McMaster made formal application on 11 February to the minister on behalf of Qantas for appointment as representatives on behalf of the Commonwealth government "for inclusion as a member of the Company to be formed for the operation of the proposed Empire Air Mail Service from Australia to New Zealand".[4] Hudson Fysh, in turn, made the first moves for the transfer of the head office of Qantas from Brisbane to Sydney. A.E. Rudder had forwarded an offer from the Shell Company offering space in their new building, which was under construction in Margaret Street. "I have confirmed with Mr McMaster on the matter," replied Fysh, "and he agrees to our securing the floor space offered."[5]

At this critical time the destiny of Imperial Airways (and of its chairman Beharrell and managing director Woods Humphery) became subject to the harsh findings of a committee set up by the British government as the result of a wide-ranging attack on British civil aviation in the House of Commons by Robert Perkins MP. Called the Cadman Committee, its report condemned both the aircraft manufacturing industry and Imperial Airways. C.G. Grey thought the report the most sensible official document yet issued on civil aviation.[6] Of Imperial Airways the report said:

> Although carriage of passengers in safety and comfort and conveyance of mails and freight have been achieved with considerable efficiency, we cannot avoid the conclusion that the management has been defective in other respects. In particular, it has failed to co-operate fully with the Air Ministry and has been intolerant of

The Qantas Empire Airways board in 1938. From left: H.H. Harman, secretary; F.E. Loxton; Fergus McMaster, chairman; A.E. Rudder, vice-chairman; F.J. Smith; and Hudson Fysh, managing director.

suggestions and unyielding in negotiations. Internally, its attitude in staff matters has left much to be desired. It seems that the managing director, presumably with the acquiescence of the Board, has taken a commercial view of his responsibilities that was too narrow, and has failed to give the government departments with which he has been concerned the co-operation we should have expected from a company heavily subsidised and having such important international and Imperial contacts. There should therefore be an immediate improvement in these respects, and this may well involve some change in directing personnel.[7]

The committee recommended the appointment of a full-time chairman, aided by one or more full-time directors. (C.G. Grey thought Woods Humphery should become chairman.) Hudson Fysh described the findings as "that fearsome and devastating happening in the history of United Kingdom Air Transport, the Cadman Report".[8] The outcome influenced him deeply and taught him, he said, in matters requiring liaison and communication with government, a lesson for life. Woods Humphery sent McMaster a copy of the evidence given by himself and Sir George Beharrell before the committee, which included close documentation of Air Ministry procrastination, particularly over the four years of negotiations on the Empire Air Mail Scheme. McMaster responded, on 11 March, that he doubted much notice of the report would be taken in Australia. It did not, he said, "lessen the sound confidence that Qantas airways has had in IAL and its chairman and yourself personally".[9] The British government, however, reacted swiftly to the committee findings. In mid-June it announced the appointment of Sir John Reith as the new chairman of Imperial Airways. Woods Humphery at once resigned.

By March 1938, as this drama was unfolding, seven QEA captains, plus two ground engineers and Arthur Baird, had completed flying boat training in England. Lester Brain had bought the twelve-foot sailing dinghy for pilot training and, despite Baird's reservations, QEA had acquired the small Saro A17 amphibian, *Cutty Sark*, for £700 to use as a trainer on the Brisbane River. On 18 March 1938, the first QEA Short S23 C-class flying boat *Coolangatta*, left Southhampton on its delivery flight to Australia. Scotty Allan was in command, with Bill Purton first officer, Eric Kydd and G.J. Aldous engineers, A.S. Patterson radio operator, and W. Drury steward. George Harman joined as passenger at Batavia, and Lester Brain at Darwin. (The S23 class had four 920-horsepower Bristol Pegasus XC engines, an all-up weight of 40,500 pounds — increased later to 43,500 pounds — and a payload of 8,200 pounds. There were fifteen passenger seats plus three cabin crew and two aircrew. The published cruising speed was 165 miles per hour and the range with this payload 760 miles. Thirty of the S23 C-class boats were produced. Six were for Australia and were named *Coolangatta, Cooee, Carpentaria, Corio, Coogee,* and *Coorong.*)[10] Meanwhile, C.O. Turner had set out financial estimates for the QEA Singapore– Sydney section if the option were adopted to operate the section with only two services per week. The results were unpromising. Turner wrote to Dismore:

> I have based them on the exclusion of stewards. Examination of the available [passenger] capacity eastbound from Singapore showed only 468 pounds per week on the Singapore–Darwin section. This is the equivalent of only one passenger seat per service on our overseas section, and it appears to us that it would be rather disproportionate to provide for a steward and buffet for only one passenger. We have therefore thought it advisable to base the estimate on excluding the buffet and steward, which gives us the equivalent of three additional seats for each service, or a further six seats a week.[11]

(The frequency was, in fact, to be three a week, allowing reasonable capacity for passengers as well as mail, and the retention of the steward.)

On 7 May McMaster took time off from Qantas affairs to write to the minister for defence, Thorby, on party political matters.

> It has come to me from a press report that there is the possibility of the appointment of another Assistant Minister and that the appointment, if made, will be a Country Party representative. You are Deputy Leader of the Country Party and I cannot too strongly urge the appointment of Fadden. Fadden is young, ambitious and far above any other Queensland member in ability, and is looked upon not only by the Country Party supporters here but also by the United Australia Party as outstanding in Queensland politics. I feel sure that any other appointment would be viewed with disfavour in Queensland. The return of the present Commonwealth Government at the next election will depend even more than in the past upon the strength of the Country Party.[12]

(Arthur Fadden went on to have a long and distinguished parliamentary career. He became prime minister for a short period in 1941, following the collapse of the Menzies government and the installation of John Curtin as prime minister.)

In May, the attention of Thorby was directed to internal

Australian air services with the appointment of an interdepartmental committee to consider Edgar Johnston's proposals for the rationalization of domestic services. In addition, it was asked "to report as to what arrangement and augmentation of internal air services will be necessary in consequence of the inauguration of the Empire Flying Boat Service, and to review the whole of the existing air services, both subsidised and unsubsidised, with the object of formulating comprehensive recommendations". The departments represented on the committee were Civil Aviation, Postmaster-General, Treasury, Commonwealth Railways, and Defence.[13]

The trans-Tasman route, the third element in the future pattern of Australia's air services, was not a high priority with the government but Thorby advised McMaster on 1 April 1938 that it had been agreed by the United Kingdom, New Zealand, and the Commonwealth governments that the service should be provided by "a Joint Operating Company comprised of interests nominated by each of the three Governments". The company was to operate the service "under an agreement with the Governments, such agreement to be supervised by a Commission representative of the three Governments". It was, wrote Thorby, "a vital condition that the whole of the capital of the Joint Operating Company shall be found from British sources. I am authorised to advise you that the Commonwealth Government has decided to nominate Qantas Empire Airways to represent the Australian interest in the Joint Operating Company, if your company is agreeable to accept this nomination."[14] Though Qantas was not greatly interested at the time in the Tasman service, it did not want any other aviation group to win government nomination.[15] The main QEA rivals had been, of course, Australian National Airways and Airlines of Australia. The government objection to ANA was its financial association with the Union Steamship Company, with which the nominee company of the New Zealand Government, Union Airways, was also closely associated; the Australian view was that the influence of the competing shipping company should be minimized. The government objection to Airlines of Australia was the controlling interest held by the British Pacific Trust, in which there were substantial United States interests.[16]

Hudson Fysh was able to advise Edgar Johnston on 13 May 1938 that "with minor variations, all the essential requirements that you specify for running-in [flying boat] services in July, and a full service in August, will be ready".[17] The move

Moving QEA files from
Brisbane to Sydney, June 1938.

of the Qantas headquarters to Sydney was also under way.
Fysh wrote to Johnston:

> As we are now almost on the eve of our departure from Brisbane,
> [here is] a line re our executives. Mr Garnsey Potts, Publicity
> Manager, occupies his office at Shell House on 20 May, Mr
> Harman, Secretary, and Mr Turner, Accountant, occupy their
> offices on 30 May. I will occupy my office from the same date or
> 6 June. I am motoring down from Brisbane. Brisbane and the
> internal route is being left a going concern and flying staff,
> ground engineers and a traffic section are being left here intact.[18]

Although the Rose Bay base was in a lamentable state of un-
preparedness, most of the QEA staff, with the office records,
moved down from Brisbane to Shell House on the weekend of
28 May. Lester Brain and Arthur Baird followed by air on 10
June when the two flying boats, *Coolangatta* and *Coogee*, were
flown down to Rose Bay.[19] Though now poised for a great

expansion of operations, Qantas also faced their first direct competition on an air route since the formation of the original company in 1920. On 28 June 1938, the first KLM service for Sydney left Amsterdam, flying DC3 aircraft as far as Batavia. There the subsidiary KNILM took over with Lockheed 14 aircraft, reaching Sydney on 5 July. Permission had been granted for two services weekly in each direction by KNILM between the Netherlands East Indies and Australia, in exchange for the QEA right to pass through Dutch territory with traffic rights.[20] The new Dutch service received generous support from the Australian press, in contrast to the general and sustained criticism of Imperial Airways.

At Imperial Airways' headquarters in London, the effect of the Cadman Committee Report had been shattering. McMaster had cabled Sir George Beharrell on 16 June: "Press reports this morning that Sir John Reith appointed chairman and that Woods Humphery has resigned. [It] most inopportune and weakening to whole organisation if Woods Humphery withdraws from active management, particularly at this stage." On the same day, Woods Humphery wrote to McMaster: "I appreciate very much the sentiments which prompted your telegram. The press report, however, is quite correct. This letter is, therefore, in the nature of a farewell one from the business sense."[21] Sir George cabled McMaster that Woods Humphery would "cease to function at the end of this month. I", he said, "am remaining on the Board."[22]

Dismore wrote to McMaster on 28 June:

> As you can well imagine, it has been heart-breaking to get a move on with things while all these political affairs have been going on, which have culminated in the loss of the head of our team. The whole organisation can best be described as "wounded". I never thought that I should experience a tragedy like this after so many years of team work. I am sending you a copy of a letter which I was impelled to send to the Prime Minister by my own sense of loyalty and fair play, and I am issuing it to the press today. I realise it is rather like throwing paper darts at an impregnable fortress but the injustice has rankled, so that I would sooner try and fail than remain silent.[23]

His letter was, of course, in vain. Woods Humphery's career with Imperial Airways was at its end.

On 1 July, the Commonwealth Parliament passed the Empire Air Services Act No. 13 of 1938, comprising the agreement between the Australian and British governments and the separate agreement between the Commonwealth and Qantas Empire Airways. Under them, Australia was to retain control over the Singapore–Darwin section; Qantas was to have no fewer than six Empire-class flying boats at its disposal on the route at any one time; there would be free interchange of aircraft between the operating companies and the various sections of the route; QEA was to be responsible for its own maintenance; the schedule would be three times a week with through journey time initially eleven days but gradually reducing to seven.[24] Timetables, stopping places, fares, and subsidies were all to be subject to government approval, and preference was to be accorded to Australian personnel. The Australian government had the right to withhold subsidy payment in any instance where a service was over twenty-four hours late.[25] (Qantas thought this a harsh and unworthy clause.)[26] All aircraft on the Sydney–Singapore section, including those owned by Imperial Airways, had to be at the disposal of the Commonwealth in case of emergency. The act provided that the working of the agreement should be supervised by a committee set up in London and representing the two governments, and that either party might withdraw before the fifteen-year agreement expired if the scheme proved persistently unsatisfactory. There was only limited criticism of the bill in the House of Representatives and in the Senate and its passage, as Hocking and Cave commented, "indicated the emergence of a policy acceptable to the nation as a whole". The agreement between the Commonwealth of Australia and Qantas Empire Airways was signed by the prime minister, J.A. Lyons, on 23 July 1938. (A third agreement, that between Qantas and Imperial Airways at company level, was still to be concluded.)

Colonel N. Falla, from Union Airways in New Zealand, wrote to McMaster following this legislative approval

having understood that this would be the prelude to the issue of fresh capital [by Qantas]. [He wrote, he said] to give you the intimation of the readiness of the Union Steamship Company to subscribe substantially. We would be prepared to proffer up to, say, £50,000 if such a subscription is in accordance with the policy of your company. I need hardly refer . . . to our joint association with your Company on the prospective Tasman service, and to the fact that, although registered in New Zealand, the Union Company has large interests in Australia.[27]

(McMaster noted on Falla's letter: "This offer was not

327

Rose Bay flying boat base, Sydney, 4 August 1938, taken during the official opening of the base by Lord Huntingfield, acting governor-general of Australia. Note that the slipway had not been completed and the intended site of the hangar was occupied by the visitors' cars. The official party was on the balcony of the white building to the left of the swimming enclosure.

accepted, for obvious reasons." Three thousand one pound shares were allotted to the Union Steamship Company.)

On 5 July 1938, the Empire flying boat *Cooee*, under the command of Captain Lynch Blosse, left Rose Bay for Singapore and the onward through journey to Southampton with Imperial Airways. Although it was the first flying boat through service from Australia, it was not the inauguration of the Empire Air Mail Scheme, as the old mail surcharge rate of one shilling and six pence per half-ounce letter was retained. A similar IAL preliminary service had left England for Australia. The Empire flying boat, *Challenger*, with Scotty Allan in command from Singapore, arrived at Darwin on 4 July, with eight press representatives on board at the invitation of Imperial Airways. They had the worst of receptions at Darwin and, as a consequence, made their views of the airline, Australian officials, and Australia's minister of defence widely known. "There were", wrote Fysh, "practically no facilities completed at that lazy and difficult port. There was not even any proper place to put passengers through the usual quarantine, immigration and customs requirements. The officials . . . insisted on their personal pound of flesh." While the officials argued over where to extract it, said Fysh, the crew and passengers were left in the flying boat at its mooring for over an hour, in a heavy swell. All the passengers were seasick. "There was a hell of a row", wrote Fysh. "The wires ran hot around the world. Darwin overnight became famous — or infamous."[28]

Scotty Allan reported that the operation of getting people ashore was carried out in darkness in a twenty-five to thirty mile per hour southerly gale, in seas at least two feet six inches high, from the exposed mooring. There were no satisfactory steps at the jetty to cope with the exceptional sea conditions and the gangway of the ship *Port Moresby* had to be used. In these conditions it had been necessary to vaccinate six people on board the *Challenger*. The engine of the refuelling barge stalled and it dragged its anchor, narrowly avoiding serious damage to the flying boat. Refuelling and engine maintenance were abandoned.[29]

McMaster issued a press statement saying that "the blame for what has become known as the 'Darwin Bungle' must be apportioned to all concerned. I am willing to admit that my Company was at fault in some respects."[30] It was a fairly magnanimous statement. The London *Daily Mail* called for the resignation of the minister for defence, Thorby, who responded with indignation. "I am sick of taking the blame for everything", he said in a statement issued in Canberra. "As far as I can see, the delay with the flying boat was due to faulty administration of the operating company."[31] According to the Brisbane *Telegraph*, the passengers arriving at Darwin had said that "conditions at Darwin were worse than at the Syrian Desert lakes and at the Persian Gulf outposts".[32] A reporter from the *Telegraph* who flew to Darwin wrote: "Where Darwin is concerned, Australia doesn't want justice. It wants mercy. This is about the most depressing introduction anyone could have to a new country. You can get a hot bath but it isn't easy. If you really insist, the hotel people will send up a girl with a tub of hot water. Arrangements here are prehistoric."[33] A harassed Darwin official said that they had done their best with a total lack of facilities. Tenders for the construction of a reception room and offices at the wharf would not close until the end of the month, he said, and they would take three months to build.[34] To compound the bitterness of the occasion for Qantas, the *Telegraph* reporter who had flown to Darwin did so on the inaugural KNILM flight from Sydney in a Lockheed Super Electra. The Brisbane *Courier-Mail*, reporting on the Dutch service, said: "This month, Brisbane was brought within eight days of London for regular commercial purposes. It seems almost incredible."[35] In the three weeks that passed before the official opening of the Empire Air Mail Scheme from London, the hullabaloo died down. QEA board minutes on 15 July recorded that "the final Agreement as between the Commonwealth of Australia and Qantas Empire Airways Limited in connection with the Empire Air Mail Scheme was submitted to the Board and it was resolved that this be signed under the seal of the Company. The Seal of the Company was thereupon affixed to the Agreement."[36] McMaster informed Colonel Falla, in New Zealand, and said that QEA "would now urge for the finalisation of the inter-company agreement with Imperial Airways".[37]

The first official flight to Australia of the Empire Air Mail Scheme left England on 28 July, carrying letters at one and a half pence per half ounce and postcards at one penny each. It reached Rose Bay without incident on 6 August, carrying two and a half tons of mail. From Australia, the flying boat service under the scheme was inaugurated when *Camilla* took off from Rose Bay, Sydney, on 4 August 1938 after the acting governor-general, Lord Huntingfield, before a crowd of more than two thousand, cut a red, white, and blue ribbon linking the aircraft with the shore. Lester Brain was in command, with eight passengers, 265 pounds of freight, and 207 pounds of mail. The Australian flag, said Fergus McMaster in his address, would now be carried by QEA flying boats all the way to England.[38] (On the service to England from Australia the letter rate was at the surcharge rate of fivepence per half ounce.)

The share issue in which Colonel Falla had been interested now went ahead. Q.A.N.T.A.S. issued a prospectus calling for public subscription of £193,681 in shares. (Paid-up capital of Q.A.N.T.A.S. was £70,819 in £1 shares at 31 August 1938.)[39]

McMaster stated formally in the prospectus that the Empire
Flying Boat Service had commenced from London on 28 July
1938 and from Sydney on 4 August 1938. The landplane service from Brisbane to London, he said, had been cancelled,
but QEA was operating a landplane service from Brisbane to
Daly Waters and from Cloncurry to Normanton. (The share
issue was oversubscribed; the 193,681 ordinary shares of £1
each were issued at par on 29 October 1938. QEA's paid-up
capital at the end of 1938, subscribed equally by the two partners, was £523,000.)[40] Fysh wrote a personal letter to
McMaster as the flying boat service began looking back to the
company's beginnings and generously contrasting
McMaster's selflessness with his own motivation. "The
pioneering work is all but forgotten," he said, "though in ten
years or so it may be revived in people's interest. It is a time
for the present. I feel that in working for Qantas I have always
had ulterior motives. I have been working for myself, for my
bread and butter, while you for so many years contributed
your time and effort for no real gain except your own self
satisfaction, and without proper payment."[41]

Now that the old overland air route from Darwin to Brisbane
had gone, the Western Australian route north from Perth
could no longer link up, as previously, with Qantas at Daly
Waters. Similarly, the southern states were no longer serviced
by the mail link of Butler Air Transport between Charleville,
in Queensland, and Cootamundra, in New South Wales
(though Butler now operated a service from Charleville to
Sydney). The incoming mails to Australia were, with the
introduction of the flying boats, distributed at Darwin, which
became the terminus for the MacRobertson Miller Aviation
Company's Western Australian route. (MMA connected with
two of the three flying boat services each week, first using
DH86 aircraft then Lockheed 10As.) The mails to South
Australia, Victoria, and Tasmania were flown south from
Darwin to Adelaide by Guinea Airways, who had operated the
1700-mile Darwin–Adelaide route since 1937 with Lockheed
Electras. (They increased their frequency from one to three
services weekly.) The route from Adelaide to Melbourne,
operated by Australian National Airways, was added to the
subsidised route category and flown by DC2 and DC3 aircraft
(which ANA adopted for almost all of its services). Qantas
continued to operate the 1628-mile route from Brisbane to Daly Waters twice weekly. The overall effect of the new Empire

Air Mail Scheme domestically was to increase substantially the volume of overseas mail carried by the internal airlines and, in turn, provide higher utilization of aircraft, additional frequencies, and better financial returns.

The company-to-company agreement between QEA and Imperial Airways for the Empire service was signed on 7 September. Under it, the flying boats were to operate as an integrated fleet over the complete route from Sydney to Southampton, but the crews were to fly only on their own sections. Each company was responsible for revenue and expenses on its own route. The initial annual subsidy payment of £169,000 sterling was to gradually increase.[42] The agreement also contained the old clause establishing the intent of the relationship: "It is the intention of both parties that each shall have a square deal . . ."[43]

A steady and continuing battle now began with both the Australian and Netherlands East Indies authorities for provision of the promised flying boat facilities, which were bad in Australia and atrocious in the East Indies.[44] Despite this handicap, the service quickly proved its regularity and popularity. The aircraft were spacious to a degree never experienced before.

> Getting up out of his chair, [wrote Fysh] a passenger could walk about and, if his seat was in the main cabin, stroll along to the smoking cabin for a smoke, stopping on the way at the promenade deck with its high handrail and windows at eye level, to gaze at the world of cloud and sky outside, and at countryside or sea slipping away below at a steady 150 miles an hour . . . On the promenade deck there was also a practical, usable space where quoits or clock golf were played . . .

The meals were sumptuous. Grapefruit and cereals, egg and bacon, bread rolls with tea, coffee, or cocoa for breakfast; then later, roast mutton with peas and potatoes, or a choice of ham, pressed beef, or ox tongue with salad, followed by Peach Melba, a cherry flan, or cheese and fruit. Looking after the passengers were the pleasant and polite stewards, "aerial pioneers of personal care and service".[45] The big boats were a delight to operate for the pilots too, both in the air and on the water. They were much more comfortable, with more crew space, and had better communications as well as the new automatic pilots.[46]

Although Lester Brain was able to report by October that the flying boats and all their gear operated very satisfactorily, there were engine troubles on all sections of the route. The

ultrahigh performance Bristol Pegasus engine, Brain commented, was a brilliant design and led the world in power-
weight ratio and fuel consumption per horsepower; but it was
not really suitable for normal Empire services. A utility engine
was preferable. "As soon as the Sydney slipway and hangar
are complete," he wrote, "we can attend to all normal maintenance and progressive certificate of airworthiness work here

Practising putting. A publicity
photograph taken on board a
QEA Empire flying boat at the
Rose Bay flying boat base in
late 1938.

333

on our own Australian-registered aircraft. An essential to sectional operation would be the carrying out of engine overhauls in Sydney." Brain concluded, however: "We have entered a period of comparatively settled operations."[47]

Fysh pressed the necessity for Qantas to carry out its own engine overhauls in Australia in letters to Edgar Johnston. "All this Company requires is to be self sufficient in the matter of engine overhaul, provision having already been made to maintain hulls and equipment", he wrote on 17 October. "We do not wish to make any additional profit but, naturally, cannot be out of pocket. The additional amount required boils down to an adjustment of subsidy between your Government and the United Kingdon." He told Johnston: "Turner, our chief accountant, leaves on 5 November for London where he will deal with accounting matters and will be about a month ... It is probable that Mr McMaster will leave a month later."[48] (The estimates which governed the finances of the new service were complex and it had proved impossible to provide the QEA board with monthly figures indicating progress. Though there was allowance for revision, thus providing safeguards, the board wanted something better.)[49]

Only a few days after Fysh wrote to Edgar Johnston, Australia suffered a major aviation disaster which was to have a profound effect on the administration of civil aviation in Australia and on the career of Johnston himself. On 25 October 1938, a DC2 aircraft of Australian National Airways, *Kyeema*, on its approach to Melbourne in bad weather, flew into Mount Dandenong. All four crew and fourteen passengers were killed. There was press and public outcry about the paucity of radio safety aids provided by the Civil Aviation Department. Parliamentarian J. Fairbairn (later to become minister for civil aviation) wrote to Fysh: "This tragedy had certainly put the press and public into a frame of mind to demand a clean-up of civil aviation, which has been due for a long time. Things may happen, I think, quickly." Fairbairn was correct. On 16 November 1938, H.V.C. Thorby wrote to the prime minister, J.A. Lyons, advising the abolition of the Civil Aviation Board and, instead, "to constitute it as a complete Government Department with a permanent head, to be known as the Controller-General of Civil Aviation". He told the prime minister he had discussed the matter with the minister for commerce, Sir Earle Page, and the attorney-general, Mr Menzies, "both of whom concur in the proposal". The alterations, he advised, "can be brought about by amending regula-

tions, there being no necessity for amending legislation. The
Ministers . . . also agree that it is hardly a matter for Cabinet,
and I would suggest that you concur in my carrying out the
above proposals at once."[50] The prime minister replied the
following day: "I do not see any objections to the plans outlined by you and should be glad if you would proceed."[51] And
so what had been the Civil Aviation Branch and part of the
Defence Department from 1929 to 1936, then the Civil Aviation Board (still under Defence) to 1938, became the Department of Civil Aviation in its own right by Government
Gazette notification on 24 November 1938. H.V.C. Thorby
became first minister for civil aviation.

In the midst of this drama Fergus McMaster, on the eve of
his visit to England, suffered a heart attack. "He will be out of
action for some months", Fysh advised Johnston on 12
November. "I must now leave for England in his place."[52] It
marked the beginning for Fysh of a period, until the outbreak
of war, of strain, drama, and responsibility. Chamberlain had
returned to London from Munich on 30 September after his
meeting with Hitler to make his announcement: "I believe it
is peace in our time." There were few who shared his belief.

Fysh was in London when QEA lost its first flying boat. On
12 December, the *Coorong* landed without incident at Darwin
in choppy seas and rising wind. The passengers were disembarked by launch and the flying boat secured for the night at
its mooring. As the wind and chop increased, Qantas station
engineer Norm Roberts became concerned. He went out to
Coorong, started the engines and ran them to ease the strain on
the mooring rope. After a time, the wind apparently not increasing, he shut the engines down and went ashore. At about
eight o'clock the *Coorong* broke loose and was blown onto the
rocks of the breakwater. Lester Brain, at the Rest House after
a day of flying, took charge of the frantic efforts at salvage. For
once the great tidal range at Darwin proved an advantage. The
Coorong had grounded at the peak of the high tide and was
made secure before salt water could penetrate the hull. It was,
however, damaged well beyond the resources of Qantas to
effect repairs and, after dismantling in the days that followed,
was sent to England by ship to Short Brothers. (*Coorong* was
fully repaired and later re-entered Qantas service.)[53]

The loss came at the worst possible time. Both Qantas and
Imperial Airways were under the greatest pressure they had
ever faced on the England–Australia route. The low cost airmail service had provoked an unprecedented public response
as Christmas approached. It was, wrote Fysh,

almost a nightmare. Nothing like it had ever been attempted before in air mail history ... Thirty-one flying boats, the Mercury seaplane and thirty-three landplanes, a total of sixty-five aircraft, were engaged on the England–Australia Empire Air Service over the busy period. In five weeks they flew 1,100,000 miles. Forty-two services were operated in and out of Sydney, and twelve of these aircraft were operated stripped of all passenger accommodation fittings, thus allowing an extra half ton of mail to be carried each trip.[54]

Concurrently, more major changes were under way for QEA's Imperial partner in England. Chairing his first annual general meeting of Imperial Airways, Sir John Reith said that the airline had been hampered by shockingly late deliveries and was operating aircraft that should have been replaced long ago. He questioned the policy of using only aircraft and engines designed and built by British manufacturers. The airline's position, he said, was neither commercial nor constitutionally satisfactory; the company was neither wholly free nor wholly secure.[55] Sir Kingsley Wood, who had succeeded Lord Swinton in May as secretary of state for air, told the House of Commons on 11 November that the government was considering the creation of a suitable instrument for British overseas civil aviation communications and was of the opinion that "this would be provided by the association of the two chosen instruments, Imperial Airways Limited and British Airways Limited, in a single public Corporation. The Government", he said, "therefore proposes to recommend to Parliament legislation which will acquire the existing undertakings of these airways."[56] Far overshadowing even these considerable matters, however, was the widespread realization that the Munich agreement had won no more than a brief respite for Britain, in which rearmament would have to accelerate. By the end of 1938, every aircraft manufacturer was straining to the limit in a national effort to increase production. Despite the changes at Imperial Airways and the even bigger changes promised, Hudson Fysh was able to write to McMaster on 14 December that "things are going fine for QEA and we have nothing to worry about. The alterations here in IAL are sad, but should result in IAL getting more done with the Air Ministry. The British interest in QEA will be stronger than ever."[57]

The sound position of Qantas as 1938 ended and war approached, reflected the great advances made by Australia as a whole in all its civil aviation activities in the decade that had passed. Measured by the yardstick of airline route mileage,

Australia as a country ranked seventh in the world. In total number of air miles flown by regular air transport companies it was sixth. There had been, since 1929, a worldwide increase in air route mileage of some 130 per cent and in miles flown of 200 per cent. Australia, however, had experienced more than double these rates. It was hardly an exaggeration to say, commented Hocking and Cave, that in the prewar years Australia was the most air-minded nation in the world.[58]

End of an Era
1939

17 On 9 January 1939, the Executive Council gave approval for the creation of the post in Australia of director-general of civil aviation. The post of controller-general of civil aviation, held by Edgar Johnston, was abolished and an acting director-general, M.W. Mehaffey, was appointed over him on 12 January. There was speculation in the press as to who would become the permanent director-general. The Brisbane *Telegraph* wrote:

> Captain Lester Brain, manager of flying operations for QEA and one of Australia's most experienced airmen, is believed to be the most favoured candidate for the post. The managing director of QEA, Mr Hudson Fysh, is also regarded as a possible choice but it is believed that both he and Captain P.G. Taylor gave early intimation that they were unavailable. Another name mentioned is that of A.B. Corbett, Deputy Director of Posts and Telegraphs for Queensland.[1]

Fairbairn had, in fact, written to Fysh after the ANA *Kyeema* crash asking if he would consider accepting the (then) position of chairman of the Civil Aviation Board if it became vacant and it was offered to him.[2] Now, at the age of forty-three, Fysh had a second job offer in England. Sir John Reith approached him to become head of operations for Imperial Airways, with a seat on the management committee. "My chairman and vice-chairman in Australia were horrified", wrote Fysh. "I turned the offer down . . . what future I had lay with QEA."[3] Fysh had been, as the year began, visiting the Bristol Company with C.O. Turner, trying to "find out the position regarding possible deliveries of large orders of spare parts for Pegasus engines", in anticipation of a national emergency.[4] The Australian government and QEA were now vitally interested in the establishment of an engine overhaul base in Australia, he told Bristols, and it was essential that the spares position should be clarified. The Bristol Company, despite enormous pressure from Air Ministry work, was helpful. It was agreed that they could put through an extra four Pegasus Type X engines for QEA with a large order received from the Air Ministry, for delivery in May or June. If, however, Qantas wanted spares in quantity, then their order would have to be placed within ten days to incorporate them into the Air Ministry production run. Delivery would then be possible about April and cost would be between thirty and forty thousand pounds. Tools and jigs that had been ordered by QEA in March 1937 were, reported Fysh, complete and were sufficient to carry out eight engine overhauls a week if necessary.[5]

Fysh had also discussed QEA operational needs, should war break out, with the deputy director-general of civil aviation, W.P. (later Sir William) Hildred. Armament, he learned, could not be carried on civil aircraft (unlike merchant ships); great importance was attached to getting mails through, for psychological reasons. Fysh urged, without success, the supply of long-range fuel tanks for the QEA boats but he did obtain Hildred's assistance in getting special delivery of the essential spares from Bristols. The preparation of a war book, to unify United Kingdom and Australian use of civil aircraft, was discussed. Despite all this activity, Fysh concluded: "After a three months stay in London, I left with much of importance unconcluded."[6] He departed for Australia from Southampton on 5 February 1939.

For the new minister for civil aviation in Australia, H.V.C. Thorby, the year had started with a detailed response by him to Qantas criticisms about the lack of government facilities on the Sydney–Singapore flying boat route. They had ranged from mooring buoy strops and marking flags for alighting areas to the Rose Bay hangar and slipway, the control building, radio services, and night landing flares. "The present control building at Rose Bay", Thorby told them, "is adequate for Government activities and for passengers. At present, at arrivals of flying boats, much inconvenience is caused by the presence of numerous children on scooters and bicycles, by nurse-girls with perambulators, and by idle on-

QEA-owned Empire flying boat at the embarkation dock at Southampton, England in early 1939. With the introduction of the flying boats in July 1938 on the Australia-UK air service, passengers remained on the same aircraft throughout their journey. Australian crews operated all flights east of Singapore while British crews were responsible for services to the west.

lookers."[7] To a criticism from Lester Brain that, at Pinkemba, "the distance between the landing pontoon and the control and traffic offices is a source of delay and expense", Thorby responded: "It is desired to observe that an elderly person walked with two suitcases from the launch to the traffic office in forty-five seconds." He did not see, he said, how any expense was involved. Fysh had complained that the lavatory accommodation was unsatisfactory. Somewhat defensively, the minister answered with comparisons. "It is admitted", he wrote, "that the lavatories are not sewered, but it is contended that the ladies' lavatory is of a superior standard, and the men's, by reason of locked closets, are cleaner than are found at railway stations."[8] On loftier matters, Fergus McMaster sent a letter of greetings to the former Qantas supporter and governor-general of Australia, Lord Stonehaven, who had been on a visit. Stonehaven thanked him: "Each Governor-General has to try to find some useful way of exercising the influence which his temporary position gives him for the benefit of the Commonwealth," he wrote, "and having concentrated on the encouragement of aviation, I am very glad to learn that you think I may have helped a little."[9]

340

C.O. Turner submitted a report to Fysh on the result of his detailed financial discussions in London with Imperial Airways after his return to Australia on 11 February. In examining the basic estimates for the Empire Agreement with IAL they had revised a number of figures and assumptions. The mileage between Singapore and Sydney was now agreed with the Air Ministry at 4,676 which, wrote Turner, was acceptable to the QEA manager of flying operations. (The previous figure had been 4,687 miles.) Speeds shown in the estimates had approximated 126 miles per hour, he reported, "while experience to date on the QEA section shows nearly 140 miles per hour". Fuel consumption, at 114 gallons per hour shown in the estimates, compared with QEA experience to date of 108 gallons per hour. The actual cost of each flying boat, wrote Turner, was agreed at £52,300 sterling, and spare engines at £1,993 each. The Qantas share of spare engines now worked out at sixteen instead of ten. "We have agreed to bear the capital cost of the additional six engines", he advised. "This will be of advantage to QEA because interest at ten per cent will be obtained on the capital involved." The cost of the preliminary financing of the purchase of all flying boats, engines, and spares had, said Turner, been borne by Imperials. This cost, he considered, was a fair charge to Imperials for use of some of the QEA boats. The extra cost of overhauling three engines per week in Australia was agreed at £16,264 per annum, which had been accepted by the Australian government. "In my view," wrote Turner, "this is a most satisfactory settlement from the point of view of QEA." On the overall accounting position with Imperial Airways he commented: "All outstanding problems between Imperials and QEA were examined and standard procedures laid down."[10]

Hudson Fysh, in turn, reported formally to the directors on the visit by Turner and himself to England. It was obvious, he wrote,

> from the extensive report on accounting matters by Mr Turner ... that the Company is protected against loss, under present arrangements, to a far greater extent than under its late landplane contract from Brisbane to Singapore. It is not inferred that the Company is not open to some business risks, but they are small in comparison with a truly commercial company. On the other side ... while enjoying such Government protection, it is hardly possible for the Company to pay a high rate of dividend to its shareholders.

Commenting on the British Government proposals to form a nationalized corporation, Fysh wrote:

> One of the objectives of the Corporation is to eliminate as far as possible Imperial Airways' complicated agreements with the United Kingdom Government, substituting something simpler and workable. Formation of the Corporation should not only provide a sounder financial basis than could be provided by IAL, but should eventually place British commercial aviation in a sounder position . . .
>
> As outlined in the report by the Chief Accountant, engine overhaul in Australia has been secured on the basis of three engines per week, the number necessary to maintain the Sydney-Singapore service. The additional cost per annum has been estimated at £16,204 and the capital expenditure at £54,630. The bulk of spares, constituting twelve months supply, and four new engines, have been ordered. The obtaining of engine overhaul in Australia has been a major objective for the past eighteen months.

Fysh reported that facilities between Sydney and Singapore were far worse than anything between Singapore and Southampton.

> Inability to night fly and make up lost time is letting down the rest of the route. The Company still largely operates under temporary and meagre facilities. Existing conditions at Koepang, Bima, Sourabaya and Batavia are inviting catastrophe and loss of life. General improvements are slow in materialising. I wish to record appreciation of the able work done by Mr Turner.[11]

(C.O. Turner was also hard at work at the time on the QEA Staff Pension Scheme in conjunction with the Australian AMP Society. It came into force on 1 June.)

Fergus McMaster's health was improving, though slowly. Harman wrote to him on 27 February to convey the board's pleasure at the news of the improvement. A.E. Rudder, a few weeks later, wrote to Mrs McMaster: "You must indeed be glad to have Mr McMaster home again. It is evident that he must make up his mind to take things quietly for a few months longer."[12] With McMaster absent, Harman was, under Fysh, shouldering an ever-increasing management load. Turner's competence and drive in dealing with the most complex agreements had been amply demonstrated. Lester Brain, in the detailed and demanding change from landplane to flying boat operations on a new and poorly equipped route, had proved outstanding; and Arthur Baird, in charge of maintenance and works, was, like Brain, at the top of his profession in Australia. The *Sydney Morning Herald* praised the airline's creditable record in a leader on 10 March 1939. "Yesterday the departure of the *Capella* signalled the hundredth flying boat service to leave Sydney and the occasion provides an opportunity to commend the high standard of punctuality achieved by Qantas Empire Airways." The *Herald* commendation, however, was directed only at the service from Australia westward, for which QEA had direct responsibility. It was critical of the Imperial Airways' performance eastbound. "On the inward journeys, unfortunately, delays have been unconscionably frequent and often lengthy, owing mainly to late arrivals at Singapore."[13]

Two days after the departure which had provoked this editorial kindliness, the *Capella* was lost. Taxiing at Batavia on 12 March, with Captain Hussey in command, *Capella* was brought in too close to the shore. Just below the surface, the forgotten remains of a wrecked frigate tore a hole in the hull. Hussey quickly drove the flying boat up on to the beach where she lay, in the shallows, filled with sea water. The water damage proved irreparable and, though *Capella* was dismantled and shipped to England, she had to be scrapped.

On 15 March 1939 Fysh advised McMaster that the position of director-general of civil aviation had been filled by A.B. Corbett. On the candidacy of Lester Brain he commented:

> As to Captain Brain . . . I should tell you that yesterday he informed me, when he knew the press had dug up the fact that he was in the running, that a Cabinet Minister had rung him up asking if he would take the position if it was offered. Brain replied that he would. I think it irregular that the Government should have approached one of our executives without informing at least one of our Board, and that Captain Brain neglected to inform me until forced by publicity to do so.[14]

The appointment of Corbett was to take effect from 3 April. The prime minister, in an official government announcement, said: "The Controller-General of Civil Aviation, Captain Johnston, will no longer be in complete control, but will have charge of one of the three branches of the Department."[15] The magazine *The Motor* described the sixty-two-year-old Corbett as "a lean, well-preserved man in excellent physical and mental mettle" with wide experience in the Postal Department, and war service in South Africa.[16] Edgar Johnston found him a man "who very much wanted to run things his own way, and didn't consult anybody much". It was a bad time for Johnston. "I never had any real contact with Corbett or the Minister", he said.[17]

This important change in the administration of Australian civil aviation came as Dutch pressures were mounting for a KLM service from Amsterdam to Sydney. (The existing service was by KNILM, the subsidiary company, from Batavia.) On March 25 the *Sydney Morning Herald* reported:

> The KLM is the chosen instrument of the Dutch Government for the establishment of the Dutch trunk lines, whereas the KNILM is the Netherlands Indies colonial line, financed by local industry. The existing Dutch air service between Sydney and London is, like the Empire service, operated by two companies. Intercontinental Airways, which is an association of the KNILM and the KLM, flies in seven and a half days between Sydney and London. The KNILM flies twice a week from Sydney to Batavia and the KLM three times a week from Batavia to London. It has been the Commonwealth Government's firm policy that an Australian company shall control the Sydney–Singapore section of the Empire service. It will find it difficult to refuse Imperial Airways permission to fly through to Sydney if it gives permission to KLM for a similar plan.[18]

The Australian government had no such plans for KLM. The minister for civil aviation, Thorby, after a flight to Singapore with Lester Brain in *Cooee*, wrote a personal note to McMaster. "You will be interested to know confidentially," he said, "that Cabinet has decided not to admit the KLM service on the Australian route."[19]

Cabinet was, however, far more concerned with the turmoil of party politics. The prime minister, Lyons, was ill and much preoccupied by the possibility of war. His brilliant attorney-general, Robert Gordon Menzies, widely regarded as the next leader of the United Australia Party and therefore the next prime minister, was constantly at odds with the ambitious but less able Country Party ministers, led by Deputy Prime Minister Earl Page. In March 1939 Menzies resigned from Cabinet and, only weeks later, Lyons died. From 4 April to 26 April, Page acted as caretaker prime minister. Menzies, elected as the new United Australia Party leader, was then commissioned to form a new government. The Country Party, under Page, refused to participate.[20]

The new prime minister, as the theoretician on Commonwealth constitutional relationships, had clear views on the limits of Australian independence in relation to the United Kingdom. For a Dominion to formulate a foreign policy and announce it, whether or not it was in line with Great Britain's, was in his judgment a suicidal line of conduct.[21] Policy in relation to any individual matter should, it was Menzies' view, be expressed to the government of the United Kingdom.[22] In a broadcast on 26 April 1939, Prime Minister Menzies stated that even in relation to affairs in the Pacific, Australia should not act "as if we were a completely separate power".[23] His views reflected a widespread feeling throughout the country that Australian nationhood, first expressed by the poets and writers before the turn of the century and much reinforced by the achievements of Australian volunteer soldiers in World War I, could be asserted without any feeling of separateness towards Great Britain. It was a national perspective that illuminated the Qantas relationship with Imperial Airways in the years before the Second World War.

Though Fergus McMaster had been slowly regaining his strength, it was by no means clear that he would be able to continue indefinitely as chairman of both QEA and Q.A.N.T.A.S. without a more marked and sustained improvement in his health. The issue of the QEA chairmanship was concerning Sir John Reith who wrote to Fysh on 18 March, asking for his views. Fysh, with the memory of McMaster's reaction to his private and personal correspondence with Woods Humphery in mind, replied:

> In regard to Board matters, you have placed me in a very awkward position indeed. As managing director it has not been my custom to comment to anyone except the chairman in regard to such matters . . . I have always tried strenuously to keep aloof from anything savouring of intrigue. If the issue was clear cut it would be different but things out here just don't seem entirely that way, and no doubt differences of opinion exist among Board members. If it becomes necessary to appoint a new Chairman, I do not know how to advise you at the moment and I think it is best left, as far as possible, to decision out here. The position is complicated . . . Apparently the position would not be filled by any other member of the Board, and Mr Rudder has been most emphatic that he will not take the job on. My own position I consider another matter. Quite frankly and openly I naturally always had the ambition to one day become Chairman in succession to Mr McMaster, but did not expect this for some years yet. The chairmanship is the top position and controls policy, expansion, political contacts etc. and, in fact, all the larger and more important things in which my main interest has been for many years. That it is wrong in principle for a managing director to become chairman I could not agree, and it should be kept in mind. I think, that we have three excellent executives in this Company in Harman, Brain and Turner. Mr McMaster appears to be far from finally failing in regard to his correspondence, and I think that things can run on as they are without danger for the present. One of the difficulties has been that it has hardly been possible to discuss with Mr McMaster the question of a possible successor.[24]

Sir John Reith, in a letter to Fysh on 9 May, replied that it was only natural, as McMaster was ill, that "we should talk about the future when you were here . . . Nobody could have thought you were guilty of any intrigue and anyhow, if you had been, I would have been inolved too." Reith signed his letter at this point and then attached two extra and separate pages to it, dealing with Fysh's personal comments.

> I don't think it is wise from either the individual or public point of view that the chief executive type such as yourself should pass to the much less onerous, though maybe more dignified position of chairman, particularly in a case like yours where you have built the thing up from the beginning, and where there is still much to do. If you were getting tired, or feeling old and bored, or anything of that sort, then the situation would be different. If you thought it had, you would need to be sure that there was somebody you would be able . . . to give the authority you have had . . . and not in fact carry on chief executive authority from the chairmanship.

Reid did not, he said, object in a general way to managing directors becoming chairmen, if they ceased to be managing directors.

> I think it is wrong in principle for the posts to be combined. And, further, it is difficult for such a managing director as you have been to stop being managing director if you moved to another post.[25]

These philosophic views on the role of the managing director from the chairman of Imperial Airways were complemented on 23 May with more specific comments on Fysh's function from his own chairman.

> In this growing business of Qantas, [wrote Fergus McMaster] you have shifted up from the position of pilot to that of head of the organisation . . . and it is difficult to say just how far your duties as managing director should go. In your position you must not in any way be lax in attending personally to essentials, particularly regarding policy and keeping in contact with Imperial Airways, Union Airways and the large airline companies of Australia, as well as the various governments. That is your essential work, as I see it. You must personally attend to that. But there is a whole lot of detailed work to be done in watching the outlay and income of the Company. This, I feel, you can only do satisfactorily by delegation to others. What they do must be ratified by yourself. That, Hudson, is the position as I see it.[26]

The entire relationship between Imperial Airways and Qantas now required revision, following the House of Commons announcement on 11 November 1938 by the secretary of state for air that a new government-owned corporation was proposed. Dismore, as assistant general manager of IAL, wrote formally to Qantas on 10 May 1939:

> The existing agreements made with Imperial Airways, a commercial company, are not altogether suitable to the new situation created by the formation of a State-guaranteed Corporation ... We wish to negotiate with you on behalf of the Corporation a new permanent agreement to replace the existing Imperial Airways–Qantas Empire Airways agreement which, while being on as favourable terms as under the existing arrangements, would be free from the complexities of the existing contract. [Dismore enclosed a draft agreement] It provides in effect for maintenance of the status quo.[27]

(Sir Kingsley Wood, on 12 June 1939, put the British Overseas Airways Corporation Bill before the House of Commons. It received Royal Assent on 4 August and provided that the new BOAC would officially take over from the older companies on 1 April 1940.)

Imperial Airways' plan to extend the Empire Service to New Zealand had also, after much argument, come closer to achievement. The QEA board had, on 23 November 1938, approved the draft heads of agreement for a company to be formed involving the participation of Imperial Airways, QEA, and Union Airways, representing the governments of the three companies. Colonel Falla, in New Zealand, was the driving force, sometimes too much so for McMaster. "There does seem an urge by Colonel Falla to act without consulting his partners on some vital matters", he wrote to Fysh on 20 May. "I do not wish Colonel Falla or any other partner to establish the principle that QEA is a minor consideration."[28] (The Australian government opposed the use of flying boats for the Tasman route on the grounds of economy but was outvoted.[29] Government enterprise was, throughout, heavily involved in the new organization. On the formation in New Zealand of Tasman Empire Airways Limited, with a share capital of £500,000, Union Airways, BOAC, and QEA took shares in the same proportions as the subsidy contributions of their countries — 39 per cent Union Airways, 38 per cent BOAC, and 23 per cent Qantas. Almost half the Union Airways shares were held by the New Zealand government, while BOAC became fully owned by the United Kingdom government in 1940. It was a cumbersome arrangement requiring heavy subsidy and a monopoly on the route for survival.[30] The outbreak of war was to delay inauguration of the service until 30 April 1940.)

On Saturday 3 June 1939, just before four o'clock in the afternoon, Capt. P.G. Taylor took off from Rose Bay in the flying boat *Guba* for a remarkable survey flight across the Indian Ocean. Undertaken to explore the possibility of an alternative air route from Australia, as a defence precaution, Taylor crossed the continent to Port Hedland in Western Australia and then set out for Mombasa, East Africa, via Cocos, Chagos, and the Seychelles. It was to prove a useful initiative. An Indian Ocean route by QEA, though not Taylor's, was to become a vital wartime communications link for Australia, though far from Fysh's thoughts at the time. Possible competition, whether from the Dutch or Australian National Airways, and the ramifications of emerging new British policy bearing on the independence of Qantas were now concerning him. He wrote to Ivan Holyman at ANA on the need to avoid unnecessary competition and received complete and confidential agreement.

> I heartily concur with the views expressed [wrote Holyman] that there is no room for Australian National Airways, Airlines of Australia and Qantas Empire Airways to be in competition for services which the Government may have in view; that is to say, I do not think we should submit quotations for any services that are operated by your Company at the present time, nor do I think you . . . should submit quotations for routes covered by this Company, without first conferring with each other. I think you can take it for granted that there will be no attempt by the Department to play either ANA or AOA against yourselves, or vice versa . . . Should at any time the Department approach us regarding routes that are at present covered by you, we will certainly advise you promptly and refrain from submitting prices unless we have your concurrence, and no doubt you will act similarly as regards our two companies.[31]

It seemed a cosy understanding, as far as competition within Australia was concerned. Externally, there was a reasurring letter from Thorby to Fergus McMaster. Though Thorby had been succeeded as minister for civil aviation on 26 April by J.V. Fairbairn, he wrote: "I have had some personal conversation with both the Minister for Civil Aviation and the Minister for External Affairs regarding the application for the KLM to enter Australia. I feel very confident that Plesman will not accomplish his one desire, that is, to enter Australia."[32]

The vice-chairman of Qantas Empire Airways, representing the interests of Imperial Airways, A.E. Rudder, was made a

348

Companion of the British Empire in the June honours list. Fysh wrote to McMaster about it and received a sad, hand-written reply on 14 June. In regard to honours for himself, he told Fysh, he was human enough to appreciate an honour from the Crown but, he wrote, "I question whether I would take much interest in a CBE". McMaster said that he had heard in a roundabout way from Canberra that both he and Fysh had been considered for honours.

> I have no doubt that you eventually will be properly recognised. You have done good, solid work for commercial aviation, and therefore for Commonwealth aviation, which means so much for the country and the Empire. I do not know when a letter from anyone has so cheered me up so much as yours, and your reference to the work I have done. In a long inactivity and illness such as mine it is impossible to avoid depressions and one feels that life at its best has just been a flimsy bubble. [My correspondence from Sydney] seemed to indicate that I should make way for someone else . . . Mr Rudder's last letter seemed to me to indicate that my resignation would be welcomed . . . I am anything but strong but am getting more into normal strength and outlook each day, since the last severe attack.[33]

McMaster, though he still had a long battle ahead of him, did not lack sympathy. Sir John Reith, in a letter to Rudder, wrote: "How much I sympathise with him in his enforced inaction."[34] Fysh wrote to him: "We miss you, and everyone is going to welcome you back to that renewed activity which I feel sure is coming."[35]

Meanwhile Fysh and Sir John Reith were corresponding about issues of potential significance to the future independence of Qantas and the relationship between the two airlines. Fysh wrote to Reith on 25 July 1939.

> Your letter shows a desire for the British Overseas Airways Corporation to take over Qantas Empire Airways operations with as little delay as possible, should this be agreed by the Commonwealth Government and Qantas, for the sake of simplification of operations and a better service. But as yet you have not got to the point of putting up a case for this. [It was logical in principle and theory, but] under present circumstances it may not work out satisfactorily, in that centralisation of control in London would probably have an adverse effect on the Australian service. It is self-evident that the actual operational results, both in landplanes and in flying boats, have been more satisfactory on the Qantas Empire Airways section than on any other . . . largely the result of the strict control of operations, as a Division closely familiar with the section and quick with action to right wrongs . . . without reference to London.

Fysh told Reith that though his views could not be taken as official, he was able to advise Reith reliably "after having had discussions with Rudder, McMaster, Loxton and the Minister for Civil Aviation, Fairbairn". The general feeling in Australia, said Fysh, was that the Imperial Airways service had not been comparable to the Dutch, but that the Qantas-operated section had held its own. "The official view out here might well be 'First set your own house in order' ", he wrote. He drew Reith's attention to the 1933 and 1937 agreements between IAL and QEA in which the whole attitude had been one of equal partnership. "There was never anything to suggest absorption of the Qantas interest in the future . . . Now, in 1939, we are confronted by a suggestion that Qantas be absorbed, and at a time when capital has but recently increased and a new sphere of operations entered upon." The Qantas shareholders, he said, had invested their money on the basis of QEA holding an attractive fifteen-year contract; QEA staff would provide problems. The minister for civil aviation, said Fysh, had advised that this suggestion to absorb Qantas "was news to him and that, even if proven desirable, would not be politically possible and might result in wrecking the Government". This, said Fysh, was also McMaster's view. He asked Sir John Reith to put the whole matter "on an official basis with QEA without delay".[36] Sir John, however, did not raise the issue directly with Qantas again, except to respond two months later: "I do not think there is much point in my arguing further for an Empire Corporation, certainly not as things are now. It was thought that Qantas might find a wider field in greater permanency than now, and with all its traditions preserved."[37] (Reith did, however, canvass the issue politically in London through the Australian high commissioner, S.M. Bruce, much to McMaster's annoyance.)

The new director-general of civil aviation, A.B. Corbett, now put forward his views to the minister, Fairbairn, on one issue that had always been central to government consideration of civil aviation — the carriage and cost of the mails. He brought to the question of whether or not there should be a surcharge on airmails a logical habit of thought and a succinct manner of expression. In comments on the interim report of the Inter-Departmental Committee on Civil Aviation, Corbett said that the opposing views expressed by representatives of the Department of Civil Aviation and Treasury, on the one hand, and the Postmaster-General's Department, on the other, were "both based on grounds which appear to be sound, according to the breadth of vision with which they are viewed". The majority view on the abolition of surcharge by the Commonwealth for first class mails on the Empire and Tasman routes (from Civil Aviation and Treasury) was that it would involve a loss of revenue which was not justified in or by existing circumstances. It was, said Corbett, a financial view and to that extent was realistic and sound. The Post Ofice "with its traditional view of service to the public" held the view, he said, that the improved service was worth the cost.

Costly mistakes had been made in the past, said Corbett, in the establishment of the Empire mail service "The position is that the flying boat service, on arrival at Darwin from England, lands the bulk of the mails and proceeds practically without loading to Sydney. On the return Sydney–Darwin route, similar conditions apply. This section of 2,384 miles is subsidised and is one sixth of the total distance from Sydney to London." The empty flying boats, argued Corbett, competed for passengers with Australian subsidized services, thus increasing internal subsidies "while the Commonwealth pays two other companies some £50,000 extra subsidy for carrying these overseas mails via Darwin–Perth and Darwin–Adelaide". Either, he said, the flying boats should terminate at Darwin or they should, if the original intention was followed, bring the mails to Sydney where subsidized services between Sydney, Adelaide, and Perth were available. A mistake was made, he concluded, that could still be corrected.

Corbett pointed out "that practically all the major costs of providing and maintaining air transport have been and will be paid for by taxpayers in some form or other". Mails carried by air, he said, "confer benefit on certain individuals who have paid a surcharge, but the general public does not benefit . . . The abolititon of surcharge eventually is inevitable. To support the present surcharge on air mail is to support a fallacy." The postal services, he pointed out, made a surplus on costs of £2,094,561 in the year ended 30 June 1938. The air service, however, carried mails nationally at a unit fee that incurred a loss. This loss plus 6 per cent on the capital invested is made good, he said, by government subsidy.

It was clear that the new director-general was a man with firm views, though he was still something of an enigma to Qantas. Fysh had been asked by the department to carry out reorganization of the Cloncurry–Normanton service in northern Queensland, but on the basis of a six monthly contract.

351

His response, "that we see difficulty and undesirable features in attempting to reorganise the Cloncurry–Normanton services for such a short period", drew criticism from McMaster.[39]

> To be quite frank with you, Hudson, your letter to the Director-General does not take the line I personally would have taken, but that is a matter of opinion and, most probably, you took the correct attitude. It is evidently the set wish of the Director-General that QEA should quote on a six months basis for Brisbane–Daly Waters, including the Cloncurry–Normanton service . . . The reasoning in your letter is absolutely sound, but he is the one calling for tenders, and I feel that you should fall in with his wishes. Personally, I would avoid conflict with the Director-General at the present time. He is an unknown factor and might possibly be one of those petty characters who, having had a disagreement with a company, will be prejudiced for all time.[40]

McMaster, though still unwell, now seemed on a steady road to recovery and welcomed his involvement in Qantas affairs. He wrote to Fysh:

> To get a knock such as I got, which was almost fatal, takes a long time to recover from. Apart from that, I have had other rather major attacks on my health . . . I am fortunate, of course, in that the trouble is more physical than mental, and that I am able to put in a good lot of time at my desk. I do not know what would happen to me if I could not have that relaxation, for it is relaxation to have something to do under these conditions. The objective of the doctor seems to be to keep me as quiet as possible, and he does not give any assistance whatsoever towards my gaining any greater physical activity . . .[41]

McMaster was certainly active in his correspondence. He wrote to QEA board member F.J. Smith about the implications of the impending formation of the new British Overseas Airways Corporation. (Smith, though representing Imperial Airways on the QEA board, did not like directorships on behalf of particular entities.) Smith replied:

> I quite agree with your views about QEA. The basic position now compared with what it was when the link was made with Imperial Airways has altered completely. I visualise that the new British Corporation might eventually wish to dominate the whole Empire service, and I quite understand your desire to "go warily". I am not comfortable about my own position on the Board; in fact I never have been. As you know, I agreed to go on the Board as representing Imperial Airways at the earnest wish of Sir Eric Geddes. I was, at the time, representing Sir Eric on the Board of the Dunlop Rubber Company, and I felt I could not well

refuse. I would have resigned from QEA some time ago except for your own personal request for me to remain.[42]

Smith's perception that "the new British Corporation might eventually wish to dominate the whole Empire service" was shared by McMaster and, once more, doubts rose in his mind about the frankness of his Imperial Airways colleagues. With characteristic openness he wrote to Sir John Reith on 21 August 1939.

I deeply dislike the fact that this, practically my first letter to you after my long illness, should be of a more of less contentious nature . . . I have kept in touch with the position resulting from the adjustments between Imperial Airways and the United Kingdom Government, and I have been assured . . . that the Agreements and Contracts entered into between Imperial Airways and Q.A.N.T.A.S. would be fully protected and honoured, both in the word and in the implied intention. I must admit, however, that I have been disturbed by the Memorandum written by yourself, as Chairman of Imperial Airways, to the High Commissioner of Australia, the Hon. S.M. Bruce, portion of which reads: "If this idea were to be approved, Q.A.N.T.A.S. [at present a holding company for the Australian interest in Qantas Empire Airways] would presumably become active again and take over from QEA the internal services in Queensland and the Northern Territory at present operated by QEA." The paragraph quoted, and also other paragraphs in the Memorandum, could give the impression that, without proper consultation, negotiations were taking place in London to displace Qantas in the Empire organisation. I will not for personal reasons stand in the way of any reconstruction in the Empire's interests . . . Whether full control of all major Empire Air Transport from one centre is sound or otherwise is a question where there could be a difference of opinion, but it would seem apparent, before Agreements and Contracts are broken and undermined, that the Services that definitely require reorganising should be the first to receive attention. Centralisation of control is spectacular, but it is a question, if Empire shipping had been confined to one company and centralised in London, whether British shipping would ever have gained the control of the seas. Shipping gained its supremacy by individualism.[43]

To Hudson Fysh, McMaster wrote: "I consider Sir John wrong, as Chairman of Imperial Airways, in writing to Mr Bruce. In re-reading the Memorandum I have been more fully impressed with what cannot be considered other than an underhand method of negotiation."[44] The reply that he received from his managing director was extraordinary in both its tone and content. "You asked me to reply by return mail if possible," wrote Fysh, "but I can hardly do this this morning owing to the semi-emergency conditions under which we are working, and I think that you, yourself, would wish to put the matter on one side till the present crisis either blows over or comes to war. I will, therefore, not reply at length till the present suspense is over." It was a blunt refusal to McMaster, and an assertion that McMaster should not press the issue he had raised. His letter then continued: "My recollection is that Sir John informed me at once of his contact with Mr Bruce, and that you can hardly take exception to Sir John's action to the extent to which you do . . . I feel it was natural for Sir John to feel out the Australian Government and ourselves as he did . . . He made it very clear that if the Australian Government or Qantas did not wish for a change there would be no change." Fysh concluded in a tone that was patronizing to McMaster and at the same time deferential in its reference to Imperial Airways. "We must also realise", he wrote, "that, after all, it is the United Kingdom which is paying the lion's share of the cost, and that we are only operators here and have little share in the big planning moves for the future of our own service."[45] It was the impatient letter of a man under great pressure of worry and work to a nuisance. It was a tone Fysh had never before used to his chairman and it contrasted markedly with his August 3 letter: "We miss you . . ."

McMaster's reply was remarkably subdued. "I took very hardly . . . your letter under reply", he wrote. "I feel sure that you did not wish the meaning to be taken out . . . that the ordinary reader would take; that is, that you would wish me to step to one side as Chairman of QEA and Q.A.N.T.A.S. Your sincerity and loyalty has been too clear over the last nineteen or twenty years for me to take those paragraphs as they could be taken. However, I regret that you did write in such a way." McMaster then addressed himself to the substance of the argument. "You will remember", he wrote, "that Mr Rudder wished definitely to keep Q.A.N.T.A.S. out of the Empire service, and to have the Australian interests represented by a 'pup' company, registered in Sydney. If Mr Rudder could have pushed Q.A.N.T.A.S. to one side he would have done so and . . . I feel sure, if we follow his advice, he will gain his objective under present conditions."[46] Fysh, seemingly aware that he had gone too far, recanted and replied: "I am trying to do my best here at a very difficult time in the Company's history, perhaps the most difficult, and I am anxious to assure you of my full loyalty to yourself personally, i.e. bringing you into the vital, larger policy questions for advice and decision, and on keeping the organisation alive . . ."[47] There was no real doubt, in this exchange, of Fysh's underlying loyalty and affection towards McMaster. It was equally clear that he now saw himself, and justifiably, as bearing almost the whole burden of leadership as the company's wartime role and organization faced fundamental review. Fysh wrote to McMaster a little later: "I realise what a tough and worrying time you are having."[48]

Fysh was, of course, under immense strain as both the United Kingdom and Australian governments prepared for what now seemed an unavoidable war. On 1 September he went with Lester Brain to Melbourne and was told of the government decision to form an RAAF squadron from four or five of the QEA flying boats. Official written advice was given to the company. They were also instructed that the service from Sydney to Singapore would cease.[49] On 2 September 1939, under instructions from the Department of Civil Aviation, Captain Crowther was recalled from Townsville in the Empire flying boat *Champion* and brought back to Sydney. On 3 September, before the public announcement of the declaration of war on Germany, Fysh wrote to McMaster: "We are anticipating a commencement of hostilities at any time. Our position over a period, should war commence and last, is still obscure. There seems a chance at the moment that our organisation will become split and scattered . . . One of the most burning questions is that of ascertaining our new income and adjusting ourselves to it. As the Empire Mail Service will have ceased, we have got to find out where our revenue will come from . . ."[50]

By 6 September it was judged that Italy and Japan would not enter the war and that Imperial Airways could continue on its route across the Mediterranean. The Empire Service was resumed from Sydney to Singapore though on a twice weekly (instead of three times per week) basis. The Australian government stipulated that five Empire flying boats should at all times be on the Sydney–Singapore section, and available for use by the RAAF if necessary.[51] (The proposal to form an RAAF squadron from QEA flying boats was abandoned.) The United Kingdom government, however, suspended the all-mails airmail principle and, to reduce mail volume, imposed an inclusive mail fee of one shilling and three pence per half ounce from 6 September. The Australian government increased its charge for outward mail to one shilling and six pence per half ounce from 5 September. On 20 September, two flying boats were handed over on charter to the Royal Australian Air Force — the BOAC boats *Centaurus* and *Calypso*, which were then in Sydney. (They went, after a rushed conversion for service at Rose Bay to No. 11 Squadron.) BOAC, in exchange, were given *Coorong* and *Corio*, which were placed under United Kingdom registration.

The romantic era of peacetime flying boat services that had operated for only a little over one year was over. On the Sydney–Singapore section of the Empire route, in the first year of flying boat operations, Qantas had carried 4,900 passengers. Freight carried had been limited by the heavy mail loadings but rose from 73,027 pounds (1937–38) to 183,839 pounds (1938–39). In only nine months of flying boat operation from 4 August 1938 the total mail carried, 307 tons, exceeded by 85 tons total mail loadings of the previous landplane service over its four years and seven months of operation. Each flying boat trip averaged some 1.36 tons of mail. Timetable regularity achieved by the flying boats was just on 94 per cent, and Qantas maintained its international record of no injuries to passengers or flying staff. The 1939 Qantas Empire Airways balance sheet to 31 March, which included eight months of flying boat operation, showed a £44,330 profit on a capital of £523,000. (A dividend of 6 per cent plus a 2 per cent bonus was paid.)[52]

Fysh now headed a QEA staff of 285. H.H. (George) Harman, under Fysh as secretary and traffic manager, had Ivan Lawson as secretarial assistant and a total of 35 in his section. On a level of equality in the organization with Harman was Lester Brain, as flying operations manager. Scotty Allan was chief pilot, with 10 captains and 10 first officers. There was a total of 43 in Brain's section. Arthur Baird, as works manager, controlled a staff of 114. His stores and spares subsection was shared by the chief accountant's section of 46, under C.O. Turner. The Brisbane–Daly Waters DH86 landplane operations continued with J. Steward as station superintendent and Eric Donaldson in charge of flying (including the Flying Doctor Service). There were 46 in this group. Fysh was paid a salary of £2,000, Brain £1,350 (including £350 flying pay), Harman £1,000 and senior flying boat captains £1,255.[53]

McMaster advised Fysh on 4 September,

> You should endeavour to keep your organisation together, whatever work it may be given to do. Keep a careful account of all expenditure and loss of normal revenue. In so far as QEA is con-

cerned, there must be no defaulting or hanging back if assistance is asked, but be sure that those responsible for asking for that assistance are not over-excited. I wish to compliment you, yourself, in getting the extra engines out, and the overhaul base in readiness. This will be a big factor for QEA, and not only for QEA but for Britain also. It is due to you personally that this work has been pushed on.[54]

McMaster's thoughts went back to the early Qantas, for Fysh had sent him a copy of an article he had written for the June 1939 issue of *Shell Aviation News*, and he commented:

> You have given too much prominence to myself and not enough to yourself and Mr Templeton. We have to recognise that it was due to the free support of Templeton right at the start that kept the movement alive. You yourself worked hard, and it was only through the determination of yourself and McGinness, with Templeton and a few others of us, that the Company was able to carry on. Yourself and McGinness worked under very stringent financial conditions, and you have always been over-generous in any publicity regarding myself.[55]

By 15 September, Fysh was able to tell Sir John Reith: "We have now settled down to the new twice weekly flying boat service and I see no likelihood of disturbance by the Australian authorities unless Japan were to come in against us. Our policy here is directed towards keeping the QEA organisation together, as long as by so doing the maximum service to the country is being rendered."[56]

The chairman's address, prepared by McMaster for the nineteenth annual general meeting in Brisbane of the original Q.A.N.T.A.S. on 27 September 1939, summarized the position of the operating company, Qantas Empire Airways, as World War II began. The newly established British Overseas Airways Corporation would, said McMaster, take over all the obligations of Imperial Airways, including those under the intercompany agreement with QEA, and that agreement would be redrawn as between QEA and the corporation. The terms would be at least as favourable and would not in any way affect the status of QEA. It was not known how the war would affect the position.

For Q.A.N.T.A.S., the holding company for Australian interests in Qantas Empire Airways, the year to 30 June 1939 had seen, said McMaster, "the largest progressive move made by the old Company, through QEA". The paid up capital was increased to £264,500 by the issue late in 1938 of 193,681 shares of £1 each as the Q.A.N.T.A.S. contribution to the additional capital needed by QEA for the purchase of the flying boat fleet. The QEA landplane service to Singapore had ceased and the Empire Flying Boat Service inaugurated under a fifteen-year contract. QEA paid up capital increased to £523,000. The total Q.A.N.T.A.S. holding in QEA was now £261,500. QEA's general reserves stood at £30,000 and its obsolescence reserve at £90,144. During the year, the QEA fleet had flown a total of 1,707,060 route-miles and a total of 5,461,986 passenger-miles. QEA had just completed its own workshops at Mascot and engine overhauls were to begin in October, with some forty people employed there. The company was sufficiently self-contained to carry on if there should be a break in the route to England.

"It would on my part amount to empty statements to try to give an opinion as to the extent to which the War is going to affect the operations or financial position of Qantas Empire Airways", wrote McMaster. "Whilst no feeling of pessimism is in my mind, I cannot give you any assurances. You can feel confident", he concluded, "that the QEA executives and staff will stand firm by the Empire."[57]

Appendix A

Qantas Fleet: Aircraft Owned and Operated, 1921–39

Aircraft Type	Registration	Constructor's Number	Aircraft Name	Acquisition	Disposal
Avro 504K	G-AUBG	D1		30 Jan. 1921	6 Nov. 1926
BE 2E	G-AUBF	C6986		18 Feb. 1921	4 Dec. 1927
Avro 547	G-AUCR	547/1		2 Mar. 1921	27 June 1922
DH4	G-AUBZ	F2682		7 Mar. 1922	Jan. 1928
Armstrong Whitworth FK-8	G-AUCF	H4561		5 Sept. 1922	12 Apr. 1923
	G-AUCS			Oct. 1923	19 Dec. 1924
	G-AUDE	F4231		5 Sept. 1922	13 Mar. 1924
Bristol F2B	G-AUEB	4965		28 Apr. 1923	3 Nov. 1927
DH9C	G-AUED	86		1 Nov. 1923	24 Mar. 1927
	G-AUEF	87		10 Nov. 1923	22 Sept. 1926
	G-AUFM[a]		*Ion*	5 Feb. 1927	21 Aug. 1928
DH50A	G-AUER	116	*Hermes*	26 Sept. 1924	
	VH-UER		*Victory*[b]	15 May 1928	20 Apr. 1934
DH50A	G-AUFA[a]	1	*Iris*	18 Aug. 1926	11 Mar. 1936
	VH-UFA[c]			24 Aug. 1936	6 Oct. 1936
	G-AUFW[a]	2	*Perseus*	11 June 1927	4 Dec. 1930
	VH-UFW				
	G-AUGD[1]	3	*Pegasus*	2 Aug. 1927	27 July 1930
	VH-UGD				
	VH-UJS[a]	6		22 Jan. 1929	July 1930
DH60 Moth[d]	G-AUFJ			22 Dec. 1926	June 1929
	G-AUFL[e]	352		21 Mar. 1927	Mar. 1929
	G-AUFR	351		21 Mar. 1927	Mar. 1929
	G-AUFU	275		8 Apr. 1927	July 1928
	VH-UFU			9 Jan. 1931[c]	14 Apr. 1932
	G-AUGH	354		12 Aug. 1927	Apr. 1928
	VH-UGH			1 June 1931[c]	16 Nov. 1932
DH60G[d]	VH-UGW	834		6 June 1929	27 Sept. 1929
				11 June 1930[c]	5 Apr. 1937

Aircraft Type	Registration	Constructor's Number	Aircraft Name	Acquisition	Disposal
	VH-UIR	894		13 Feb. 1929	
	VH-UJM	986		3 June 1929	
	VH-ULQ	976		13 Aug. 1929	Apr. 1930
	VH-ULR	977		16 Aug. 1929	26 Nov. 1929
DH60M[d]	VH-UNB	1408		22 Dec. 1929	10 Apr. 1930
	VH-UNP	1407		17 Mar. 1930	
	VH-UOI	1478		17 June 1930	16 Sept. 1930
	VH-UOK	1494		19 June 1931	
	VH-UOT	1530		26 Aug.	
	VH-UQV	783		13 Mar. 1933	9 Mar. 1934
DH50J	G-AUHE[a]	4	*Atalanta*	Mar. 1928	
	VH-UHE				3 Oct. 1934
	G-AUHI[a]	5	*Hermes*	12 May 1928	4 Sept. 1928
	VH-ULG[a]	7	*Hippomenes*	3 Aug. 1929	14 July 1935
DH61	VH-UJB	334	*Apollo*	Mar. 1929	2 Feb. 1935
Giant Moth	VH-UJC	333	*Diana*	Mar. 1929	22 July 1935
DH80	VH-UPA	2022		29 Sept. 1930	9 June 1937
Puss Moth	VH-UPQ	2085		24 Dec. 1930	7 Dec. 1933
DH83	VH-URI	4084		15 Feb. 1924	30 Apr. 1952
Fox Moth	VH-USL	4096		29 June 1935	1 Jan. 1938
	VH-UUS	4044		June 1942	27 July 1943[f]
	VH-UZC	4048		2 Feb. 1937	27 July 1943[f]
	VH-UZD	4040		2 Feb. 1937	3 Oct. 1949
DH86	VH-USC	2307	*Canberra*	13 Oct. 1934	18 July 1938
Commonwealth	VH-USD	2308	*Brisbane*	22 June 1935	9 Aug. 1938
Class	VH-USE	2309	*Sydney*	22 Jan. 1935	20 Feb. 1942
	VH-USF	2310	*Melbourne*	7 Jan. 1935	28 Sept. 1940[f]
	VH-USG	2311		15 Nov. 1934	15 Nov. 1934[g]
	VH-UUA	2306	*Adelaide*	22 Jan. 1935	14 Sept. 1938
DH90	VH-UTJ	7562		3 Oct. 1940	18 Oct. 1946
Dragonfly	VH-UXB	7513		23 Oct. 1936	25 Feb. 1947
Saro A17	VH-UNV	17/2		15 Oct. 1937	5 Apr. 1938
Cutty Sark					
Short S23	VH-ABA	S876	*Carpentaria*	June 1938	Aug. 1942
Empire Flying	VH-ABB	S877	*Coolangatta*	18 Mar. 1938	26 July 1940
Boat				23 July 1943	11 Oct. 1944
	VH-ABC	S849	*Coogee*	Sept. 1938	8 June 1940
	VH-ABD	S851	*Corio*	Oct. 1938	Sept. 1939
	VH-ABE	S851	*Coorong*	Sept. 1938	Sept. 1939
	VH-ABF	S878	*Cooee*	20 Apr. 1938	Aug. 1942

Note: The Australian register of civil aircraft was introduced in 1921 following the International Convention for the Regulation of Aerial Navigation which was signed by many nations on 13 October 1919. Under this convention only one letter was used to denote nationality and all countries of the British Empire used the letter G, followed by a hyphen and four letters. Australia was indicated by the letters AU following the hyphen and thus all early aircraft of Qantas start with the letters G-AU.

In 1928 the International Commission for Air Navigation revised the system and allocated the primary letters VH to Australia. These letters were followed by a hyphen and three further letters. In making the change the old registration was followed as closely as possible, thus G-AUBG became VH-UBG.

Where G, which now stands for Great Britain only, features in this list after 1930, it refers to aircraft operated by Qantas but owned by an organization in Great Britain. The aircraft were not transferred to the Australian register.

Acquisition and disposal dates do not always coincide with Aircraft Register action. Accurate acquisition dates are not available for many aircraft hence approximate dates are used. These may be date of acceptance from the vendor (the true acquisition date), date of arrival in Australia, or date of accession to the register. Conversely, disposal dates may be date of acceptance by the purchaser, date of departure from Australia, or date of transfer or cancellation of the registration.

aBuilt by Qantas at Longreach.

bChange of name.

cRepurchased by Qantas.

dQantas acted as agents for de Havillands. Some of these aircraft were registered in Qantas's name only for that purpose and would not have formed part of the Qantas fleet. Present research has not permitted segregation of these aircraft.

eLater modified to DH60X.

fImpressed by RAAF.

gCrashed during delivery flight from United Kingdom.

Appendix B

QEA Summary of Aircraft Accidents, 1921–39

Date	Aircraft	Crew	Location	Category	Nature of Accident	Damage to Aircraft	Cause of Accident	Injuries Sustained
2 Mar. 1921	Avro 547 G-AUCR	P.J. McGinness	Mascot	Serious	Directly attributable to design weakness of under-carriage originally designed for Avro 504K	Undercarriage, wings, and propeller	Structural failure	Nil
2 Aug. 1921	504K G-AUBG	P.J. McGinness	Ingham	Serious	Forced landing in cane field	Wings and fuselage railed to Sydney for repairs	Broken throttle lever	Nil
12 Dec. 1921	504K G-AUBG	P.J. McGinness	Elderslie	Minor	Landing	Wing tip and undercarriage	Rough terrain	Nil
25 Feb. 1923	AWFK8 G-AUCF	H. Fysh	Jericho	Serious	Stalled in attempted take-off from too small a ground	General damage	Human error	Nil
6 June 1923	DH4 G-AUBZ	F. Huxley	Guildford Park	Serious	Landed through bush telephone line	General damage	Human error	Nil

Date / Aircraft	Pilot	Location	Severity	Circumstances	Damage	Cause	Casualties
13 Sept. 1923 FK8 Armstrong-Whitworth G-AUDE	G. Matthews	Blackall	Serious	Forced landing owing to engine failure	Extensive but repairable; railed to Longreach but not repaired	Broken gudgeon pin	Nil
18 Dec. 1923 F.2.13 Bristol Fighter G-AUEB	A.W. Vigers	Longreach	Serious	Went on nose landing Longreach aerodrome	Wings and propeller; aircraft repaired	Faulty landing	Nil
25 July 1925 DH9C G-AUEF	L.J. Brain	Maxwelton	Serious	Forced landing because of approaching darkness	Undercarriage, propeller, and leading edge of wing	Forced landing owing to approaching darkness	Nil
24 Sept. 1925 DH9C G-AUED	N. Evans	McKinlay	Minor	Struck aerodrome fence taking off	Undercarriage and propeller	Human error	Nil
24 Sept. 1926 DH9C G-AUEF	L.J. Brain	Cloncurry	Serious	Engine cut out during take-off	Undercarriage and propeller	Engine failure	Nil
20 Oct. 1926 DH50A G-AUER	C. Matheson	Kynuna	Not serious	Taxied into washway	Undercarriage	Human error	Nil
20 Feb. 1927 DH50A GK-AUER	L.J. Brain	McKinlay	Serious	Overturned during take-off	Undercarriage and propeller	Struck fence and came to rest in adjoining paddock; boggy aerodrome	Nil
24 Mar. 1927 DH9C G-AUED	A.D. Davidson	Tambo	Destroyed	During approach aircraft stalled and crashed	Total loss	Aircraft stalled during landing	One crew, two passengers killed
12 May 1927 DH60 Moth	N. Evans	Cloncurry	Minor	Forced landing on inadequate area	Undercarriage and propeller	Human error	Nil
5 Feb. 1928 DH9C G-AUFM	L.J. Brain	Camooweal	Serious	During take-off aircraft failed to lift, ran through fence	Undercarriage and both wings	Faulty take-off on indifferent aerodrome	Nil
6 Apr. 1928 DH60 G-AUFR	N. Evans	Cloncurry	Serious	Engine failure		When landing on a football field, aircraft ran through a fence	Nil
4 Sept. 1928 DH50J G-AUHI	C.W.A. Scott	Adelaide	Destroyed	Shortly after taking off, bad weather encountered; aircraft crashed in the hills	Destroyed by impact and fire	Going into heavy cloud against orders	One crew killed (engineer)
13 Dec. 1928 DH50	E. Donaldson	Vindex	Semi-serious	Aircraft blown over on ground	Undercarriage, wings, and propeller	Weather	Nil
1 Feb. 1930 DH60	A. Baird	Corona	Minor	Wheel collapsed	Undercarriage and propeller	Structure failure	Nil
12 May 1930 DH50J	A. Baird	Winton	Minor	Taxied into washway	Undercarriage and propeller	Human error	Nil

Date	Aircraft	Crew	Location	Category	Nature of Accident	Damage to Aircraft	Cause of Accident	Injuries Sustained
26 Sept. 1930	DH50A G-AUJS	E. Donaldson	Cloncurry	Serious	Abandoned take-off after type burst	Undercarriage, propeller, and wings	Type failure	Nil
25 Dec. 1932	DH61 VH-UJB	A. Baird	Tambo	Serious	During a taxi test aircraft swung and entered deep gully	Starboard longerons extensively damaged	Airport surface muddy	Nil
14 Jan 1934	DH50A G-AUFA	E.G. Donaldson	Dajarra	Serious	Take-off, local temperature over 100°F	Extensive wing, undercarriage, and fuselage damage	Engine failure owing to air-lock in petrol system	Nil
30 Oct. 1934	DH50J VH-UHE	N.H. Chapman	Vindex	Destroyed	Flew into ground	Destroyed by fire	Possible pilot fatigue	One crew and two passengers killed
15 Nov. 1934	DH86 VH-USG	D.R. Prendergast & M.V. Creetes	Barsdale	Destroyed	Accident resulted in grounding of all DH86 aircraft pending investigation by DCA. Note: This aircraft was not Qantas property at time of accident but was being delivered for the opening of the Aust. Eng. Service	Destroyed by impact	Investigation revealed pilot was in lavatory at the time; shortly after take-off from Longreach got into a flat spin and crashed	Four crew killed
20 Dec. 1934	DH61 VH-UJC	G.U. Allan	Camooweal	Serious	When taxiing tail skid caught on concealed stone	Tail skid structure torn from fuselage	Field condition	Nil
16 Jan. 1935	DH61 VH-UJC	H.B. Hussey	Pt. Stuart	Serious	During take-off wheels fell into a ditch; aircraft tilted onto its nose	Propeller and wing leading edge	Poor condition of field	Nil
8 Jan. 1936	DH83 VH-URI	E.C. Sims	Wandoola	Serious	Aircraft did not lift during take-off; struck stumps at far end of field	Lower wing extensively damaged; one longeron broken at wing root; propellor destroyed	Aerodrome; boggy surface of the field	Nil
11 Jan. 1936	DH86 VH-USC	R.B. Tapp	Singapore	Serious	While landing during rain aircraft overran the field, struck railway line at aerodrome boundary	Starboard mainplane and propellers extensively damaged; starboard engine cowlings and accessories also damaged; starboard undercarriage wrecked	Pilot error, overshot and unable to go around again owing to poor visibility	Nil
27 Apr. 1936	DH86	R.B. Tapp	Sourabaya	Serious	On landing starboard tyre burst and stripped from its rim; wheel rim dug	Four longerons fractured 6 inches from stern post;	Structural failure; starboard tyre burst on landing	Nil

Date	Aircraft	Pilot	Location	Extent of damage	Circumstances	Damage	Cause	Injuries
27 June 1936	DH86 VH-UUA	H.B. Hussey	Roma	Serious	After landing the starboard tyre burst; aircraft swung violently to starboard	Empennage extensively damaged; starboard dowty leg badly damaged	Structural failure; starboard tyre burst after landing	Nil
19 Mar. 1937	DH86 VH-USC	H.B. Hussey	Concurry	Serious	During landing aircraft swung and undercarriage collapsed	Empennage	Loss of control	nil
18 Aug. 1937	DH86 VH-UUA	R.S. Adair	Winton	Serious	After a crosswind landing aircraft had run about 450 yards before starboard undercarriage leg collapsed	Starboard dowty leg fractured; starboard lower mainplane slightly damaged, two propellers bent	Structural failure; undercarriage strained or damaged on this or some previous trip	Nil
7 Nov. 1937	DH86 VH-USD	E.C. Sims L. Grey	Darwin	Serious	During take-off port inner engine failed after aircraft had covered more than one half of the available run; take-off was abandoned and undercarriage collapsed on attempted ground loop to avoid striking fence	Rear end of fuselage broke off forward of stern port; port lower mainplane and aileron extensively damaged	Engine failure; port inner engine failed during take-off	Nil
1 Jan. 1938	DH83 VH-USL	S.L. Ashley	Winton	Destroyed	Aircraft caught in a violent wind storm while tied down at aerodrome	Destroyed	Weather; tie-down pegs torn from the ground by wind storm	Nil
5 Apr. 1938	Saro-Amphibean VH-UNV	W.H Crowther	Pinkenba	Destroyed	When alighting on water the amphibean nosed over and capsized	Destroyed	Pilot error; failed to retract undercarriage before alighting	Two crew slightly injured
25 Dec. 1938	DH90 VH-UXB	E.G. Donaldson	Mt Isa	Serious	Swung during take-off	Undercarriage structure damaged	Inherent fault with this type of aircraft	Nil
27 Feb. 1939	DH83 VH-URI	D. Tennent	Mitchell River	Serious	During latter part of landing run aircraft ran into ditch and overturned	Propeller and mainplane damaged	Weather; pilot forced to land in field and not found for seven days	Nil
Not recorded	DH83 VH-URI	K. Berry	Alexandra Downs	Serious	When landing aircraft overturned	Wing spars fractured, fuselage damaged	Brakes on during landing, lost for four days before being found	Nil
12 Mar. 1939	Empire Flying Boat G-ADUY	H.B. Hussey	Batavia	Serious	While taxiing to the buoy the flying boat struck a submerged object; hull was holed and boat sunk	Hull, wings, and engines extensively damaged by water and salvage attempts	Striking a submerged pontoon not charted by Dutch Harbour authorities	Nil

Notes

In citing sources in the notes, abbreviations have generally been used. Sources frequently cited have been identified by the following:

McMP   McMaster Papers*   ⎫

HFP   Hudson Fysh Papers   ⎬ see p. xiv for location

EJP   Edgar Johnston Papers ⎭

QR   *Qantas Rising*

* Among the McMaster Papers is an unfinished narrative of the early years of Qantas put together by Fergus McMaster. It is referred to in the notes as the "McMaster narrative".

Prologue

1. McMP.
2. *Graziers' Review*, 16 April 1924, p. 53.
3. McMP.
4. *Graziers' Review*, 16 April 1924, p. 53.
5. McMP.
6. McMP.
7. Ward, *Nation for a Continent*, p. 120.
8. Ibid., p. 123.
9. Ibid., p. 188.
10. Ibid.
11. Gibson, *Australia and Australians in Civil Aviation: An Index to Events from 1823 to 1920*. Qantas, 1971. This valuable index, compiled by members of the Qantas Research and Information Bureau under the direction of Ron Gibson and with the enthusiastic support of the then Qantas chief press and information officer, John Ulm (son of aviation pioneer C.T.P. Ulm) provides the source for references concerning civil aviation events in Australia to 1920. I give the main references actually cited in that work (though not all of them) for those who may not have access to the Ron Gibson work itself; the Bland Papers, Mitchell Library, Sydney; *The Empire*, Sydney, 25 February 1860.

12. Melbourne *Argus*, 2 February 1858; London *Times*, 23 January 1858.
13. Annual Report of Aeronautical Society of Great Britain, 1878, pp. 30 et seq.
14. Cole, *Henry Williams*, pp. 173-182.
15. "Lawrence Hargraves Notebooks", *Journal of Proceedings of the Royal Society of New South Wales* 6, no. 1 (1909-15).
16. Ibid.
17. *Sydney Morning Herald*, 10 December 1909.
18. *Motor in Australia*, 10 October 1909, p. 22; *Sydney Morning Herald*, 10 December and 20 December 1909.
19. Adelaide *Register*, 18 March 1910; Adelaide *Observer*, 26 March 1910; *Journal of the Aviation Historical Society of Australia*, 12 October 1958.
20. Melbourne *Argus*, 16, 19, 22 March 1910.
21. Davies, *World's Airlines*, pp. 4-5.
22. *Sydney Morning Herald*, 23 May 1911.
23. *The Queenslander*, 4 February 1911.
24. Sydney *Sun*, 13 January 1911.
25. Melbourne *Argus*, 20–25 February 1911.
26. *Nepean Times*, 30 September and 7 October 1911.
27. Mackenzie, *Solo*.
28. *Flight*, 9 November 1912, p. 1029; *Melbourne Age*, 28 January and 3, 7, 9, 12 February 1914; *Harry George Hawker: A Pioneer of Australian Aviation* (Melbourne: Department of Civil Aviation, 1953).
29. Mackenzie, *Solo*, pp. 17-19.
30. Fysh, *QR*.
31. Stroud, *Air Transport*.
32. Marduel letters in the possession of Qantas.
33. Fysh, *QR*, p. 69.
34. Ibid., p. 73.
35. Ibid., p. 85.
36. Handwritten report by Hudson Fysh, McMP.
37. Kellaway to Fysh, McMP.
38. Fysh, *QR*, p. 87.
39. Ibid., p. 88.
40. John Fysh recollection; interview with author.
41. McMP.
42. McMP.

Chapter 1

1. Fysh, *QR*, p. 92.
2. Alexander, *Australia Since Federation*, p. 59.
3. Ward, *Nation for a Continent*, p. 127.
4. Ibid., p. 27.
5. McMP.
6. Davies, *World's Airlines*, p. 17.
7. Allen, *K.L.M.*, p. 10.
8. McMP.
9. McMP.
10. McMP.
11. McMP.
12. A.D. Allen, 19 Castlereagh St, Sydney to A.W. Campbell, 26 October 1920, McMP.
13. *The Morning Bulletin*, Rockhampton.
14. McMP.
15. McMP.
16. McMP.
17. McMP.
18. McMP.
19. Prospectus, 14 October 1920, McMP.
20. Comment by McMaster, McMP.
21. Fysh, *QR*, p. 100.

22. Frank Cory letter, 29 January 1921, McMP.
23. *The Morning Bulletin*, Rockhampton, 3 February 1921.
24. Letter to McMaster from State Government Insurance Office, 19 January 1921.
25. Fysh, *QR*, p. 102.
26. McMaster narrative, McMP.
27. McMaster narrative, McMP.
28. McMaster narrative, McMP.
29. McMaster address, McMP.

Chapter 2

1. Frank Cory interview with author.
2. Provisional Directors' Report, 21 May 1921, McMP.
3. McMP.
4. McMP.
5. McMP.
6. McMP.
7. McMP.
8. McMP.
9. Report of Fysh to McMaster, McMP.
10. McMP.
11. McMaster to Campbell, 3 March 1921, McMP.
12. Cory to Campbell, 24 February 1921, McMP.
13. McMaster to Campbell, 3 March 1921, McMP.
14. Frank Cory interview with author.
15. Fysh to McMaster, 26 April 1921, McMP.
16. McMP.
17. McMP.
18. McMP.
19. Capt. E.C. Johnston, Civil Aviation Board, Department of Defence, McMP.
20. McMP.
21. *Aeronautics*, 24 March 1921.
22. Melbourne Argus, 23 November 1921.
23. *Aeronautics*, May 1921.
24. Lieutenant Colonel Holt in *Aeronautics*, May 1921.
25. McMP.
26. Hansard, 22 November 1921.
27. Fysh to McMaster, 8 June 1921, McMP.
28. C.J. Brabazon to McMaster, 19 June 1921, McMP.
29. McGinness to McMaster, 1 August 1921, McMP.
30. Fysh, *QR*, p. 110.
31. Ibid., p. 116.
32. McMaster narrative, McMP.
33. McMaster narrative, McMP.
34. McMP.
35. Fysh, *QR*, p. 116.
36. Ibid.
37. Brinsmead, 28 September 1921, McMP.
38. McMP.
39. McMaster narrative, McMP.
40. McMaster narrative, McMP.
41. McMaster narrative, McMP.
42. McMaster narrative, McMP.
43. Australian Press Association story, 3 November 1921.
44. Hansard, 22 November 1921.
45. McMP.
46. McMaster narrative, McMP.
47. McMaster narrative, McMP.
48. McMaster narrative, McMP.

49. Hansard, 22 November 1921.
50. Hansard, 22 November 1921.
51. Telegram from Hon. Chas McDonald, 27 November 1921, McMP.
52. McMP.
53. J.E. Deane, secretary of the Prime Minister's Department, 15 December 1921, McMP.
54. Fysh letters, McMP.
55. McMP.
56. Captain Edgar Johnston interview with author.
57. Fysh, *QR*, pp. 118-19.
58. McMaster narrative, McMP.
59. McMaster narrative, McMP.
60. Fysh telegram to McMaster, 29 January 1922, McMP.
61. McMaster narrative, McMP.
62. McMaster narrative, McMP.
63. Fysh telegram, 2 February 1922, McMP.
64. Letter from Fysh in Melbourne, 3 February 1922, McMP.
65. Letter from Brinsmead (Department of Defence), 8 February 1922.

Chapter 3

1. Fysh to McMaster, 3 February 1922, McMP.
2. Fysh, 7 March 1922.
3. Frank Cory interview with author.
4. C. Vickey (4 Bridge St, Sydney) to McMaster, 24 February 1922.
5. Telegram from Fysh to McMaster, 22 March 1922.
6. Fysh, *QR*, pp. 120-21.
7. Ibid., p. 121.
8. Fysh telegram, 19 April 1922, McMP.
9. Fysh telegram, 24 April 1922, McMP.
10. Griffin letter, 26 June 1922, McMP.
11. McMP.
12. McMP.
13. Griffin letter, 1 September 1922.
14. McMP.
15. McMP.
16. McMP.
17. McMP.
18. McMP.
19. McMP.
20. McMP.
21. McMaster telegram, 6 October 1922, McMP.
22. McMP.
23. McGinness telegram, 2 November 1922, McMP.
24. Fysh, *QR*, p. 127.
25. McMP.
26. Fysh, *QR*, p. 127.
27. Frank Cory interview with the author.
28. Fysh, *QR*, p. 127.
29. McMaster to McGinness, 28 October 1922, McMP.
30. Fysh, *QR*, p. 128.

Chapter 4

1. Fysh, *QR*, p. 133.
2. Log book of G-AUDE (given to Capt. R.J. Ritchie by Sir Hudson Fysh and in his possession).
3. Jack Hazlett interview with the author.

4. Jack Hazlett interview with the author.
5. McMP.
6. McMP.
7. McMP.
8. McMaster narrative, McMP.
9. McMP.
10. McMP.
11. Jack Hazlett interview with the author.
12. McMP.
13. Miller, *Early Birds*, p. 101.
14. Ibid.
15. Ibid., p. 103.
16. Fysh, *QR*, p. 141.
17. McMaster narrative, McMP.
18. Jack Hazlett interview with author.
19. Jack Hazlett interview with author.
20. McMaster narrative, McMP.
21. McMaster narrative, McMP.
22. McMP.
23. McMP.
24. Fysh to McMaster, 14 June 1923, McMP.
25. Miller, *Early Birds*, p. 104.
26. Ibid.
27. Manager's Report, 30 June 1923, McMP.
28. Fysh to McMaster, 14 June 1923, McMP.
29. Fysh to McMaster, 21 June 1923, McMP.
30. Fysh to McMaster, 21 June 1923, McMP.
31. Fysh, *QR*, p. 147.
32. McMP.
33. McMP.
34. McMP.
35. McMP.
36. Minutes of Directors' Meeting, 17 November 1923, McMP.
37. McMaster to Campbell, 1 December 1923 and Campbell to McMaster, 5 December 1923, McMP.
38. McMaster narrative, McMP.
39. Fysh, *QR*, p. 152.
40. McMP.
41. McMP.

Chapter 5

1. Fysh, *QR*, p. 154.
2. Ibid.
3. Ibid., p. 158.
4. McMP.
5. Fysh, *QR*, p. 161.
6. Directors' Meeting, 19 March 1924, McMP.
7. McMaster to Fysh, 29 February 1924, McMP.
8. *Graziers' Review*, 16 April 1924.
9. Davies, *World's Airlines*, p. 34.
10. Fysh to McMaster, 20 May 1924, McMP.
11. Ibid.
12. Fysh to McMaster, May 1924, McMP.
13. *Graziers' Review*.
14. Fysh to McMaster, 11 October 1924, McMP.
15. R. Miller to McMaster, 4 October 1924, McMP.
16. McMP.
17. McMP.
18. Qantas Circular, January 1926, McMP.

19. Ibid.
20. Ibid.
21. Fysh, *QR*, p. 176.
22. McMP.
23. McMP.
24. *Aircraft*, August 1926.
25. Fysh, *QR*, p. 178.
26. Ibid.
27. Ibid., p. 181.
28. Hocking and Haddon-Cave, *Air Transport*, p. 17.
29. Ibid.
30. Fysh, *QR*, p. 152.
31. Ibid., p. 193.
32. Manager's Report, 6 April 1927, McMP.
33. Ibid.
34. Ibid.
35. Ibid.

Chapter 6

1. Seventh Annual Report, 1 October 1927, Qantas Library.
2. Fysh to the collector of customs, 12 February 1927, McMP.
3. Fysh to the collector of customs, 12 February 1927, McMP.
4. Fysh, *QR*, p. 189.
5. Ibid.
6. Hocking and Haddon-Cave, *Air Transport*, p. 8.
7. Ibid.
8. Fysh report, 2 November 1928, McMP.
9. Fysh, *QR*, p. 198.
10. McMP.
11. McMP.
12. Miller, *Early Birds*, p. 137.
13. Hocking and Haddon-Cave, *Air Transport*, p. 11.
14. Ibid.
15. Fysh, *AR*, p. 206.
16. McMP.
17. McMP.
18. McMP.
19. McMP.
20. McMaster to Scott, 21 October 1928, McMP.
21. Scott, *Scott's Book*, p. 138.
22. Fysh, *QR*, p. 197.
23. Manager's Report, 30 January 1929, McMP.
24. Ibid.
25. Manager's Report, 2 November 1928, McMP.

Chapter 7

1. McMP.
2. Directors' Meeting, 7 March 1929, McMP.
3. Ibid.
4. Fysh, *QR*, p. 128.
5. McMaster narrative, McMP.
6. Manager's Report, 1 May 1929, McMP.
7. Ibid.
8. Evidence of Kingsford Smith before the Air Inquiry Committee, May 1929, McMP.
9. Finding of the Air Inquiry Committee, paragraph 55, McMP.

10. McMP.
11. McMP.
12. *Aircraft*, 30 April 1929.
13. Ibid.
14. Air Inquiry evidence, McMP.
15. Evidence of Ulm before the Air Inquiry Committee, McMP.
16. Fysh, *QR*, p. 229.
17. *Aircraft*, December 1925.
18. Hocking and Haddon-Cave, *Air Transport*, p. 85. (Report of Imperial Air Communications Special Sub-Committee, Section XVI of Cond. 2768.)
19. Hocking and Haddon-Cave, *Air Transport*, p. 185.
20. Edgar Johnston interview with the author, 1982.
21. *Aircraft*, 31 July 1929.
22. Ibid.
23. Hansard, 23 August 1929.
24. Manager's Report, 19 June 1929, McMP.
25. Annual General Meeting, 19 June 1924, McMP.
26. McMP.
27. Fysh, *QR*, p. 233.
28. McMP.
29. McMP.
30. McMP.
31. Fysh to McMaster, 24 November 1929, McMP.
32. McMP.
33. Letter from Fysh to McMaster, 22 November 1929, McMP.
34. McMP.
35. Telegram from Fysh to McMaster, 7 January 1920, McMP.
36. McMP.
37. McMP.
38. Fysh, *QR*, p. 236.
39. Letter from McMaster to Norman White, 8 August 1930, McMP.
40. McMP.
41. Norman White to McMaster, 2 August 1930, McMP.
42. *Longreach Leader*, 31 October 1930.
43. *Aircraft*, 31 July 1930.
44. Harman to McMaster, 4 November 1930, McMP.
45. Fysh report to McMaster, McMP.
46. *Longreach Leader*, 31 October 1930.
47. Ibid.
48. Fysh circular to pilots, HFP.
49. Hansard, 22 November 1921.

Chapter 8

1. *Aircraft*, 1 October 1930.
2. *Aircraft*, 30 November 1930.
3. McMP.
4. McMP.
5. Allen, *K.L.M.*, p. 23.
6. Davies, *World's Airlines*, p. 23.
7. Higham, *Imperial Air Routes*, p. 137.
8. McMaster letter to directors, 24 February 1931, McMP.
9. Fysh, *QR*, p. 240.
10. Fysh to McMaster, 30 March 1931, McMP.
11. HFP.
12. McMP.
13. Fysh, *QR*, p. 244.
14. *Aircraft*, 4 April 1931.
15. *Aircraft*, July 1931.
16. *Aircraft*, 1 June 1931.

17. *Aircraft*, 31 July 1931.
18. Ibid.
19. *Aircraft*, 1 July 1931.
20. McMP.
21. McMP.
22. Fysh, *QR*, p. 245.
23. Ibid.
24. Qantas Library.
25. Fysh, *QR*, p. 243.
26. Telegram from Fysh to McMaster, 22 November 1931, HFP.
27. HFP.
28. Woods Humphery to Fysh, 16 December 1931, HFP.
29. HFP.
30. Templeton to Fysh, 3 December 1931, HFP.
31. Templeton to Fysh, 3 December 1931, HFP.
32. HFP.
33. McMaster to Templeton, 23 December 1931, McMP.
34. HFP.

Chapter 9

1. HFP.
2. EJP.
3. EJP.
4. EJP.
5. EJP.
6. EJP.
7. EJP.
8. EJP.
9. Fysh, *QR*, p. 245.
10. Ibid.
11. Memorandum re proposed merger, 27 February 1932, EJP.
12. Ulm to Fysh, 4 February 1932, EJP.
13. Ulm to Johnston, 4 February 1932, EJP.
14. McMP.
15. McMP.
16. *Aircraft*, 1 March 1932.
17. M.L. Shepherd (secretary of Defence Department) to Qantas, 24 March 1932, EJP.
18. Brearley to Fysh, 17 March 1932, HFP.
19. Brearley to Fysh, 17 March 1932, HFP.
20. HFP.
21. HFP.
22. McMP.
23. EJP.
24. EJP.
25. HFP.
26. "Notes, Suggestions and Recommendations concerning the establishment and operation of the Australian Section of the Australia–England Air Route and Subsidised Air Services Within Australia", by C.T.P. Ulm, joint managing director, on behalf of Australian National Airways Limited, 7 April 1932, McMP and EJP.
27. Brearley to Ulm, 11 April 1932, HFP.
28. Brearley letter, 18 April 1932, McMP.
29. Ulm to Johnston, 11 April 1932, EJP.
30. Ulm to Johnston, 20 April 1932, EJP.
31. Letters from McMaster to Fysh, 3 April and 10 April 1932, HFP.
32. McMP.
33. McMP.
34. Hocking and Haddon-Cave, *Air Transport*, p. 4.

35. Ibid, p.7.
36. HFP.
37. HFP.
38. HFP.
39. HFP.
40. HFP.
41. HFP.
42. Copy of Larkin proposals, 24 May 1932, McMP.
43. HFP.
44. McMP.
45. McMP.
46. McMP.
47. McMP.
48. Hocking and Haddon-Cave, *Air Transport*, p. 80.
49. EJP.
50. EJP.
51. Speech on 4 July 1933, HFP.
52. EJP.
53. HFP.
54. McMaster to Fysh, 17 September 1932, McMP.
55. Ibid.
56. HFP.
57. HFP.
58. HFP.
59. Fysh to McMaster, 20 December 1932, McMP.
60. McMP.
61. Fysh to McMaster, 17 December 1932, McMP.
62. McMaster to A.E. Rudder, 21 December 1932, McMP.
63. EJP.

Chapter 10

1. Fysh, *QR*, p. 250.
2. HFP.
3. McMP.
4. Fysh, *QR*, p. 257.
5. Ibid.
6. HFP.
7. HFP.
8. Fysh, *QR*, p. 257.
9. Cable from Fysh to Cameron, 13 February 1933, HFP.
10. Fysh to Rudder, 20 April 1933, McMP.
11. Copy of WAA bulletin transcribed by Fysh in letter to Rudder, 22 April 1933, McMP.
12. Note by McMaster, McMP.
13. HFP.
14. EJP.
15. Ulm to Johnston, 20 June 1933, EJP.
16. McMP.
17. Stroud, *Air Transport*, pp. 96-103.
18. HFP.
19. *Aircraft*, 1 June 1933.
20. *Aircraft*, 1 August 1933.
21. Edgar Johnston to Kingsford Smith, 7 June 1933, EJP.
22. *Aircraft*, 1 September 1933.
23. *Wings*, 1 September 1933.
24. Brisbane *Telegraph*, 26 June 1933.
25. Brisbane *Telegraph*, 26 June 1933.
26. Qantas *Gazette*, June 1933, HFP.
27. *Sydney Morning Herald*, 27 June 1933.
28. *Wings*, 1 September 1933.

29. McMaster to A.E. Rudder, 30 June 1933, McMP.
30. Report of Annual General Meeting for year ending 30 June 1933.
31. HFP.
32. HFP.
33. Fysh to McMaster, 30 August 1933, HFP.
34. HFP.
35. *Parliamentary Debates*, 1933.
36. McMP.
37. Editorial, *Sydney Morning Herald*, 27 June 1933.
38. Brisbane *Courier Mail*, 14 September 1933.
39. Fysh to Pearce, 8 June 1933, HFP.
40. *Sydney Morning Herald* report, 25 September 1933.
41. Ibid.
42. *Aircraft*, 16 September 1933.
43. Brisbane *Sunday Mail*, 1 October 1933.
44. Brisbane *Courier Mail*, 16 October 1933.
45. Brisbane *Telegraph*, 23 October 1933.
46. *Evening Standard*, 20 October 1933.
47. Brisbane *Sunday Mail*, 22 October 1933.
48. *Labor Daily*, 26 October 1933.
49. Brisbane *Telegraph*, 28 October 1933.
50. EJP.
51. EJP.
52. Annual Report, 3 October 1933, Qantas Library.
53. Fysh, *QR*, p. 257.
54. Ibid., p. 258.
55. Ibid.
56. HFP.
57. Fysh, *QR*, p. 256.
58. Fysh report, 24 October 1933, HFP.
59. HFP.
60. HFP.
61. Qantas *Gazette*, 30 November 1933, Qantas Library.
62. Brisbane *Courier Mail*, 11 November 1933.
63. HFP.
64. Fysh, *QR*, p. 255.
65. Ibid., p. 255.
66. Ibid., p. 260.
67. Ibid., p. 260.
68. Fysh to McMaster, 9 February 1934, HFP.

Chapter 11

1. HFP.
2. Air Convention Bulletin, January 1934.
3. Air Convention Bulletin, March 1934.
4. EJP.
5. HFP.
6. Brisbane *Courier Mail*, 26 October 1933.
7. J. Stannage to Edgar Johnston, 9 March 1934, EJP.
8. EJP.
9. Edgar Johnston interview with the author, 1982.
10. EJP.
11. Fysh, *QR*, p. 264.
12. Harman to Fysh, 31 January 1934, HFP.
13. HFP.
14. Brisbane *Telegraph* report, undated, HFP.
15. *Sydney Morning Herald*, 21 April 1934.
16. Ulm to Edgar Johnston, 27 April 1934, EJP.

17. EJP.
18. Rudder to Fysh, 20 April 1934, HFP.
19. McGinness telegram, 23 April 1934, HFP.
20. *Sydney Morning Herald*, 21 April 1934.
21. McMP narrative.
22. QEA board minutes, 1 May 1934, HFP.
23. HFP.
24. Fysh to Brain, 21 April 1934, HFP.
25. Fysh to Tapp, 6 June 1934, HFP.
26. *Longreach Leader*, 16 June 1934.
27. Brisbane *Courier Mail*, 4 July 1934.
28. Sydney *Sun*, 12 July 1934.
29. Brisbane *Telegraph*, 17 July 1934.
30. *Aircraft*, 1 January 1934.
31. Brisbane *Courier Mail*, 1 June 1934.
32. *Melbourne Herald*, 27 September 1934.
33. EJP.
34. HFP.
35. Fysh, *QR*, p. 266.
36. Fysh to Mrs Chapman, 24 November 1934, HFP.
37. HFP.
38. Bill Crowther interview with the author, 18 January 1983.
39. Qantas *Gazette*, 30 October 1934.
40. Fysh, *QR*, p. 266.
41. Fysh, *Qantas at War*, p. 6.
42. Author's interview with A.J. Quin Harkin, then chief accountant of Imperial Airways.
43. *The Bulletin*, 7 November 1934.
44. *The Times*, 5 November 1933.
45. London *Daily Telegraph*, 5 November 1933.
46. Brisbane *Courier Mail*, Special Cables, 6 November 1934.
47. Hocking and Haddon-Cave, *Air Transport*, p. 88 (quoting statement of Sir George Pearce).
48. *Aircraft*, 1 December 1934.
49. Brisbane *Telegraph*, 15 November 1934.
50. Fysh, *Qantas at War*, pp. 3-8.
51. Brisbane *Telegraph*, 16 November 1934.
52. Brisbane *Courier Mail*, 21 November 1934.
53. Fysh, *Qantas at War*, p. 10.
54. Brisbane *Courier Mail*, 21 November 1934.
55. Fysh, *Qantas at War*, p. 6.
56. Brisbane *Courier Mail*, 21 November 1934.
57. Brisbane *Courier Mail*, 21 November 1934.
58. Fysh, *Qantas at War*, p. 9.
59. Mrs Rodgers to Edgar Johnston, 20 December 1934, EJP.
60. Johnston to Mrs Ulm, 7 January 1935, EJP.
61. Mrs Ulm to Johnston, 10 January 1935, EJP.
62. Kingsford Smith to Johnston, 8 February 1935, EJP.
63. Johnston to Fysh, 25 May 1934, EJP.
64. Brisbane *Telegraph*, 11 December 1934.
65. Higham, *Air Routes*, p. 84.
66. Secret paper, 11 March 1935, submitted to the Australian Cabinet, EJP.
67. Paper by the acting controller of civil aviation to the secretary, Defence Department, 6 March 1935, outlining the views of Edgar Johnston, controller, prior to his departure overseas, EJP.
68. HFP.
69. Woods Humphery to Fysh, 25 September 1934, HFP.
70. Fysh to Woods Humphery, 31 October 1934, HFP.
71. HFP.
72. HFP.
73. HFP.
74. Woods Humphery to Fysh, 2 January 1935, HFP.
75. Fysh to Woods Humphery, 24 November 1934, HFP.

76. HFP.
77. McMaster to Woods Humphery, 17 December 1934, HFP.
78. Fysh to Woods Humphery, 31 December 1934, HFP.
79. HFP.
80. EJP.
81. McMP.
82. McMP.
83. McMP.
84. *Parliamentary Debates* (Commons), 20 December 1934.
85. McMP.
86. McMP.
87. HFP.
88. McMaster to Geddes, 22 January 1935, HFP.
89. HFP.
90. Fysh, *Qantas at War*, p. 12.
91. Brisbane *Courier Mail*, 17 January 1935.
92. Brisbane *Courier Mail*, 17 January 1935.
93. Fysh, *Qantas at War*, p. 12.
94. Johnston to Fysh, 23 January 1935, EJP.
95. Johnston to Fysh, 4 February 1935, EJP.
96. Geddes to McMaster, 15 February 1935, McMP.
97. Fysh to Johnston, 28 December 1934, HFP.
98. Johnston to Fysh, 4 January 1935, HFP.
99. HFP.
100. Fysh, *Qantas at War*, p. 14.
101. Telegram, 29 January 1935, HFP.
102. Johnston to Fysh, 4 February 1935, McMP.
103. Johnston to Fysh, 29 January 1935, EJP.

Chapter 12

1. EJP, February 1935.
2. Brisbane *Courier Mail*, 23 June 1934, EJP.
3. Fysh to Johnston, 12 June 1934, EJP.
4. Fysh to Johnston, 19 July 1934, EJP.
5. KNILM to Fysh, 21 July 1934, EJP.
6. Fysh to KNILM, 6 August 1934, EJP.
7. Fysh to Johnston, 11 August 1934, EJP.
8. Johnston to Fysh, 23 August 1934, EJP.
9. Johnston to Fysh, 10 September 1934, HFP.
10. Fysh to Johnston, 20 September 1934, HFP.
11. Woods Humphery to Plesman, 23 November 1934, HFP.
12. Woods Humphery to Fysh, 23 November 1934, HFP.
13. Fysh to Woods Humphery, 28 December 1934, HFP.
14. Fysh to Dismore, 22 December 1934, HFP.
15. Fysh, *Qantas At War*, p. 39.
16. Ibid., p. 40.
17. Ibid.
18. Ibid., pp. 42-43.
19. Interview with author, 1982.
20. Hocking and Haddon-Cave, *Air Transport*, p. 34.
21. Managing Director's Report, 24 January 1935, HFP.
22. Fysh to Woods Humphery, 8 February 1935, HFP.
23. Confidential Memorandum to Cabinet, PMG Department, 4 March 1935, HFP.
24. Paper by acting controller of civil aviation, 16 March 1935, EJP.
25. Secret Cabinet Paper, Defence Department, 11 March 1935, EJP.
26. Woods Humphery to Fysh, 2 April 1935, HFP.
27. Woods Humphery to Fysh, 9 April 1935, HFP.
28. Fysh to Woods Humphery, 9 April 1935, HFP.

29. Fysh draft paper, 31 March 1935, HFP.
30. Draft chairman's address, 31 March 1935, HFP.
31. Fysh to Woods Humphery, 9 April 1935, HFP.
32. QEA Organisation Notes, 1935, HFP.
33. Rudders Ltd. to Fysh, 11 April 1935, HFP.
34. Fysh to Rudders Ltd., 15 April 1935, HFP.
35. Fysh, *Qantas at War*, p. 32.
36. Kingsford Smith to Johnston, 19 February 1935, EJP.
37. Woods Humphery to Fysh, 23 April 1935, HFP.
38. Johnston to Fysh, 7 May 1935, HFP.
39. Fysh to Johnston, 7 May 1935, HFP.
40. Fysh, *Qantas at War*, p. 45.
41. Ibid., p. 54.
42. Operational Memorandum by Lester Brain, 1935, HFP.
43. Fysh, *Qantas at War*, p. 54; and interview with author, 1982.
44. Rudder to Fysh, 15 July 1935, HFP.
45. McComb to Johnston, 31 May 1935, EJP.
46. Memorandum, Department of Defence, 26 April 1935, EJP.
47. Group Capt. G.R. Macfarlane Reid to Johnston, 27 May 1935, EJP.
48. Fysh to Woods Humphery, 10 May 1935, HFP.
49. Minister Parkhill to QEA, 29 May 1935, EJP.
50. QEA to Minister Parkhill, 6 June 1935, EJP.
51. McMaster's annotated luncheon menu, 10 May 1935, McMP.
52. Annotated menu and notes by McMaster, McMP.
53. McMaster to Johnston, 6 June 1935, EJP.
54. Air Vice Marshall R. Williams to Fysh, 10 June 1935, HFP.
55. Fysh to McComb, 12 June 1935, HFP.
56. Brisbane *Telegraph*, 30 June 1935.
57. Johnston to secretary, Department of Defence, 26 June 1935, EJP.
58. Johnston to McComb, 2 July 1935, EJP.
59. Johnston to McComb, 5 July 1935, EJP.
60. Brisbane *Telegraph*, 8 July 1935.
61. *Sydney Morning Herald*, 9 July 1935.

Chapter 13

1. *Sydney Morning Herald*, 17 May 1935.
2. Melbourne *Argus*, 6 June 1935.
3. Unidentified press clipping, 20 June 1935, McMP.
4. Kingsford Smith to Minister Parkhill, 24 June 1935, EJP.
5. McComb to Johnston, 9 July 1935, EJP.
6. Ibid.
7. Johnston to McComb, 12 July 1935, EJP.
8. Johnston to Fysh, 12 July 1935, EJP.
9. Johnston to secretary, Department of Defence, 13 July 1935, EJP.
10. Rudder to Woods Humphery, 16 July 1935, HFP.
11. Transcript of London Conference, 17 July 1935, EJP.
12. Johnston to McComb, 20 July 1935, EJP.
13. Memorandum by McComb, 17 July 1935, EJP.
14. Johnston to McComb, 20 July 1935, EJP.
15. Woods Humphery to Fysh, 23 July 1935, HFP.
16. McMaster to Geddes, 29 July 1935, HFP.
17. McMaster to Rudder, 22 July 1935, McMP.
18. Fysh to Woods Humphery, 6 August 1935, HFP.
19. Departmental Memorandum, 2 August 1935, EJP.
20. Fysh to Johnston, 8 August 1935, EJP.
21. Johnston to McComb, 14 August 1935, EJP.
22. McComb to Johnston, 30 July 1935, EJP.
23. Fysh to Woods Humphery, 15 July 1935, HFP.
24. Woods Humphery to Fysh, 30 July 1935, HFP.

25. Cable from New Zealand government to acting prime minister, 5 August 1935, EJP.
26. McComb to Johnston, 13 August 1935, EJP.
27. London *Daily Express*, 5 August 1935.
28. Ibid.
29. Fysh to Johnston, 8 August 1935, HFP.
30. J.V. Fairbairn to Fysh, 19 August 1935, HFP.
31. Board resolution by McMaster, 23 August 1935, HFP.
32. Johnston to McComb, 14 August 1935, EJP.
33. Confidential memorandum by Johnston, 30 August 1935, EJP.
34. Fysh to Dismore, 31 August 1935, HFP.
35. Geddes to McMaster, 2 September 1935, HFP.
36. Rudder to McMaster, 10 September 1935, McMP.
37. Fysh to McMaster, 25 September 1935, HFP.
38. Geddes to McMaster, 22 October 1935, McMP.
39. Fysh, *Qantas at War*, p. 64.
40. Fysh to Johnston, 26 October 1935.
41. *Sydney Morning Herald*, 17 May 1935.
42. Unidentified press clipping, McMP.
43. McMaster to Geddes, 26 November 1935, HFP.
44. Geddes to McMaster, 30 November 1935, HFP.
45. Hocking and Haddon-Cave, *Air Transport*, pp. 88-89.
46. Fysh to Johnston, 28 November 1935, HFP.
47. *Sydney Morning Herald*, leader, 6 December 1935.
48. Fysh to G.U. Allan, 16 December 1935, HFP.
49. Geddes to McMaster, 13 December 1935, McMP.
50. Fysh to Johnston, 24 December 1935, HFP.
51. Fysh to Sir Donald Cameron, 30 December 1935, HFP.
52. Fysh to McMaster, 27 December 1935, HFP.
53. McMaster to Minister Parkhill, 27 December 1935, HFP.

Chapter 14

1. Johnston to Fysh, 3 January 1936, EJP.
2. Parkhill to McMaster, 3 January 1936, McMP.
3. Fysh, *Qantas at War*, p. 99.
4. Brisbane *Telegraph*, 2 February 1936.
5. *The Bulletin*, 12 February 1936.
6. Brisbane *Telegraph*, 3 February 1936.
7. Fysh to Dismore, 4 February 1936, HFP.
8. Woods Humphery to Fysh, 4 February 1936, HFP.
9. Fysh to Woods Humphery, 8 February 1936, HFP.
10. Woods Humphery to Fysh, 8 February 1936, HFP.
11. McGinness to Johnston, 13 January 1936, EJP.
12. Johnston interview with the author, 1982.
13. Stannage to Johnston, 9 and 17 January 1936, EJP.
14. Fysh to Johnston, 5 February 1936, HFP.
15. Brain to Johnston, 11 February 1936, EJP.
16. Brain to Fysh, 25 January 1936, HFP.
17. Fysh to Woods Humphery, 25 February 1936, HFP.
18. Fysh to Johnston, 10 February 1936, HFP.
19. Fysh to Woods Humphery, 3 March 1936, HFP.
20. Johnston to Fysh, 4 March 1936, HFP.
21. Parkhill to McMaster, 3 March 1936, HFP.
22. McMaster to Parkhill, 5 March 1936, McMP.
23. Parkhill to McMaster, 25 March 1936, McMP.
24. Fysh to Johnston, 2 April 1936, EJP.
25. McMaster to Parkhill, 27 March 1936, McMP.
26. Woods Humphery to Fysh, 24 February 1936, HFP.
27. Woods Humphery to Fysh, 18 March 1936, HFP.

28. Fysh to Dismore, 17 March 1936, HFP.
29. Fysh, *Qantas at War*, p. 100.
30. A.E. Hempel to Fysh, 6 April 1936, HFP.
31. Imperial Airways, *Outline Specification for a Flying Boat Airway*, 1936, HFP.
32. Notes by McMaster, April 1936, McMP.
33. Fysh to Rudder, 20 April 1936, HFP.
34. Brackley, *Memoirs of a Pioneer of Civil Aviation*, p. 474.
35. Fysh, *Qantas at War*, pp. 118-9.
36. Brain to Fysh, 28 June 1936, HFP.
37. Fysh to Woods Humphery, 2 June 1936, HFP.
38. Fysh to Williams, 11 June 1936, HFP.
39. Williams to Fysh, 17 June 1936, HFP.
40. Fysh to C.G. Grey, 16 June 1936, HFP.
41. Brisbane *Courier-Mail*, 26 June 1936.
42. *TRANSIT*, 1981: interview with Sir Norman Brearley by Syd Cauveren.
43. Fysh to Brain, 27 July 1936, HFP.
44. Fysh to Brain, 26 February 1936, HFP.
45. Brain to Fysh, 4 June 1935, HFP.
46. Ibid.
47. Fysh to Woods Humphery, 7 July 1936, HFP.
48. Fysh to Brackley, 8 July 1936, HFP.
49. Brackley to Fysh, 25 July 1936, HFP.
50. Fysh to Brain, 10 August 1936, HFP.
51. Brain to Fysh, 7 September 1936, HFP.
52. Fysh to Woods Humphery, 11 August 1936, HFP.
53. Woods Humphery to McMaster, 24 August 1936, McMP.
54. Woods Humphery to McMaster, 24 August 1936, HFP.
55. McMaster to Woods Humphery, 17 September 1936, HFP.
56. Woods Humphery to McMaster, 9 October 1936, McMP.
57. McMaster to Woods Humphery, 26 October 1936, McMP.
58. Fysh to Woods Humphery, 5 October 1936, HFP.
59. Fysh to Dismore, 6 October 1936, HFP.
60. Fysh to Cobby, 13 October 1936, HFP.
61. Cobby to Fysh, 4 November 1936, HFP.
62. Fysh to McMaster, 28 November 1936, HFP.
63. Johnston to Fysh, 22 October 1936, HFP.
64. McMaster to Woods Humphery, 10 December 1936, McMP.
65. Ibid.

Chapter 15

1. Brisbane *Courier-Mail*, 12 January 1937.
2. McMaster to Woods Humphery, 14 January 1937, McMP.
3. *Sydney Sun*, 14 January 1937.
4. McMaster to Woods Humphery, 21 January 1937, McMP.
5. Press statement by Prime Minister J.A. Lyons, 9 February 1937, EJP.
6. Hocking and Haddon-Cave, *Air Transport*, p. 116.
7. McMaster press statement, 29 January 1937, McMP.
8. Johnston to Fysh, 26 April 1937, HFP.
9. Note by McMaster, 1937, McMP.
10. Managing Director's Report, 31 March 1937, HFP.
11. Operations Reports, 1936.37, HFP.
12. McMaster to Woods Humphery, 1 June 1937, McMP.
13. Unidentified press clipping, July 1937, McMP.
14. Penrose, *Wings Across The World*, p. 101.
15. Fysh, *Qantas at War*, p. 140.
16. J.A. Lyons to Woods Humphery, 24 June 1937, HFP.
17. Annex A, Pacific Conference Papers, Section 11, No. 14, EJP.
18. Handwritten note by McMaster on typed text of letter to J.A. Hunter, assistant minister, 9 July 1937, McMP.

19. McMaster to Hunter, 9 July 1937, McMP.
20. Ibid.
21. Ibid.
22. McMaster to Woods Humphery, 9 July 1937, McMP.
23. Fysh report, 14 July 1937, HFP.
24. McMaster to Menzies, 15 July 1937, McMP.
25. Johnston interview with author, 1982.
26. McMaster to Menzies, 27 July 1937, McMP.
27. Re-Organisation of Internal Services: Report of Controller-General to Minister, 5 August 1937, EJP.
28. *Smith's Weekly*, 7 August 1937.
29. Fysh, *Qantas at War*, p. 145.
30. Fysh to McMaster, 6 September 1937, McMP.
31. McMaster to Woods Humphery, 20 August 1937, McMP.
32. Dismore to McMaster, 1 September 1937, McMP.
33. McMaster to Woods Humphery, 3 September 1937, McMP.
34. McMaster to C. Minter, Messrs Minter Simpson & Co, Sydney, 1 October 1937, McMP.
35 McMaster to Woods Humphery, 19 October 1937, McMP.
36. Fysh, *Qantas at War*, p. 147.
37. Fysh to Johnston, 24 September 1937, HFP.
38. McMaster to Parkhill and Menzies, 20 October 1937, McMP.
39. Menzies to McMaster, 25 October 1937, McMP.
40. Parkhill to McMaster, 15 November 1937, McMP.
41. McMaster to Woods Humphery, 16 November 1937, McMP.
42. Brain to McMaster, 20 November 1937, McMP.
43. Woods Humperhy to McMaster, 24 November 1937, McMP.
44. Woods Humphery to McMaster, 29 November 1937, McMP.
45. Fysh, *Qantas at War*, p. 144.
46. *Sydney Morning Herald*, 2 December 1937.
47. *Sydney Morning Herald*, 26 November 1937.
48. Higham, *Britain's Imperial Air Routes*.
49. Woods Humphery to McMaster, 3 December 1937, McMP.
50. McMaster to Woods Humphery, 16 November 1937, McMP.
51. Thorby to J.A. Hunter, 3 December 1937, McMP.
52. Fysh, *Qantas at War*, p. 144.
53. Fysh press statement, December 1937, HFP.
54. Fysh to Johnston, 15 December 1937, HFP.
55. Brain to Fysh, 22 December 1937, HFP.

Chapter 16

1. Fysh to Johnston, January 1938, HFP.
2. Johnston to Fysh, 7 February 1938, HFP.
3. Thorby to McMaster, 9 February 1938, McMP.
4. McMaster to Thorby, 11 February 1938, McMP.
5. Fysh to Rudder, 18 March 1938, HFP.
6. Penrose, *Wings Across the World*, p. 107.
7. Report of the Cadman Committee, February 1938, copy EJP.
8. Fysh, *Qantas at War*, p. 142.
9. McMaster to Woods Humphery, 11 March 1938, McMP.
10. Fysh, *Qantas at War*, p. 125.
11. Turner to Dismore, 22 April 1938, McMP.
12. McMaster to Thorby, 7 May 1938, McMP.
13. Memorandum by Johnston, May 1938, EJP.
14. Thorby to McMaster, 1 April 1938, McMP.
15. Fysh, *Qantas at War*, p. 137.
16. Hocking and Haddon-Cave, *Air Transport*, p. 91.
17. Fysh to Johnston, 13 May 1938, HFP.
18. Fysh to Johnston, 14 May 1938, HFP.

19. Fysh, *Qantas at War*, pp. 159-60.
20. Ibid., pp. 167-68.
21. Woods Humphery to McMaster, 16 June 1938, McMP.
22. Beharrell to McMaster, 16 June 1938, McMP.
23. Dismore to McMaster, 28 June 1938, McMP.
24. Hocking and Haddon-Cave, *Air Transport*, p. 21.
25. Ibid., pp. 89-90.
26. Fysh, *Qantas at War*, p. 127.
27. Falla to McMaster, 1 July 1938, McMP.
28. Fysh, *Qantas at War*, p. 166.
29. Report by G.U. Allan, 1938, HFP.
30. Brisbane *Telegraph*, 7 July 1938.
31. Thorby press statement, Canberra, 3 July 1938, McMP.
32. Brisbane *Telegraph*, 7 July 1938.
33. Brisbane *Telegraph*, 8 July 1938.
34. Brisbane *Telegraph*, 6 July 1938.
35. Brisbane *Courier Mail*, 11 July 1938.
36. Minutes of meeting of directors, Sydney, 15 July 1938, McMP.
37. McMaster to Falla, 15 July 1938, McMP.
38. Fysh, *Qantas at War*, pp. 164-65.
39. Smith and Johnston to McMaster, 31 August 1938, McMP.
40. Fysh, *Qantas at War*, p. 157.
41. Fysh to McMaster, 11 August 1938, HFP.
42. Fysh, *Qantas at War*, p. 129.
43. Ibid.
44. Ibid., p. 176.
45. Ibid., pp. 172-73.
46. Notes prepared by Captain Crowther and given to the author, 1982.
47. Brain to McMaster, 12 October 1938, McMP.
48. Fysh to Johnston, 17 October 1938, HFP.
49. Fysh, *Qantas at War*, p. 218.
50. Thorby to Lyons, 16 November 1938, McMP.
51. Lyons to Thorby, 17 November 1938, McMP.
52. Fysh to Johnston, 12 November 1938, HFP.
53. Fysh, *Qantas at War*, p. 174.
54. Ibid., pp. 178-79.
55. Penrose, *Wings Across the World*, p. 112.
56. Ibid., p. 113.
57. Fysh to McMaster, 14 December 1938, HFP.
58. Hocking and Haddon-Cave, *Air Transport*, p. 36.

Chapter 17

1. Brisbane *Telegraph*, 14 March 1939.
2. Fysh, *Qantas at War*, p. 181.
3. Ibid., p. 200.
4. Fysh report, 2 January 1939, HFP.
5. Ibid.
6. Fysh, *Qantas at War*, p. 187.
7. Thorby to QEA, 3 January 1939, HFP.
8. Ibid.
9. Stonehaven to McMaster, 24 January 1939, McMP.
10. Turner Report to Fysh, 11 February 1939, HFP.
11. Fysh report to directors, 21 February 1939, HFP.
12. Rudder to Mrs McMaster, 29 March 1939, McMP.
13. *Sydney Morning Herald*, 10 March 1939.
14. Fysh to McMaster, 15 March 1939, HFP.
15. Brisbane *Telegraph*, 16 March 1939.
16. *The Motor*, April 1939.
17. Johnston interview with author, 1982.
18. *Sydney Morning Herald*, 25 March 1939.

19. Thorby to McMaster, 20 February 1939, McMP.
20. Younger, *Australia and the Australians*, p. 578.
21. Watt, *The Evolution of Australian Foreign Policy 1939-1965*, p. 20.
22. Ibid.
23. *Sydney Morning Herald*, 27 April 1939.
24. Fysh to Reith, 24 April 1939, HFP.
25. Reith to Fysh, 9 May 1939, HFP.
26. McMaster to Fysh, 23 May 1939, HFP.
27. Dismore to Fysh, 10 May 1939, HFP.
28. McMaster to Fysh, 20 May 1939, HFP.
29. Johnston interview with the author, 1982.
30. Fysh, *Qantas at War*, p. 230.
31. Ivan Holyman to Fysh, 9 June 1939, HFP.
32. Thorby to McMaster, 28 June 1939, McMP.
33. McMaster to Fysh, 14 June 1939, HFP.
34. Reith to Rudder, 3 July 1939, HFP.
35. Fysh to McMaster, 3 August 1939, HFP.
36. Fysh to Reith, 25 July 1939, HFP.
37. Reith to Fysh, 28 September 1939, HFP.
38. Corbett report to minister, 24 July 1939, EJP.
39. Fysh to Corbett, 6 June 1939, HFP.
40. McMaster to Fysh, 10 June 1939, HFP.
41. McMaster to Fysh, 14 August 1939, HFP.
42. F.J. Smith to McMaster, 20 June 1939, HFP.
43. McMaster to Reith, 21 August 1939, HFP.
44. McMaster to Fysh, 22 August 1939, HFP.
45. Fysh to McMaster, 26 August 1939, HFP.
46. McMaster to Fysh, 6 September 1939, HFP.
47. Fysh to McMaster, 3 October 1939, HFP.
48. Fysh to McMaster, 11 October 1939, HFP.
49. Managing Director's Report, 23 September 1939, HFP.
50. Fysh to McMaster, 23 September 1939, HFP.
51. Managing Director's Report, 23 September 1939, HFP.
52. Fysh, *Qantas at War*, p. 216.
53. Ibid., pp. 220-21.
54. McMaster to Fysh, 4 September 1939, HFP.
55. McMaster to Fysh, 7 September 1939, HFP.
56. Fysh to Reith, 15 September 1939, HFP.
57. Draft Chairman's Address to 19th Annual General Meeting of Q.A.N.T.A.S.,
    27 September 1939, McMP.

General Bibliography

Alexander, F. *Australia Since Federation*. 3rd ed. London: Nelson, 1976.

Allen, R. *Pictorial History of K.L.M. Royal Dutch Airlines*. London: Ian Allan, 1978.

Baitsell, J.M. *Airline Industrial Relations: Pilots and Flight Engineers*. Boston: Harvard University, 1966.

Behr, J. *Royal Flying Doctor Service in Australia 1928-1979*. Manuscript in the possession of Federal Council of the Royal Flying Doctor Service of Australia.

Bennett-Bremner, E. *Front-Line Airline: The War Story of Qantas Empire Airways Limited*. Sydney: Angus and Robertson, 1944.

Brackley, F.H., comp. *Brackles: Memoirs of a Pioneer of Civil Aviation*. Chatham: W. & J. Mackay, 1952.

Brogden, S. *Australia's Two-Airline Policy*. Carlton, Vic.: Melbourne University Press, 1968.

Butler, C.A. *Flying Start: The History of the First Five Decades of Civil Aviation in Australia*. Sydney: Edwards & Shaw, 1971.

Carter, I.R. *Southern Cloud*. Melbourne: Landsdown Press, 1963.

Corbett, D. *Politics and the Airlines*. London: George Allan & Unwin, 1965.

Crome, N.C. *Qantas Aeriana*. Edited by N.C. Baldwin. Sutton Coldfild: Francis J. Field, 1955.

Davis, R.E.G. *A History of the World's Airlines*. Lonond: Oxford University Press, 1964.

Donne, M. *Leader of the Skies: Rolls-Royce: The First Seventy-Five Years*. London: Frederick Muller, 1981.

Friedman, J.J. *A New Air Transport Policy for the North Atlantic: Saving an Endangered System*. New York: Atheneum, 1967.

Fysh, H. *Qantas at War*. Unedited manuscript. Mitchell Library, Sydney.

Fysh, H. *Qantas Rising*. Sydney: Angus and Robertson, 1965.

Fysh, H. *Taming the North*. Rev. and enl. ed. Sydney: Angus and Robertson, 1950.

Fysh, H. *Wings to the World: The Story of Qantas 1945-1966*. Sydney: Angus and Robertson, 1970.

Gibson, R.J. *Australia and Australians in Civil Aviation: An Index to Events from 1832 to 1920*. Vol. 1. Sydney: Qantas Airways Ltd., 1971.

Harvey-Bailey, A. *Rolls-Royce — the Formative Years 1906-1939*. Historical Series no. 1. Derby: Rolls-Royce Hertiage Trust, 1982.

Higham, R. *Britian's Imperial Air Routes 1918 to 1939: The Story of Britain's Overseas Airlines*. London: G.T. Foutlis & Co. Ltd., 1960.

Hocking, D.M. and Haddon-Cave, C.P. *Air Transport in Australia*. Sydney: Angus and Robertson, 1951.

Jackson, A.J. *Avro Aircraft Since 1908*. London: Putnam, 1965.

Mackenzie, R.D. *Solo: The Bert Hinkler Story*. Sydney: Jacaranda Press, 1962.

Miller, H.C. *Early Birds*. Adelaide: Rigby, 1968.

Mollison, J. *Playboy of the Air*. London: Michael Joseph, 1937.

Moody, J.D. *Qantas and the Kangaroo Route*. Ph.D. thesis, Australian National University, Canberra, 1981.

Munson, K. *Pictorial History of BOAC and Imperial Airways*. London: Ian Allan, 1970.

Pattison, B. and Goodall, G. *Qantas Empire Airways Indian Ocean Service 1943-1946*. Footscray, Vic.: Aviation Historical Society of Australia, 1979.

Penrose, H. *Wings across the World: An Illustrated History of British Airways*. London: Cassell, 1980.

Scott, C.W.A. *Scott's Book: The Life and Mildenhall-Melbourne Flight of C.W.A. Scott*. London: Hodder and Stoughton, 1934.

Shaw, A.G.L. *The Story of Australia*. London: Faber & Faber, 1955.

Smith, C.B. *Amy Johnson*. London: Collins, 1967.

Stroud, J. *Annals of British and Commonwealth Air Transport 1919-1960*. London: Putnam, 1962.

Thomas, M. *Out on a Wing: An Autobiography*. London: Michael Joseph, 1964.

Turner, P. St. J. *Pictorial History of Pam American World Airways*. London: Ian Allan, 1973.

Ward, R. *A Nation for a Continent*. London: Heinemann, 1979.

Watt, A. *The Evolution of Australian Foreign Policy 1938-1965*. London: Cambridge University Press, 1967.

Younger, R.M. *Australia and the Australians: A New Concise History*. Adelaide: Rigby, 1970.

Index

387